THE GOD OF WAR

THE LOCHLAINN SEABROOK COLLECTION

AMERICAN CIVIL WAR
Abraham Lincoln Was a Liberal, Jefferson Davis Was a Conservative: The Missing Key to Understanding the American Civil War
Confederacy 101: Amazing Facts You Never Knew About America's Oldest Political Tradition
Confederate Blood and Treasure: An Interview With Lochlainn Seabrook
Everything You Were Taught About African-Americans and the Civil War is Wrong, Ask a Southerner!
Everything You Were Taught About the Civil War is Wrong, Ask a Southerner!
Give This Book to a Yankee! A Southern Guide to the Civil War For Northerners
Lincoln's War: The Real Cause, the Real Winner, the Real Loser
The Great Yankee Coverup: What the North Doesn't Want You to Know About Lincoln's War!
The Ultimate Civil War Quiz Book: How Much Do You Really Know About America's Most Misunderstood Conflict?
Women in Gray: A Tribute to the Ladies Who Supported the Southern Confederacy

CONFEDERATE MONUMENTS
Confederate Monuments: Why Every American Should Honor Confederate Soldiers and Their Memorials

CONFEDERATE FLAG
Confederate Flag Facts: What Every American Should Know About Dixie's Southern Cross

SECESSION
All We Ask Is To Be Let Alone: The Southern Secession Fact Book

SLAVERY
Everything You Were Taught About American Slavery is Wrong, Ask a Southerner!
Slavery 101: Amazing Facts You Never Knew About America's "Peculiar Institution"

CHILDREN
Honest Jeff and Dishonest Abe: A Southern Children's Guide to the Civil War
Saddle, Sword, and Gun: A Biography of Nathan Bedford Forrest For Teens

NATHAN BEDFORD FORREST
A Rebel Born: A Defense of Nathan Bedford Forrest - Confederate General, American Legend (winner of the 2011 Jefferson Davis Historical Gold Medal)
A Rebel Born: The Screenplay (film about N.B. Forrest)
Forrest! 99 Reasons to Love Nathan Bedford Forrest
Give 'Em Hell Boys! The Complete Military Correspondence of Nathan Bedford Forrest
Nathan Bedford Forrest and African-Americans: Yankee Myth, Confederate Fact
Nathan Bedford Forrest and the Battle of Fort Pillow: Yankee Myth, Confederate Fact
Nathan Bedford Forrest and the Ku Klux Klan: Yankee Myth, Confederate Fact
Nathan Bedford Forrest: Southern Hero, American Patriot - Honoring a Confederate Icon and the Old South
Saddle, Sword, and Gun: A Biography of Nathan Bedford Forrest For Teens
The God of War: Nathan Bedford Forrest as He Was Seen by His Contemporaries
The Quotable Nathan Bedford Forrest: Selections From the Writings and Speeches of the Confederacy's Most Brilliant Cavalryman

QUOTABLE SERIES
The Alexander H. Stephens Reader: Excerpts From the Works of a Confederate Founding Father
The Quotable Alexander H. Stephens: Selections From the Writings and Speeches of the Confederacy's First Vice President
The Quotable Jefferson Davis: Selections From the Writings and Speeches of the Confederacy's First President
The Quotable Nathan Bedford Forrest: Selections From the Writings and Speeches of the Confederacy's Most Brilliant Cavalryman
The Quotable Robert E. Lee: Selections From the Writings and Speeches of the South's Most Beloved Civil War General
The Quotable Stonewall Jackson: Selections From the Writings and Speeches of the South's Most Famous General
The Unquotable Abraham Lincoln: The President's Quotes They Don't Want You To Know!

CONSTITUTIONAL HISTORY
The Articles of Confederation Explained: A Clause-by-Clause Study of America's First Constitution
The Constitution of the Confederate States of America Explained: A Clause-by-Clause Study of the South's Magna Carta

VICTORIAN CONFEDERATE LITERATURE
Rise Up and Call Them Blessed: Victorian Tributes to the Confederate Soldier, 1861-1901
The God of War: Nathan Bedford Forrest As He Was Seen By His Contemporaries
The Old Rebel: Robert E. Lee As He Was Seen By His Contemporaries
Victorian Confederate Poetry: The Southern Cause in Verse, 1861-1901

ABRAHAM LINCOLN
Abraham Lincoln: The Southern View - Demythologizing America's Sixteenth President
Lincolnology: The Real Abraham Lincoln Revealed in His Own Words - A Study of Lincoln's Suppressed, Misinterpreted, and Forgotten Writings and Speeches
The Great Impersonator! 99 Reasons to Dislike Abraham Lincoln
The Unholy Crusade: Lincoln's Legacy of Destruction in the American South
The Unquotable Abraham Lincoln: The President's Quotes They Don't Want You To Know!

CIVIL WAR BATTLES
Encyclopedia of the Battle of Franklin - A Comprehensive Guide to the Conflict that Changed the Civil War
Nathan Bedford Forrest and the Battle of Fort Pillow: Yankee Myth, Confederate Fact

PARANORMAL
Carnton Plantation Ghost Stories: True Tales of the Unexplained from Tennessee's Most Haunted Civil War House!
UFOs and Aliens: The Complete Guidebook

FAMILY HISTORIES
The Blakeneys: An Etymological, Ethnological, and Genealogical Study - Uncovering the Mysterious Origins of the Blakeney Family and Name
The Caudills: An Etymological, Ethnological, and Genealogical Study - Exploring the Name and National Origins of a European-American Family
The McGavocks of Carnton Plantation: A Southern History - Celebrating One of Dixie's Most Noble Confederate Families and Their Tennessee Home

MIND, BODY, SPIRIT
Autobiography of a Non-Yogi: A Scientist's Journey From Hinduism to Christianity (Dr. Amitava Dasgupta, with Lochlainn Seabrook)
Britannia Rules: Goddess-Worship in Ancient Anglo-Celtic Society - An Academic Look at the United Kingdom's Matricentric Spiritual Past
Christ Is All and In All: Rediscovering Your Divine Nature and the Kingdom Within
Christmas Before Christianity: How the Birthday of the "Sun" Became the Birthday of the "Son"
Jesus and the Gospel of Q: Christ's Pre-Christian Teachings As Recorded in the New Testament
Jesus and the Law of Attraction: The Bible-Based Guide to Creating Perfect Health, Wealth, and Happiness Following Christ's Simple Formula
Seabrook's Bible Dictionary of Traditional and Mystical Christian Doctrines
The Bible and the Law of Attraction: 99 Teachings of Jesus, the Apostles, and the Prophets
The Book of Kelle: An Introduction to Goddess-Worship and the Great Celtic Mother-Goddess Kelle, Original Blessed Lady of Ireland
The Goddess Dictionary of Words and Phrases: Introducing a New Core Vocabulary for the Women's Spirituality Movement
The Way of Holiness: The Story of Religion and Myth From the Cave Bear Cult to Christianity

WOMEN
Aphrodite's Trade: The Hidden History of Prostitution Unveiled
Princess Diana: Modern Day Moon-Goddess - A Psychoanalytical and Mythological Look at Diana Spencer's Life, Marriage, and Death (with Dr. Jane Goldberg)
Women in Gray: A Tribute to the Ladies Who Supported the Southern Confederacy

Five-Star Books & Gifts From the Heart of the American South

SeaRavenPress.com

THE GOD OF WAR

Nathan Bedford Forrest
As He Was Seen By His Contemporaries

COLLECTED, ARRANGED, & EDITED BY THE AUTHOR, "THE VOICE OF THE TRADITIONAL SOUTH," COLONEL

LOCHLAINN SEABROOK
JEFFERSON DAVIS HISTORICAL GOLD MEDAL WINNER

Diligently Researched and Generously
Illustrated for the Elucidation of the Reader

2018
Sea Raven Press, Nashville, Tennessee, USA

THE GOD OF WAR

Published by
Sea Raven Press, Cassidy Ravensdale, President
PO Box 1484, Spring Hill, Tennessee 37174-1484 USA
SeaRavenPress.com • searavenpress@gmail.com

Copyright © 2018 Lochlainn Seabrook
in accordance with U.S. and international copyright laws and regulations, as stated and protected under the Berne Union for the Protection of Literary and Artistic Property (Berne Convention), and the Universal Copyright Convention (the UCC). All rights reserved under the Pan-American and International Copyright Conventions.

1st SRP paperback edition, 1st printing, June 2018 • ISBN: 978-1-943737-65-9
1st SRP hardcover edition, 1st printing, June 2018 • ISBN: 978-1-943737-66-6

ISBN: 978-1-943737-65-9 (paperback)
Library of Congress Control Number: 2018943908

This work is the copyrighted intellectual property of Lochlainn Seabrook and has been registered with the Copyright Office at the Library of Congress in Washington, D.C., USA. No part of this work (including text, covers, drawings, photos, illustrations, maps, images, diagrams, etc.), in whole or in part, may be used, reproduced, stored in a retrieval system, or transmitted, in any form or by any means now known or hereafter invented, without written permission from the publisher. The sale, duplication, hire, lending, copying, digitalization, or reproduction of this material, in any manner or form whatsoever, is also prohibited, and is a violation of federal, civil, and digital copyright law, which provides severe civil and criminal penalties for any violations.

The God of War: Nathan Bedford Forrest As He Was Seen By His Contemporaries, by Lochlainn Seabrook. Includes endnotes and bibliographical references.

Front and back cover design and art, book design, layout, and interior art by Lochlainn Seabrook
All images, graphic design, graphic art, and illustrations copyright © Lochlainn Seabrook
All images selected, placed, manipulated, and/or created by Lochlainn Seabrook
Cover images and design copyright © Lochlainn Seabrook
Cover photo: N. B. Forrest Equestrian Monument, formerly located at Memphis, Tennessee

All persons who approve of the authority and principles of Colonel Lochlainn Seabrook's literary work, and realize its benefits as a means of reeducating the world about the South and the Confederacy, are hereby requested to avidly recommend his books to others and to vigorously cooperate in extending their reach, scope, and influence around the globe.

The views on the American "Civil War" documented in this book are those of the publisher.

PRINTED & MANUFACTURED IN OCCUPIED TENNESSEE, FORMER CONFEDERATE STATES OF AMERICA

Dedication

TO ALL THOSE WHO READ AND ENJOY MY BOOKS.

Epigraph

Mounted on his big sorrel horse, sabre in hand, sleeves rolled up, his coat lying on the pommel of his saddle, looking the very God of War, General Forrest rode down our line as far as we could see him. I remember his words, which I heard more than once: "Get up men. I have ordered Bell to charge on the left. When you hear his guns, and the bugle sounds, every man must charge, and we will give them hell!"[1]

Confederate Private John Milton Hubbard, 1911

"Forrest in Close Quarters," from a painting owned by Col. V. Y. Cook.

CONTENTS

Notes to the Reader: 11
Introduction, by Lochlainn Seabrook: 17

CHAPTER 1   1863-1895: 23
CHAPTER 2   1896-1897: 57
CHAPTER 3   1898-1900: 95
CHAPTER 4   1901-1903: 132
CHAPTER 5   1904-1905: 163
CHAPTER 6   1906-1909: 195
CHAPTER 7   1910-1913: 231
CHAPTER 8   1914-1917: 259
CHAPTER 9   1918-1932: 294
CHAPTER 10 POEMS ABOUT FORREST: 318

Appendix A Forrest's Letter to a Confederate Soldier's Father: 337
Appendix B The Passing of Forrest's Wife Mary Ann: 338
Appendix C Blacks Compliment Forrest UCV Commander: 339
Appendix D President T. Roosevelt Eulogizes the South: 340
Appendix E A Southerner and a Yankee Address Blacks: 342
Appendix F A Brief Biography of N. B. Forrest II: 343
Notes: 344
Bibliography: 349
Meet the Author: 354

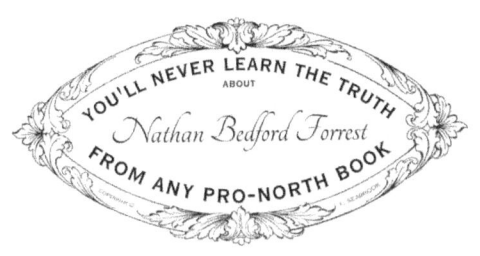

NOTES TO THE READER

"NOTHING IN THE PAST IS DEAD TO THE MAN WHO WOULD
LEARN HOW THE PRESENT CAME TO BE WHAT IT IS."

WILLIAM STUBBS, VICTORIAN ENGLISH HISTORIAN

THE TWO MAIN POLITICAL PARTIES IN 1860

☛ In any study of America's antebellum, bellum, and postbellum periods, it is vitally important to understand that in 1860 the two major political parties—the Democrats and the newly formed Republicans—were the opposite of what they are today. In other words, the Democrats of the mid 19th Century were Conservatives, akin to the Republican Party of today, while the Republicans of the mid 19th Century were Liberals, akin to the Democratic Party of today.[2]

Thus the Confederacy's Democratic president, Jefferson Davis, was a Conservative (with libertarian leanings); the Union's Republican president, Abraham Lincoln, was a Liberal (with socialistic leanings).[3] This is why, in the mid 1800s, the conservative wing of the Democratic Party was known as "the States' Rights Party."[4]

Hence, the Democrats of the Civil War period referred to themselves as "conservatives," "confederates," "anti-centralists," or "constitutionalists" (the latter because they favored strict adherence to the original Constitution—which tacitly guaranteed states' rights—as created by the Founding Fathers), while the Republicans called themselves "liberals," "nationalists," "centralists," or "consolidationists" (the latter three because they wanted to nationalize the central government and consolidate political power in Washington, D.C.).[5]

The author's cousin, Confederate Vice President and Democrat Alexander H. Stephens: a Southern Conservative.

Since this idea is new to most of my readers, let us further demystify it by viewing it from the perspective of the American Revolutionary War. If Davis and his conservative Southern constituents (the Democrats of 1861) had been alive in 1775, they would have sided with George Washington and the American colonists, who sought to secede from the tyrannical government of Great Britain; if Lincoln and his Liberal Northern constituents (the Republicans of 1861) had been alive at that time, they would have sided with King George III and the English monarchy, who sought to maintain the American colonies as possessions of the British Empire. It is due to this very comparison that Southerners often refer to their secession as the Second Declaration of Independence and the "Civil War" as the Second American Revolutionary War.

Without a basic understanding of these facts, the American "Civil War" will forever remain incomprehensible. For a full discussion of this topic see my book, *Abraham Lincoln Was a Liberal, Jefferson Davis Was a Conservative: The Missing Key to Understanding the American Civil War*.

THE TERM "CIVIL WAR"

☞ As I heartily dislike the phrase "Civil War," its use throughout this book (as well as in my other works) is worthy of explanation.

Our entire modern literary system refers to the conflict of 1861 using the Northern term the "Civil War," whether we in the South like it or not. Of course, this is purposeful, for America's book industry, which determines everything from how books are categorized and

The American "Civil War" was not a true civil war as Webster defines it: "A conflict between opposing groups of citizens of the *same* country." It was a fight between two individual countries; or to be more specific, two separate and constitutionally formed confederacies: the U.S.A. and the C.S.A.

designed to how they are marketed and sold, is almost solely controlled by Liberals, socialists, globalists, collectivists, and communists, individuals who will do anything to prevent the truth about Lincoln's War from coming out. An important aspect of this wholesale revisionism of American history is the use of the phrase "Civil War," which Yankee Liberals thrust into the public forum even as big government Left-winger Lincoln was diabolically tricking the Conservative South into firing the first shot at the Battle of Fort Sumter in April 1861.

The progressives' blatant American "Civil War" coverup continues to this day, one of the more overt results which pertains to how books are coded, indexed, and identified.[6] Thus, as all book searches by readers, libraries, and retail outlets are now performed online, and as all bookstores categorize works from or about this period under the heading "Civil War," honest book publishers and authors who deal with this particular topic have little choice but to use this deceptive term. If I were to refuse to use it, as some of my Southern colleagues have suggested, few people would ever find or read my books.

Add to this the fact that scarcely any non-Southerners have ever heard of the names we in the South use for the conflict, such as the "War for Southern Independence"—or my personal preference, "Lincoln's War." It only makes sense then to use the term "Civil War" in most commercial situations, distasteful though it is.

We should also bear in mind that while today educated persons, particularly educated Southerners, all share an abhorrence for the phrase "Civil War," it was not always so. Confederates who lived through and even fought in the conflict regularly used the term throughout the 1860s, and even long after. Among them were Confederate generals such as Nathan Bedford Forrest, Richard Taylor, and Joseph E. Johnston, not to mention the Confederacy's vice president, Alexander H. Stephens.

In 1895 Confederate General James Longstreet wrote about his military experiences in a work subtitled, *Memoirs of the Civil War in America*, while in 1903 Confederate General John Brown Gordon entitled his autobiography, *Reminiscences of the Civil War*. Even the Confederacy's highest leader, President Jefferson Davis, used the term "Civil War,"[7] and in one case at least, as late as 1881—the year he wrote his brilliant exposition, *The Rise and Fall of the Confederate Government*.[8] Authors writing for *Confederate Veteran* magazine sometimes used the phrase well into the early 1900s,[9] and in 1898, at the Eighth Annual Meeting and Reunion of the United Confederate Veterans (the forerunner of today's Sons of Confederate Veterans), the following resolution was proposed: that from then on the Great War of 1861 was to be designated "the Civil War Between the States."[10]

Confederate General James Longstreet was just one of many Southern officials who referred to the conflict of 1861 as the "Civil War."

A WORD ON EARLY AMERICAN MATERIAL

☛ In order to preserve the authentic historicity of the antebellum, bellum, and postbellum periods, I have retained the original spellings, formatting, and punctuation of the early Americans I quote. These include such items as British-English spellings, long-running paragraphs, obsolete words, and various literary devices peculiar to the time. However, I have corrected misspelled names to prevent confusion, and also *where possible*, inaccurate dates and locations (the inevitable result of old faulty memories). Bracketed words within quotes are my additions and clarifications, while italicized words within quotes are (where indicated) my emphasis.

PRESENTISM

☛ As a historian I view *presentism* (judging the past according to present day mores and customs) as the enemy of authentic history. And this is precisely why the Left employs it in its ongoing war against traditional American, conservative, and Christian values. By looking at history through the lens of modern day beliefs—and, just as heinous, fabricating obviously fake history based on emotion, opinion, and political ideology—they are able to distort, revise, and reshape the past into a false narrative that fits their ideological agenda: the liberalization *and* Northernization of America, the enlargement and further centralization of the national government, and total control of American political, economic, and social power, the same agenda that Lincoln championed.[11]

Judging our ancestors by our own standards is unfair, unjust, misleading, and unethical.

This book rejects presentism and replaces it with what I call *historicalism*: judging our ancestors based on the values of their own time. To get the most from this work the reader is invited to reject presentism as well. In this way—along with casting aside preconceived notions and the bogus "history" churned out by our left-wing education system—the truth in this work will be most readily ascertained and absorbed; truth that has been rigorously researched and forensically uncovered by myself using the scientific method. As Confederate Colonel Bennett H. Young noted in 1901:

> History is valuable only as it is true. Opinions concerning acts are not history; acts themselves alone are historic.[12]

LEARN MORE

☛ Lincoln's War on the American people and the Constitution can never be fully understood without a thorough knowledge of the South's perspective. As this book is only meant to be a brief introductory guide to these topics, one cannot hope to learn the complete story here. For those who are interested in additional material from Dixie's viewpoint, please see my comprehensive histories listed on pages 2 and 3.

Keep Your Body, Mind, & Spirit Vibrating at Their Highest Level

YOU CAN DO SO BY READING THE BOOKS OF

SEA RAVEN PRESS

There is nothing that will so perfectly keep your body, mind, and spirit in a healthy condition as to think wisely and positively. Hence you should not only read this book, but also the other books that we offer. They will quicken your physical, mental, and spiritual vibrations, enabling you to maintain a position in society as a healthy erudite person.

KEEP YOURSELF WELL-INFORMED!

The well-informed person is always at the head of the procession, while the ignorant, the lazy, and the unthoughtful hang onto the rear. If you are a Spiritual man or woman, do yourself a great favor: read Sea Raven Press books and stay well posted on the Truth. It is almost criminal for one to remain in ignorance while the opportunity to gain knowledge is open to all at a nominal price.

We invite you to visit our Webstore for a wide selection of wholesome, family-friendly, well-researched, educational books for all ages. You will be glad you did!

Five-Star Books & Gifts From the Heart of the American South

SeaRavenPress.com

Loyalty to the truth of Confederate history

U.D.C. MOTTO, 1921

INTRODUCTION

"No soldier can be relied on for faithful service who expects to live until the close of the war."[13] — GEN. N. B. FORREST, C.S.A.

Only the unread, uneducated, and indoctrinated are offended by the name Nathan Bedford Forrest. Those who *are* familiar with him, however—in particular, those who have read my other books on the immortal Southern hero—not only respect and even love him, they are in awe of him. If you are learning about Forrest for the first time here, rest assured, you will quickly find yourself in the latter category!

To begin your conversion to Forrestism, there is only one thing you need to know: this outstanding American, who had no military training and yet won nearly every battle he engaged in, was without question *the most remarkable cavalry leader in world history*. This single fact alone makes him worthy of adulation and study. And yet there is much more.

While the genuine story of Nathan Bedford Forrest was long ago deleted from our history books, then rewritten by Liberals, socialists, and South-haters in order to heap shame on the South and justify Lincoln's War on the Constitution, the real man remains untouched and untarnished, still burning brightly like gold in a freshly opened ancient Egyptian tomb.

The famed "God of War" and all-American icon, Nathan Bedford Forrest.

Thanks to God's providence, the words of his contemporaries have not been suppressed or even altered by enemies of the South. And it is from this rich cornucopia of 19th and early 20th-Century material that I have drawn the reminiscences of Forrest found in the present volume.

Forrest's contemporaries, of course, were mainly the Confederate officers and privates who served under or with him. But this group also includes the Union soldiers who fought against him, as well as the women whose honor, homes, and towns he saved and whose fathers, husbands, grandfathers, sweethearts, sons, and brothers he returned at the end of the War. As this collection will show, he also had scores of supporters from foreign lands, many of them high ranking military leaders and teachers, a trend that continues into the present day.

Forrest's accomplishments on the field of action are beyond reckoning (he was the only soldier on either side of the War to rise from private to lieutenant general), while his successes in the world of business were extraordinary (born in dire poverty, by the start of Lincoln's War he was worth at least $50 million in today's currency).[14] A dyed-in-the-wool Conservative (then a Democrat), an ardent right-wing political activist, and an inveterate constitutionalist (who always carried a weapon), he was also a faithful, industrious, and protective husband, and a passionate father whose children, grandchildren, and even great-grandchildren—he would have been proud to learn—later contributed important work in support of the Southern Cause: conservatism. (His grandson, for example, Nathan Bedford Forrest II, served as Adjutant General and Chief of Staff of the Sons of Confederate Veterans.) There can be no doubt that if we had had ten or even five Forrests on the Confederate side, today the South would be living proud and free under the most equitable and prosperous government the world has ever known: *The Confederate States of America*—a title taken from the nickname of the original U.S.A. (as it was planned, formed, and intended by the Conservative Founding Fathers).[15]

The men and women included in *The God of War* were certainly well aware of the many wonderful attributes and characteristics of this invincible Southern warrior and loyal American Conservative—who one Confederate soldier rightly referred to as "the leading spirit in the revolution"[16]—and they left behind scores of testimonies as evidence.

Liberals and other South-haters, who focus solely on Forrest's dealings with slavery (a business which he engaged in for only a few years) and his alleged associations with the Ku Klux Klan (the postwar Klan was a *temporary* pro-Constitution organization with no connection to today's *permanent* KKK),[17] will be disappointed to find that of the nearly 200 Forrest admirers I have included here, almost none discuss or even mention these topics. The reason is simple enough: they are insignificant aspects of a superbly lived life that was centered around patriotism, conservatism, Christianity, constitutionalism, individualism, self-reliance, marriage, family, traditionalism, charity work, military duty, civic duty, and the American work ethic.

These facts, along with the amazing adventure that was Forrest's real life story, are why his legacy will never be forgotten, replaced, or overthrown. This book is part of my effort to ensure that it does not.

In closing let me leave you with the words of an unknown Victorian writer, who aptly summarized the thoughts and feelings of traditional Southerners and American patriots—then and now:

> Southern children ought to know of the imperishable grandeur of Gen. Lee, of the magnificence in battle of Stonewall Jackson and Albert Sydney Johnston, of the daring bravery of Forrest, of Morgan, and of Cheatham. The renown of the Confederate soldier is not told in splendid monuments; it rests in the hearts of the Southern people, and there it must be kept fresh and green forever. They want their children to receive facts. From facts no conclusions can be drawn derogatory to the courage of Southern soldiers or to the genius and military prowess of Southern generals.[18] — THE NASHVILLE AMERICAN, CIRCA 1898

Now, turn the page dear reader, and be prepared to experience every emotion as you pour over the personal reminiscences of the many champions of Confederate General Nathan Bedford Forrest. Not the mythological monster fabricated by South-loathing Liberals, but the real Forrest; the one known by his contemporaries as "a man of unimpeachable integrity, high moral courage, and constructive citizenship";[19] a true all-American hero and one of the great Southern icons; the man I justly call "the John Wayne of Dixie." His friends, business associates, and wartime "band of brothers" loved him because they knew him. Their shared memories will now give you a chance to get to know him as well. Let the Forrest Festival begin.[20]

LOCHLAINN SEABROOK
Nashville, Tennessee, USA
June 2018
In Nobis Regnat Christus

Nathan Bedford Forrest

Born at Chapel Hill, Tenn., July 13, 1821
Confederate Private at Memphis, Tenn., June 21, 1861
Lieutenant Colonel (Company of Tennessee Cavalry), July 10, 1861
Colonel (Forrest's Regiment Cavalry), March 10, 1862
Brigadier-General, July 21, 1862
Major-General, December 4, 1863
Given command of all cavalry of the Army of Tennessee, November 6, 1864
Lieutenant-General, March 2, 1865
Final (official) surrender, May 9, 1865
Died at Memphis, Tenn., October 29, 1877 (age 56)

The GOD of WAR

Note: Dates only specify the year an entry was published in the sources available to me, and do not necessarily indicate the actual year it may have first appeared in public.

1

1863-1895

THE BOLD & BRILLIANT FORREST

☛ Tullahoma, [Tenn.], May 5, 1863. — Wartime dispatch addressed to Governor John Gill Shorter, Montgomery, Ala.: By a rapid concentration of forces in North Alabama I have driven out the heavy column of the enemy recently marauding there. Some 1,800 [Union] cavalry, however, passed our left and made a desperate dash to destroy our communications and depots in Georgia. By a bold and brilliant movement not surpassed in the war Forrest, with half their number, pursued rapidly and fought them running for five days, without forage or food, except what he could hastily gather in that wild mountain region. He has finally killed or captured the whole party.[21] — CONFEDERATE GENERAL BRAXTON BRAGG

FORREST & THE SOUTHERN CAUSE

The only known photo of Gen. Nathan Bedford Forrest from wartimes.

☛ I feel that we should educate our children in the true faith while we live, so that when we have bivouacked on the other shore our cause will live. By "our cause" I mean the right to self government and American manhood. Let us teach them to love the Republic our fathers bequeathed us, the Republic of equal rights for all the States. Teach them that the followers of Sidney and J. E. Johnston, Forrest, Wheeler and Hood, fought for the preservation of civil liberty against centralism [liberalism] and the downfall of American liberty.[22] — P. A. GREEN

AN EARLY REMINISCENCE OF FORREST
☞ In February, 1841, when I was but ten years of age, I remember well a small company of volunteers which marched out of the town of Holly Springs, Mississippi, to the relief of Texas, then threatened by invasion from Mexico. In that little band stood Bedford Forrest, a tall, black-haired, gray-eyed youth, scarce twenty years of age, who then gave the first evidence of the military ardor he possessed. The company saw no fighting, for the danger was over before they arrived, and the men received no pay. Finding themselves in a strange country, without friends or money, Forrest, with the characteristic energy which distinguished him in after life, split rails at fifty cents per hundred and made the money necessary to bring him back to his family and home.[23]
— CONFEDERATE GENERAL JAMES RONALD CHALMERS

THE THUNDERBOLT OF WAR
☞ [General Forrest was the] thunderbolt of war and a superb soldier.[24]
— COLONEL RICHARD HENRY LEE

HOW THEY STOOD PICKET UNDER FORREST
☞ One day in 1864 orders came to the regiment for a detail for scout and picket duty, and the instructions accompanying the orders were for the detail to proceed along a certain road until the enemy was discovered, then stop, hold him in check if possible, but under all circumstances to inform the General of the whereabouts and strength of the enemy. All know that when "old Bedford" [General Forrest] issued orders he intended them to be obeyed, and promptly, too. So worn out as the men were it was not long before the party, under command of Lieut. Garner, started on what might prove a wild goose chase, and was just as likely to prove a tiger hunt, with lots of tiger in it. Of one thing the men were sure, they would go until they found the enemy if he was on that road.

Every old soldier knows that on such expeditions he always picked out a mate. One of the men, Burns, a youngster in point of years, but an old soldier, and one of the best that Forrest had, picked out Dick Townsend for his chum. Townsend was riding a gray, almost white, horse. This part of it Burns did not like at all, but decided he would rather risk Townsend with a white horse than any other man there, with a less objectionably colored horse. But I'll let Burns tell the rest.

We had ridden ten or twelve miles when, just after dark, we came up to an old fellow's house and asked him if there were any yanks about, and he told us that they were camped just across the creek about half a mile ahead. We went on quietly, keeping a good lookout, and sure enough, when we got near the creek we could hear dogs barking. They always had dogs about their camps: why, we never could tell, unless it was because the negroes followed them and the dogs followed the negroes. At any rate, the dogs were always there. We halted, and could distinctly hear them talking: and after listening long enough to be sure that we had accomplished our mission, we fell back down the road about a quarter [mile] and put out a picket.

It came Townsend's and my turn to go on late, and we went to the top of the hill with a lot of orders, mostly "nots"—namely, not to talk, not to smoke, not to make the least noise, and not to shoot, if possible to avoid it, and not, under any circumstances, to dismount, but to sit quietly on our horses and watch. I do not know how long I had been there when I got so sleepy it seemed to me I should fall off of my horse. I leaned over, and in a whisper asked Townsend if he was sleepy too. He said he was nearly dead. Finally, we could stand it no longer, and got down off our horses and began walking back and forth in front of them as far as the halters would let us, but this didn't do any good. Looking around I saw that the road was raised—that is, it was higher than the ground on either side of it. I told Townsend that I was going to sit down on the ground and rest. We both sat down, putting our feet in the ditch. There were plenty of weeds growing close up to the side of the road. I leaned over and put my head down on my hands as they rested on my gun. I did not expect nor intend to go to sleep, but I was completely fagged out. I don't know how long I had been in the position described when something passed by through the weeds with a whisk, a whisk that waked me instantly. It was right under my nose when I saw it, and I tell you the truth when I say it nearly scared the life out of me. It scared me so bad I yelled, "Hellfire, what's that?" as loud as I could, and then I saw it was nothing but a coon. Almost instantly we were on our horses listening, but the yanks never heard a word, or if they did they made no sign. As soon as we found we hadn't alarmed them we got to laughing, and really after the scare was over it was about as funny an adventure as any that happened to me during the war. It shows how little it takes to scare a fellow almost to death when he is tired out and expecting to be scared anyhow. Just before day we withdrew, but Townsend and I laughed all day over that terrible fright.[25] — "SCOUT"

SHORT BIOGRAPHICAL SKETCH OF FORREST

☞ Born in Bedford [now Marshall] County, Tenn., July 13, 1821; died in Memphis, Tenn., October 29, 1877. He removed to Hernando, Miss., in 1842, and was a planter until 1852, when he removed to Memphis.

General Forrest was one of the most remarkable men developed by the war. In fighting he was the Stonewall Jackson of the West. United States Senator John W. Daniel, of Virginia, in his great speech as orator for the United Confederate Veterans, at their reunion in New Orleans, in April, 1892, said: "Forrest, the 'Wizard of the Saddle,' oh what genius was in that wonderful man! He felt the field as Blind Tom touches the keys of a piano.[26] 'War means killing,' he said, 'and the way to kill is to get there first with the most men.' There is military science—Napoleon, Stonewall and Lee—in a nutshell. He was not taught at West Point, but he gave lessons to West Point." Erroneous statements have been published, even in Encyclopedias, concerning his illiteracy.

Stonewall Jackson. Forrest was often compared to the great military leader from Virginia.

His lovely Christian wife [Mary Ann] died in Memphis only a year or two since.[27] Of his family now living there are Captain William Forrest and his three children—Mary, Bedford, and William.[28] — SUMNER ARCHIBALD CUNNINGHAM

IF ONLY . . .

☞ I regard Forrest as the greatest cavalry officer in our war. I firmly believe had Stonewall Jackson lived and been given 50,000 infantry, and Forrest given 15,000 cavalry, they would have wiped the thing out and "carried the war into Africa," instead of standing on the defensive and being worn out, as we were.[29] — H. R. HILL

FORREST'S CAPTURE OF WOOLFORD

☞ I belonged to Forrest's old brigade, Company A, 11th Tennessee Cavalry. After the battle of Chickamauga we were camped at Cleveland, Tenn., and [Union Col.] Woolford[30] [was camped] at Philadelphia [Tenn.], eight miles south of Loudon [Tenn.]. We started one morning, and rode all day and all night. The next morning surrounded Woolford.

He was ready for "the fun." The 11th was in line behind the artillery, the 4th in our rear, the 8th on our right, the 9th and 10th on the road between Philadelphia and Loudon to cut off their retreat. Forrest hadn't occupied a road running west, and when it got too hot for the boys in blue they started west. Forrest saw the gap, and ordered our regiment (the 11th) to dash across the road. It was about half a mile from us. At the same time the 4th took our place in the line. We got in about 200 yards of the road when [Confederate] Col. Holman ordered my company A and Company B to charge. We went at them like wild men, firing our revolvers, and with the old Confederate yell we went through their line, still shooting and yelling, Col. Holman at the same time coming down on the other ride of the road. They whirled back for town. With the old 11th Tennessee still after them, they rushed through Philadelphia for Loudon. Here they met the 9th and 10th. The only thing they could do was to surrender. We got 500 prisoners, 7 pieces of artillery, 82 wagons, 600 stand of small arms, with all of their camp equipage. This was before the siege at Knoxville. [Confederate Gen. James] Longstreet was then on his march from Chattanooga. He came up in a few days. Then we drove them into Knoxville, where we cut their line in two. After the battle I saw some dead yanks in the [river] branch and pulled some of them out.[31] — GEORGE W. YOUNGBLOOD and J. T. MARTIN

REUNION OF FORREST'S ESCORT

☞ The annual reunion of Forrest's Escort are events of unusual interest, because the personal intimacy of the members has been maintained through the three decades that have intervened. Besides, they have the pride of having done "more hard fighting than did the escort of any other general in the war."

The exercises at the beautiful Cumberland Park, near Nashville, were exceedingly pleasant. . . . On this occasion the peculiar characteristics of Forrest were a theme. Terrible as was the man in battle, he manifested much more faith in prayer than may be supposed from his general reputation. He would digress from command in trying ordeals to ask: "Chaplain, are you praying?"

At the close of the last reunion near Nashville, [Confederate] Majs. [Gilbert Vincent] Rambaut and Charles W. Anderson and Capts. J. C. Jackson and George Dashiell sat with a . . . [journalist] through a pleasant dinner hour in the city. Replies to questions about how they happened to be with Forrest brought out some interesting reminiscences.

Maj. Rambaut was with him from the first, and Capt. Dashiell had been selected because he was a Memphian. He was taken from [Gen.

Benjamin F.] Cheatham's staff. Maj. Charles W. Anderson had been engaged in the transportation department, but he felt so outraged by the vandalism of the enemy at his own home that he determined to engage in field service, and soon after applying to Forrest he wrote an official paper so concisely that the General determined to make him his secretary.

Gilbert V. Rambaut.

Capt. John C. Jackson was an infantry officer, and was so badly wounded at Shiloh that his further service in that department was despaired of, but he would not conform to orders to go on post duty. His only remedy was to resign his commission. This he did, and then went to Gen. Forrest and requested a place with him. He told him that their fathers were neighbors and that he would like to serve under him, but the General told him that he could give him nothing [no rank]. Capt. Jackson explained that he had only expected a place as a private soldier. After some months a vacancy occurred, and Forrest was glad to appoint him as lieutenant. When the gallant Montgomery Little, captain of his escort, was killed, Capt. Nath Boone was the First Lieutenant, and he suggested to Forrest the promotion of Lieut. Jackson to captain. When the General reported the suggestion Jackson was surprised, but did not accept until he had conferred with Boone and had, also, the unanimous accord of the men.

Capt. Jackson gave an account of Forrest at Parker's Cross Roads, which may never have been in print. This was while Jackson was serving as a private. The Federals were greatly superior in numbers, and engaged the Confederates front and rear. Two [Confederate] companies had been sent to the rear, and Jackson went in search of them, but soon reported that he found the yankees instead. The General [Forrest] started instantly in that direction, with Jackson only by his side. There were six ammunition wagons, of the sixty-five captured a few days before, in the road crossing, and when they reached that point, Jackson said "I wouldn't go any farther if I were you." Forrest turned his face, and, with eyes flashing, said, "Sir?" and instantly spurred his horse, which leaped over a wagon tongue, and in a moment he was confronted by a group of Federals who stepped from behind a barn, when the officer demanded his surrender. With a presence of mind amazing, Forrest said, "All right, I'll go back and get what few men I have left"; and he rode off as deliberately as a farmer going from his plow. On reaching his escort, not faraway, he said in a kind of hiss, "Charge them, boys! charge them!" and with his escort company he cut his way out, when anything but a complete surrender seemed hopeless. He got nearly all of his command across the Tennessee [River] quickly.

The suggestion is being made to erect bronze statues of Gen. Forrest in Memphis, in Nashville, and in Chattanooga.[32] — SUMNER ARCHIBALD CUNNINGHAM

FORREST'S OLD REGIMENT

☛ I have long since thought of writing a short history of Forrest's old regiment . . . . I had the honor of being a member of it from the formation at Memphis, Tenn., to its surrender at Greensborough, Ala. Forrest did not enter the service at the head of a Tennessee Regiment of calvary, as is frequently published. Half of his command was from other States. We had Overton's and Logan's companies from Kentucky; Kelley's and Becoats' companies from Alabama; and Gould's from Texas; besides, May's company, though organized at Memphis, was largely of Mississippians, Arkansians, and Texans. Then, too, McDonald's company made up at Memphis, contained some Arkansians.

With seven companies we started from Memphis to the seat of war in Kentucky. N. B. Forrest was Lieut. Colonel, and Rev. David C. Kelley was Major. Hambrick succeeded Kelley to the captaincy of his company. Our first halt was at Fort Donelson, where we did some scouting down the Cumberland River. We were next ordered to Hopkinsville, Ky., where we established permanent camps, and from this point we made frequent scouts, west to the Ohio, and north to Green rivers.

Our first battle of any note was Sacramento, a Kentucky village. Cavalry did the fighting on both sides. This fight lasted but a very short time. The forces were about equal, but the enemy had the advantage of being on the defensive. The head of our column came within range of his guns before we had formed, compelling our men to form under a distressing fire. But form we did, and drove the blue coals pell mell through the village, and into a boggy lane where a great many of them were killed and captured. This battle had a splendid effect in our regiment, causing men and officers to confide in and respect each other. We were convinced that evening that Forrest and Kelley were wise selections for our leaders. And in all the battles that followed in which these two men were actors, they well sustained the reputation made on the field of Sacramento.

Kelley's motto was thus: "In the path of duty there is no danger"; and thus "The duty of a soldier is to obey orders." Forrest made that path of duty plain, Kelley walked in it amid the roar of artillery, the rattle of musketry, even mid the groans of the dying as calmly as he had formerly walked to his pulpit on Sabbath morning. D. C. Kelley was one of the bravest men I ever saw. I never saw him manifest the least sign of fear or excitement on any field of battle, and I was with him on many. I give here one incident. It happened at the siege of Fort Donelson. It was when the enemy tried to pass the Fort with his fleet. Our regiment being cavalry could not be used in defense of the fort. So we were placed back to wait for orders. During this bombardment and when it looked like the furies of hell were turned loose on us, I looked down the line, and saw Kelley sitting on a camp stool leaning against a tent pole reading his Bible. My curiosity was at once excited, and wondering if it were possible for a man to be interested even in reading God's word under such circumstances, I walked to where he was, stood close to him until I was satisfied that he was deeply interested in the Book.

David C. Kelley.

I went back and called some comrades' attention to it, and after going close to him they returned in perfect amazement, that any man could be so composed amid such roaring of cannon shots, and screaming shells. Why, the very earth was quivering under us.

But I started to write the history of the regiment, not of one man. We were badly broken up at Donelson, only a part of us getting away. A number of the brave boys fell on that bloody field, and among the number my captain, Charles May. Oh, how sad we were when he fell with six holes through and near his heart; either of which would have been fatal! He indeed fell in the thickest of the fight, with sixteen of his company dead and wounded around him.

May's charge at Donelson deserves to go down to history among the most daring deeds ever performed on any field of carnage. True, it was reckless and unwise; but they were obeying orders. It is a wonder that the order was ever given; but a greater wonder is that any of us who went with Charlie May into that horrid hollow that cold, icy evening ever rode away again. No braver boys than those who fell around May in that charge—braver men never died on field of battle.

Forrest left Fort Donelson next morning with a part of his regiment.

Gould and Logan remaining with their companies, and also some men from other companies. Capt. Overton stayed, but his Lieut. Crutcher came out with most of his men.

We went thence to Nashville, and next to Huntsville, Ala., at which place a great many of us were furloughed for recruiting purposes. Our next camp was at Burnsville, Miss., where we secured several new companies, and a number of recruits for the old companies. At this place the regiment was reorganized. Forrest was made Colonel, Kelley, Lieutenant Colonel, and Balch, Major. From Burnsville we went to Shiloh, and were actors on that bloody field. When the army fell back to Corinth we remained between the lines nearly all the time that [Braxton] Bragg occupied Corinth. We followed the army to Tupelo. At this point Forrest left us and went to Tennessee as a Brigadier [General]. After this Kelley left us, as did the two Alabama companies. Balch was promoted to Lieutenant Colonel, and E. B. Trezevant to Major.

Under General Frank Armstrong we made campaigns into North Alabama and West Tennessee, fighting almost continually, taking active part in the battles around Iuka, and also at Corinth. Balch left us and Trezevant succeeded him. We were next ordered to [join] Forrest at Columbia, Tenn. All but the Tennessee companies were then taken from us, and two of these, mere fragments, were put into May's old company with the writer in command, leaving just two of the old companies, McDonald and Blantor.

Col. Trezevant was also ordered to take command of the 10th, its Colonel being absent at the time. This was a new regiment, and had seen but little service.

Soon after this the battle of Thompson Station [Tenn.] was fought. Col. Trezevant was ordered to make a flank movement to prevent the enemy from getting back to Franklin in case of his defeat. The regiment was dismounted, and suddenly we came in close proximity to the enemy. The firing commenced almost simultaneously, and oh, what a rapid fire it was! The Tenth was armed with double barreled shot guns, except my company, which had carbines, and in easy range did terrible execution. While the battle was at white heat I turned to speak to Trezevant of how gallantly the men were bearing themselves, and I noticed that he looked pale. I stepped closer and said, "Colonel, are you hit?" The reply was, "Yes, Captain, I am killed. Take charge of the regiment." Putting my arm around him to assist him to the ground, I was ordered by General Forrest immediately to move the regiment forward. Leaving my friend and the hero, I obeyed, and never saw the form of that gallant man any more. I learned that he lingered until the evening, and then gave up his noble life. No braver man or truer friend ever buckled on sabre in defense of Southern soil and Southern honor than Col. E. B. Trezevant.

During our retreat to Chattanooga, the old battalion was reformed. Captain McDonald being the senior officer. The battalion was composed of four companies—A, B, C, and D. A was a Memphis company, transferred from infantry called the Bluff City Grays, and commanded by Captain Philip T. Allen. These men were veterans when they came to us, and we found them as brave as the bravest. Company B, McDonald's old company, commanded by Capt. J. G. Harbor; Company C, May's old company, commanded by Capt. J. C. Blanton; and Company D, commanded by Capt. Bill Forrest [N. B. Forrest's son]. This company was a detail from the old regiment as an escort for General Forrest.

We now took the name of McDonald's Battalion. We did a great deal of scout duty and much hard fighting around Chattanooga. We participated in the great battles of Chickamauga, fought the yankee cavalry at and above Charleston in East Tennessee, and went with Gen. Joe Wheeler around the yankee army north of the Tennessee river. On this campaign we lost our beloved commander, Major McDonald, who was killed, as was Captain May, in a foolish charge at Farmington, Tenn. McDonald was a Scotchman, and as brave a man as ever bore that honored name. He was a line officer, having excellent military ability, and was fast gaining the confidence and admiration of his superiors. But alas, alas, at one of those places where superiors failed to have proper information, McDonald, with his battalion, was ordered to make the charge, which was gallantly done, into the very jaws of death, without the remotest chance of success. Col. Jas. T. Wheeler, of Tennessee, who commanded the brigade at the time, told me afterwards that when he transmitted the order to McDonald he turned away weeping, and refused to witness the terrible charge made by McDonald and his brave men.

Miss Bessie Louise Cox, Maid of Honor for Forrest's Cavalry Corps.

Philip T. Allen was our next commander. After the Wheeler campaign Forrest was ordered to the Mississippi Department. Bragg giving him the old battalion, Morton's battery and his escort, commanded then by Captain Jackson. This little command was placed under Lieut. Col. Crews, and ordered from Rome, Ga., to Okolona, Miss., at which place we met Forrest, and marched directly to Jackson, Tenn., entering the enemy's lines at Saulsbury, Tenn. Our object was to get recruits and rations, which we did, and more, too. The enemy made sure they would bag Forrest. They swarmed thick and fast around us, and fighting was almost incessant. The old battalion and escort had to protect the long wagon train and unarmed men that we had gathered. Of course Morton's Battery assisted usably when they could get there, but our movements were so rapid, and sometimes through byways, that it was impossible to have Morton every time we were attacked.

Allen fell seriously wounded at Lagrange, in a hand-to-hand fight with a full regiment, outnumbering us more than two to one; but, instead of their getting our wagons, we got theirs. By the way, I note a little incident that happened at this fight. After the yankees had retired from the field, Forrest ordered me to pursue them with the battalion, which I did at a gallop. Coming to a short bend in the road on a hill, I saw the enemy formed in line of battle, evidently preparing to charge us. I caught Forrest by the shoulder, saying: "General, they have got us; they are going to charge!"

He checked his horse and asked: "How many men have you?"

My reply was, not more than thirty; that most of the men had stopped to pillage the yankee wagons.

His orders were: "Bring them into line at a gallop," which was instantly done.

By the time the lines were formed, he asked, in a loud voice, for a white handkerchief. A man answered from the ranks that he had one. Forrest then, in a loud voice, said to the man: "Put it on a stick and go down there and tell them yankees that if they do not surrender I will kill the last one of them."

The man started, and so did the yankees, on a perfect stampede. We actually caught some of them. Certainly no man but Forrest would ever have thought of playing such a trick on the enemy. We were at that time in their clutches, if they had but known it. A bold charge at the time by that yankee command would have captured Forrest. We could not possibly have escaped. But the charge was not made, and we rode away to fight them again at Moscow, where we forced our way through them and saved our recruits and supplies, taking all into Mississippi.

The old battalion was then consolidated with Jeff Forrest's [the General's younger brother] Regiment. However, this did not last long. Shortly after this, near Como, Miss., the officers of the battalion were all placed under arrest, charged with mutiny. General Forrest was absent at Mobile at the time. Still, his act was the cause of the trouble. Just before his departure for Mobile he sent a supernumerary officer to take command of us (Allen, our senior captain, being at the time absent and wounded). We felt it our duty to contend for the rights of our wounded brother officer; hence the arrest for mutiny. But when Forrest returned he gave us what we asked for, Philip T. Allen, Major, commanding, and [we] were ready for battle again.

Soon after this Col. D. C. Kelley came back to us, and new companies were added, and it was a full regiment again. We then went with McCulloch's Brigade to Montevallo, Ala., but were ordered back immediately to take part in the Cross Roads fight. Col. Kelley, with part of the regiment, was in the battle. We reached Mississippi, in time for the fight at Harrisburg. In this battle your scribe got a wound that laid him on the shelf for several months. After this, and before I had rejoined them, the old boys turned up in Memphis one morning. When I found them again they were on the Tennessee river, near Paris Landing.

A few days after I got there we had a fight with some gunboats. I must here tell the part that we took in that novel affair. While the regiment was under the bank fighting the gunboat, there was a steamboat run within range of our guns, having on her some yankees, and she was forced to surrender. I was ordered by Colonel Kelley to take charge of the boat and run her to a landing. On reaching the landing Colonel Kelley came aboard and told me Forrest's orders were that we run the steamboat across the river and bring him that gunboat, and he asked me what I thought of it. I told him I thought it "mighty ticklish" business, that the old regiment could fight on land, but we were inexperienced in naval matters, though if the "old Tycoon" said so we would have to turn mariners and try it. So Company C, with D. C. Kelley as admiral (I reckon) left our moorings and started out on our first naval expedition, and I really thought it would be our last. Col. Kelley stood in the pilot house with a cocked pistol to direct the yankee pilot. Lieut. Jim Sutherland, with pistol in hand, stood by the engineer. I was ordered to keep the men on the alert. I knew that one broadside from the gunboat would have sent the admiral and Company C to the bottom of the river, but the thing turned out differently than any sane man would have expected. The yanks ran the bow of their boat into the bank and deserted her without shutting off steam or taking anything with them, not even their dead and wounded. They also left us a splendid dinner, cooked and on the table.

We attacked the gunboat by a hawser to the transport and turned it across the river. We now had a fleet of two transports and a gunboat. They were placed in charge of an old steamboat captain and ordered to accompany the expedition to Johnsonville, but when unprotected by our guns en route, an attack was made by an overwhelming Federal fleet, and we lost our capture. I learn that Col. Kelley still has in his possession the side arms of the officer commanding on the captured boat. That officer, as he delivered the arms, said, "I surrender to the commander of the sharpshooters who made it impossible for me to handle my boat. I could otherwise have run the gauntlet of the artillery."

The next day, I think it was, the fleet was lost. From this place we went to Johnsonville, on the Tennessee river, and assisted in the destruction of a great many of the enemy's boats and large quantities of army stores. We then joined Hood at Florence, Ala., went on that campaign to Nashville and back to Mississippi, taking an active part in the battles fought on the trip from Mississippi to Alabama to look after General Wilson, but Forrest's ranks had become too thin to check such numbers as Wilson had. So the end came, but there were but few of the old regiment to surrender.

The large majority of those who started with Forrest from Memphis in the beginning were in their graves yes, dead on the field of honor. The remnant [that was] left stacked their arms with sad hearts and wended their way to desolated homes. Since then the majority of that remnant has passed away, and it won't be long until all will "cross over the river and rest under the shade of the trees."[33] Thank God, I have never met one of the regiment who had apology to make for the part he took in that war.[34] — CONFEDERATE CAPTAIN J. C. BLANTON

GENERAL FORREST AMONG CIVILIANS
☛ Every living soldier of Forrest's West Tennessee Cavalry remembers the Sixth Tennessee Federal regiment, commanded by [Union] Col. F. H. [Fielding Hurst], of Purdy, McNairy County, Tennessee, a regiment of cavalry unknown to fame by any gallant deeds or meritorious conduct on the battlefield, and one which the war records of the rebellion alone have preserved from merited oblivion.

It may be truthfully said of this regiment that it did more plundering, burning, robbing, and running and less fighting, than any regiment in the Federal army, Fifth Tennessee Federal Cavalry only excepted.

On one of Forrest's campaigns, from Mississippi into West Tennessee, and soon after leaving Corinth, he learned that Hurst and his regiment had evacuated Purdy, and that before leaving they had laid in ashes the homes of absent Confederate soldiers, also those of a number of citizens who were known to be in sympathy with the South.

Wilson's Sixteenth Regiment, of our command, and Newsom's, also, were composed of men from McNairy and adjoining counties, and Forrest knew that unless timely steps were taken to prevent it there would be trouble when he reached Purdy.

When within a few miles of that place he directed me to take a sergeant and five men from his escort, dash on into Purdy, and place a guard around the residence of Col. Hurst.

On entering the town, blackened wall's, lone chimneys, and charred remains of buildings gave abundant evidence of Hurst's cowardly vandalism. Learning from a citizen that his residence was in the suburbs, and directly on our line of march to Jackson, we were soon at its front.

Five year old W. Bennett Jr., Mascot of Troop A, Forrest's Cavalry.

Dismounting and entering the portico of his dwelling, I tapped lightly on the door with the hilt of my saber. In a moment or so it was opened by a lady, when I asked, "Is this Mrs. Col. Hurst?" She tremblingly answered, "Yes, sir."

I noticed her agitation, also that on opening the door her countenance quickly changed, manifesting on the instant both surprise and alarm.

Hastening to relieve her apprehensions, I said, "We are not here to harm you, but have been sent for your protection. Although Gen. Forrest has not reached Purdy, he is aware of the ruin and devastation caused by your husband's regiment, and has sent me in advance of his troops to place a guard around your house. This guard is from his own escort, and will remain with you until all of our command has passed, and I assure you that neither your family or anything about your premises will be disturbed or molested."

Giving the officer of the guard instructions, I turned to her, and was in the act of raising my cap before mounting my horse, when, brushing away tears she could no longer repress, she said, "Please, sir, say to Gen. Forrest, for me, that this (referring to the guard) is more than I had any right to expect of him, and that I thank him from my heart for this unexpected kindness. I shall gratefully remember it and shall always believe him to be as generous as he is brave."

Returning to the town, I rejoined the General as he was entering the public square, where he halted and was soon surrounded by citizens of the place, among them the venerable father of Col. D. M. Wisdom, of our command, who said, "You see, General, the marks of Col. Hurst's last visit to our town, and you are also aware that a large number of our citizens are Union people, and they are greatly alarmed for fear of retaliation on the part of your command.

Forrest's reply was characteristic and stripped of his habitual way of emphasizing matters: "I do not blame my men for being exasperated, and especially those whose homes have been laid in ashes, for desiring to revenge such cowardly wrongs, but I have placed a guard around the home of Hurst, and others need feel no uneasiness. Orders have been issued to my command that no Union citizen of this town must be insulted, much less harmed, and this order was accompanied by my personal request that it be obeyed to the letter, and I am sure no soldier of my command will disobey the one, or disregard the other. Of one thing, however, the Union friends of Hurst and his cowardly regiment of Tennessee renegades may rely upon. If we ever are so fortunate as to find them just once in my front, I will wipe them off the face of the earth. They are a disgrace to the Federal army, to the State, and to humanity."

Ever after this, whenever it was known that Forrest was on the move, that [Union] command stood not on the order of its going. They well knew that whenever they confronted Forrest there would be a long account to settle.

During my service as a staff-officer of Gen. Forrest from October, 1862, to the surrender, he fought every [Union] cavalry commander and much of the infantry of the [U.S.] army of the Cumberland, also that of the Mississippi—[Yankee] Generals Kilpatrick, Stanley, Mitchell, Wilder, McCook, and Minty, of the former, and Grierson, Hatch, Mower, Warren, and Winslow, of the latter, yet for none of these commanders do we cherish the slightest feeling of either disrespect or resentment. I bear cheerful testimony now to the dash, the gallantry and soldierly bearing of these officers, and regret that for the credit of the State of Tennessee, the names of [Yankee officers Col.] Hurst and Gen. William Sooy Smith cannot be added to the list. Truth forbids it, for we never met them where they should have been—at the front.

Before the war they were men of prominence, both of them lawyers of recognized ability. When our army was forced out of Tennessee they had regiments of cavalry ostensibly to fight for the Union, yet history and the "Records of the War of the Rebellion" fail to show their participation in a single battle of any note, nor in all the reports of Federal army commanders have I been able, so far, to find one word of commendation of either of them.

Retribution, as marked as it is just, always follows the cowardly and vindictive use or abuse of power. Shirking both danger and duty on the field, they hounded, plundered, arrested, abused and insulted a helpless and defenseless people, and as a consequence, both have long since sunk into obscurity, despised and execrated by thousands who suffered from their cruel deeds, unrelieved by a single brave or noble act on the battlefield or off of it.[35] — CONFEDERATE MAJOR CHARLES W. ANDERSON

THE GIRL WHO PILOTED FORREST

☛ It was Emma Sansom, a courageous girl in a home remote from other habitations on Black Creek, a stream with perilous fords near Rome, Ga., who volunteered to go with the Confederates when in hot pursuit of [Union] Gen. [Abel D.] Streight at the time of his capture. She heard Gen. Forrest express intense concern about fording the stream, and as her father and brothers were away in the war, she wanted to do "some service" herself, and importuned her mother, who objected, but yielded when that "wizard of the saddle," as

Emma Sansom.

perhaps no other could have done, thrilled her with his need for a guide at once. It is said that she asked Gen. Forrest on the way to let her ride in front, as she might be some protection to him against the bullets. The young girl had no thought that it would give her fame beyond all that she had ever done or could hope to do, and that she was mounting behind the General who was fast upon making the most noted captures of the war, save only those great events when our main armies surrendered from sheer exhaustion in '65.

Miss Sansom married in her mature years, but has long since crossed another dark stream, and may have conferred [in Heaven] with General Forrest, who has done likewise, but who had previously made peace with all his enemies.[36] — SUMNER ARCHIBALD CUNNINGHAM

MILITARY CHARACTER OF GENERAL FORREST

☛ No soldier of modern times so forcibly impressed his singular and magnetic individuality upon all surroundings as did Gen. N. B. Forrest. Naturally great, nature's God designed him for the accomplishment of great purposes. He was untutored in the arts and sciences, and unlearned in the strategy of war as taught by theory; he followed in battle no chartered precept, but relied always upon the unerring dictates of his own great reason. Possessed of a native strategy all his own, he cared for no chartered precedent. He based his combinations and dispositions of troops on the topographical and geographical surroundings. So great was the almost resistless force of his individual magnetism that he impressed every man in his command with the firm conviction that victory would perch upon his standard ere the battle was fought, and no leader was ever followed to battle with blinder confidence on the part of his soldiery. Having passed through all official grades to that of Lieutenant General [one rank shy of full General], he commanded when the war closed a cavalry corps of twenty thousand men trained to fight wherever and whenever they met the enemy. In moral elan and efficiency as veteran soldiery, they were not inferior to the "Old Guard" of the First Napoleon. Under his leadership and direction the infantry and cavalry arms of the service were combined in one body, which he fought either on foot or horse as the topography of the country and the character of the enemy required, and he moved his large body of horses from place to place with a rapidity never before equalled, and with an ever abiding confidence that the day would be won. He shirked no responsibility however great, and was actuated in all he did by no purpose other than the good of his country. He commanded not only the respect and confidence of his troops, but also that of the citizens of all the states in which he operated. The greatness of his soul manifested itself on all occasions. He never seemed to value his life in a worthy cause. He was ever at the front, and was thereby enabled to detect the first waver of the foe and take advantage of it. Cowardice in either officers or men he thoroughly despised, while few general officers honored the brave man in the private's jacket as he did. There were privates in his old regiment and in his escort for whom he had as much respect, and whom he treated with as much consideration, as he did regimental commanders. No more knightly soul than his ever lived on this earth. In battle it was his greatest pleasure, sabre in hand, to seek hand to hand personal encounter with some foeman more daring than his comrades, and few there were who, thus engaged, escaped his terrible blade.

  Loving his native South as the child loves the mother from whose gentle breast it draws its life, there was no sacrifice which he deemed too great to make in her service. Subordinated for the first two years of the war to the direction of his inferiors, he bore this indignity

uncomplainingly, setting an example to officers and men worthy of their highest and best emulation. Serving in battle often next to his person, although but a boy, I enjoyed his friendship and confidence to an extent perhaps not bestowed by any other general officer on a private. I know that God never made a man who regretted more sincerely an injustice done to either officer or soldier, and that he suffered most keenly from the consciousness of it, also that he was ever ready to make the most generous reparation. During the first years of the war he was greatly hampered by the military authorities of the Confederate government. The President himself [Jefferson Davis] attached too great importance to training of the United States Military Academy. It was only in the last year of the war that Mr. Davis was pleased to recognize the great ability of Forrest and to assign him to high command. Then it was that the country received the benefit of his genius. Like Jackson, he was a soldier of the school Napoleonic, originating his own plans and carrying them out in his own way [usually in the saddle]; like Jackson, he fought battles and won victories. In Mississippi, Alabama, Tennessee, and Kentucky, the theater of his operations, he met his enemy and destroyed him, as did Jackson in the valley of Virginia. The student of military history will search in vain for a figure more worthy of his enthusiastic admiration.[37]
— HARRY W. RHODES

GENERAL N. B. FORREST IN 1864

☞ In the light of history there stands out in clear relief the figure of Lieutenant-General Nathan Bedford Forrest, the most remarkable man our Civil War developed, and the greatest fighter of which the world has an authentic record. Endowed with a physical frame which resisted fatigue and exposure, a muscular organization developed into athletic proportions by reason of the hard manual labor necessity compelled him to perform from the earliest years of boyhood until he was a man, he possessed that quality of mind which never entertained the fear of personal disaster, nor in the flurry of hand-to-hand combat, nor the excitement or confusion of battle, lost for an instant the calm appreciation of what was transpiring. Quick to perceive in the rapidly shifting scenes of battle the opportunity for a fatal blow, he struck as the lightning flashes, blinding and withering. Before his sudden onslaught, to waver was rout; and in his tireless and unrelenting pursuit, rout became panic.

Without education and absolutely without any knowledge of war gleaned from the study of what others had accomplished, he evolved and put into execution the tactics and the strategy of the most famous generals in history. In his terse phraseology: "The way to whip 'em, is to get there first with the most men," and although his greatest victories were won with forces numerically inferior, he so fought his men that where he struck, he was equal to or stronger than his adversary. He realized the value of boldness even when akin to rashness, and, when possible, he attacked notwithstanding the disparity of numbers. When the enemy was about to charge, or was charging, his rule was to go at them at once. He knew that the excitement of a forward movement inspired even the timid

John Allan Wyeth.

with courage; while to stand in the open to receive the thundering onslaught of a cavalry charge, was a severe test of the courage of the bravest, and demoralizing to the timid. The *active defensive* was in him an intuition. Moreover, he fought his artillery as if they were shot-guns, charging right up to the opposing lines, their double-shotted contents at short range dealing death and disaster. Although his soldiers were called "mounted infantry" and "Forrest's Cavalry," they were neither infantry nor cavalry. There was not a bayonet in his command, and early in the war the sabre was discarded for the repeating pistol. They fought on horse or foot to suit the conditions.

It is probable that not a regiment he commanded could have made a correct tactical manoeuvre on foot in action; and beyond the formation by fours and the evolution into line for the charge, the cavalry manual was practically obsolete. With the men he led, strict discipline was impossible; and yet they fought with the steadiness of trained veterans, under the wonderful influence of one who inspired the timid with courage, and the brave with the spirit of emulation.

He said, "War means fighting, and fighting means killing," and when the enemy were not hunting him, he was hunting for them. Ever in the thickest of the fray, it is a marvel that he lived to see the war end. If ever man had a charmed life, such was his. The missile of the assassin, the gun and sabre of the open and honorable foe, turned from their mortal purpose. He was on over one hundred different occasions under fire, and these include the bloody and hotly contested battles of Fort Donelson, Shiloh, Chickamauga, Franklin, and Nashville. "Twenty-seven horses were shot under him," states [Confederate] Gen. James R. Chalmers; and a famous writer, himself a soldier.

[Confederate] Lieut. Gen. Richard Taylor says: "I doubt if any commander since the days of lion-hearted Richard has killed so many of his enemies as Forrest." His word of command as he led the charge, was, "Forward, men, and mix with them!" Though torn with bullets, and hacked in countless places with the sabre, or hurled from his horse in [the] death struggle of the melee, his life was spared to serve to the end the cause [conservatism] which no man better served than he.[38]

I consider General Forrest the most wonderful man in the history of our Civil War, and am sure everybody in the South and every Confederate soldier should be glad of an opportunity to do something toward perpetuating his marvelous achievements.[39] — DR. JOHN ALLAN WYETH

TRAGIC INCIDENT AT CHICKAMAUGA

☛ The death of [Confederate] Capt. F. P. Gracey, of Clarksville, brought to mind a tragic incident of the battle of Chickamauga.

Capt. Gracey was then a lieutenant in command of a section of Napoleon guns of Cobb's Kentucky Battery [C.S.], attached to Breckenridge's Division. On the last day of the battle, this division was the extreme right of Bragg's Infantry, while Forrest, with Armstrong's division of his Cavalry, fought the day out dismounted, "touching elbows" with Breckenridge during the morning, and in the evening with a portion of Walker's reserve corps under Generals Walthall and Govan.

Before the battle began, Breckenridge and Forrest were riding together to the front. On nearing the line of battle they found Gracey's section of artillery in reserve in the rear, the nature of the ground preventing Gen. Helm from using all of his guns. Forrest (who believed in putting every man and gun in the fight) applied for the loan of Gracey's section; and it was ordered at once to the front and into position. Skirmishing soon began, and as the Generals were separating, Breckenridge reined in his horse, and said: "With you on my flank, Gen. Forrest, I shall suffer no uneasiness as to my right being turned by the enemy to-day. But mind you, General! don't lose Gracey and my Napoleon guns."

The battle soon waxed hot, the enemy was driven back, and about ten o'clock Armstrong swung his right brigade under the brave and gallant Dibrell to the left and front, capturing the Federal Hospital at Cloud's Spring, thus gaining the enemy's rear, and also possession of the Lafayette road, upon which Grainger's [Union] corps was moving to the assistance of [Union] Gen. [George H.] Thomas, but whose advance was greatly retarded by our mounted division of Cavalry commanded by

[Confederate] Gen. [John] Pegram unsupported by any Infantry.

Forrest withdrew from this road, but massed his artillery, consisting of Morton's, Huggin's and Huwald's batteries, and Gracey's section, upon a glady ridge running parallel with and about six to eight hundred yards from it. Waiting quietly until Grainger's column was fairly in his front, every gun was put into action, and so severe and telling was their fire that Grainger was compelled to abandon the open road, change direction, and seek shelter behind the foot hills of Missionary Ridge, between Cloud's Spring and McDonald's.

Towards sundown, artillery firing had ceased on our left, and occasional rapid discharges of musketry was all that could be heard in that direction. An artillery duel, however, had been going on for some time between Gracey's section—a section of Morton's rifle guns, and a Federal battery on a hill near McDonald's.

About six p.m., with no enemy in his front, Forrest considered the battle ended for the day, and directed me to order Morton and Gracey to cease firing, also to thank Gracey for his gallant and efficient services, and order him to limber up his guns and report back to his command. Reaching Morton first, his guns were silenced. I then rode to Gracey's position and gave him the same

Mattie Dortch Wood (right) of Nashville "was ardently devoted to the Confederacy and true to the cause [conservatism]. It was her one desire that these principles be instilled into her children. She was always pleased to talk to them about the war, and with pride she often told of meeting and talking with General Forrest as he was on his way to Murfreesboro."

order, and delivered the General's complimentary message. After thanking me, he remarked that one of his pieces was loaded, and he would like to get permission to discharge it, as it was unsafe to move with it, the gun being hot. I took the responsibility of ordering him to change the direction of the piece, so as not to invite a renewal of the engagement with the yankee battery, elevate it as high as possible and discharge it, which he did.

As is well-known, Gen. Thomas withdrew his command through McFarland's Gap to Rossville, beginning the movement as early as 5:30 p.m., and completing it before eight o'clock, of which fact Bragg was entirely ignorant until the next morning. On that morning (the 21st of September, '62), Forrest was ordered to mount his command and push the enemy on to Chattanooga on the Lafayette road; but before starting, he directed me to take a detachment of Cavalry and a detail from the escort to act as couriers cross Missionary Ridge, and get on the line of the Federal retreat, and join him in the direction of Rossville. Unwilling to lose time by going back to McFarland's Gap, I determined to make the crossing at the depression above Cloud's Spring. In ascending we soon approached the Cloud house. There I saw that a cannon shot had gone through the left front room. It had entered two or three feet above the floor level. In an instant it occurred to me that Gracey's last shot did it. Halting for a moment, inquiry was made of the Assistant Surgeon in charge. He said that the shot struck the building about six o'clock—that it came from the last cannon fired the evening before, and in its passage through the house it killed a wounded officer; and he pointed to the shattered relics of a cottage bedstead on which the officer lay at the time. The church at Cloud's, and the grounds around the spring were filled with Federal wounded, and were plainly in view from the position of our batteries, but the Cloud mansion was above the spring and completely hidden by a grove of trees.

This discharge from Gracey's gun causing death, induced [Union] Gen. W. C. Whitaker of Grainger's Corps, to incorporate in his report of the battle of Chickamauga this erroneous and unjust charge: "With alacrity and enthusiasm, the men marched under a hot sun, and through clouds of dust up the Lafayette road until they found the Rebel mounted Infantry drawn up in line of battle to intercept our progress. They had already readied the rear of Thomas' command, and had possession of his field hospital, which they had inhumanly shelled while filled with our wounded, killing my personal friend, the gallant Dick Rockingham, Lieutenant-Colonel of my brave old regiment, the Sixth Kentucky [U.S.], who was lying wounded in it."

If Gen. Whitaker is still living, it may interest him, as well as the surviving friends and comrades of Col. Rockingham, to know that his death was caused by the accidental destination of a ball from an elevated unaimed gun, fired solely to render it safe for removal from the field, and not from any "inhuman shelling," as charged in his report. In using the past tense ("had inhumanly shelled"), Gen. Whitaker charges that such shelling had been done, and his friend killed before he and his command reached the hospital grounds on their way "almost at a double-quick" to the relief of Gen. Thomas. In justice to my old commander, and the brave officers and men of his batteries, I must say that the charge is untrue. When Dibrell swung his brigade on to the Lafayette road and captured the hospital at ten o'clock in the morning his batteries were in the rear of the division, and not a cannon shot was fired during the movement.

With the record of the splendid fighting done by Gen. Whitaker's brigade that same evening on the flank of Thomas, and his own gallant conduct on the field, as attested by his division and corps commanders, he cannot, if he be as just as he was brave, fail to make a manly withdrawal of the charge, which does great injustice to a brave commander and as gallant troops as ever formed in line of battle. But whether this be done or not, as a staff officer of Gen. Forrest, and with him, too, from "start to finish" in this great battle, and knowing, also, the facts of Col. Rockingham's death to be just as I have stated them, I cannot permit the charge to go into history uncontradicted.[40] — CONFEDERATE MAJOR CHARLES W. ANDERSON

FIRST IMPRESSION OF FORREST AT CHICKAMAUGA

☛ [It was at the Battle of Chickamauga that,] for the first time, I met General Forrest on a battle field. In the midst of the indecision of the moment, among the first who arrived at our guns, I noticed a splendidly mounted, magnificent looking man, commanding in stature and appearance, in full Confederate gray uniform, who seemed to be a general officer. He was unattended, and riding among the men. I heard him say to them: "Rally here, Louisianians, or I'll have to bring up my bobtail cavalry to show you how to fight!" This call revealed the man to me; and I recognized in his face the lineaments I had often heard described as peculiar to Forrest. He looked like some knight-errant dropping into our midst from out of some battle picture of romance; some Richard Coeur de Lion—some Black Douglas. That knightly apparition ever since has been ineffaceably mixed in my recollection.[41]
— CONFEDERATE GENERAL J. A. CHALARON

CHICKAMAUGA REMINISCENCES

☛ ... My Company, the "Maynard Rifles," was organized some time before the war; it was composed of merchants, lawyers, doctors, etc., mostly men of thirty years of age and upwards, who armed, uniformed and equipped themselves in all things for the field, and were well drilled, especially in the skirmish drill, in the use of the Maynard rifle, a patent "breech-loader" then just coming into use. We used these weapons for the first time in battle at Shiloh. Our great cavalry hero, Gen. N. B. Forrest, was a private in our Company when the war commenced.

I witnessed a very uncommon touching scene, on the day of Chickamauga, which I never saw before or after; at different times, a soldier wounded in the arms, leading another to the rear with both eyes shot out. I often saw wounded soldiers carrying off a worse wounded companion. The night after the battle one of Gen. Bragg's couriers brought me his dispatch to the War Department at Richmond to be telegraphed from Ringgold. The instrument of the operator with me would not work, and we were in a quandary; when an officer of Gen. Morgan's Cavalry, I think his name was Gardner, a Canadian, who had aided Gen. Morgan in tapping wires, etc., in his Northern raids, hearing of the trouble, produced his instrument, connected with the wires, and in a few minutes the dispatch was telegraphed. It was written in pencil, short and distinct, but ended, after telling of the defeat of the enemy, the capture of guns and prisoners, "the enemy still confronts us." Gen. Bragg did not realize the complete victory, and had he followed the urgent advice of Forrest, could have finished it by the destruction or capture of Thomas. I have that dispatch and other army papers yet.[42] — CONFEDERATE MAJOR B. J. SEMMES

THE TRUE STORY OF FORT PILLOW

☛ After the return of Gen. Forrest's command from his expedition to Paducah, Ky., his Adjutant General, Major [John P.] Strange, was attacked with hemorrhage of the lungs, and when ready for the move against Fort Pillow his condition was so critical that Gen. Forrest thought it best to leave Col. Galloway and his son, Willie Forrest, at Jackson with him; hence, I was the only staff officer with Gen. Forrest in his expedition against that fort.

[Confederate] Gen. [James R.] Chalmers, with Bell's and McCulloch's brigades, and four small pieces of artillery, moved out from Jackson on the morning of the 10th of April, 1864. Gen. Forrest, with escort, and a detachment under Lieut. Col. Wisdom, followed later. On reaching Brownsville he directed Gen. Chalmers to make a forced march on the night of the 11th, and if possible to reach Fort Pillow by or before day on the morning of the 12th (in order to take the garrison by surprise), and to attack at once on arrival.

Gen. Forrest rested a few hours at Brownsville, and followed Chalmers. When within eight or ten miles of the river we heard the first cannonading at the fort, and knew then that Gen. Chalmers was at work. Our march was quickened, and some three or four miles from the fort we were met by a courier with a dispatch from Gen. Chalmers, stating that he had driven the enemy into their works and the rifle pits around the fort, and, as I now remember, expressing the opinion that they could not be assaulted and captured except with heavy cost. This dispatch put us in a trot, and Gen. Forrest was soon on the ground and in command.

As everything was comparatively quiet, our jaded horses were rested for a few moments, while the General held a short conference with Gen. Chalmers. After which, unaccompanied except by myself, he made a rapid circuit around the landside of the fort from the Federal horse lot to Coal Creek above, returning to our starting point over a diminished distance from the works. In returning we were subjected to a constant and dangerous fire from the parapets.

The General's horse was wounded, and my own pulled up dead lame after leaping a small ditch. I supposed him shot also, but it proved [to be] a strain. Going at once to the Escort's position in rear of the Federal horse lot, I dismounted private Lucas, of that company, took his horse, and rejoined the General as he was returning alone from a re-examination of the ground over which we had ridden, and as we galloped rapidly around and down toward the river, a second horse was shot [out from] under him and killed.

In these examinations he found a ravine almost encircling the fort, and that from the high ground over which we had ridden, sharpshooters could command most of the area inside the fort, and could enfilade its retreating angles, and render them untenable or the occupation exceedingly hazardous.

He also discovered that the ravine once gained by our troops, they would be just as well fortified as were the enemy, one party being inside and the other just outside of the same earthworks. His plan of action was quickly determined, was speedily communicated to Gen. Chalmers, and by him to his brigade commanders, and preparations and dispositions made at once for its execution.

Under signals from the fort, the [Union] gunboat *New Era* lay abreast of the mouth of the ravine below the fort, and was constantly shelling us. By the General's directions, I moved a section of artillery to the high bluff below the mouth of the ravine, where a plunging fire would necessarily drive her from her position. Of this movement she was doubtless advised by signal from the fort, as she steamed up the river and out of range before we could open fire on her.

While absent on this duty, strong lines of [our] sharpshooters had been thrown forward to the high ground previously referred to, and when I rejoined the General our whole force, under a terrific fire from the artillery and small arms of the garrison, was closing rapidly around the works. Bell's brigade was on the right, extending from the mouth of Coal Creek southward; McCulloch's brigade on the left, extending from the ravine below the fort northward, his right joining the left of

Bell's line abreast of the fort.

When Gen. Chalmers had gained this desired position, which was done rapidly and handsomely, but with the loss of some brave officers and men, Gen. Forrest determined, in order to save further loss of life, to demand a surrender. He knew the place was practically in his possession, as the enemy could not depress their artillery so as to rake the slopes around the fort with grape and canister, and the constant and fatal fire of our sharpshooters forced the besieged to keep down behind their parapets. He believed the Federal commander fully recognized the situation, and that he would accept an offer to surrender in preference to an assault by a force much larger than his own, and in full view. Bugles were sounded for a truce and a parley, and a white flag sent forward with a demand for the immediate and unconditional surrender of all the Federal troops at Fort Pillow.

N. B. Forrest Sponsors and Maids of Honor, U.S.C.V. The N. B. Forrest Camp Adjutant, N. B. Forrest II (the General's grandson), is pictured bottom center.

The smoke of approaching [Union] steamers ascending the river had been visible for some time. Three of them were now nearing the fort. Gen. Forrest ordered me to take a detachment from McCulloch's brigade and move to the bluff, and prevent them from landing. I at once detached three companies, about one hundred and fifty men, and moved them rapidly to a position within sixty yards of the south entrance of the fort, descending by a path and occupying some old rifle pits on the face of the bluff, which were built by the Confederates in 1861 for protecting their water battery. These pits were washed out, broken, and in many places filled in by caving banks from above, yet afforded some protection.

The channel of the Mississippi River at Fort Pillow runs close under the bluff, and as the foremost steamer neared our position I directed one of the men to fire at her pilot house. A second shot from another secured attention at once, and she sheared off toward the bar across the river. This steamer was the *Olive Branch*, crowded from forecastle to hurricane deck with Federal soldiers. She was closely followed by the *Hope*, and the *M. K. Cheek*, both of which adopted the course of the leading steamer, making for the bar on the west side of the river, and all of them passing up to the position of the gunboat *New Era*, which lay midstream just above the fort.

The bugler of the Thirteenth Tennessee Federal Cavalry had taken advantage of the truce to recover his trappings from his horse, which he had left tied in a small gulch or ravine leading from the fort toward the river. As I rode to the head of it I discovered him, with his back to me, busily engaged in securing his gum cloth and coat. I waited quietly until he turned to regain the fort. His astonishment and trepidation can well be imagined at finding a six shooter levelled at his face and an able bodied "Reb" behind it. Ordering him to hand me his carbine butt end foremost, and then to untie his horse and lead him out ahead of me, I rode down and around to the General's position, who was then with much impatience awaiting an answer to his final demand for a surrender.

As there were no [Yankee] steamers in sight coming from below, I remained with him until the final and emphatic refusal of the garrison to surrender was received.

I had in the meantime communicated to him the position of the gunboat, also that two large empty barges were cabled to the shore in [the] rear of the fort, which might be utilized by the garrison, under her protecting fire, as a means of escape. I was equally particular in impressing upon him the hazardous position of the detachment on the face of the bluff, (out of sight of, and entirely separated from, the balance of the command), and that in the event of any failure to carry the works by assault, a sortie from the south entrance of the fort in their rear, with the gunboat and its cannon and marines in their front, their destruction or capture would certainly follow.

He fully recognized their isolated and exposed position, but, ignoring the contingency, he directed me to return to my position at once—to take no part in the assault, but to prevent any escape from the garrison by barges or otherwise—to pour rifle balls into the open ports of the *New Era* when she went into action, and, to use his last expression, "fight everything blue betwixt wind and water until yonder flag comes down."

Returning at once, all necessary orders were given to the senior officer of the detachment, and by him they were passed along the trenches. I took a position in speaking distance of him, and where, by remaining mounted, I could see the fort flag; preferring to expose myself and horse to the expected fire of the *New Era* to that from the parapets of the fort, from which I was not fifty yards distant, but fully protected by an intervening ridge, around the head of which I had intercepted the bugler.

From this position I had a full view of the entire water line in [the] rear of the fort, and much of the sloping bank above it. Owing to the conformation of the bluff, its brow in the rear of the fort was not visible, but nearly all the slope from the water line to within twenty or thirty feet of the top of the bluff in the rear of the fort was in plain view.

This was the situation as taken in while anxiously awaiting the sound of [Jacob] Gaus' well-known bugle. It soon came; was repeated along the line, and at once followed by the yells of our men, and a terrific discharge of the batteries and small arms of the fort. In a few moments a portion of the garrison rushed down toward the river, and upon them we opened a destructive fire. The yells of our troops as they mounted the parapets could be plainly heard above the din and rattle of musketry, and in a moment more the whole force of the garrison came rushing down the bluff toward the water with arms in hand, but only to fall thick and fast from the short range fire of the detachment temporarily under my command, which threw them into unutterable dismay and confusion. This fire, with that of the whole assaulting line, was, for the few moments it lasted, most destructive and deadly. The moment the federal colors came down, I ordered firing to cease at once, and it was promptly done. Directing the commanding officer to bring his men up out of the pits and report to his regiment, I dashed into the south entrance of the fort. Everything was in confusion and the dead and wounded were lying thick around, but there was no firing anywhere.

I met the General between the flagstaff and the entrance, and his first words were: "Major, we drove them right to you, and I cut their flag down as soon as I could get to it."

No one under such circumstances could accurately give the time of these transactions, but I am satisfied in my own mind that it was less than fifteen minutes from the time our bugles sounded until their colors came down, and less than two minutes from the time they were lowered until

firing had ceased, and I had joined the General inside the works.
Every soldier who has ever participated in work of this kind knows that such actions must be short, sharp and desperate, to be successful.

Gen. Forrest's first order was to wheel around and move out the cannon of the fort so as to command the river. He could have opened fire at long range upon the *New Era*, as she steamed away up the river, but instead of doing so, directed me to take Capt. Young, the Federal provost marshal, and a white flag, and endeavor to open communication with her, with a view of delivering the Federal wounded and securing surgical aid for them until they could be removed.

With a flag we followed her up the river bank, waving her to stop and send a boat ashore. She paid no attention whatever to our signals. Doubtless her commander thought our flag a ruse to effect his capture, and his vessel soon disappeared around the point above the fort.

Members of the N. B. Forrest Camp, U.C.V., Chattanooga, Tenn., 1900.

Returning and reporting to the General our failure to communicate with the *New Era*, he at once caused details to be made of all the unwounded Federals, under their own officers, to first bring into the huts and houses on the hill all their wounded comrades, and then to proceed at once to bury their dead.

When the wounded and dead had been removed from the face of the bluff, a detail of our own men was sent down to gather up all the small arms thrown down by the garrison. I went with this detail myself, and inspected and handed over to our ordinance officer two hundred and sixty-nine rifles and six cases of rifle ammunition, all of which were gathered up on the face of the slope from the fort to the water's edge. The six cases of cartridges were piled against the upturned roots of an old tree, with their tops removed, ready for immediate distribution and use.

Gen. Forrest remained on the ground until late in the evening, hoping to be able to deliver the wounded to some steamer, should any approach the fort; but as none ventured to come in sight, he gave full directions to and turned over the command to Gen. Chalmers, and, moving out on the Brownsville road with his escort, we encamped at a farmhouse about seven or eight miles from Fort Pillow.

As we were mounting our horses next morning (the 13th) en route to Jackson, a heavy cannonading began at the fort. The General at once directed me to take ten men from the escort and, with Capt. Young (who was still with us), to proceed back to Fort Pillow and again attempt negotiation with the Federal fleet for the removal of their wounded.

On arrival I caused all of Gen. Chalmers' details, at whom the gunboats were firing, to be at once withdrawn, and accompanied by Capt. Young only, with a white flag, rode down to the water's edge. The [Union] gunboat *Silver Cloud* discovered us and our flag, ceased firing, and steamed slowly in shore. When within hailing distance her engines were stopped, and her commander, through his trumpet, asked, "What was wanted?" I asked him to send an officer ashore, and I would deliver my communications in writing. Seeing him run out and launch a small boat into the river, I dismounted from my horse and wrote briefly what was desired; but, on turning around, found the small boat nearing our position with the United States flag at its bow and six armed marines and an officer aboard. Waving him back, and calling his attention to our white flag, I told him that I could hold no parley with him until he returned to his vessel, hoisted a white flag, and returned with his oarsmen unarmed. This he readily did, and on his return a communication was given him, requesting the landing of the *Silver Cloud* in order to negotiate for a truce, and for the delivery of all the wounded of the garrison, and assuring the commander of his safety in landing under a white flag; but, if unwilling to land, to send a boat back and I would go on board to complete the desired arrangements.

As soon as my message was delivered, [Union] Capt. Ferguson lowered his colors, ran up a white flag, and landed his vessel. Going on board, I was furnished by the purser with pen and paper, and in a short time an agreement was made for a truce from 9 o'clock a.m. to 5 o'clock p.m. All the conditions named were accepted by Capt. Ferguson, and the articles drawn up in duplicate and signed by both parties: after which I went ashore, sending a dispatch at once to Gen. Chalmers' headquarters, notifying him of the truce, and that, for fear of a collision, none of his troops must be allowed to come within the old Confederate rifle intrenchments, but suggesting that he and staff come down whenever his duties would permit. I then sent four of my men to clear the fort and its surroundings of all stragglers, and to allow no one to remain on the grounds but surgeons and their assistants.

Allowing time for the men to carry out these orders, I notified Capt. Ferguson to run out his stagings, and that the fort and all its surroundings were now in his possession. Several [Union] steamers were in sight awaiting developments and signals. They were signalled to drop down and land, and in a short time the removal of the wounded to the steamer *Platte Valley* began.

I remained at her gangways, taking a full and complete list of the wounded as they were carried on board, placing a guard at the stage planks of the other steamers, to insure the delivery of all the wounded upon one vessel.

[Union] Capt. Young, who was left ashore in charge of Sergt. Eaton, of the escort, learned that his wife was on one of the steamers just landed, that she was in great stress of mind as to his fate, and asked permission (under guard) to go on board, assure her of his safety, give some instructions as to his private affairs, and bid her farewell. I placed him under parole of honor to report back to me at 2:30 p.m., and allowed him to go at once. He accepted the parole, with many thanks for my kindness, and reporting promptly at the designated hour, was sent out to Gen. Chalmers' headquarters to join his comrades as a prisoner of war.

James R. Chalmers.

Permission was given to all the passengers on the three steamers to visit the fort, and all of them did so, many of them bringing back in their hands buckles, belts, balls, buttons, etc., picked up on the grounds, which they requested permission to carry with them as relics or mementoes of Fort Pillow. All such requests were cheerfully and pleasantly granted.

Gen. Chalmers and staff came down and remained an hour or more, and notified me that he was withdrawing his command to Brownsville, and offering to leave a detachment to accompany me after the truce, which I declined, because I thought we could soon overtake them. With the prisoners and fort artillery I thought they could not move very rapidly. I did not know then that one brigade and the prisoners and artillery were already half way to Brownsville, or I would most certainly have accepted a stronger escort.

Before the expiration of the truce all the wounded had been placed on the *Platte Valley*, and a receipt in duplicate taken from them, signed by Capt. Ferguson, of the *Silver Cloud*. I was, as may be well imagined, worn down and exhausted, and when my duties were over a couple of lieutenants of the Federal army on the *Platte Valley* insisted on my taking a parting glass with them at the bar of that steamer, which I of course did, little thinking at the time that my acceptance of their hospitality and their courtesy would cost them their commissions. For this courtesy and kindness, one officer was cashiered and the other reduced to the ranks.

A while before five o'clock I suggested to Capt. Ferguson the departure of the passenger steamers yet at the landing, and stated to him that after the truce I should proceed to burn all the buildings at Fort Pillow; that they had been preserved for the accommodation of the Federal wounded, and their existence was no longer necessary or desirable. When the steamers had all left, I assured Capt. Ferguson that there was no Confederate force within two miles of the fort, and that he could let go his lines and depart at his leisure, and without fear of molestation.

I then saluted him an adieu, and with my little squad rode slowly up the bluff.

The men with me were dismounted, and set to work scattering and distributing loose straw, hospital beds and bunks through all the buildings. We waited until the *Silver Cloud* let go her lines and swung out into the river. As she lowered her white flag the torch was applied, and as she ran up her colors the last buildings left at Fort Pillow burst into flames. We then mounted our horses and bade Fort Pillow a lasting adieu.

My concluding thoughts: The fearful loss of life at Fort Pillow is alone chargeable to the total incapacity of its commanding officer, and to the fatal and delusive promise or agreement made by [Union] Capt. Marshall, of the gunboat *New Era*, with Maj. Bradford—that is, that when whipped the garrison was to drop down under the bluff, and the *New Era* would give the rebels cannister and protect and succor them. Maj. Booth, who commanded Fort Pillow, was killed early in the morning by a bullet through the brain. His death placed the command in the hands of Maj. W. F. Bradford, of the Thirteenth Tennessee Federal Cavalry, a man without any military capacity whatever; and, if reports were true of him, his conduct as a soldier, as well as the violation of his parole after capture, show him as destitute of honor as wanting in military skill and ability.

When he found himself surrounded by a force thrice his own, and knew that his works were no longer defensible against an assault by such numbers, his plain duty was to surrender the fort and save further loss of life. Nor can he be excused for relying upon the promise of Capt. Marshall, after seeing and knowing that the movement of two howitzers to the low bluff had driven the *New Era* from the only position in which her promised aid could have been at all available.

Marshall did know, and Maj. Bradford ought to have known, that with the channel of the river right under the bluff, and a broad bar with shallow water right opposite the fort, the *New Era* could not get sufficient "offing" to elevate her guns and do any damage to parties on top of a bluff at least eight feet above the water line.

Yet, with all this, the sequel shows that Maj. Bradford, relying upon the promise of Capt. Marshall, refused the third and last demand of Gen. Forrest for his surrender; and when assaulted and driven from the works, he retreated *with arms in hands, and ammunition provided and placed under the bluff*, only to find that the *New Era*, instead of dropping down and giving the Rebels grape and canister, steamed quickly out of harm's way, leaving the duped commander and the deluded garrison to their fate.

How far Capt. Marshall could have aided the garrison no one can say, but it would have been far better for his name and fame had he moved his vessel promptly into action, and perished in attempting to do as he promised, than live and know that his violated promise, and his abandonment of the garrison, first led and then left hundreds of his countrymen and comrades to a swift and sweeping destruction.

I have never hesitated to assert, as I do now, that, numbers considered, the detachment temporarily under my command did, by far, the most fatal and destructive, as well as the *very last firing* done at Fort Pillow. It was enfilading, a terribly short rifle range, and began with the retreat of the very first [Union] troops that left the fort, and continued steadily and rapidly *until the Federal flag came down*. In our position under, or on the face of the bluff, one could only know when the fort was in our possession by the falling of its colors or a special messenger. The former was the quicker,

Nathan Bedford Forrest III, the great grandson of General Forrest. Born 1905 in Memphis; killed in action over Kiel, Germany, in 1943, while serving with American forces.

and under my orders, as soon as it fell, firing was promptly stopped, and, ordering the detachment to report back at once to its regiment, I was with the General in less than two minutes after the flag came down.

The charges against Gen. Forrest and his men of massacre and butchery at Fort Pillow are outrageously unjust and unfounded. He did everything in his power to induce a surrender and avoid an assault. Thrice was a surrender demanded, and as often refused. There never was any surrender, therefore no massacre after surrender, as has been so erroneously and widely charged.

I take occasion here to say that in my long service with Gen. Forrest, his kindness to the vanquished, the unarmed and unresisting foe, was a marked characteristic of the man. He believed and always said and felt, that "war meant fight, and fight meant to kill," but never in all his career did a Federal soldier throw down his arms and surrender, that did not receive at once his consideration and protection. He captured many thousand Federals, and there is not one living to-day who can truthfully say that he was ever mistreated or ever insulted by Nathan Bedford Forrest.[43] — CONFEDERATE MAJOR CHARLES W. ANDERSON

Z

1896-1897

FORREST'S MARKSMANSHIP

☛ At Stevenson, Ala., Gen. Forrest sighted a man [Union soldier] on top of a stockade, half a mile off; he seemed to be so defiant, 'tis said that Forrest dismounted, got hold of one of Morton's pieces of artillery and took aim; he cut that man half in two.[44] — BROMFIELD LEWIS RIDLEY

APPEARANCE & CHARACTERISTICS OF FORREST

☛ Lieutenant-General N. B. Forrest, who was my immediate commander during the first year of the war, if not the greatest military genius, was certainly the greatest revolutionary leader on our side. He was restrained by no knowledge of law or constitution; he was embarrassed by no preconceived ideas of military science. His favorite maxim was: "War means fighting, and fighting means killing." Without the slightest knowledge of them, he seemed by instinct to adopt the tactics of the masters of military art.

On December 28th, 1861, Forrest, with 300 men, met the enemy for the first time, about 450 strong, near Sacramento, Ky. This fight deserves special notice, not only because of its success and the confidence inspired in the raw Confederate cavalry, but because it displayed at once the chief characteristics and natural tactics which were subsequently more fully developed and made Forrest famous as a cavalry leader. He had marched his command twenty miles that day when he found a fresh trail where the enemy's cavalry had passed. Putting his command at a gallop, he traveled ten miles further before he struck the rear guard. His own command was badly scattered, not half up with him, but without halting he rushed headlong at them, leading the charge himself. When he had driven the rear guard on to the main body, and they turned on him with superior force, he quickly dismounted his men and held the enemy in check until his command came up, and ordered them to attack in flank and rear. This movement was successful, and the retreat of the Federals soon began. Quickly mounting his men, he commenced one of his terrible pursuits, fighting hand to hand with pistol and sword, killing one and wounding two himself, continuing this for miles, and leaving the road dotted with living and dead.

[Confederate] Major D. C. Kelley, who then for the first time saw his superior under fire, describing the wonderful change that took place in his appearance, says:

> His face flushed until he bore a striking resemblance to a painted Indian warrior, and his eyes, usually so mild in their expression, flashed with the intense glare of the panther about to spring on its prey. In fact, he looked as little like the Forrest of our mess-table as the storm of December resembles the quiet of June.

General Chalmers relates: "Some of the notable points in Forrest's manner of fighting, were (1) reckless courage in making the attack, a rule he invariably followed and which tended to intimidate his adversary; (2) the quick dismounting of his men to fight, showing that he regarded horses mainly as a rapid means of transportation for his troops; (3) his intuitive adoption of the flank attack, so demoralizing to the enemy even in an open field, and so much more so when made, as Forrest often did, under cover of woods which concealed the weakness of the attacking party; (4) his fierce and untiring pursuit, which so often changed retreat into rout and made victory complete; (5) following, without knowing it, [Charles James] Napier's precept of the art of war, he was always in front making personal observations. This practice brought him in many personal conflicts and exposed him to constant danger, and he had 27 horses killed and wounded under him in battle. This practice led to imitation by his general officers, and at Hart's cross-roads, the day before the battle of Franklin [II], I witnessed Forrest with two division and three brigade commanders, all on the skirmish line.

"At Shiloh, Forrest, without orders from any superior officer, had pushed his scouts to the river and discovered that reinforcements of the enemy were coming. I was then in command of an infantry brigade, which by some oversight had not received the order to retreat; about midnight, Forrest awoke me, inquiring for Generals Beauregard, Bragg and Hardee, and when I could not tell him, he said in profane but prophetic language, 'If the enemy come on us in the morning, we will be whipped like hell!' He carried this information to headquarters and, with military genius, suggested a renewal at once of our attack; but the unlettered colonel was ordered back to his regiment."

Guard of Honor, from Troop A, Forrest's Cavalry, early 1900s.

I recall an anecdote strikingly illustrative of the esteem in which Forrest was held by the people, and he always told it on himself with great delight. When Bragg was retreating from Tennessee, Forrest was among the last of the rear guard. An old lady ran out of her house to the gate as he was passing, and urged him to turn back and fight. As he rode on without stopping, she shook her fist at him and cried, "Oh! you great, big, cowardly rascal! I only wish old Forrest were here; he would make you fight!"

One of the greatest secrets of Forrest's success was his perfect system of scouts. He kept reliable scouts all around him and at great distances and often, even day's in advance, he was informed of movements that were about to be made.

Near West Point, (1864) Forrest soon came up to where I was standing on the causeway, leading to the bridge, and, as it was the first time I had ever been with him in a fight, I watched him closely. His manner was nervous, impatient and imperious. He asked me what the enemy were doing, and I gave him the report just received from Colonel Duff, in command of the pickets. He said sharply, "Well, I will go and see myself." He started across the bridge, which was about thirty yards long and then being raked by the enemy's fire. This struck me at the time as a needless and somewhat braggadocio exposure of himself, and I followed him to see what he would do. When he reached the other bank, the fire of the enemy was very heavy and our men were falling back, one running without hat or gun. In an instant Forrest seized and threw him to the ground, and, while the bullets were whistling around him, administered a severe thrashing with a brush of wood.

General Joseph E. Johnston said if Forrest had been an educated soldier, no other Confederate general would have been heard of.

Dr. J. B. Cowan, of Tullahoma, Tenn., who was chief surgeon to Forrest's Cavalry during the war, and was intimately associated with Forrest, says that at the battle of Okalona, where Forrest's brother Jeffrey was killed, his grief was over powering when he realized that the brother whom he idolized, and who, being a posthumous child, had been tenderly reared and carefully educated by the elder brother, was mortally wounded. Although the Federals were in flight with Forrest pursuing, he seemed for a moment to forget the great responsibility of his position as a commander, in the agony of this sudden affliction. He dismounted, picked up his dying brother and held him in his arms as he would a child, until his lifeblood was spent. The wound was of such a character that surgical relief was impossible, and he bled to death within a few minutes. The rough soldier kissed his dead brother tenderly, with tears streaming from his eyes, laid him gently upon the ground, took one last look, and then his expression of grief gave way to one of almost ferocity; he sprang to his horse, shouting to [Jacob] Gaus, his bugler, "Blow the charge!" and swept ahead of his men in the direction of the retreating enemy. Dr. Cowan followed as close behind him as he could keep in the pursuit, and the faithful escort were well up with their great leader. Half a mile or so down the road they suddenly came upon the enemy, who had determined upon a stand. A piece of artillery was placed to sweep the road by which they must approach, and the Federals, dismounted, had taken a strong position on either side of the road. As soon as they were observed, the Federals fired upon them, and Dr. Cowan remonstrated with the General for thus exposing himself. Forrest remarked, "Doctor, if you are uneasy, you can ride out of range"; and the General continued in this position, making a careful survey of the enemy's position. His horse was killed under him, and he mounted

Confederate Gen. John Adams perished at the Battle of Franklin II, not far from Forrest and his troops.

another, belonging to one of the escort who had just then ridden up. While Forrest was riding a little further on, on the side of a little eminence, this horse was also killed. Satisfied with the reconnaissance, which had only occupied a few minutes, he drew his saber and shouted to the escort, "Move up!" This plucky body of sixty men followed with equal bravery their daring and now reckless leader.

It seemed to me then that the General, maddened by grief at the loss of his favorite brother, wanted to go with him. It was only the matter of a moment when the General and his escort were mixed up with the Federals in a fearful melee. I put the spurs to my horse, ran back in the direction from which we had come to hurry up help, met Colonel McCulloch with a portion of his Missouri regiment, and said to him, "Colonel, for God's sake hurry down the road as fast as you can. The General and his escort are down there in a hand to hand fight, and I am afraid he will be killed before you can get there!" Forrest slew three men with his sword in this terrible fight before the Federals yielded and fled from the field.

General Richard Taylor, who later in the war was placed in command of the department in which Forrest operated, says in his book, *Destruction and Reconstruction*, "some months before the time of our first meeting he had defeated Sturgis at Tishimingo, and he soon repeated his defeat of General Grant at Okalona.

"Okalona was fought on an open plain, and Forrest had no advantage of position to compensate for great inferiority of numbers, but it is remarkable that he employed the tactics of Frederick at Leuthen and Zorndorf, though he had never heard these names. Indeed, his tactics deserve the closest study of military men. When asked to what he attributed his success in so many actions, he replied, 'I got there first with the most men.' I doubt if any commander since the time of lion-hearted Richard, has killed so many of his foes as Forrest. His word of command was unique, 'Move up, and mix with 'em!' While cutting down many a foe with long-reaching arm, his keen eye watched the whole fight and guided him to the weak spot. Yet, he was a tender-hearted, kindly man. The accusations of his enemies that he murdered his prisoners at Fort Pillow and elsewhere are absolutely false. These negroes told me of Forrest's kindness to them."

In the closing campaign at Selma, in April, 1865, General Taylor says: "Forrest ordered his brigades to the Catawba crossing, leading one in person. He was a host in himself, and a dangerous adversary to meet at any reasonable odds. With one brigade, Forrest was in Wilson's path; he fought as if the world depended on his arm, and sent to advise me of the deception practiced on two of his brigades, hoping to stop the enemy if he could with the third, the absence of which he could not account for. After Selma fell, he appeared horse and man covered with blood, and announced the enemy at his heels, and that I must move at once to escape capture. I felt anxious about him, but he said he was unhurt and would cut his way through."

If Forrest was terrible and relentless in battle, he was by nature gentle, tender and affectionate. His love for children was very strong. My personal friend, Colonel R. B. Kyle, of Gadsden, on the 25th of June 1895, gave me in writing the following personal reminiscence of the great soldier: "About May 7th, 1863, as Forrest was returning from the capture of Streight, at Rome, he stayed all night at my house. Forrest's terrific pursuit of Streight, and the capture of his large command with a force only one-third as numerous as the enemy, had, of course, filled the country through which Streight had passed with the idea that Forrest was a tremendous fighter, and gave me the impression that his mind would be occupied only with things concerning the war; but the only thing that seemed to concern him while in my house for almost a day and all night, was my little two-year-old boy, to whom he took a great fancy, holding him on his lap and carrying him around the place in his arms. The little child showed great fondness for him and loved to stay with him. The next day, when Forrest rode away in the direction of Guntersville, he took the little fellow two or three miles on the road with him, holding him on the saddle in front of him, and I rode along with Forrest this distance in order to bring the child home to his mother. He kissed the little fellow tenderly as he bade him good bye and, turning to me, said, 'My God, Kyle, this is worth living for!'

"I again met Forrest in the fall of '63 on board a train en route to

Braxton Bragg.

Montgomery, Ala., to meet President Davis, with whom he had some correspondence, and who had asked Forrest to come to Montgomery, as he wanted to see him personally. We renewed our acquaintance, and in conversation he told me he would not serve [any] longer under Bragg. He said that he was not competent to command any army; that the [C.S.] army had whipped the Federals badly at Chickamauga, and that he, with his command, had followed them almost to the suburbs of Chattanooga; that they were demoralized, and could have been captured, and that he rode back himself, after sending couriers and getting unfavorable replies, and found General Bragg asleep. He urged that they move on in pursuit of the enemy at once, as their capture was certain. Bragg asked how he could move an army without supplies, as his men had exhausted them. Forrest's reply was, 'General Bragg, we can get all the supplies our army needs in Chattanooga.' Bragg made no reply, and Forrest rode away disgusted."[45] — DR. JOHN ALLAN WYETH

A HEROINE OF THE SOUTH
☛ The famous raid of General Streight with two thousand men, near Rome, Ga., resulting in his capture through the intrepidity of a Miss Emma Sansom, was an instance of female prowess long to be remembered. Amidst the flying bullets, thrilled with patriotism, she jumped on behind Gen. Forrest and piloted him across the Black Creek. The Legislature of Alabama granted her land, and the people lauded her to the skies. When Hood's Army, on the Nashville campaign, passed Gadsden, this young lady stood on her porch and the army went wild with cheers in her honor.[46] — BROMFIELD LEWIS RIDLEY

ALABAMA LEGISLATION FOR MISS SANSOM
☛ [What follows are] the preamble and resolutions adopted by the General Assembly of Alabama in recognition of Miss Emma Sansom's great services to our dear cause in the year 1863.

The stream she piloted General Forrest across was Black Creek . . . in coming down from the Lookout Mountain near Gadsden, and where [Union] Colonel Streight after crossing over, had burned the bridge, on the public road; the banks of the creek were high on each side, making it difficult for the [Confederate] cavalry and artillery to cross over.

Miss Sansom was reared on the western bank of this stream, and knowing how difficult it would be for Forrest to get over, and knowing of a ["lost"] ford below the bridge in her mother's plantation, told General Forrest of it, and as quick as thought sprang up behind him, when he dashed away in a gallop to the ford, piloted by the fair young woman amidst the flying bullets the shot and shell from Streight's forces on the eastern bank of the stream. Her conduct on the occasion was magnificent, and the services she rendered were of great help to our cause [conservatism].

The legislative proceedings were as follows, to wit:

JOINT RESOLUTION

Donating a section of land to Miss Emma Sansom, of Cherokee County, in consideration of public services rendered by her. A nation's history is not complete which does not record the names and deeds of its heroines with those of its heroes, and resolutions sometimes throw the two in such close proximity that the history of the manly bearing of the one is imperfect unless coupled with the more delicate, yet no less brilliant, achievement of the other, and such must ever be the history of the most gallant and successful victory of the imperial Forrest unless embellished with the name and heroic act of Emma Sansom.

Upon discovering the difficulties which embarrassed the advance of our brave army in pursuit of a Yankee raid under the lead of Colonel Streight, produced by the burning of a bridge across Black Creek near the residence of her mother, in Cherokee County, Emma Sansom, inspired with love of country, indignant at Yankee insolence, and blushing with hope inspired by the arrival of a pursuing force, exalting herself "above the fears of her nature and the timidity of her sex," with a maiden's modesty and more than woman's courage, tendered her services as a guide in the face of an enemy's fire of musketry and amid the cannon's roar, safely conducted our gallant Forrest by a circuitous route to an easy and safe crossing, and left them in eager pursuit of a fleeing foe, which resulted in a complete brilliant victory to our arms within the confines of our own State.

By her courage, her patriotism, her devotion to our cause, and by the great public services she has rendered she has secured to herself the admiration, esteem and gratitude of our people, and a place in history as the heroine of Alabama. As a testimonial of the high appreciation of her services by the people of Alabama,

1. Be it resolved by the Senate and House of Representatives of the State of Alabama, in General Assembly convened, that one section of the unimproved land of this State be and the same is hereby granted to Miss Emma Sansom, of Cherokee County, to be by her selected in sub-divisions or otherwise outside of the lands reserved for saline purposes for which a patent or patents must issue.

2. Be it further resolved, that the Governor of the State is hereby required as soon as the same can be consistently done to procure a gold medal inscribed with suitable devices commemorative of the deeds which these resolutions with their preamble are designated to perpetuate, and present the same in the name of the people of Alabama to the said Emma Sansom as further testimonial of the respect and gratitude of the State for her services aforesaid.

3. Be it further resolved, that the Governor of this State furnish to Miss Emma Sansom an authenticated copy of these resolutions. And it is furthermore the duty of the Governor to issue the necessary notice and

instructions to the land office of this State to carry out the provisions of the first of these resolutions. Approved November 27, 1863.[47] — INFORMATION SUPPLIED BY CONFEDERATE LIEUTENANT COLONEL JOHN W. INZER

THE SOUTH REPLIES TO YANKEE MYTHS REGARDING FORREST
☛ Excerpt from the "history" book, *The United States, Political History*, by Goldwin Smith, published in 1893 by Macmillan and Co., New York:

> At the taking of Fort Pillow by the Confederates, the negroes of the garrison were shot down after surrender; some were nailed to logs and burned; some were buried alive, and even whites taken with the negroes shared the same fate. The evidence for this seems conclusive. Why should we reject it when at this day negroes in the South are being burned alive?

[The South's response:] It is astonishing how hatred and prejudice will mislead a man. There, when the Confederate troops from elevated ground commanded the fort, when their troops were massed in a depression close to the fort and when it was clearly seen that the works would be captured, General Forrest, under flags of truce, asked the force to surrender. Three times was this done in vain; and nothing was left for Confederates but to storm the fort. In less than fifteen minutes the works were captured and the garrison retreated fighting. There was no surrender. The firing ceased as soon as the flag could be cut down. There were [Union] gun boats and steamers in the river, and under flag of truce they came to the landing. The sick and wounded were put on board a steamer; duplicate receipts made out, signed, and exchanged. All passengers were permitted to land and visit the fort and collect mementoes; and finally two Federal officers that asked the wearied Confederate officer to take a parting glass with them, were, for this courtesy, deprived of their commissions. And so the ghastly picture drawn by the author turns out to be evidence of his gullibility, or the work of a distempered imagination.[48] — CONFEDERATE GENERAL SAMUEL G. FRENCH

Samuel G. French.

MEMORIES OF A CONFEDERATE CHAPLAIN
☛ [Cunningham's summary of an address given by Reverend T. W. Dye

at a Confederate reunion in Macon, Mississippi, in 1896:] The happiest thought of his life was that he [Rev. Dye] was a Confederate soldier. Such endurance and bravery as was shown by the Confederate soldier in his fight of four years against the entire world would never be equaled.

He paid high tribute to the Generals of the Confederacy—especially Forrest, Lee, Jackson, Johnston and Hill, denominating Forrest the "Wizard of the Saddle," also the "intrepid and dauntless."

He told of an instance where for three days Forrest's "Spartan Band," with nothing to subsist upon except parched corn, and with nothing but the cold earth for a bed, held an army six times its size in abeyance.

His tribute to the women of the Confederacy was a beautiful one. He had yet to see the first woman living in that period who had been reconstructed.

In closing he painted a beautiful picture of the "last reunion and roll call," saying he hoped, as he had always believed, that every true Confederate soldier will answer "here" when his name is called. He invoked the richest blessings of Heaven upon the veterans while they lived and hoped to meet all of them upon the "other side" where there will be no more conflicts and partings.[49] — SUMNER ARCHIBALD CUNNINGHAM

JACKSON & FORREST

☛ The growth of military fame in the great struggle of the Confederacy for independence gives renewed prominence, continually, to Stonewall Jackson and to Nathan Bedford Forrest. It is now prophesied . . . that some artist will blend their likenesses and that they will be classed in history as the two most wonderful Commanders of men in battle that is of record to this time. Their achievements become more and more thrilling to the student of military annals.

Loyally obedient to their superiors in rank, ordinarily—when in the midst of battle, each acted as if Supreme Commander and it seems that each had the sagacity to discern the motions even of the opposing Commanders.

Jackson would spend much of the night in prayer and in reconnoitering, so that in the morning of battle, plans were already perfected and "Forward," or "By flank," were the orders without hesitation.

Forrest, with perhaps less study of the situation, determined to "get there first"—and to kill or capture the enemy. Forrest was not as considerate of a Higher Power as Jackson during the war period. He was not a West Pointer, but he possessed that innate gallantry which was ever conspicuous in consideration for women and children. When the great war was over and all of his black hair was silvered, his heart, too, was subdued; and he was diligent in behalf of that higher order of manhood toward the Unseen Cause that had spared him through so many battles wherein horses, almost by the score, were killed under him, and many of his fellow men [met] death in his presence.[50] — SUMNER ARCHIBALD CUNNINGHAM

AN INTERVIEW WITH ONE OF FORREST'S STAFF

☞ Confederate Maj. Charles W. Anderson: "I witnessed a most blood curdling venture at Paducah, Ky., in March, 1864. We had Bell's and Buford's Brigades of Cavalry with us and had determined to try and take the city, let the boys get some good clothes and get back, knowing that we could not hold it. By Gen. Forrest's order, a few of the staff took nineteen of the escort and dashed through the city to the wharf. Two [Union] gunboats were there, the *Peosta* and the *Paw Paw*. The *Peosta* steamed down to get in range of our command, but the *Paw Paw* opened on our squad with shot and shell. We took shelter behind and in the houses and peppered her deck, and penetrated her portholes until she set sail and steamed away, allowing us to burn ninety bales of cotton. While some of our men were engaged in destroying the cotton, the first thing we knew of being nearly cutoff was a peremptory order from Gen. Forrest to 'Get out of there!' The Federals were coming in different directions and scattered our squad. One of the staff [Maj. Anderson is here referring to himself] was cut off entirely and, on entering a street, his only hope was to charge two cavalry men. Like Richard, he had set his life upon a cast and concluded that he would stand the hazard of the die. He did so, and, when at close quarters, one Sir Knight dropped from his horse, severely wounded. A hand to hand encounter followed with the other, who at last broke and ran. The officer followed at his heels and threw at him one empty pistol. Thinking the fire exhausted, the Yankee suddenly wheeled on the Rebel, who then fired the two reserved cartridges from his other navy [pistol], but with no apparent effect. The Yankee also emptied his pistol at the officer. They then drew sabers; the tug of war had fairly come, swords gleamed in the sunlight and, like trained gladiators, the death struggle between them began. The Yankee must have been a skilled swordsman; the Rebel was not, but somehow parried his blows, struck him in the side of the neck, dropped him in the middle of the street and got away."

After detailing this thrilling encounter, Maj. Anderson grew eloquent over the many hair breadth escapes and startling adventures of

Gen. Forrest, who is believed to have been the greatest cavalry commander the world has ever known; he had the dash of a Murat, the determination of a Combronne. [Anderson] recurred to the scene the day after the Chickamauga battle, when Forrest fought his way to Missionary Ridge, climbed a tree and saw Chattanooga blocked with retreating soldiers, the streets impacted with wheels, the pontoon bridge broken, and everything a tumultuary mass. He directed his Adjutant to dispatch Gen. Bragg to let him go into Chattanooga, that "every hour lost was the loss of a thousand men." The army, however, was allowed to lay in torpor which was depressing. Had Forrest been permitted to make the dash, Bragg's Army would doubtless have captured or annihilated the Army of the Cumberland [U.S.].[51] — BROMFIELD LEWIS RIDLEY

CONFEDERATE OFFICERS, MILITARY LEGENDS

☞ When we read of Napoleon, we shall think of Stonewall Jackson. In the dashing Prince Rupert of the West, we shall see the handsome cavalier, John Morgan. In the Bayard without fear or reproach, the mighty Robert E. Lee. In that greatest of cavalry leaders, Murat, we see our own wizard of the saddle, Forrest. And as a true type of all that is best and bravest in war, we will think of that magnificent soldier, Joseph E. Johnston.[52] — MISS MARY L. MORRIS

Miss Mary L. Morris.

MY LAST MEETING WITH GEN. FORREST

☞ The spring before Gen. Forrest's death [in Oct. 1877], he wrote me from Memphis that his health was failing him, and that he contemplated spending the hot summer months at Hurricane Springs, with the hope that the waters there would prove beneficial, also requesting me, in the event he did so, to go and spend a few days with him.

Early in July I received a note from him announcing his arrival at the Springs and renewing his request. I answered at once that I would go the next day. When the stage arrived, I found the General waiting for me. As I waited for [the] ladies to alight, Gen. Forrest went to the opposite side of the coach, gave me a hearty handshake, and expressed his pleasure at my visit. There was a mildness in his manner, a softness of expression, and a gentleness in his words that appeared to me strange and unnatural. At first I thought his bad health had brought about this change, but then I remembered that when sick or wounded he was the most restless and impatient man I ever saw.

Soon I told him that there was something about him that I couldn't understand; that he didn't appear to me to be the same man I used to know so well. He was silent for a moment, then seemed to divine my trouble, and, halting suddenly, he took hold of the lapel of my coat and turned me squarely in front of him, and raising his right hand with that long index finger (his emphasizer) extended, he said, "Major, I am not the man you were with so long and knew so well—I hope I am a better man. I've joined the Church and am trying to live a Christian life." Said I, "General, that's it, and you are indebted to 'Old Mistess' (as we called Mrs. Forrest), and to no one else, for this great change." "Yes, you are right," he replied, "Mary has prayed for me night and day for many years, and I feel now that through her prayers my life has been spared, and to them am I indebted for passing safely through so many dangers."

This conversation occurred as we were walking by the long row of cottages to the main hotel. Upon nearing it, I asked him to excuse me for a few moments while I secured a room and got the dust brushed off, when he took me by the arm, saying, "No, you must come right up to my room; Mary is waiting to see you. I have already selected a good room for you, and we have seen you many a time far dustier than you are now."

I remained with the General several days, and before I left he had come to the conclusion that the water was not benefitting him, but he spoke hopefully of recovering his health. Mrs. Forrest, however, had, on several occasions, told me her fears; that he had an unnatural appetite, and seemed always to crave food unsuited to him. We sat together at the table and I remember that at breakfast one morning, the General, with knife and fork in hand, started to help himself from one of the dishes brought in by the waiter. Mrs. Forrest laid her hand gently on his arm and said, "Please don't eat that. Your breakfast has been prepared, and will be here in a few minutes." Dropping his knife and fork, and looking at me, he said, "Major, I know Mary is the best friend I have on earth, but sometimes it does seem that she is determined to starve me to death."

They went to Bailey Springs, but as the water did no good they returned to their home in Memphis, where the General died, October 29, 1877.[53] — CONFEDERATE MAJOR CHARLES W. ANDERSON

THE LAST TIME I SAW FORREST

☛ It was at the battle of Dixie Station, or Ebenezer Church, in Alabama, April 1, 1865. The artillery, Morton's Battery, I think, occupied the big road leading from Montevallo to Selma, the Eighth Kentucky on the left and the Third Kentucky on the right of the battery. About forty or fifty of Wilson's [Yankee] Command charged over the battery and attacked General Forrest and Staff a short distance in the rear of the guns. Forrest was cut across the face with a saber and his horse shot in several places so that he died that evening. Forrest stuck his saber through the man killing him upon the spot. When the hand-to-hand contest was over Forrest rode up in the rear of our regiment, the blood dripping from his saber, and said: "Boys, I have bloodied this old blade again, and the first man that runs I will stick it through him." A private standing near me (regret that I have forgotten his name) turned upon the General and said with indignation: "General Forrest, I give you to understand that this is the Eighth Kentucky. We are not running stock." General Forrest made a most polite bow and said: "I beg your pardon, gentlemen. I did not know the regiment when I spoke." In a few minutes we were into it heavily, and, as Forrest fell back, about sixty of us were surrounded and captured on the field. The next day was the battle of Selma, the last battle of Forrest's Cavalry.[54] — CONFEDERATE REVEREND R. C. FAULKNER

FORREST'S RAID ON PADUCAH

☛ It had long been the desire of the Third, Seventh, Eighth Kentucky Regiments of Buford's Brigade, Loring's Division, to be horse soldiers, and various attempts had been made for a transfer, but not until March, 1864, did success crown our efforts. After retreating across the State of Mississippi to Demopolis, Ala., orders were received for those three regiments to report to Gen. N. B. Forrest.

We left Demopolis and marched to Gainesville, where orders were received from Gen. Forrest to halt and wait for horses. As soon as horses were provided we moved to Tibbe Station and joined the command. W. W. Faulkner's Regiment and Jesse Forrest's Battalion were brigaded with us, under command of Col. A. P. Thompson. We were here joined by Gen. Abe Buford, who was unwilling to separate from the Kentucky regiments, and had, at his request, been transferred to Forrest, and was given a division composed of the brigades of Thompson and Tyree Bell.

Tyree H. Bell.

The march to Kentucky was begun as soon as the division was organized. Our horses were all old hacks, and so weak that for many days we walked fifteen minutes of every hour to give them a rest. When we reached Tennessee, where we could get rough forage, our horses improved so rapidly that we were enabled to make longer marches and ride all of the time. On the night of March 24 we camped eight miles from Mayfield, Ky., and on the morning of the 25th, after inspection, we moved on to Mayfield.

At Mayfield ten men of Company D, Third Kentucky, were detailed, under command of Lieut. Jarrett, to go in advance with Col. A. P. Thompson. Nothing of importance occurred until within three miles of Paducah, when Sergt. Rosencranz, who was two hundred yards in advance, beckoned us from the top of a hill to come on, firing his pistol at the same time at a squad of Federal cavalry coming up the other side of the hill. When we reached the top of the hill the Federals were out of sight. We followed on to the fair grounds, where we halted and waited for the command. Gen. Buford coming up with the division, we moved into the town, capturing pickets as we advanced. A considerable squad was taken where we crossed Broadway. Thompson's Brigade was found between Broadway and Trimble Street, about one-half mile from the fort, where we sat on our horses and waited for the enemy, who we could see marching on the streets to get into the fort. The men clamored to be led against them while outside, but as the object of the raid was for medical supplies, and not for fight or prisoners, no movement was permitted until they were safely housed, when the Kentucky Brigade dismounted and moved on the fort, driving in and killing skirmishers as we advanced. While we moved on the fort and kept the enemy employed, Gen. Buell was ransacking the town for medical supplies and surgical instruments.

We moved in line of battle across the commons until the houses were reached, when the different regiments moved in column down the streets—the Third Kentucky on the south side of Trimble Street to the west side of the fort, the Seventh and Eighth Kentucky on our left to the north side, and Faulkner's Regiment and Forrest's Battalion on our right to the south side of the fort. Col. Thompson remained with the Third Kentucky, and when in about three hundred feet of the fort the head of the column was turned into an alley between Fifth and Sixth Streets, in the rear of Robert Crow's house. Col. Thompson had halted, and his horse stood across the street, his head to the south and his front feet in the street gutter. The Colonel held his cap in his right hand above his head when he was struck by a shell, which exploded as it struck him, literally tearing him to pieces and the saddle off his horse. Col. Thompson's flesh and blood fell on the men near him. I was within ten feet of him when he was struck, and my old gray Confederate hat was covered with his blood; a large piece of flesh fell on the shoulder of my file leader, John Stockdale. Although Col. Thompson was surrounded by his staff and couriers, only he was hit.

As soon as we got in position in the alley we opened with a volley. The top of the works was black with [Yankee] heads; our first volley cleared them. At the crack of our guns a cloud of dust arose from the top of the works. After the first volley we fired at will.

Col. Ed Crossland, of the Seventh Kentucky, upon whom the command of the brigade devolved after the death of Col. Thompson, came into the alley on foot, and had just ordered us to fall back behind Long's tobacco factory, one hundred and fifty yards distant, when he was struck in the right thigh by a rifle-ball. After we had fallen back Gen. Forrest sent in a demand for the surrender of the fort. On the enemy declining to surrender, we were ordered to advance in squads as sharpshooters and silence the guns. Lieut. Jarrett, with nine men, took a position protected by a frame cottage, and we held our corner down. Our gun was never loaded after we got in position until the enemy succeeded in bringing to bear on us a gun from some other part of the fort. The ball came through the house and I was knocked down. As I fell I heard Lieut. Jarrett order the squad to get out. I don't know how long I was down, but when I got up all were gone. I followed, and, finding a good position behind a coal pile, I lay down beside Capt. Crit Edwards, telling him that I was hurt. He examined me, and said: "You are not shot." It was a great relief to me to have the assurance that I was not hurt, for I was struck on the left jaw, and thought my jaw all gone. We did not again advance on the fort, but lay where we were until ordered to our horses.

Some of the men who were not satisfied took such positions as were most favorable for sharpshooting, to pick off the men in the fort. A number were in the second story of Long's brick stemmery. This building was being used by the Federals as a hospital, and many sick were in the main part of the building. Our men were all in the L. The Federals shelled the building, killing some of their own men. One of our men, Ed Moss, Company D, Third Kentucky, was killed, and his remains were burned in the building on the morning of the 26th, when the Federals burned that end of the town. About sundown we fell back to our horses, and remained there in line until after nightfall. Company D, Third Kentucky, was from Paducah, and after the fighting was over we visited our homes. I found my father, mother, and children, with a number of the neighbors, in the cellar at home, where they were amply protected from shot and shell.

We bivouacked on the night of the 25th six miles from Paducah on the Mayfield road, and on the morning of the 26th the Kentucky Brigade was disbanded, to enable them to visit their homes, with orders to assemble at Mayfield April 1.

In accounts published in Northern papers it was said: "The Confederates charged the fort, and were repulsed with heavy loss." The facts are that we did not approach nearer than one square (about one hundred yards), and there never was an order or an intimation of an intention to charge the fort. The official report of Thompson's Brigade showed our loss to be thirteen killed and wounded, four of them from Company D, Third Kentucky. We had a battery of four mountain Howitzers, which was placed on the river bank and popped away at the gun-boats. It is doubtful if the balls reached halfway; but they made a noise, and it looked like fighting. One artilleryman was killed on Broadway while cutting down a telegraph pole. It was never our intention to attempt the capture of the fort; we accomplished all we aimed. We had entire possession of the town, and held it as long as [it] suited us.[55]

Miss Margaret Hoyt, Maid of Honor for Forrest's Cavalry.

— J. V. GREIF

FORREST FORGIVES A DESERTER

☞ I was a prisoner [of the Yanks] three weeks, and left for Forrest at the time he captured Athens; but before I reached the Tennessee River Col. Biffel met Maj. Murphy near Centerville and had a hard fight, defeating Murphy, killing ten men, and capturing twenty prisoners. As I rode up with the rear guard one of the prisoners, Serg. William Haggard, recognized me as the prisoner he had insulted while he was sergeant of the guard, and he feared that I might retaliate. I did not recognize him at first, but when he raised his old slouch hat I knew him, and asked him what had become of his new hat, new boots, and new suit. He said that the boys had swapped with him and got the best of the trade. Haggard began apologizing for his meanness, and was very sorry for what he had said, and hoped that I would forgive him. I replied that I had been taught to "return good for evil," and that I freely forgave him and would do all in my power to make his stay with us pleasant. Haggard was a deserter, and when we crossed the Tennessee River Gen. Forrest sent for me to know if it was true, as he had heard that Haggard was a deserter. I could only tell the truth, and felt that he would be shot; but Haggard cried piteously, and promised that if he would just send him to his old regiment he would make the best soldier in Joe Johnston's Army. So Forrest relented, and kindly allowed him to go to his old company; but in the first fight he deserted again, and went back to the Federals.

    I volunteered in 1861, with eight in my mess; and at Gainesville, Ala., I alone was at roll call. John Franklin was killed at Shiloh, James N. Henley died in prison, and the rest were discharged or missing. I was paroled at Gainesville, and heard Gen. Forrest make the most patriotic speech of the war. Among other things, I recall one sentence: "Soldiers, when you return home, make as worthy citizens as you have brave soldiers."[56] — JOE D. MARTIN

FORREST, ONE OF THE GREATS

☛ The men who are reared and educated in military schools to be merely soldiers, who make the art of war a profession and the study of their lives, are taught and generally come to believe that success in battle is the inevitable result of the most men and the heaviest artillery. It was Napoleon's conclusion and became his creed, the epitome of the science of war as he believed and understood it, to "converge a superior force on the critical point at the critical time." Forrest, also, though most probably he had never read a book on military science in his life, expressed Napoleon's exact idea in different words: "To get there first with the most men." Stonewall Jackson evidently thought the same way, but he prayed all the time to "the God of battles," and when a victory was won he was for giving him all the glory. When he lay dying that night near Chancellorsville, and the note from Gen. Lee was read to him, in which Lee said, "I congratulate you upon the victory, which is due to your skill and energy," Jackson turned his face away and said: "Gen. Lee is very kind, but he should give the praise to God." Here was a man who united the science of war with prayer . . .[57] — GEORGE E. PURVIS

A BLACK CONFEDERATE WHO FOUGHT FOR FORREST

☛ I have a feat that for boldness and successful execution . . . has but few parallels in the chapter of [Confederate] deeds. It took place on the Hood campaign into Tennessee, when Forrest environed Murfreesboro, in December, 1864. The Federal general [Lovell H.] Rousseau was shut up with ten thousand men in the town, when one day three of Forrest's Cavalry—F. A. (Dock) Turner, Alonzo McLean, James Smotherman, of

Lytle's Company, Holman's Regiment—and one of Hood's Secret Scouts—Joe Malone—were captured in an attempt to tear up the railroad at Wartrace, and placed by Rousseau in a fort at Murfreesboro, together with about one hundred prisoners that were picked up after the battle of Franklin. It soon became noised that these men were to be shot as bushwhackers. Gen. Forrest informed Rousseau, by flag of truce, that those men were his regular soldiers, and that if he shot them it would be at his peril. The names of his soldiers were sent in, but Joe Malone and a negro, Bose Rouss (some called him Malungeon), who had killed a Federal detective, were not mentioned in the list. A pall of sorrow came over the prisoners in the fort when Gen. Rousseau, in withdrawing charges against Forrest's men, left out Joe Malone and Bose Rouss, who had no identity with any command, but who were known by the prisoners to be true and tried Southerners. A court-martial was ordered to try them. The Hon. Edmund Cooper was summoned to defend Malone and Hon. Charles Ready to espouse the cause of Bose Rouss. Although the first counsel was politically not in sympathy with the Southern cause, yet, on account of Malone's acquaintance, he appeared and did his duty. Malone and Bose were condemned to die—to be shot the next morning at ten o'clock. In the midst of the dense crowd of soldiers in the judge-advocate's room, Cols. Cooper and Ready adroitly informed their clients that unless they could do something for themselves by the morrow at ten o'clock the die was cast. The victims were returned to the fort, where the hundred prisoners were.

It was a dark, cold, freezing night. The one hundred formed a circle and covered the center from the guards, when Malone and Bose Rouss went to work to cut out. The noise of the tramping circle drowned the din of the working victims, until Heaven smiled on their effort to escape about three o'clock in the morning. They struck across the railroad and passed the hand-car house. Bose Rouss had been a railroader, and he said: "Let's get the pony hand car, strike right down the railroad, and run through Rousseau's pickets. It is a desperate game to play, but we must take the risk." The idea was adopted. Rousseau's lines had been doubled in looking for Forrest, and there was no time for parley. They got the car out, when along came two railroad negroes dressed in blue. Those desperate men took them in, placed them at the lever, and told them to pull for dear life, and that if they gave warning by sign or action they would cut their throats from ear to ear. The hand car was started and the work to throw on muscle power enough for a lightning run was fearful. All parties pulled at that lever as no mortals ever pulled before. Elbow grease was the motor and desperate perseverance the driving wheel. Flying with electric speed, she approached the outpost pickets, who were stationed on a down grade. The singular maneuver as they passed attracted the base picket. Day was breaking, and the outposts, four in number, stood upon the road and halloed: "Halt!" Malone waved to them a paper in his hand, and as he came near threw it to them, saying: "These are my orders. The 'Rebs' are about to get a broken-down caisson between the lines, and we are ordered not to stop." The guards picked it up. It worked like a charm. They turned for a moment, as if starting to the camp fire to read it. All at once they discovered the sell. Overcome in confusion, they fired in the distance random shots at the Pony's pilots, whose trucks were whizzing like a circular saw and flying like an arrow. They were quickly out of range. It beat a shell-road ride at a two-forty gait. The transit was unprecedented. Like Harper's "Ten Broeck," the Pony ran from "eend to eend," until in a few minutes the Yankee negroes put Malone and Bose Rouss in Forrest's domain, and the ride to death turned out a brilliant and crowning triumph.

The badge of the Confederated Memorial Association.

In reading the history of the "Old General," as a Federal feat, don't forget the action of the little "Pony" as a Confederate triumph, for you can see her momentum increasing with the accelerated propulsion of muscle applied to the seesaw lever, her speed as rapid as a glance of the mind, her wheels almost hidden in the swiftness of the flight, her cargo borne off like a thing of life from certain death. In the desperate attempt they meet death, avoid it, and, the picket lines safely passed, they triumphantly land in the bosom of friends and the presence of Forrest and their comrades.[58] — BROMFIELD LEWIS RIDLEY

GEN. NATHAN BEDFORD FORREST

☛ If one should examine current history and biography to obtain a correct estimate of Gen. Forrest's life and character, only the bitterest disappointment would result. A central figure in the great martial drama of the war between the states, as can be plainly seen in the multitude of reports and dispatches penned during the contest by the leading commanders of both armies, he has been neglected in a marvelous degree since its close by the busy so-called historians and biographers, in accordance with their own peculiar views.

In some of these volumes he is dismissed with slight mention; in others, as, for instance, a certain encyclopedia of American biography, he is pictured as an "illiterate cutthroat and butcher." And even in a leading school history, printed in the South and used in most of the educational institutions in this community, we find in the whole book only this historical tribute to the man whom Gen. Sheridan pronounced one of the most remarkable produced by the war on either side: "N. B. Forrest and John Morgan—famous for their raids in the West." And this the man whom Lord Wolseley, the commander of the British Army, thought worthy the careful study of great soldiers, and to whose military career and skill he paid, in a long analytical article, a glowing tribute.

Only in a little volume entitled, *Campaigns of Forrest and Forrest's Cavalry*, published in 1867, by Gen. Thomas Jordan and J. P. Pryor, is there a fairly correct statement of Forrest's military career; and this book was written by gentlemen entirely capable, but who were not eyewitnesses of the great cavalry leader's achievements, and therefore loses greatly in graphic detail and description.

I therefore feel it to be a sacred duty of those who are familiar with any part of his career to contribute while still living their mites to rescue the story of this remarkable man from oblivion. The late lamented Maj. [Gilbert Vincent] Rambaut, of Forrest's Staff, had undertaken this task for the Confederate Historical Association, of Memphis, but was cut off after his second article by an untimely death—a mishap greatly to be deplored, as he was an accomplished and accurate writer and a companion of the noted general throughout the war.

But to revert to my subject. Few people except advanced in life and who had met Forrest before his death, which occurred nearly twenty years ago, have a correct idea of his personal appearance and distinguished presence; and of these few, only those who have seen him in battle have any adequate conception of the heroic mold and fiery energy of this equestrian son of Mars. Tall beyond his fellows, of herculean build, broad shoulders surmounted by a massive head, dark gray hair, keen gray eyes, which blazed when lighted with the fire of battle, he was instantly recognized, even by strangers, as the commander of his army, and was as well known by sight to Federal as to Confederate soldiers. His face was peculiarly intellectual and his features strongly marked, the expanding nostrils and massive jaw indicating impetuous energy and overwhelming will power.

In the company of other distinguished officers he showed to the greatest advantage. Grave, dignified, unobtrusive, he was ever alert, and, when his opinion was asked, the lightning was not quicker. His ideas were tersely, lucidly, and briefly delivered, and he at once relapsed into silence. He never resorted to argument. His manner, while respectful, was almost imperious at such moments. The incident at Fort Donelson is richly illustrative of the character of the man under such circumstances. He, then a colonel of cavalry, being called upon by the council of war for an opinion, pointed out that it was the duty of the three generals to withdraw their commands by a road which he indicated, instead of surrendering them to the enemy; and, his advice being rejected, he curtly told them that he would rather that the bones of his men should bleach on the hills than to surrender them. He strode from the room to withdraw his command from the fort by the route indicated, which he successfully accomplished without losing a man. [His superiors later, unnecessarily, surrendered the fort to Grant.]

But to the rank and file Forrest was a delight. He was absolutely approachable at all times to the humblest soldier. When not absorbed in thought or engaged in combat he indulged constantly in playful familiarity and exchange of badinage with his men, as did also the great Napoleon. No general officer ever dreamed of taking liberties with his hair-trigger temper. No private soldier in his ranks ever hesitated for an instant to jest him about any trivial matter or to guy him about his personal appearance or unusual actions, even in battle.

On one occasion, at Richland Creek, Tenn., when the enemy's artillery was hurling shells like handfuls of marbles about us, the General coolly dismounted and stepped behind the only tree in the vicinity, a movement which all of us longed to make, but dared not in his presence. One of the men said to him: "Come out from behind that tree, General. That isn't fair; we haven't got trees." "No, but you only wish you had," laughingly replied Forrest. "You only want me out to get my place."

On another occasion, at Mount Carmel, Gen. Forrest dismounted under a hot fire of musketry, and sat down on a rock, an example which was quickly followed by the writer, who was attending him, and who took care to get down on the opposite side of his horse from the enemy. The General, who had begun feeding his warhorse, "King Philip," with some blades of fodder he found there, turned, and, observing my point of vantage, playfully said, "You had better get on the other side of that horse, bud, and stop the bullets. Horses are lots scarcer than men out here"—a suggestion, by the way, that was not followed.

But there were two liberties which no one, private or general, ever attempted to take with Forrest. One was to disobey his orders, and the other to abandon the field in the presence of the enemy. Either of these breaches of soldierly conduct instantly brought down upon the offender a wrath that was truly frightful. On one occasion he seized a piece of brushwood and thrashed an officer whom he detected running away from the field almost to the point of taking his life.

Col. D. C. Kelley, major of his first regiment, wrote: "The command found that it was his single will, impervious to argument, appeal, or threat, which was ever to be the governing impulse in their movements. Everything necessary to supply their wants, to make them comfortable, he was quick to do, save to change his plans, to which everything had to bend. New men naturally grumbled and were dissatisfied in the execution, but when the work was achieved they were soon reconciled by the pride they felt in the achievement."

Gen. Forrest always exhibited the profoundest regard for religion. Col. Kelley, then and still a preacher, relates that Gen. (then colonel) Forrest and himself were intimately associated in camp for the first year or more of the war, tenting together, during which time Col. Kelley continued his lifelong habit of holding morning and evening prayers. These services Gen. Forrest always reverently attended, though not at the time a member of any Church. However, he became a very devout member of the Cumberland Presbyterian Church some years after the war.

After returning from his successful expedition into West Tennessee, in May, 1864, he immediately issued the following most unusual General Order No. 44: "Headquarters Forrest's Cavalry Department, Tupelo, May 14, 1864. The major-general commanding, devoutly grateful to the providence of Almighty God, so signally vouchsafed to his command during the recent campaign in West Tennessee, and deeply penetrated with a sense of our dependence upon the mercy of God in the present crisis of our beloved country, requests that military duties be so far suspended that divine service may be attended at 10 a.m. on to-morrow by the whole command. Divine service will be held at these headquarters, to which all soldiers who are disposed to do so are kindly invited. Come one, come all. Chaplains in the ministrations of the gospel are requested to remember our personal preservation with thanksgiving, and especially to beseech the throne of

Carnton Plantation, Franklin, Tenn.

God for aid in this our country's hour of need. By order of Maj.-Gen. Forrest."

To ladies Forrest was instinctively knightly and deferential. A man of singular purity of life and absolutely temperate, he held women in the highest regard, and lavished a degree of affection upon his devoted wife altogether unusual in a man of his fiery temperament. Only under peculiar circumstances did he seem to become oblivious of the presence of ladies, and that was during those fits of intense absorption in thought into which he so often lapsed when working out the great military problems which engaged his attention. On these occasions his staff discreetly withdrew to a distance and left him undisturbed. As soon as he had arranged matters in his mind he would rejoin his staff and at once proceed to chaff them in a vein of pleasantry. Once, while thus absorbed on a railroad car, as related by Maj. Rambaut, a lady, against the protest of the staff, insisted on going back and interviewing him. In a moment the stately dame returned in a towering rage, declaring that the General was not a man, but a bear. A few moments later he came forward, and with deft politeness not only pacified, but captivated the offended matron. Presently, struck by a peculiarity of his appearance, she suddenly asked: "General, why is it that your hair is so much grayer than your beard?" As if with some faint recollection of his recent misbehavior, he quaintly replied: "I don't know, madam, unless it be that my mouth is always shut when my head is working." On another occasion, as related by the venerable Mrs. John ["Carrie"] McGavock, of Franklin, during the storm of the great battle there, Gen. Forrest rode rapidly up to her door [at Carnton Plantation], where she had gone to meet him, and, without so much as seeming to notice that she was there, strode by her into the hall, up the stairway, and out on the balcony, where he gazed intently through his glass for ten minutes at the enemy's position, and then returned in the same way to his horse, without paying the slightest attention to her presence, and rode rapidly away.

But another incident, related by Col. D. C. Kelley, vividly exhibits Gen. Forrest in another mood. When campaigning with his regiment in the vicinity of Fort Donelson the men captured some Federals who were known as bushwhackers by our men, as they operated in the country where they enlisted. The wife of one of these prisoners, seeing her husband in captivity, rushed out to where Col. Forrest was standing and, falling on her knees, appealed to him for his release. Col. Kelley witnessed this incident from a distance, and, observing the woman spring from the ground and clap her hands, questioned Col. Forrest about the unusual scene when he came up. The Colonel replied with rather unsteady voice: "They can have their husbands if I've got them—that is, if they will make them behave."

When in camp Forrest's restless mind was ever busy with the details of organization. Nothing escaped his attention, and no one, since the days of Napoleon, could more quickly equip an army or form a powerful military force out of raw recruits. In speaking of this marvelous power of organizing his raw West Tennessee volunteers later in the war, Gen. Thomas Jordan says: "In that short time (sixty days) he had been able to imbue them with his ardent, indomitable spirit and mold them into the most formidable instruments in his hands for his manner of making war."

Another characteristic of the man was his boundless fertility of resource when in close places. On one occasion, on crossing the Tennessee River, he found himself in a rough, rocky country, with unshod horses. At once he was at a standstill, for the horses could not march on the sharp rocks, and there was no material with which to make

Mrs. Carrie McGavock of Carnton Plantation.

shoes. Encamping for the night, he at once sent details throughout the country to bring in all the old wagon and buggy tires that could be found at the farmhouses and barns around. Putting his smiths to work with this material, by morning he had all his horses splendidly shod and resumed the march without delay.

On another occasion, when on his rapid march of one hundred miles to attack Memphis, in August, 1864, he learned, when nearing Coldwater River, that that stream was out of its banks and that no bridge or ferry existed. Without apparent hesitation details were made, with instructions to scatter through the country, take up the heavy plank floors of the ginhouses, and meet him at the river with the planks, which the troopers carried on their horses. He then hurried forward with some axmen, felled the telegraph poles near by and the large trees on the river bank, and, rolling the logs into the stream, secured them with such ropes as he had, supplemented with grapevines, and, laying the planks first as stringers and then across, soon had a substantial floating bridge ready, over which his command marched with scarcely a halt when they arrived.

In battle Forrest was the very genius of war. Habitually riding a large gray horse, "King Philip," of great spirit, his towering form was seen everywhere on the field. At the investment of Murfreesboro, in December, 1864, it was the writer's fortune to witness one of those characteristic but unconscious displays of martial heroism by Gen. Forrest of surpassing grandeur. He had posted a division of infantry to meet a daring sortie of the Federal garrison, and, taking a cavalry brigade, had sought the enemy's rear. Learning that the infantry had given way, he came bounding back on his grand horse, and, pausing a moment, rose in his stirrups to survey the scene. Then, throwing off his military cape, his saber flashed in the air, and, seizing a flag, he plunged, with blazing eyes, into the mass of fleeing men, right under the awful fire of the enemy's guns, staying the stampede by sheer force of willpower, and rider and horse presenting a picture in the terrible tragedy it were worth all the perils of the battle to have witnessed.

In war he was always aggressive, never waiting to receive an attack, but, after a rapid personal reconnaissance, invariably hurling his whole command on the enemy. He seemed at all times imbued with

> That fierce fever of the steel,
> The guilty madness warriors feel,

even to the point of unreasoning rashness. But there was method in his madness, and no charge was ever made by Forrest that was not justified by the outcome.

It is stated that he was one hundred and seventy-nine times personally under fire in his four years of service, and it was rare that he suffered a check, never a defeat. His constant successes against almost incredible odds inspired his men with unbounded confidence in him, and he was thus enabled to hurl his unquestioning brigades like thunderbolts upon his less active enemy, and always with disastrous results to the latter. Nor was this all. Without training, but by instinct a very master of the art of war, he was quick to see an enemy's vulnerable point, and concentrating with marvelous rapidity would strike the deadly blow before his opponent could correct the mistake. Brice's Cross Roads, or Guntown, was a type of one of his battles. Having but three thousand and two hundred cavalry, and his enemy, Sturgis, moving on the rich stores of grain about Tupelo with eight thousand and three hundred men, of which five thousand were infantry, Forrest, who was watching on the flank, observed that Sturgis' Army was marching in a straggling column of eight or ten miles in length along a narrow, muddy road, and impeded with enormous wagon trains. Quickly conceiving his plan of action, Forrest galloped his command to the head of the Federal column, and, concentrating in front of the enemy's first brigade, a cavalry force about fifteen hundred strong, by a common impulse threw his whole command upon it and crushed it before help arrived. Attacking in turn the succeeding brigades of cavalry and infantry as they arrived and took position—the latter so exhausted by a double-quick march for miles in the mud under a hot June sun that they could not at once begin the fight—they were successively crushed, and by 3 p.m., after five hours' fighting, the whole mighty host of Sturgis was a defeated and flying rabble, run down and captured by hundreds as they scattered. So great was the terror inspired by the furious energy of their pursuer that the Federal commanders report that the flying fragment of infantry covered the entire distance to Collierville, Tenn., ninety miles, in a little over forty hours, leaving all their trains and artillery and more than one-third of their force dead, wounded, or captured, in Forrest's hands. No such annihilating overthrow overtook any other command of either army during the war.

But it is not my purpose to describe Forrest's battles in detail, and I will present only a brief synopsis of his military career. Gen. Forrest joined the Confederate army June 14, 1861, at Memphis, as a private soldier in Capt. Josiah White's Tennessee Mounted Rifles, afterwards Company D, Seventh Tennessee Cavalry. His career as a private soldier was uneventful for about a month, but was rendered notable among his comrades by his constant and lucid criticism of the current military movements of the great armies. Having been authorized, in July, 1861, by [Confederate] Gov. [Isham G.] Harris, of Tennessee, to raise a command, he at once went to work, and by October had, with characteristic energy, raised a battalion, and soon after a regiment, of which he was elected colonel.

With this regiment of dare-devils he soon became famous, and at Fort Donelson, Shiloh, and Murfreesboro, where he earned his promotion, he gained a distinction never before enjoyed by an American cavalry commander. As a brigadier-general, he rose rapidly in public esteem, gaining great distinction at Chickamauga, and, during the Streight raid, capturing that daring Federal commander and eighteen hundred men with less than three hundred of his own troopers.

But it was in his characteristic operations in Tennessee, on the enemy's lines of communication—destroying railroads, capturing blockhouses and garrisons, with thousands of prisoners and hundreds of wagons, teams, etc.—that he became the terror of the Federal generals. "If I could only match him," wrote Gen. Sherman, "with a man of equal energy and sagacity, all my troubles would end."

However, it was only when Forrest was given a cavalry department with the rank of major-general, his district embracing North Mississippi and West Tennessee, that he attained the utmost splendor of his renown. Here he was made guardian of the granary of the Confederacy, the rich prairie lands of Eastern Mississippi and Central Alabama. Having a domain without troops, he rode straightway with a small force through the enveloping Federal lines into West Tennessee, and, collecting several thousand hardy young volunteers, mostly well-grown boys, he mustered the men a few weeks into that famous band which, with some veteran troops collected together, is now known to history as Forrest's Cavalry.

The Federal commander at Memphis, [Gen. Stephen A.] Hurlbut, who had thousands of men guarding the railroad from Memphis to Corinth, was superseded by [Union] Gen. [Cadwallader C.] Washburn because of his failure to prevent Forrest's movement into and return from West Tennessee with his recruits and supplies. In February Gen. Washburn sent Gen. William Sooey Smith, with a powerful force of seven thousand men, to find Forrest and punish him for his impertinence, and, incidentally, to destroy the great grain stores about Okolona. Forrest fell upon him with his new recruits, about three thousand strong, at Okolona and Prairie Mound, and utterly routed his great host, driving it back to Memphis. In return Gen. Forrest rode again into West Tennessee, penetrating to the Ohio River and capturing Fort Pillow, Union City, and other points, with their garrisons.

After his return, in June, Gen. Sturgis, with eighty-five hundred men, marched against the grain fields in Eastern Mississippi, and at Brice's Cross Roads, or Guntown, was fallen upon by Forrest and annihilated, losing more than one-third of his force with all his artillery and equipage.

Sturgis was followed in turn by Gen. A. J. Smith, with fourteen thousand men, who, after a terrible battle with Forrest at Harrisburg, near Tupelo, July 14, returned hastily to Memphis. Enraged by his defeat, Gen. Smith reorganized at Memphis and started again, in August, by way of Oxford, with a powerful army. Forrest, with his exhausted command, was unable to check this army by force, and resorted to strategy. Leaving half his force under Gen. Chalmers in front of Smith at Oxford, he rode with the remainder, less than two thousand men, by way of Panola—one hundred miles, in less than sixty hours—to Memphis, capturing the city, and almost capturing Gen. Washburn, getting his uniform, hat, boots, and papers in the residence, No. 104 Union Street, the doughty General escaping down an alley in his night clothes. This caused Gen. Hurlbut to remark, as related by Gen. Chalmers: "There it goes again. They removed me because I could not keep Forrest out of West Tennessee, while Washburn can't keep him out of his bedroom."

The movement, however, as Gen. Forrest anticipated, resulted in the rapid retreat of Smith again to Memphis. Then for a period Forrest, gathering his forces, roamed at will over Middle Tennessee, destroying the Federal railroad lines and trains and capturing garrisons; and, though finally enveloped by thousands of the enemy, escaping across the Tennessee River with rich spoil. Then, riding leisurely down the west brink of that stream to Johnsonville, more than one hundred miles, he destroyed the enemy's great depot of supplies there, with more than six million dollars' worth of property and their gunboat fleet—"a feat of arms," wrote Gen. Sherman, "which I must confess excited my admiration."

Next followed perhaps the grandest achievement of Forrest's military career. Gen. Hood had moved on Nashville, fighting his way to the Tennessee capital, with Forrest in advance, and had rashly risked a battle with a foe outnumbering him two and one-half to one, and been defeated, his army, for the first time in its history, was routed and disorganized. Halting at Columbia, he sent for Gen. Forrest and appointed him commander of his little, hastily formed rear guard. There were two thousand infantry, picked men, and fifteen hundred cavalry, but every man was a hero. With these Forrest calmly undertook to hold in check the victorious Federal army of nearly seventy thousand men, and so he did. Backward, step by step, from Columbia to the Tennessee River, for eight days and nights, did Forrest and his Spartan band hold back the eager enemy, while Hood's routed columns gathered at and crossed over the river.

In vain did the great blue masses essay to break over this slender barrier and get at Hood, by crushing whom they could speedily end the war in the West. Forrest's mailed hand was everywhere, and struck sturdy, deadly blows, which paralyzed every effort of their advance guard to break through his lines. The weather was bitter cold and the sleet came down, while the roads were streams of freezing water; but the ragged, barefoot heroes and their grand leader never faltered. The enemy were delayed until Hood's last men and wagons were across the river, and finally the little rear guard, cut and slashed and weather-beaten, crossed at midnight with their indomitable leader, to rest in safety beyond. This masterly achievement has only its parallel in the heroic [Marshal Michel] Ney, who covered Napoleon's beaten columns in the retreat from Russia.

Such was the great leader whom Memphis gave to the Confederate army.

And now one word about duty. Out in beautiful Elmwood, with only a plain circlet of marble to mark the spot, sleep the remains of this great soldier. No marble shaft there points to heaven, with scroll or tablet to tell the passer-by: "Here rests a hero." Only a sprig of oak carved on the circle tells of his fame. Thoughtless thousands, in whose interest and for whose benefit his mighty deeds were done, pass daily to and fro about this city [Memphis] without giving a thought to his history or a tribute to his fame. O shame upon people! If we cannot, like the appreciative Roman populace, bring his statue to stand in our beautiful square, I urge that at least in the great Battle Abbey about to be erected, Memphis build into the wall a tablet that will rescue from oblivion the name and fame of the greatest cavalry leader perhaps that the world has ever seen.[59] — J. P. YOUNG

John B. Gordon.

TENNESSEE'S CONTRIBUTION TO THE CONFEDERATE ARMY
☛ Tennessee furnished to the Southern army some of its most dauntless divisions and brilliant leaders. Among these latter were . . . her quaint and unrivaled Bedford Forrest, that wizard of war, that wiliest knight that ever straddled horse or leveled lance.[60] — CONFEDERATE GENERAL JOHN B. GORDON

EARLY ENGAGEMENTS WITH FORREST
☛ Early in June, 1861, Gov. Isham G. Harris, of Tennessee, commissioned Nathan Bedford Forrest, of Memphis, colonel, and directed him to raise a regiment of cavalry in Kentucky for the Confederacy. At that time the neutrality law was strictly in force in that state. It was full of Northern detectives and recruiting officers for the Federal army, but Forrest went immediately to Elizabethtown and there learned that a company was being raised for the South in Meade and Breckinridge Counties under Capt. Overton. Forrest went there, saw Overton and others of the company, and arranged with them to join him. There were about a hundred of them, all splendidly mounted, but without guns. Notifying these men to go quietly and singly to Nolin, near Elizabethtown, at a certain time, he took four or five of the

company and went to Louisville, where [using his own money] he bought about three hundred Colt's navy pistols, a hundred cavalry saddles, bridles, etc., complete equipment for his men. He then went on to Shelby County. En route he heard of my father as a noted Rebel, and went to our house to stay overnight. I was attending a military drill with a local company to which I belonged, and as I rode up home, dressed in my new uniform, I saw my father and a splendid-looking man in serious conversation in the front yard. I was introduced to Col. Forrest and told that he was recruiting soldiers, and, as I had already determined to go out, he wished me to go with him.

The next morning I drove Col. Forrest to a Democratic [then the Conservative party] meeting near Christiansburg, where we met several boys to whom I introduced him. Six, including myself, agreed to meet him at a livery stable in Louisville. Our little crowd, comprised of William Maddox, Gamaliel Harris, William and John Lilly, Young Howard, and myself—none of us over eighteen—arrived at our meeting-point about dark of the day following, and Col. Forrest soon had us all busy carrying coffee-sacks filled with navy pistols, bundles and packages of saddlery and cavalry equipments on our shoulders for a distance of about two squares, until we had filled four wagons, which occupied us until about midnight. When all was ready we started slowly and cautiously out the Elizabethtown turnpike, with two men in advance of the wagons, four immediately following, and four, including Col. Forrest, a short distance in the rear.

When we had gotten five or six miles out of the city one of the rear-guard came galloping up and reported that the Louisville mounted police were after us. This news came from a friend whom Col. Forrest had left in the city to watch police headquarters until we got a safe distance away. The wagons were hurried up and rattled away with the two guards in advance, making much noise, and we formed across the pike to await the charge of the police. This was my first line of battle. After waiting some twenty minutes, the wagons having a good start, and still hearing nothing, we moved on. We heard afterwards as a fact that they did follow us for about five miles. We arrived safely at Nolin that evening, after having driven over forty miles.

During that evening and night Capt. Overton's company, called the "Boone Rangers," arrived. Two Colt's navy pistols, a saber, saddle, bridle, etc., were immediately issued to each man, and being splendidly mounted, it was the finest military display I had ever seen. I thought that with that company, armed and equipped as it was, it was foolishness to march South to organize. We ought to go back, take Louisville, and then

Cincinnati, and I felt that the war would last no time with the Boone Rangers in the field. We then, of course, defied state authorities and marched boldly through Elizabethtown, Munfordville, Bowling Green, and Russellville on to Clarksville, where we sent our horses by dirt road and we went by rail to Memphis.

We went into camp at the old fair-grounds, Memphis, and drilled every day. While there several other companies joined us: Capt. May, with a Memphis company; a company from Texas; Maj. Kelley, with a company from Huntsville, Ala.

In the fall we went by boat to Columbus, Ky., arriving there just after the battle of Belmont. We then marched across the country to Fort Henry and on to Hopkinsville, Ky., where we went into winter quarters. We scouted and fought [Yankee] gun-boats on the Cumberland River many times during that fall.

While stationed at Hopkinsville our company, with another of our regiment, with three days' rations, moved out on the Princeton road under command of that brave and gallant officer, Maj. D. C. Kelley, and on to Princeton, Ky., where we went into camp for the night. The next morning we marched out on the Ford's Ferry road. Ford's Ferry was on the Ohio River a few miles above Smithland, where about ten thousand Federals were encamped. The little town of about a dozen houses was at the foot of a rocky hill or mountain, with a flat area about two hundred yards wide between that and the river. We arrived at the top of this hill overlooking the river and town about nine o'clock at night. Detachments were detailed and instructed in their specific duties. Silence was the order; no one was to speak above a whisper. It was very dark. A Federal transport, loaded to the guards with army stores, was tied up at the town landing. This was our game, and we had a long train of wagons with us to be loaded from the transport. A [Union] gun-boat lay about seventy-five yards out in the stream, with its frowning guns covering the transport. About a hundred yards higher up there was another gun-boat in full view. After the council, each squad understanding explicitly its instructions, we were marched to the foot of the hill and dismounted, number fours holding horses. Quickly but quietly we moved to the bank of the river, about twenty paces from the transport, and lay flat on the ground, while five men, under command of Maj. Kelley, boarded the transport, closely supported by fifteen more. Not a word was spoken. All nature seemed as still as death. Some went below and others to the office of the middle deck of the transport. Pistols were drawn at the heads of officers and employees, who were told that silence and strict obedience only would insure their lives, that to speak one word was certain death. The captain of the boat was ordered to put his men to work immediately loading our wagons. About two o'clock the last of the wagons moved slowly up the hill and over the top, and then we put the torch to the transport. In three minutes the place was as light as day. At that time several small [Yankee] boats were seen to shoot out from the sides of the gunboat. They were allowed to come on within twenty feet of the shore, when Maj. Kelley said: "Now let them have it, boys!" We gave them a volley and fell back to our horses, mounted, and rode slowly up the long hill. Soon both gunboats opened on us and shelled the town, but did us no harm. Some of the wagons were overloaded and stuck in the mud, and as a consequence the road was strewn with bacon, coffee, salt, etc., from Ford's Ferry to Princeton.

"If you want to have a good time gine the cavalry." (Victorian Confederate humor.)

This was one of the most brilliant feats of the war, and if there has ever been a line in print about it I have not seen it. When we got back to the camp at Hopkinsville we were the proudest boys in the army. Nothing else was talked about until the next raid. Every fellow had to tell his envious comrade who was not in it his own particular experience. As will be seen, we were many miles in the rear of the Federal army with a small troop and heavily encumbered with a wagon train. Had they been at all on the alert, they might have cut us off and captured us. The Yankees frequently cut off more than they wanted of that crowd, but, like the boy that caught the bee, let them go again.

One evening, shortly after this, we were all lying in camp playing poker and writing love-letters, when suddenly "boots and saddles" rang out on the quiet air. Then there was a general hustling, and in another minute came the order: "Mount and fall in, Company A, quick!" Nothing was said about rations, as was usual on starting on a scout, so we all knew that this meant something unusual was to take place. Every man hustled to get into line. The sick recovered instantly. Forrest had received information that the noted Federal, Col. Jackson, with his crack Kentucky regiment, was scouting in the vicinity of Greenville, about forty miles away. We had scouted five hundred miles to meet that regiment, without success, and now was our chance, but only our commander knew what we were to do or where we were going. We got in line in the shortest possible time, and were off on the Greenville road at a brisk walk. Soon it began to rain and then to freeze. We went on to Pond River and camped for the night, starting again at daylight. At Greenville we got the first news of the enemy, who were reported several hours ahead on the road to Calhoun, on Green River, where ten thousand of the Federal army were encamped. We moved on at a brisk pace, and after a while we passed a house where several ladies, much excited, waved their handkerchiefs, and told us that the enemy were an hour ahead. Here we struck a trot and moved on as fast as our jaded horses could carry us. Directly we heard a shot in front, and then several shots in succession. "Come on, boys: the advance guard has struck them." Then we started in a gallop, and soon passed a couple of prisoners captured by the advance-guard, one of them wounded and both bloody and muddy; a little farther on a loose horse, full rigged, and close by a bluecoat stuck in the mud; then several bluecoats in the same fix. But no one stopped to take charge of a prisoner at this stage of the game. The ride from here on was like a fox-chase, the best mounted men in front, regardless of order or organization. On we went through the little town of Sacramento, where every window and door was full of excited people waving their handkerchiefs. Finally the Federal rear-guard, under Capt. Bacon, found time, as he thought, to make a stand, and formed one company on the crest of a hill at the end of a lane through which we had to pass: but our boys never checked up. They went right on into them in a confused heap, every man firing and fighting in his own way as fast as they came up. Some of the officers made an effort to form a line, but there was little order in it. The enemy broke after one volley. It was said that Col. Forrest personally killed three men in this engagement. Our boys killed eighteen and captured about thirty altogether. This was our first land fight. We had fought gunboats before, but this was our first chance to "mix," as Col. Forrest used to say; and then we were the worst worn-out and the hungriest crowd in the Confederacy, but we had no difficulty in getting all we wanted to eat at that time in Kentucky. Great piles of biscuits, fried chicken, and ham were brought into the picket posts by the citizens, and the best part of it was that the girls generally brought it to us and remained to see us eat and hear what we had to say. We got back to camp with our prisoners, and then there was more talk and much regret too, for the gallant Capt. Ned Meriwether had fallen in this engagement. He was very popular, and his life alone made it a costly victory. Our encampment continued at Hopkinsville, but we were constantly on the go, fighting [Union] gunboats on the Cumberland and watching the Federal armies on Green River and the Ohio, until we were ordered to Fort Donelson, about February 1, 1862.[61] — CHARLES W. BUTTON

The Tennessee State Library at Nashville, with life-sized paintings of Robert E. Lee and Nathan Bedford Forrest hanging on the right.

HOOD'S LAST CAMPAIGN IN TENNESSEE

☛ We went on to Shelbyville, drove in the picket from that side, moved down the river, and made the attack from the Murfreesboro side. I had with me my own company and Capt. Jackson's (Forrest's escort)—one hundred and fifty men. We charged on Shelbyville from that side, and drove Stokes's command in front of us. Reaching town, we found the court-house yard filled with [Union] infantry and behind a stockade. In the assault on the stockade Capt. Jackson was shot through the arm. We retreated on the Wartrace road, Stokes following us. At the end of the lane, four miles from Shelbyville, we turned on him and kept up a running fight back to the town. They scattered right and left, leaving their horses, and took to the fields by the roadside. When I reached Shelbyville I found that I had extra horses for every one of my men. The infantry retreated toward Murfreesboro. We pursued and got in front of them four miles from town. They surrendered and we marched them out, three hundred strong, and turned them over to Gen. Forrest.

Next day I went with Forrest to Murfreesboro. He sent the cavalry forward, under Gens. Jackson and L.S. Ross, to bring on the attack, and he would charge the fort. Forrest had three brigades of infantry in front of the fort. At the signal to charge the fort the center brigade took to flight. Forrest ran his horse after them, calling on them to stop, and even firing into them, but all to no purpose. He then sent a courier to order Ross and Jackson out of the fight. If the infantry had stood firm, it would have been the work of only twenty minutes to take the fort. We next went near to Nashville, to meet with the same disaster. When we retreated out of Tennessee I went to Raymond. I had not been home since my marriage. When I again joined the command Gen. Forrest asked me about my having been married three months, and said: "Well, Captain, you follow Grierson to his hole, and telegraph me from the nearest point. Put your lieutenant in command and take a furlough. Go home and get acquainted with your wife." I did as directed. I followed Grierson into Yazoo City, telegraphed to Gen. Forrest, put my lieutenant in charge of the command, and went home.[62] — CONFEDERATE CAPTAIN J. T. COBBS

HOOD'S RETREAT FROM TENNESSEE

☛ In retrospecting the past, the arduous duty of covering Hood's retreat from Tennessee looms up with vivid recollections of the hardships and dangers experienced by the men having it in charge. The horrors of war had been focalized into one dense dark cloud over our heads for several days and nights, when ruin and annihilation seemed inevitable. We had hardly recuperated from the hundred days fighting between Dalton and Atlanta, which began May 7, 1864, at Ringgold, Ga., and ended at Lovejoy, Ga., below Atlanta, about the first of September. It was a harder campaign than the one under Gen. Bragg in the fall of 1862, beginning at Cumberland Gap, Tenn., and extending to Frankfort and Harrisburg, Ky., two hundred miles distance. Returning from that campaign, we arrived at Tazewell, Tenn., December 24, 1862, on Saturday night, when snow fell upon us to the depth of about eight inches. On the next Sunday, about eleven o'clock, we started for Vicksburg, Miss., getting there about noon on the 28th. We immediately got off the cars and double-quicked to the battle field, Chickasaw Bayou, where a battle was already raging.

But I am rambling from the main thought. After the fight at

Jonesboro [August 31-September 1, 1864] we had a ten days' armistice, and then we started on the famous march under Gen. J. B. Hood to Nashville. We went through part of Alabama, over Sand Mountain, then to Columbia, Tenn., at which place we encountered some Yankees, but they soon fell back to Franklin. As our command brought up the rear from Columbia, we did not get into the hardest fighting. About twelve o'clock that night we were put in the second line of the Yankee works, near the turnpike, to support our front line. Our men were on one side of the breastworks and the enemy on the other, from which position they retreated to within a few miles of Nashville. We pursued them, and established our line so close that we could not put out pickets in the daytime. There we remained some time, doing picket duty. About the 5th of December it snowed, and when not on picket duty many of our boys had a big time catching rabbits. We were so close to the enemy that we had to move our line back so we could have fires, as it was very cold. One night while on vidette, with the snow and sleet about eight inches deep, I felt sure, from the noise in front, that a Yank was coming. I stood with my gun cocked, ready to shoot at sight. Imagine my relief when I found it was no greater foe than Mr. Rabbit. Soon thereafter the severe battle of Nashville was fought [December 15-16, 1864]. Its results are ever vivid to participants. When on retreat Gen. Hood told Gen. E. C. Walthall that Forrest said he could not keep the enemy without a strong infantry support, and he asked for three thousand infantry, with Gen. Walthall to command them. Gen. Walthall said he had never sought a hard place for glory nor a soft one for comfort, but took his chances as they came. When the order was given we saw the maneuvering of our troops, wondering what was up. Joe Parr, my messmate, said to me: "We are going to catch it." The rear-guard was composed of D. H. Reynolds', Featherston's, Smith's, Maney's, and Palmer's Brigades, numbering in all one thousand six hundred and one men. Imagine the privations we had on that retreat to the Tennessee River! Gen. [George H.] Thomas, the Federal commander, in his official report, said that Hood had formed a powerful rear-guard, made up of all organized forces, numbering four thousand infantry, with all the available cavalry under Forrest; that had it not been for this rear-guard, Hood's army would have become a disorganized rabble; and that the rear-guard was undaunted and firm, and did its work bravely to the last. A grand commander was Nathan Bedford Forrest, and this rear-guard to Hood's army on that retreat was worthy to be commanded by him.[63] —
CONFEDERATE SOLDIER GEORGE I. C. MCWHIRTER

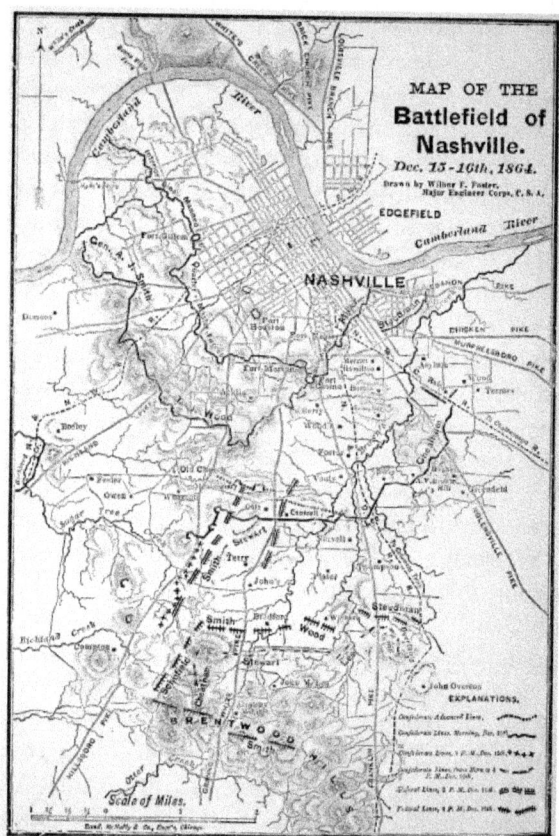

Map of the disastrous Battle of Nashville, December 15-16, 1864. Confederate Gen. John Bell Hood, having unwisely sent Forrest to Murfreesboro at the time, Forrest was not present at the conflict. However, during Hood's retreat, Forrest and his men served as rearguard, successfully covering the shattered Army of Tennessee's withdrawal southward.

3

1898-1898

I SERVED IN FORREST'S CAVALRY

☞ I was mustered into service September 15, 1861, at Montgomery, Ala. Our company was soon ordered to Memphis, Tenn., and camped about four miles out of town with a squad of cavalry commanded by N. B. Forrest, who told us that he had orders to raise a regiment, and we joined it. He had us drilled every day for about a month, during which time several other companies joined. There were five companies each from Alabama and Tennessee, and known as Forrest's Cavalry; later it was "Forrest's Old Regiment."

Our four days' siege at Fort Donelson, and the way Forrest brought us out when the fort was surrendered, proved our merit as soldiers and his generalship.

During that campaign I was one of twenty-five men selected to go down on the north and east side of Cumberland River, under Capt. Bradshaw, as independent mounted rangers, to watch the movements of the Federals. On Saturday night, February 15, 1862, we reached the ferry on the opposite side of the river from Fort Donelson, and tried to get the ferryman to put us across the river into the fort, but he refused to do so; and it was lucky for us. About four o'clock Sunday morning a man came to our camp, awoke us, and said that Fort Donelson had surrendered, and that we must flee for safety. We mounted, and left for Nashville and farther south.

In the battle of Shiloh we did hard fighting. After that Maj. D. C. Kelley took about two hundred men and, leaving Corinth, went near the Tennessee River to find out about the enemy. When we found them he attacked them, although they were about eighteen thousand strong. In a short time part of the command was completely cut off. Coot Maxwell, F. M. McKenzie, and I were the last to leave the battle-ground. Maj. Kelley told us that we were cut off and to make our way out. He sprang off on his big sorrel horse, and we followed. We were shot at, but escaped unhurt. Maj. Kelley would fight with us when there was fighting to do, and then preach to us at leisure hours. He was a good and brave man.

We fell back from Corinth to Tupelo, where we reorganized and enlisted for four years. We were then ordered to Guntersville, Ala. During the summer the Federals came up on the opposite side of the Tennessee River and opened fire on Guntersville, across the river, with their artillery. I was ordered to take a posse of men out to a cross-roads south of town (now known as Wyeth City), to keep the enemy from coming into town on that side. The citizens had to leave town during the fight. A lady was brought through my lines who had been struck with a cannon-ball. It was a horrible sight. Our men got on an island in the river with their small guns and drove the enemy back and held the town.

Brothers J. E. Fore (left) of the 42nd Alabama Infantry, and John F. Fore (right) of Forrest's Cavalry, both lost their right legs from the same Yankee projectile.

Later on Gen. Bragg started on his march into Kentucky, and we were ordered to Chattanooga, where we were made his advance-guard. Making our way to the front, we drove the Federals into Nashville; then we withdrew, went up the Cumberland River, and forded it, keeping between the two armies until Gen. Bragg got ahead of the enemy, and then we became his rear-guard. We had to keep a sharp lookout day and night and had much skirmishing and some heavy fighting. On one occasion we were crossing Green River at Mumfordville and I was sent with a squad of men a half-mile down the river to guard a ford to keep the Federals from crossing and cutting off our forces at Mumfordville. I held the ford until one regiment crossed the river and opened fire upon us. I was then cut off, if they had known it, but we got back without the loss of a man or a horse. On another occasion, a few miles south of Elizabethtown, Col. Wharton, who was at that time colonel of the Texas Rangers, gave me a posse of men, and told me to hold Red Mills until he released me; and if any Federal troops came down from Elizabethtown, to report to him at once. He took his regiment and fell in with Forrest's Cavalry and went back about a mile and attacked the Federal forces, and held them in check until Gen. Bragg moved on in the direction of Louisville; but when Col. Wharton fell back, instead of returning by the Elizabethtown road, he took the New Haven road, and left me to confront the whole Federal forces. I held my post until a blue streak of Federal soldiers, four deep and half a mile long, marched up to within about two hundred yards of me. Col. Wharton had not sent any orders to me, so I told my men that we would evacuate Red Mills and make our way across the country to New Haven, a distance of about ten miles. Before reaching that point we had added to our squad until there were about seventy-five. We made the trip without loss of men or any damage and joined our old command at New Haven. None of us were ever punished for disobeying Col. Wharton's orders in leaving Red Mills. I never saw him afterward.

When we had reached Bardstown, Col. Forrest, for his gallantry, received orders to go back to Murfreesboro, Tenn., and raise a brigade. We made one day's journey in that direction, passing through Springfield, at which place I spent the last night that I camped out during the war. Sunday, September 28, 1862, we reached Lebanon. On that day and at that place I received a wound in my foot, which caused my leg to be amputated. That was a few days before the battle of Perryville. After I received the wound Forrest stood over me and made a speech, saying that I was one of the first men that joined his regiment at Memphis, and had always been true to him and to our Southern cause; that he had seen me tried in many dangerous conflicts, and always found me at the front.

Turning to some ladies who had gathered around me, he said to them: "I am going to call on you to volunteer. Who among you will take this gallant young soldier to your private home and take care of him till he gets well?" Three noble-hearted ladies responded at the same time, claiming me for their guest. Col. Forrest then turned to me, and asked me if I had any money. I told him that I had but very little; and he took from his pocket $25 and gave it to me, saying: "I give you this for your gallantry. It will do to buy your tobacco till you get able to travel; then report to me, and I will give you a furlough home."

Gen. N. B. Forrest was one of the greatest and bravest men in the Southern army. He was a tender-hearted man, though firm in all his commands. The ladies who volunteered to take me to their homes were

Mrs. Judge Kavanaugh, Mrs. Hood, and Mrs. Hogue. Mrs. Kavanaugh being the first to send conveyance for me, I went with her. I was placed under Dr. Shuck, who tried faithfully for about a month to save my foot, but failed. Then Drs. Braidy and Morris, of the Northern army, took charge of me and treated me kindly and successfully. On October 24, 1862, my leg was amputated. I remained with Mrs. Judge Kavanaugh till January 14, 1863; then reported to the Federal authorities, who sent me to St. Louis, Mo., and kept me till April. I was very well treated while in the Northern prison, and made friends everywhere I traveled. I was sent from St. Louis to City Point, Va., and exchanged about the 1st of May, 1863. Thus ended my war career.[64] — JOHN F. FORE, C.S.A.

THE THUNDERBOLT OF WAR
☞ Confederate Gen. Dabney H. Maury was one of the first to learn of Forrest's innate power as a commander, and named him the "Thunderbolt of War."[65] — SUMNER ARCHIBALD CUNNINGHAM

A JOKE ON FORREST
☞ Dr. J. B. Cowan, well known, especially among the Tennessee veterans, and who was chief surgeon to Gen. N. B. Forrest, . . . told of a trick he played on Forrest's chief engineer. The command, only a little before the surrender, camped for a night by the Tombigbee River. The General, for [good] reason, wanted to know how much the water would rise during the night, and directed that the engineer attend to it. Next morning, when he inquired about the matter, the Doctor said: "At a stand [still]."

"No!" yelled Forrest; "I saw a boulder last night that is now out of sight."

In vindication of the engineer, reply was made that he drove a nail into a flatboat just at the edge of the water, and the water stood exactly as before. Of course this joke did not stand long. Proper information was given, and the surgeon provided the engineer, who had faithfully discharged his duty, a little wine for the stomach's sake.[66] — SUMNER ARCHIBALD CUNNINGHAM

FORREST'S CAVALRY VETERANS
☞ At a meeting of the survivors of Forrest's Cavalry held in the Fogg School-Building, at Nashville, Tenn., June 24, 1897, the report of the Committee on Constitution and Permanent Organization was adopted, and is as follows:

Article 1. The objects of this association are to bring together annually the soldiers who may at any time have served under the command of Lieut.-Gen. Forrest for good fellowship, the collection of accurate historical data, and the creation of a memorial worthy of our great commander.

Article 2. Membership in this association shall in nowise be inconsistent with membership in any local camp or bivouac of Confederate Veterans.

Article 3. All veterans of Forrest's Cavalry shall be entitled to membership on the payment of $1 per annum dues. When individual members can not attend the annual reunion, any twenty veterans may unite in sending one delegate to represent them in all business coming before the annual meeting, said delegate being entitled to cast twenty votes.

Article 4. The officers shall be a Commander, with the rank of major-general, with three Brigadier-Generals, and an Assistant Adjutant and Quartermaster-General, with the rank of colonel—to be elected annually. These officers, with one manager to be chosen by the survivors of each brigade and battery (who were at any time under Forrest's command), shall constitute an Executive Committee to transact all business *ad interim*, subject to the approval of the annual reunion.

Article 5. The surviving members of Gen. Forrest's staff will form the staff of the Commanding-General, in the positions and with the rank held at the surrender at Gainesville, Ala., during their natural lives. An election was held to fill the offices indicated in the institution, which resulted as follows: Major-General H. P. Lyon; Brigadier-Generals, D. C. Kelley, R. M. McCullough (another Brigadier-General to be elected by the Executive Committee); Assistant Adjutant and Quartermaster-General, with the rank of colonel, George L. Cowan.

George L. Cowan.

The association adjourned to meet one year hence at Atlanta, Ga., at the time of the Confederate reunion. It is requested and urged by the General commanding that all survivors of Gen. Forrest's command meet at Atlanta and join the association. If those who can not attend will send their address, name of company and regiment, with $1, to George L. Cowan, Franklin, Tenn., they will be enrolled as members.[67] — CONFEDERATE MAJ.-GEN. H. B. LYON and QUARTERMASTER GENERAL GEORGE L. COWAN

A BRAVE TEXAS RANGER

☛ In the year 1864 I was living with my aged father within four miles of Woodbury [Tenn.] on the old stage road between there and McMinnville. One day Forrest's Cavalry came up the road, and were surrounded by Federals on all sides. A short but desperate battle was fought, and Forrest's men were at last obliged to retreat. A Texas Ranger was brought into our house with his leg shot off by a cannon-ball. The surgeon dressed his wound as quickly as possible, and then left him. One by one, his comrades rode up to the door and bade him farewell, saying: "Good-by, D." His name was John D. Rugley. He died in a few hours, and was buried in one of the grand old hills of Cannon County. He was never conscious of anything after being shot. That brave Ranger's grave is marked by a tall rock that I put over him, and bears the inscription: "John D. Rugley, a Texas Ranger." I was only fifteen years old at this time.[68] — SANDY ELKINS

U.D.C. CHAPTER NAMED AFTER FORREST

☛ Touched by the same enthusiasm that extends throughout our beloved Southland, a number of Brownsville [Tenn.] representative women met in April for the purpose of organizing a chapter of Daughters, which they called after the noble Forrest.

With a present enrollment of sixteen, and the interest of the people aroused in keeping the truth before all generations, the chapter anticipates a bright future.

The officers of Forrest Chapter are: Mrs. Carey A. Polk, President; Mrs. T. B. King and Miss Laura Bradford, Vice Presidents; Miss April Mulherun, Recording Secretary; Miss Harriet Moses, Corresponding Secretary; Miss Mary Livingston, Treasurer.

Mrs. Carey A. Polk.

Forrest Chapter was a worthy auxiliary in the annual reunion of veterans at Johnson's Lake, and assisted in arranging a most excellent programme. [Confederate] Gen. [William B.] Bate was the orator of the day, and was presented by the President of the chapter with a handsome floral Confederate flag, made by Miss Mulherun.[69] — SUMNER ARCHIBALD CUNNINGHAM

THE HEROINE EMMA SANSOM JOHNSON
☞ The same spirit that animated the men of the South in the war of 1861-65 was manifested by the women where opportunity offered. Our heroines, it will be well to remember, had nothing but the spirit of true patriotism to prompt them to deeds of daring. They were not aspirants for promotion to office, but acted solely from a love of country and of home. Such was the case of Emma Sansom, a fifteen-year-old girl, who volunteered to face the bullets and shells of [Union] Gen. Streight, riding behind Gen. Forrest at Black Creek to show him a ford where he could cross the stream after Streight had burned the bridge across the creek to delay the pursuit of Forrest's command.

In the last days of April, 1863, Gen. Streight, of the Federal army, started with about twenty-four hundred men from Tennessee to raid North Alabama. He crossed the Tennessee River near Decatur, Ala., and crossed Sand Mountain via Brooksville, in Blount County, and Walnut Grove, in Etowah County, entering the Coosa Valley at Gadsden—all in Alabama—on the 2nd day of May, 1863. When he reached Black Creek, two miles west of Gadsden, he crossed his army over and fired the bridge behind him. One or two days after Streight left Tennessee Gen. Forrest heard of his raid, and at once started in pursuit, taking with him parts of two or three regiments, three hundred and fifty men in all, and two pieces of flying artillery, and overtook Streight at Black Creek after the bridge had been fired. Mrs. Sansom, a widow, lived on the road near the bridge, and after Streight had passed her house she saw smoke rising from the bridge. She at once started with her fifteen-year-old daughter, Emma, to extinguish the flames, but as she neared the bridge she found that it was guarded by [Union] pickets. Returning toward her home she met Gen. Forrest, who advanced to the brow of the hill, thus drawing the pickets' fire, and one of his men was killed. Forrest then asked Mrs. Sansom if there was any speedy way of crossing the stream. To this inquiry Miss Emma promptly stated that she knew where there was an old ford above the bridge, and that she would show him where it was, volunteering to mount behind him on his horse and show him the way. Her mother protested against this, as the bullets and shells were flying thick along the route that she would necessarily have to go in order to reach the ford; but, nothing daunted, Miss Emma climbed the corner of a rail fence and mounted behind Gen. Forrest, who rode swiftly across the field in plain view of the enemy, by her direction, to the old ford, and, finding it satisfactory, rode back through the hail of shot and shell. He delivered Miss Emma back to her mother, remarking to Mr. Gabriel Hughes, who had just arrived, that the young lady's brave and courageous act was unparalleled, and that she deserved the gratitude of the country and a pension from the government. By this act of Miss Emma's pursuit was facilitated by at least two hours, and it enabled Forrest to overtake Streight, who was within twenty-five miles of Rome, Ga., and attack and capture him, with his twenty-four hundred men.

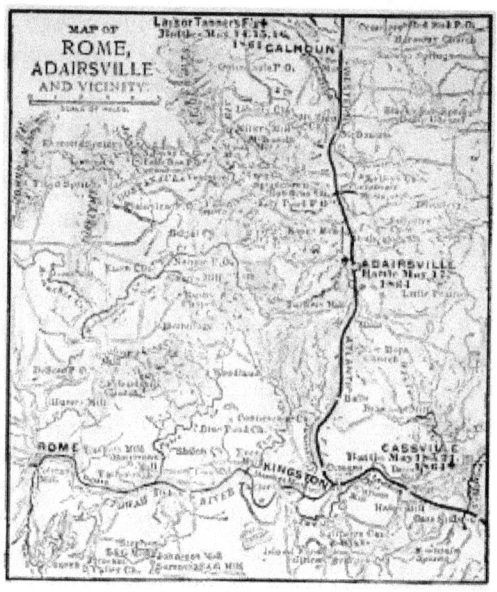

Map of the Rome, Georgia, area, part of Forrest's theater of operations.

The main object of Streight's raid was to burn the iron furnaces in Cherokee County, Ala., which he had done, then to destroy the public works and the city of Rome, Ga.; and it is not doubted that but for Miss Sansom's heroic service he would have succeeded in completing his purposes.

It has been stated that Miss Sansom received a large donation of land from the State of Alabama. The Legislature of Alabama did pass an act donating to her a section of land, but she never obtained a title to it, and at the surrender of course all public lands in Alabama belonged to the United States government. It is a fact, confirmed by the statement of Mrs. Emma Sansom Johnson (that is her name now) to the writer, that she has never received one dollar from any source in consideration of the circumstances related.

Mrs. Johnson is a widow with several children, and is in feeble health. She is not blessed with the comforts of life which she richly merits. She now lives at Calloway, Tex. She was impelled by a love of the cause, of her country, and her home, having four brothers fighting under the "stars and bars" at that time. The brave men of the South owe to Mrs. Johnson material assistance commensurate with the assistance she so cheerfully and daringly rendered unto our great cause. If our men do not respond to her needs, I feel that the Daughters of the Confederacy will take the matter in hand and give her the material aid that she needs and so justly deserves.[70] — MISS OLLIE G. WOODLIFF

FORREST, STREIGHT, & SANSOM
☛ In the spring of 1864 the Federal general Streight, with some two thousand mounted infantry, made a rush from the Tennessee River near Florence, Ala., to destroy the iron works belonging to the Confederacy at Montevallo, Ala., and Rome, Ga. The Confederate general N. B. Forrest, the "Wizard of the Saddle," with about the same force as Gen. Streight, was fronting Gen. Dodge; but, quickly realizing Streight's intentions, he left some eight hundred in front of Gen. Dodge, and with about twelve hundred more started in hot pursuit of Streight. The brilliancy and intrepidity of this running fight of four days and nights, scarcely stopping, is one of the heroic things of the war. They fought day and night. The first night they fought four battles in the mountains—one at eight o'clock, one at ten, one at twelve, and one at two in the morning—Streight retreating on Rome all the time, and Forrest trying to annihilate him. It is a matter of history how Forrest, on the second day, had to drop all his men but six hundred on account of their broken mounts, and with these followed and fought Streight day and night till he finally forced him and some seventeen hundred of his men to surrender almost in sight of his destination. The heroic deed of the girl, Emma Sansom, at the Black Creek bridge, caused the Governor of Alabama to have struck for her a gold medal, and the Legislature of the State granted her, by special act of that body, a section of public land.[71] — JOHN TROTWOOD MOORE

FORREST SAVES A BLIND HORSE & A SACK OF CORN
☛ I read again to-day the account of Gen. Streight's raid . . . [and] the brave deed of the fifteen-year-old girl, Emma Sansom, who sprang up behind Gen. Forrest and, amid a hail of bullets from the enemy, piloted him to a ford where he could cross his men after the Federals had burned

the bridge.

I was then living in North Alabama, and nearly in sight of the road Streight traveled. On that morning I had been called to conduct a funeral service over the remains of a very dear friend, Thomas Barbee, a brother of Rev. Dr. J. D. Barbee, of Nashville. I had nearly reached the place, a distance of eight miles, when I encountered an old and wealthy citizen, who was under great excitement, moving his mules, horses, cattle, bacon, and negroes out into the woods. Upon asking him what was up he cried out, "Yankees, Yankees!" and told me that three thousand had camped at Daniel Hodge's the night before. Of course our funeral congregation was broken up.

On arriving at home I saw that my wife and a half-grown negro boy had our old blind gray horse and were trying to move to a place of greater security [and hide] some shelled corn which we were saving for bread. A sack had come untied and the corn had spilled, and they were standing over it in a good deal of trouble. It was good news that the Yankees had swept by and that Forrest was close after them. I was chaplain of the Twenty-Fourth Tennessee regiment, and greet all the old boys who may see this, wherever they are scattered.[72] — REVEREND J. W. CULLUM

GEN. FORREST'S ORDER TO COL. BAXTER SMITH

☛ I write of an incident that occurred during the battle that Forrest had with the Federals at Murfreesboro [Tenn.] in 1862. I was at home on sick leave just after the battle of Fishing Creek. My health improving, I joined the Texas Rangers and Morgan's men, who were scouting the country near Nashville and trying to ascertain when Gen. Buell would advance his forces. About fifteen of us young men banded together and made our ways out from Nolensville, Triune, and Sparta, and met Gen. Forrest in McMinnville as he was coming down on Murfreesboro with about twelve hundred men. I persuaded the boys to join the battalion of Col. Baxter Smith, then a Major. We soon realized that we had a leader who knew his business. About five miles from Murfreesboro we were halted and ordered to "dismount, fix saddles, and tighten girts." This we did, remounted, and galloped into Murfreesboro just about daylight. The Texas Rangers engaged the Ninth Michigan. Quite a number of Federals collected at the courthouse, and Col. Morrison, of the Second Georgia, undertook to dislodge them. Gen. Forrest in the meantime hastily collected six companies, Col. Baxter Smith's four companies being of the command. Gen. Forrest, placing himself at the head of these six companies, moved out about two miles from town to attack the

Third Minnesota, about twelve hundred strong. Think of it—three hundred and fifty cavalry charge twelve hundred infantry! The charge was disastrous to us. Our men fell back, and Gen. Forrest raged. The writer's horse was shot in the head, and the blood spurted so freely that he got off, expecting his horse to drop; but realizing his danger, he remounted and rode out safely. Gen. Forrest re-formed his men, rode out in front, and, in a clear, distinct voice, said: "Col. Smith, lead the charge." I shall never forget the impression made on my mind at that moment. Col. Smith had taken Trim Brown and myself on his staff for the fight, and we had to follow him. Col. Smith tied his bridle reins, and, with sword in one hand and pistol in the other, started out in a gallop, and led his command right on into the midst of the enemy; and it was a hand-to-hand fight for about one hour, until the enemy retreated, leaving all their tents and baggage.

Baxter Smith.

Gen. Forrest captured the entire Federal force, consisting of about twenty-five hundred or three thousand men, a large quantity of army stores, mules, and wagons. We carried them to McMinnville; paroled the men and sent the officers back South. Gen. Forrest gave the men their band, and they serenaded us with the good old songs of "Dixie," "Bonnie Blue Flag," "The Girl I Left Behind Me," and other Southern airs.

How our hearts filled with joy and pride when we thought of the victory we had won! Armed with shotguns and any other that we could get, and without artillery, while the enemy had the latest improved Enfield and Springfield rifles and a splendid battery of artillery. The battery that was captured that day was taken and used by Gen. Forrest during the remainder of the war, and was known far and near as the famous Morton Battery, being a regular terror to the enemy. It was commanded by Capt. John W. Morton, of Nashville, Forrest's Chief of Artillery.

God bless the old gray-haired Confederates who have had such hard times in this world of disappointments; and when the great Master sounds the last trumpet, may they all be found with "palms of victory" in their hands, "praising God, from whom all blessings flow."[73] —
CONFEDERATE CAPTAIN FRANK BATTLE

DEFENDING THE ACT DONATING LAND TO EMMA SANSOM

☛ The subject of this bill should address itself to every patriotic Southern heart. It is one which should engross the sympathy and enthusiastic advocacy of every man who lives in our glorious Southland. Gen. Streight, with 2,400 picked men, was on a raid through Alabama, bound for Montevallo and Rome, Ga., where he expected to destroy iron works of the Southern Confederacy. Terror and desolation followed in his wake, and the citizenship along his route fled before his devastating forces. Forrest, the "wizard of the saddle," that incomparable military genius, had invested the enemy at Corinth. When he heard of Streight's raid, he swiftly sped in pursuit of the Yankee general. Crossing the river at Decatur, he overtook him in the mountains of North Alabama. Then followed four fierce fights in the night, and the reverberating of the cannon, and the cracking of musketry told terrible tales of fierce and raging battle. Streight, being pursued, crossed over Black Creek, one of the most turbid and rapid mountain streams in all the land, and burned the bridge behind him. The stream was swollen on this occasion, and for the first time in his life the gallant Forrest was daunted. He had about given up in despair, when out from a nearby mountain cottage, like a startled wild doe, sprang a beautiful mountain maid of fifteen years, who said to him: "Gen. Forrest, I know where there is an old ford, and I will pilot you to it." Her mother protested, and insisted that it was "unladylike" of her to do so. But she replied, "I am not afraid to trust myself with so brave a man as Gen. Forrest," and she sprang up on his horse behind him with alacrity.

They crossed over safely, and upon arriving on the other side, she followed Gen. Forrest in the trenches and waved her bonnet at the Yankee forces, who, seeing it was a woman, shouted cheers at her signal bravery. It is familiar to all how Gen. Forrest, with three hundred men, captured Streight and his force of twenty-four hundred.

The brave men who assembled in this hall as representatives, who had fought on the battlefield, and who met the succeeding term of the General Assembly, donated to this Alabama heroine a section of land, but the carpetbag administration [of Liberal President Ulysses S. Grant] that followed deprived her of her just rights. Is there a man who will say that Emma Sansom did not render valuable service to our army in aiding Forrest to capture the raider Streight?

Yet you [critics] say all this is but sentiment! Even so. Inspired by a kindred impulse, I love to wander alone beneath the starlit heavens, and there in silence and in solitude commune with the God of my soul. If you would prostitute the universe of sentiment, then filch from the sweet flowers "the perfume of their breath." Take the roses from the cheeks of fair women, and the spark from their scintillating orbs. I feel that I should be recreant to a patriotic and intelligent constituency, did I not lift up my humble voice in behalf of this pending measure. I speak for the good people of Democratic [then Conservative] Madison, the [Alabama] county that sent more soldiers to the war than she had voters at the polls, and devoutly trust that Emma Sansom will receive equity at your hands. She is no longer young. The roses in her cheeks have faded; she is in destitute circumstances, and often wants for the necessities of life. The patriotic women of Dixie have perpetuated in silent grandeur on the capitol campus the memory of those who so bravely died for what they thought was right, but "nothing dies that memory rocks to sleep." Sir, my noblest heritage from father was that of being his son—the son of an ex-Confederate captain. Co-patriots, let us enact this bill. Let us say to the old Confederates, "We confirm your actions of the past"; let us vindicate the right. Let us restore Emma Sansom to her just deserts! Let us give her a home in Alabama, that she may live in independence. Let us, gentleman, make her declining years as happy and as full of comfort as were her girlhood days in brilliant, matchless, womanly courage, love, and reverence for her country.[74] — JOHN H. WALLACE

FORREST'S BLUFF

☞ We knew that [Union Gen. William S.] Rosecrans was trying to get our arsenal at Rome, Ga. One day word was brought in that a [Union] cavalry brigade had passed through Tuscumbia, and we made after them. We followed them as fast as we could until they got to Salt Hill, and we were much surprised to see them turn off and go up the hill instead of going straight on. They turned and faced us, and we had fight. Presently I heard Gen. Forrest shouting in that peculiar voice of his: "Boys, we must get out of this." I had never heard Forrest speak of retreating before, and it frightened me. After we had fallen back a little way I saw Forrest behind a fence, storming up and down with a pistol, threatening to shoot the first man who crossed that fence. The retreat had to stop. Forrest had hit on a new plan. He called out: "Boys, we've got to bluff them!" The way he "bluffed" them was by dividing his command and sending them in at Col. Streight and his men in detachments from several points at once. Four or five flags of truce came flying in on the Indiana colonel, supposed to have come from various Confederate generals who were miles away. At last Col. Streight said to the bearer of the summons: "I have already surrendered to several of your generals. Now what do you want me to do?" As a matter of courtesy, and so as not to make the humiliation too great, Forrest consented to let the Union men march down into a hollow and surrender where the bulk of the Confederate troops could not see them. Of course there wasn't any bulk there. And that was how the 1,962 men of Streight's command laid down their arms to the 416 of Forrest's.[75] — DR. WHITSITT

Map of the Atlanta Campaign, the area of "one hundred days' fighting," showing the great battlefield of North Georgia as it appeared in 1864 on the line of the Western and Atlantic Railway. Forrest devoted much Confederate time and blood to the region along the Tennessee-Georgia border.

INCIDENT AT CAHABA

☛ . . . Forrest fought Wilson's raiders stubbornly at an old Baptist church called Ebenezer (since called the battle of Ebenezer), between Maplesville and Plantersville, Ala. They made the next stand in Selma, where there were breastworks, and another battle was fought. The Confederates were scattered, and the Yankees came on down as far as Cahaba. We lived on the main road leading from Cahaba to Linden, Ala. About dark one of my neighbors notified me to be on my guard, as the Yankees would certainly be there that night. I was alone except for my five sleeping little ones and an old servant who had volunteered to do all in his power to protect us. I placed lighted lamps in the rooms, and seated myself on the front porch to wait. About eleven o'clock I heard the clatter of horses' feet crossing the bridge, the clanking and jingling of sabers and spurs, and quickly they were at the gate. With the first "Halloo" my heart gave a bound, for I knew they were our men. It was Capt. [Nathan] Boone [of Forrest's Escort] who addressed me: "Well, madam, are you frightened to death?" I replied: "No, sir; but I am so glad that you are not Yankees. Was Gen. Forrest killed? We heard today that he received a severe saber cut over the left ear." He said: "No, madam; Gen. Forrest was well this evening. I am the man who has the saber cut." His head was bound in a large towel. Soon a courier came inquiring for Gen. Forrest's horse that was wounded and had been ordered to my house. I told him we had sent the horse to the house of a neighbor, and I called a negro to accompany him there. When they reached the house the horse had been sent farther for safe-keeping, and to this day I had never heard of the horse or the courier or the captain of Gen. Forrest's escort. . . . Gen. Forrest left a glove at Plantersville, and it is now in possession of Mr. Perry McGhee, Stanton, Ala.[76] — MRS. MARY A. HAMMER

John S. Bowen.

REUNION OF THE 22nd MISSISSIPPI

☛ [The] survivors of the Twenty-Second Mississippi Regiment [attended] a reunion . . . held at Stafford's Well, near Winona, Miss., on June 23, 1899. This regiment was mustered into service at Iuka, Miss., early in 1861, to serve "for three years or during the war," and it served until the final surrender of all the armies, April 26, 1865, at Greensboro, N.C.

In the early part of the war it was in the brigade of Brig. Gen. John S. Bowen, of Missouri, and although it was afterwards transferred from his command, yet an enthusiastic attachment between Gen. Bowen and the regiment began when it was in his command and continued until his death. The area of the regiment's service was in Kentucky, Tennessee, Georgia, Alabama, Mississippi, Louisiana, and North Carolina, and it was engaged in most of the important battles that were fought in that territory, among which were Shiloh, Chickasaw Bayou, Corinth, Champion Hills, Big Black, Vicksburg, Baton Rouge, New Hope Church, Resaca, Peach Tree Creek, Kennesaw Mountain (July 22), and in all the fierce battles in the Sherman campaign from Dalton to Atlanta. It was with Hood at Franklin and Nashville in the Tennessee campaign, and volunteered under Gen. Forrest, and covered Hood's retreat in the winter of 1864 from Nashville to the Tennessee River. It was under Forrest at Sugar Creek, Tenn., and captured a number of Federal cavalry horses, which the men rode to the Tennessee River. This was the last fight Forrest was engaged in, covering Hood's disastrous retreat, and he gave the Federals such a good licking that they did not attempt to follow him again.

Survivors of the Twenty-Second Mississippi Regiment, C.S.A.

The good grub, blankets, and overcoats we captured that miserable, cold winter's day will never be forgotten by the writer as long as memory lasts. This regiment was engaged for over four years in active service, covering a large territory, from Louisiana to Kentucky and from Mississippi to North Carolina: marched thousands of miles, was engaged in over one hundred battles and skirmishes, where men were killed and wounded, and surrendered with two hundred and eighteen men out of an enlistment of twelve hundred. The few survivors of this once formidable regiment are now scattered over many of the States of the Union, North and South.[77] — PHIL CHEW

PLANNING FORREST'S MONUMENT AT MEMPHIS
☛ October 13, 1899, the Confederate Memorial Association held a meeting to devise a plan to aid in the Forrest monument movement, which the Confederate Historical Association and Veterans are urging so strenuously. A final conclusion was reached to assess ourselves, each lady present pledging $5, and a goodly sum for this worthy cause was at once entered upon the Treasurer's books; and, furthermore, each member promised to see others and secure cooperation along this line, and we confidently believe we shall secure a handsome sum as our contribution. We hope the day is not far distant when we can invite our friends to participate in the ceremonies of unveiling a fitting monument to commemorate our inimitable Forrest.[78] — MRS. KELLAR ANDERSON

EXCERPT FROM A LOUISVILLE, KENTUCKY, REUNION SPEECH
☛ There will be here some who rode and fought with the peerless, fearless Forrest, and who on that terrible day at Tishomingo Creek sabered and slew many of the multitude who had been sent to destroy him, and followed that untutored soldier, whose brilliant strategy and magnetic leadership won for him the world's applause.[79] — CONFEDERATE COLONEL BENNETT H. YOUNG

A BLESSING FOR GEN. FORREST
☛ The impression prevalent about our great cavalry general does not credit him with much religious sentiment, yet there were many things in his career which showed a deep reverence for genuine religion. One of his most trusted officers was Col. D. C. Kelley, a Methodist preacher, who maintained his Christian character consistently all through the war, and who was one of the wariest and most dashing of his subordinate commanders. For Col. Kelley he had the profoundest respect, recognizing his sincere piety as well as his splendid courage.

A little incident told me directly after the war will illustrate the tender side of Gen. Forrest's nature. It was told to me by members of my grandfather's family. My mother's father lived six miles south of the little village of Charlotte, in Dickson County, Tenn., on a farm which was granted to his father for services as captain in the Revolutionary war. He was nearly ninety years old at the beginning of the civil war. Though he had loved the Union devotedly, he deeply regretted that he could not fight for the South. He believed in her cause [conservatism] with all his heart. He had his old rifle cleaned and placed where he could lay his hands on it, should occasion arise for him to use it against an invading foe.

On one of his expeditions into Tennessee—I think it was on the way to Fort Donelson in 1863—Gen. Forrest spent a night at my grandfather's, and, by his considerate attention, won the old man's heart. The next morning, when the General and his personal attendants were ready to start, the old gentleman, though nearly blind, must needs accompany him part of the way. So, taking his staff in his hand and one of his grandchildren to lead him, he walked along by the General's horse until they came to the main road at the edge of the farm. When the General stopped to bid his host good-by the escort rode on. The old man asked him to get off his horse, which he did. He then asked him to kneel down. Then, laying his hands on the General's head and lifting his sightless eyes to heaven, the old patriarch solemnly invoked the blessing of God on Gen. Forrest, on his men, and on the cause for which he was fighting. The General's face was bathed in tears as he remounted his horse. In a year my grandfather was laid in his grave. Gen. Forrest lived to win many victories during the war, and afterwards he became a humble Christian. It may be that prayer was one of the influences that kept him safe through many dangers and finally led him to that Saviour in whom the old man trusted.[80] — CONFEDERATE REVEREND J. H. MCNEILLY

Bishop T. F. Gailor.

THIRTY-FOUR YEARS AFTER THE END OF THE WAR
☞ Forrest is no longer in the North denounced as the butcher of Fort Pillow, but is there recognized and esteemed as the greatest cavalry leader of American history. . . . Where are the soldiers in all history who were the superiors of Forrest and his men?[81] — BISHOP THOMAS FRANK GAILOR

REMINISCENCES OF GEN. FORREST IN MIDDLE TENNESSEE
☞ I see that the [United] Daughters of the Confederacy unveiled at Franklin, Tenn., on the 30th of November, one of the handsomest

monuments that has been erected in the South. I regret that I was unable to be present, as that monument stands upon the very spot of ground where I enlisted in the noble cause of the Confederacy March 22, 1861, in the Williamson County Grays, which formed a part of the First Tennessee Regiment. We left in a short time thereafter for Virginia, under that grand old commander, Gen. Robert E. Lee, in Northwestern Virginia. We tramped from Valley Mountain to Cheat Mountain, then back to Valley Mountain, and from there to Big Sewell and Little Sewell Mountains; thence back to Green Brier Bridge, and from there to Winchester, Va., where we joined Stonewall Jackson; from there to Hancock, Md., back to Romney, thence back to Winchester. In January, 1862, we were transferred to the Army of Tennessee, under Gen. Albert Sidney Johnston at Shiloh, routing Gen. Grant on Sunday, April 7, 1862. The unhappy result after that grand man's death is known.

From there the Army of Tennessee was sent back to Chattanooga, and there reorganized and moved to Kentucky, where we fought the great battles of Perryville and Richmond. Again reorganizing, we moved back to Murfreesboro, Tenn., where we fought the great battle in December, 1862. We fell back from Murfreesboro, where Bragg was succeeded by Gen. Joseph E. Johnston, to Shelbyville, Tenn.

In the spring of 1863 I served as aid-de-camp on my uncle's (Gen. Preston Smith) staff; but was transferred to the staff of Gen. Forrest, and returned with him from Shelbyville to Spring Hill, Tenn., where he organized his cavalry command.

Well do I remember at daybreak when he moved on Franklin, emptying the jail at that place of many of our noble boys, and, on our way out, as advance guard, passing Dr. Cliff's office, opposite what was known as the old factory store, from the porch of which a United States flag was waving. I attempted to remove it. Instantly a musket was placed in my face by a woman, who cried: "Hands off!" It is needless to say I obeyed. The shelling was terrific from Figures Hill, where the great Federal forts were erected, and in crossing the public square a twenty-pound shell exploded, killing several horses and wounding a few men. We broke across the street to make our escape, passing through what was known as Moss Sutler's store, going out the back door. Gen. Forrest was in command. We all made good our escape, and returned to Spring Hill with the loss of only eight of our brave boys. We had killed and wounded more than one hundred Yankees in less than one hour passing around and through the town, besides liberating comrades from the jail.

A few days after this grand raid, at Spring Hill Gen. Forrest said to me, "I am invited to Columbia by Mrs. Galloway to dine with her," and asked me how I should like to go. My answer was that I knew the girls very well and would enjoy it. "Have our horses saddled, and we will ride in," was his answer. On our arrival at Columbia we left our horses at Jim Guest's livery stable, and walked up to Mrs. Galloway's, who lived just back of the Athenaeum. While we were at dinner the door bell rang, and the announcement was made at the table by a servant that a [Confederate] soldier (Lieut. [Andrew W.] Gould) wished to see Gen. Forrest. I was instructed by the General to tell him that he would see him in Maj. Severson's office in the city hall building at 3 o'clock. I went to the door and delivered the message. Returning to the dining room, I enjoyed the splendid dinner and the social chat with the young ladies. The General and I bade the family adieu, going to Severson's office on our way back. The General asked me if I had one of those pocket knives that I got at Franklin, and I gave him one—a three-bladed knife with one long blade and two small ones. Entering the clerk's office, I took a seat to enjoy a cigar given me by Miss Galloway. The

Alexander P. Stewart fought with Forrest during the Middle Tennessee campaign.

General passed down the hall, and as he entered the third room to the rear Lieut. Gould sprang out, drew his pistol, and shot the General in the thigh. [Note: later it was learned that Gould's attack was due to his erroneous belief that Forrest had once humiliated him.] Immediately the General stabbed him with the big blade of the knife, driving the handle and all into his lung. Lieut. Gould, while running down the hall, passed me, and I made a grab for him, tearing the lapel from his coat. He ran up the street to Engle's tailor shop, the General and I after him. The General was caught by Col. Jim Edmonson and several of his command, trying to hold him. I ran to Guest's stable for our pistols, secured them, and returned in a very few minutes and gave the General his pistol. We rushed to Engle's tailor shop, where Lieut. Gould was confined. There was an enormous crowd in the streets and in the store. The General gave command to clear the way, and in he went. Lieut. Gould was lying upon the cutting table in the rear of the store, with a doctor attempting to examine his wound. Off the counter he rolled and out the back door.

He fell in the yard, supposed to be dead. The General pulled his navy on him. I took him by the arm, raising the same, and remarked: "Don't shoot; he is dead." He handed me his pistol, telling me to take charge of his body, which I did, having him removed to Taylor's hotel. He revived after the knife was removed, and lived for a few days.[82]

Gen. Forrest was taken by Col. Edmonson and others to the Galloway residence, and the bullet removed from his thigh, which, though very painful, was a slight wound. It was soon dressed, and we were in our saddles and on our way back to Spring Hill. The day after we moved on Triune, Tenn., where the right wing of Rosecrans's army was stationed, some 24,000 strong, routing the entire command just at daylight. There I received a slight wound in the hip. We made good our escape, after killing and wounding as many as we had in our entire command.

I could go on and note many other reminiscences from 1861 to 1865 that my old comrades would enjoy. It is well on occasions like this to trace the history of our country from the downfall of the Confederacy to the present time. It is still the old South, born again, more prosperous, more beautiful, and more lovely than of yore. Great as the Confederacy was in war, still greater has her people proved themselves in peace.

Henry H. Smith.

When the war ended and the last Confederate laid down his arms almost, if not quite, one million of our foes were still in the field, with unlimited resources, and we were helpless in the hands of our conquerors. Yet in less than ten years the State and local governments in the entire territory embraced in the Confederacy were irrevocably in the hands of the ex-Confederates [that is, the Northern Liberals' effort to "reconstruct" the South ultimately failed]. The annals of the Confederates and the Confederacy have become among the brightest pages in the history of our common country. Gen. N. B. Forrest is no longer denounced in the North as the butcher of Murfreesboro, Fort Pillow, and many other important places, but is there recognized and esteemed as one of the greatest cavalry leaders in American history . . .[83] — CONFEDERATE CAPTAIN HENRY H. SMITH

A BORN LEADER & FIGHTER
☛ Forrest was a born leader of men and a born fighter, and knew the art of war by instinct as correctly as Caesar, Napoleon, or Alexander, or Grant. It was all intuition to him, and he knew it instinctively—that which others learned by books.[84] — JOHN TROTWOOD MOORE

ATTENTION, FORREST'S CAVALRY
☛ General Order No. 2. Headquarters of Forrest's Cavalry Corps, Murfreesboro, Tenn., March 5, 1900.

1. The Major General Commanding hereby gives notice to Commanders of the three brigades constituting Forrest's Cavalry Corps, C. S. A., that a rendezvous of all Confederate veterans, either cavalry or infantry, who at any time served under the command of Gen. Forrest will take place at Baldwin, Miss., June 10 next.

2. Brigade Commanders will report at once to these headquarters a roster of their full staff, mentioning also an officer especially detailed to go to Baldwin for the purpose of aiding all preparations necessary to make this reunion a success.

3. In addition to the anniversary celebration of the great victory at Tishomingo (Brice's Cross Roads), it is especially desired that Brigade Commanders will appoint an officer whose duty it shall be to devote himself to securing facts of history marking the career of our great commander; also to set on foot or aid in prosecuting plans for the erection of an equestrian statue to Gen. N. B. Forrest. By order of Maj. Gen. D. C. Kelley, Commanding.[85] — CHAS. W. ANDERSON, A. A. G.

FORREST'S REPUTATION AMONG THE YANKS
☛ [Confederate] Gen. [Philip D.] Roddey's Cavalry operated in North Mississippi, Alabama, and Tennessee, and the boys used to get off some good jokes at their expense, claiming they acted on the principle that "he who fights and runs away will live to fight another day." At the battle of Sulphur Trestle, Tenn., Forrest captured, after a hard fight, several hundred prisoners. While they were stacking arms an Irish Yankee wanted to know, "Bejasus, who do we surrender to?" One of the boys answered: "Gen. Forrest." "Well, why in the divil didn't you let us know? We would have surrendered an hour ago."[86] — RUFE ADAMS

FORREST'S CHIEF OF ARTILLERY—JOHN WATSON MORTON
☛ Although it is as a cavalry general that the name of Forrest is best known, students of his great career from the time he enlisted as a private to when he finished as a lieutenant general best appreciate the genius of

the man in his wonderful, resourceful versatility in handling men and molding them to his purposes in a great variety of emergencies. When he went into the army his knowledge of things military was less than that of the average volunteer; and yet did there ever live a commander who could take a body of men, as did he, untutored, undrilled, and unskilled, and make them to the enemy's imagination so dreadfully persuasive and, in fact, so terribly effective? His troopers, as horsemen, were the peers of any that ever wielded the saber. Dismounting them, he used them successfully against as hardy infantry as ever met a charge, and taught the military world new lessons in cavalry tactics. He made infantrymen of cavalrymen and cavalrymen of infantrymen with results equally brilliant.

The greatest marvel in Forrest's career, and that which was most surprising to professional military chieftains and critics, was his intuitive comprehension of the value of artillery. He entered the army knowing no more about artillery tactics than a crusader of the Middle Ages; and yet he achieved unprecedented victories with that arm of service that were new revelations of his genius. Keenly observant of the qualities of his men, Gen. Forrest made instant use of any special individual aptness. He never better illustrated the soundness of the judgment that inspired the enthusiastic confidence of his men than in his choice of lieutenants—his brigade commanders, his department chiefs, his staff officers, and particularly in his choice of a chief of artillery. For this vital post he selected, against the young man's modest demurring to be chosen over older officers, John W. Morton, then a delicate stripling. But Morton, a smooth-faced boy, had at Fort Donelson won the praise of the generals commanding and absolutely fought his way into Forrest's special esteem. He went with Forrest, and was given his first battery of guns, captured from the enemy on the West Tennessee raid of 1862. Thereafter Gen. Forrest not only gave to Capt. Morton implicit confidence, but not infrequently relied upon the judgment of the youthful cannoneer commander as to the best service to be had from his guns. It was immediately after the battle of Chickamauga that Capt. Morton went with Forrest into his Mississippi Department.

John W. Morton.

The General had referred to the artillery captain as the "little bit of a kid with a big backbone." He had delighted the General by keeping his guns in pace with the swiftest movements of his flying expeditions. Morton's batteries lumbered and thundered where sabers gleamed and carbines and pistols flashed in the headlong charge. His guns were the van of the victorious columns at Brice's Cross Roads, where they went into action with the celerity of the skirmish lines. On the Tennessee River and in the Johnsonville campaign—the most unparalleled performance of our civil or any other war—when Forrest struck a crushing blow at one of Sherman's largest depots of supplies, Morton, with his batteries led the way, and, with Gen. Forrest's approval, selected the positions from which they effected the capture of two gunboats, a heavily laden transport, and destroyed at Johnsonville military stores worth, according to an official Federal report, over $2,500,000, in addition to a fleet of eleven steamers, barges, gunboats, and transports, whose sunken hulls may yet be seen at Johnsonville when the river is low—voiceless but eloquent witnesses of the completest victory and most extraordinary campaign of the war.

Forrest's artillery, with Morton ever at their head, was in the van of Hood's advance into Tennessee, and while at Franklin and Nashville the Confederate infantry, despite their utmost valor and sacrifice, were overwhelmed by numbers, Morton and his guns successfully broke up the outposts, destroying railroads and blockhouses of the enemy's outer lines, and then joined the stricken army in time to aid in saving it from annihilation.

When the sad retreat of Hood's bruised and battered battalions made their bleeding way beyond the Tennessee River, Walthall and Forrest, with Morton's artillery, held the swarming hosts of pursuers at bay, and the shells of the never-yielding batteries, until the last pale and bloody regiment was safe on the Southern bank of the river, ever shrieked defiance and hurled destruction into the foremost ranks of outnumbering foes.

And when, at last, the Confederate leaders decided to quit the terribly unequal struggle, whose continuance meant the further desolation of the land they loved—already scarred and blighted by four merciless years of war—there was no organization, of those who wore the gray and furled the stars and bars for the last time, so well equipped and ready for fight as Morton's batteries of guns, all captured from the enemy.

Their chief was yet so young at the surrender, that when he went home he took a course at school, pursuing the studies that had been interrupted by the war.[87] — SUMNER ARCHIBALD CUNNINGHAM

GEN. FORREST'S SCHOOL TEACHER
☛ Col. John Laws came from Hillsboro, N.C., to Tennessee in 1826 or 1828, and settled at Chapel Hill. After it was made a part of Marshall County he became its representative for three terms in the State Legislature. One of these was in 1861, when the State seceded. Col. Laws was a militia officer in the old North State and in Tennessee. Upon coming to Tennessee he engaged as a teacher, and one of his students became a renowned military hero. He was a lifelong Democrat [then a Conservative], and when the Federals occupied the State went South. One day while riding on a road near Corinth, Miss., he was passing a group of officers, when one of them hailed him cordially, and asking if he knew him, said, "You ought to know me; you have whipped me often enough," and added, "I am Bedford Forrest." He then urged his old teacher to spend the night with him. Col. Laws was asked once if Forrest was a bright student. He replied: "Bedford had plenty of sense, but would not apply himself. He thought more of wrestling than his books; he was an athlete."[88] — SUMNER ARCHIBALD CUNNINGHAM

ONE OF FORREST'S SCOUTS
☛ . . . Comrade H. Wohlleben, of Oxford, Miss., who served through the war with Gen. Forrest, . . . was often sent by him on perilous secret service. On one occasion he was sent into the Federal camp at Rienzi to get the strength and position of the enemy. Disguised as a farmer's boy, he went in, spent the night with them, got all the information desired, and before day mounted a horse belonging to one of the pickets and made a dash for liberty. He was followed nearly eight miles, so closely that he was forced to abandon his mount and take to the woods, finally succeeding in making his way back to his command. Comrade Wohlleben, it is stated, was engaged in forty-seven battles and skirmishes, and escaped without a scratch until the battle of Franklin, where he was severely wounded in the ankle. Two years ago he journeyed to New York to get his old war-time friend, Dr. Wyeth, to perform an operation for his relief. Comrade Wohlleben has the bullet, his old six-shooter, and jacket of gray—relics of the past that he prizes highly.[89] — SUMNER ARCHIBALD CUNNINGHAM

"ONE OF THE SHREWDEST TRICKS OF THE WAR"
☛ I have [an] . . . incident worth relating that took place at Sacramento, Ky. It was the only time I ever saw a hand-to-hand contest with sabers. Bill Terry, of my regiment, was killed by a saber thrust whilst he was warding off other blows. I recollect in connection with the Streight raid

William S. McLemore

that there were but two regiments up when Streight surrendered. These, with parts of Forrest's escort and Ferrell's artillery, were the only troops in seventy miles of us. The two regiments were Biffle's and ours. The Biffle's Fourth Cavalry Regiment was known as both the Ninth and Nineteenth. These, with the escort and artillery, numbered in all about five hundred effectives. Col. Streight captured a soldier of my command (William Haynes) and asked him how many troops Forrest had. Haynes, knowing Forrest's game of bluff, replied: "Roddey's Brigade, Biffle's, McLemore's, Buford, Bell, Lyon, and others." Upon Haynes's representation, Streight turned to his staff and said, "Gentlemen, we are gone up." Forrest, you know, had scattered his troops, not knowing where Streight would strike. When we got upon Streight's heels a flag of truce was sent to him by some of Forrest's escort, demanding a surrender. The reply was: "I will not surrender unless you have more men than I!" In an interview that followed, as Forrest's officers came up for instructions, he disposed of their commands so as to leave an impression of great force. I tell you, this capture of seventeen hundred men by five hundred of us was one of the shrewdest tricks of the war, and was played to success.⁹⁰ — CONFEDERATE COLONEL WILLIAM S. MCLEMORE

REUNION OF FORREST'S CAVALRY CORPS

☞ The reunion of Forrest's Cavalry on June 10-11 [1900] at Brice's Cross Roads was possibly the most enjoyable and satisfactory ever held by a body of Confederates. It was conspicuously pleasant, as every old soldier knew his comrades and could remember accurately the many marches, battles, and campaigns of Gen. Forrest. The people were most hospitable at Corinth, Baldwyn, and Tupelo, and on the battlefield of Brice's Cross Roads there was never a more bountiful dinner set for any people; it was not only abundant, but was excellently prepared and graciously served by the fair women of that neighborhood. There were fully 6,000 present and enough provisions left over to have fed as many more. One of the managers remarked that "the heavy rains and muddy roads embarrassed those who had the dinner in charge, and they didn't have a fair chance." The gallant Gen. [Edmund W.] Rucker, like all the other soldiers, was overwhelmed with good things, and remarked:

"Well, we will come again and give you a chance."

The three members present on Gen. Forrest's staff (Maj. C. W. Anderson, Capt. George Dashiell, and Capt. John W. Morton) were introduced by Col. Kelley, Major General Commanding. Gen. Rucker, Judge A. W. Hawkins, Hon. M. H. Meeks, Col. Baxter Smith, and others delivered appropriate addresses.

The accomplished Miss Cayce, sponsor for Mississippi, delivered a most beautiful address of welcome, which was gracefully and appropriately responded to by Miss Laura May Barksdale, granddaughter of Maj. J. P. Strange, sponsor for Tennessee. Miss Ford, granddaughter of Maj. Strange, and Miss Weatherford were Miss Barkdale's maids of honor, who added much to the social features of the occasion.

The battlefield of Brice's Cross Roads was visited by many of the old soldiers who had not been on this historic ground since the brilliant and ever-memorable victory of Forrest and his men. Most of the Confederate and Federal soldiers had been removed from where they were hastily buried at the time. Two soldiers, one J. C. Jourdan, First Sergeant Moreland's Battalion, was buried near the Phillips house with two cedar trees to mark his resting place; the other J. S. King, Rice's Battery, was killed at the last position taken by the artillery which closed the fight. This position was two and a half miles from Brice's Cross Roads, and was stubbornly contested, the enemy charging to within a few yards of the guns.

Gen. Lyon, opportunely hurrying up to the right of the artillery with a portion of his command dismounted, raised a yell, and with double-shotted canister from the artillery the enemy were driven from the field. It was soon ascertained why this obstinate stand was made; only a few hundred yards farther on a large number of wagons and ambulances had been abandoned by the enemy.

Miss Laura May Barksdale, Sponsor for Forrest's Cavalry.

Three members of Morton's Artillery were wounded; the gallant Lieut. Tully Brown had his horse killed, and a number of artillery horses were killed and wounded at the last position. This closed the fight of the 10th.

The artillery was constantly on the front and often in advance of the main line from the time it reached the field until the close of this most remarkable engagement. About two miles from Brice's Cross Roads the artillery had taken the lead. It could move faster than the cavalry, as the commands fought on foot and had to remount and reform, whilst the artillery had only to limber to the front and move forward. Four guns had been passed to the front and placed in position on a wooded ridge to the left of the main road. The enemy had taken position on a parallel ridge across an old field about half a mile distant. The artillery opened a vigorous fire, and was replied to by a storm of missiles from small arms. Leaves and limbs were clipped, and trees skinned, bullets striking the tires and axles of the guns. Two men caught the lead. Not a skirmisher or single support of any kind was present. Forrest was, however, not long in reaching us. Having dismounted, he walked up the hill to the guns, when Capt. Morton, saluting, said: "General, it is pretty warm here. They'll hit you. You had better step lower down the hill." Instantly, expecting a reprimand as to this suggestion, Capt. Morton apologized by saying, "Please excuse me, General, I don't mean to say where you shall go," and turned to his guns. Gen. Forrest, without a word, walked a short distance down the hill and took a seat at the root of a tree. The two guns from Morton and two from Rice's Batteries had hot work here. Within fifteen or twenty minutes Gen. Forrest called to Capt. Morton to come to him, when he said: "See the head of my column coming up the road. I will take command of that force and charge across that field, strike them on the flank, and double them up on that road," pointing to the place. "When you hear Gaus sound his bugle for the charge, take your artillery and charge down the road, and give them hell right yonder," pointing to the place where he said he was going to "double them up."

Forrest did exactly as he said he was going to do. The artillery was advanced rapidly down the road to within one hundred and fifty or two hundred yards of the enemy's lines, speedily put into action, and directed double-shotted canister upon the enemy's disordered lines as they crowded and "doubled up" in their efforts to reach the road. Forrest's wonderful genius was shown in the success of the movement, and by the number of dead and wounded at the point where he said he would "double them up."

This was possibly the only time in the history of any battle where the general commanding gave an order to charge with artillery without support.

The people of Tupelo, one of the most enterprising towns in North Mississippi, gave the veterans a fine welcome. The battlefield of Harrisburg, only about two miles distant, was visited, and a great many who were wounded on that bloody ground found the spot where they caught the enemy's lead. It was in this fight that a section of Morton's Battery, commanded by Lieut. Tully Brown, had seven out of eight men wounded at one gun, his own horse killed and a number of artillery horses killed and wounded, and the guns pulled off by Eb Titus's company. Rice's Battery was badly disabled and had to be pulled from the field by the gallant Kentuckians. Thrall's Battery was ordered to Rice's relief, and did valiant service. Harrisburg was one of the most desperately fought battles of Forrest's Cavalry. Gen. Stephen D. Lee was in command. Nearly every field officer of Bell's, Mabry's, and the Kentucky brigades were killed or wounded, and many companies of those commands came out of that battle commanded by sergeants or corporals, the officers all having been killed or wounded.

The people of North Mississippi are properly grateful to Gen. Forrest for his protection of that rich country. It is said that [Union] Gen. Sturgis remarked: "I was only anxious to reach Columbus, Miss., the center of secession and aristocracy of the South. I would not have left one brick above another." This refined, hospitable, and patriotic people were spared. Sturgis never reached Columbus.

Tully Brown.

Dr. John A. Wyeth . . . says: "This was the most brilliant victory of Forrest's most remarkable campaigns." [Union] Gen. [Cadwallader C.] Washburn, in his official report, says: "It took Gen. Sturgis's army ten days to march from Memphis to Brice's Cross Roads, and only one day and two nights to return to Memphis." Muster rolls captured on the day of the battle gave 10,265 active for duty in the Federal command, with twenty-two pieces of artillery. Forrest's force was 3,200, with only 2,400 actively engaged, as one-fourth were horse holders. There were but two batteries of four guns each under Capt. John W. Morton, chief of artillery. Forrest captured as many men as he had in the fight, killed and wounded nearly as many more, captured all of their artillery except one gun, two hundred and fifty wagons and ambulances, and scattered the balance of Sturgis's army all over a large area.[91] — SUMNER ARCHIBALD CUNNINGHAM

WOMEN'S FORREST STATUE ASSOCIATION

☞ The following are the officers of the Women's Forrest Statue Association: Mrs. T. J. Latham, Chairman of the Executive Committee; Mrs. J. Harvey Mathes, Vice Chairman; Mrs. James M. Greer, Secretary; and Mrs. Charles M. Drew, Treasurer.

To the honor of Tennessee, the Memphis women's organizations have resolved on the erection of a monument to Gen. N. B. Forrest. If ever matchless genius, the most daring courage, indomitable will and marvelous success secured imperishable fame for any hero, surely it belongs to our own "wizard of the saddle." Napoleon said: "In war men are nothing, a man everything." Truly was this exemplified in Gen. Forrest. It is well known that the military genius of Forrest was acknowledged in Europe before it was recognized in America, and that both Gens. Grant and Sherman realized his wonderful capacity before it was appreciated by the Confederate generals. The present generation is the one to claim the privilege of perpetuating in bronze, or marble, the heroic deeds of this son of Tennessee, and now is the time to begin, and this is the year to finish the work.

Mrs. T. J. Latham.

Mrs. Latham accepted the Presidency of the Tennessee State Division of the United Daughters of the Confederacy, with the pledge and condition that the first work should be for the Forrest monument, believing that with the promised aid of many veterans and camps early success would be achieved.

We confidently appeal to every camp and veteran, and U.D.C. Chapters, and public-spirited citizens, for contributions.

Contributions should be sent to Mrs. C. M. Drew, Treasurer, or to Mrs. J. M. Greer, Secretary of the Women's Forrest Statue Association.

The circular is signed by George W. Gordon, Major General Commanding Tennessee Division, U.C.V. [United Confederate Veterans]; John P. Hickman, Adjutant General, Chief of Staff; John W. Morton, Colonel; W. W. Carnes, Lieutenant Colonel; and J. S. Galloway, Major on Gen. Gordon's Staff; J. W. Crawford and W. A. Collier, Colonels on Gen. Stephen D. Lee's Staff; and Pres. Young, Secretary Confederate Historical Association. Also by Mesdames M. C. Goolett, J. P. Hickman, M. H. Cliff, J. Harvey Mathes, Vice Chairman

Forrest Statue Association; Mrs. T. J. Latham, State President; and Mrs. Frances Kirby-Smith, Vice President, U.D.C. for Tennessee.[92] — SUMNER ARCHIBALD CUNNINGHAM

THE FORREST MONUMENT MOVEMENT
☛ Special Order No. 2. Headquarters Forrest's Cavalry, Murfreesboro, Tenn., September 3, 1900.
In pursuance of the expressed purpose of Forrest's Cavalry at their recent reunion held on the battlefield of Brice's Cross Roads, the Major General Commanding has determined to press during the present year the collection of funds for the Forrest monument [at Memphis]. With this in view, he hereby appoints the following officers of his staff as the Monumental Committee of this corps—viz., Col. Charles W. Anderson, Adjutant General, Murfreesboro, Tenn.; Col. W. A. Collier, Chief of Staff, Memphis, Tenn.; Col. George S. Cowan, Chief Quartermaster, Franklin, Tenn. This committee is not only instructed, but is hereby fully authorized to carry on this work by the use and adoption of such means, measures, and methods as in their judgment are deemed necessary to success.[93] — CHARLES W. ANDERSON, ASST. ADJT. GEN.

BATTLE OF TISHOMINGO CREEK
☛ The place is known as Brice's Cross Roads, but the post office is Bethany. I am unable to explain why so little mention has been made of this engagement even by Southern writers. It was a signal Confederate victory. The slight mention made of it by Northern writers is easily explained, for it was a humiliating defeat. Gen. Grant in his official report of the operations of the war dismissed it with a few sentences.
To guard against any injury to his communications, he states:

> Gen. Sherman left what he supposed to be a sufficient force to guard against Forrest in West Tennessee. He directed Gen. Washburn, who commanded there, to send Brig. Gen. Samuel Davis Sturgis in command of his force to attack Forrest. On the morning of the 10th of June Gen. Sturgis met the enemy near Guntown, Miss., was badly beaten and driven back in utter rout and confusion to Memphis, a distance of about one hundred miles, hotly pursued by the enemy.

The battle occurred about six miles from Guntown, at the crossing of the Ripley and Fulton road with that from Pontotoc to Jacinto.
At this Cross Roads in 1864 was the residence of Mr. William Brice, a large two-story building; also the dwelling of Dr. A. G. Smythe, then unoccupied. Across the road from Brice's house was an unoccupied

storehouse, and near by was the Associate Reformed Church of Bethany. The place was about half a mile east of Tishomingo Creek [thus the conflict is also known as the Battle of Tishomingo Creek]. My home was then with my father, Dr. E. Agnew, nearly three miles from the Cross Roads toward Ripley, where I still reside. The Cross Roads were sometimes called "Brice's Cross Roads," because his dwelling was the principal building there. It is so styled in Sturgis's official report in 1864. We had no mails. Our intelligence of current events was generally derived from rumors, and these were, as a rule, unreliable.

On June 5 three Federal regiments of cavalry passed through Ripley, taking the Rienzi road, camping three miles from there. They fed off of Yancey, who was said to be ruined. This force was estimated at from fifteen hundred to three thousand men. A large infantry force, said to number ten thousand, was reported to be at Salem, coming on. What this move meant we could not imagine. Russell's Tennessee Regiment was following this cavalry, watching their movements.

Forrest, with his main forces, passed up by the Cross Roads, Tuesday evening, the 7th. The trains on the Mobile and Ohio Railroad that night and the next morning brought up his artillery; and it was evident that he was moving toward Corinth.

That evening (the 7th) [Edmund Winchester] Rucker's Brigade, consisting of [W. L.] Duckworth's Tennessee and Duff's and [James Ronald] Chalmers' Mississippi Regiments, had a fight four miles south of Ripley, fell back and camped at Kelly's Mill on the Tallahatchie, and on Wednesday they went to Baldwyn.

On Thursday, the 9th, we learned that Rucker's Brigade had gone from Baldwyn toward Rienzi. Forrest's command was then all above us.

Friday, the eventful 10th of June, a negro man came in and reported that the Yankees had camped the night before at Stubbs's farm, seven miles from us, in the direction of Ripley. Some scouts had called at Mr. J. O. Nelson's during the night, and warned them of the impending danger. It was not known whether they would go by the Baldwyn or the Guntown road.

I took charge of my father's mules and horses, and with some negroes to help care for them and a little brother thirteen years old, went into a dense thicket a mile and a half southwest of our home, where we hoped to hide our stock and save them from seizure by the Federal troops if they came our way. My father hid in the woods north of his dwelling, where he remained safely till the day after the battle. The anxiety with which we watched and listened can be imagined. From our hiding place we heard a mysterious roaring noise made by the advancing

Federal army. Not long after, one of our own negroes, who came skulking through the woods, told us that the Yankees were then at my father's home; that the yard was "black with Yankees;" that they had taken everything we had to eat, and that about fifty wagons were in the road in front of the dwelling; also that there were thousands of negroes with the Yankees. We listened intently, and anxiously awaited developments. Soon a volley of small arms was heard—the first shots of the day. The advance guard of Sturgis's force had encountered a squad of Confederate cavalry. This occurred in Dry Creek bottom.

We will never forget: The Confederate Cemetery at Covington, Georgia, 1898.

Hon. Newnan Cayce, of Columbus, Miss., has told me that he was with that reconnoitering detachment of cavalry. They fell back and reported the advance of the Federal force. Ere long cannon began to roar in a southeastern direction, near the Cross Roads. The battle, beginning about 10 a.m., raged long and doubtfully, and it was after five o'clock before the Federals retreated.

Sturgis established his headquarters in Mr. Brice's house. His cavalry was under the command of [Union] Gen. Benjamin H. Grierson, and consisted of two brigades (Waring's and Winslow's) numbering 3,300 men, with six pieces of artillery and four mountain howitzers. His infantry was under McMillan, and consisted of three brigades—Wilkins', Hoge's, and Bouton's. The last was of negro troops. The infantry numbered 4,400 men, with twelve pieces of artillery. Sturgis estimated his force at 8,000, in round numbers, and the estimate is regarded as a low one. He had twenty-three regiments in all.

Forrest's force consisted of 3,500 men, comprised in four brigades, commanded by Lyon, Rucker, Johnson, and Bell—all cavalry. With the main part of his force he was in Booneville the night of the 9th. I have understood that Forrest was not sure of Sturgis's movements until during that night, when scouts reported him camped at Stubbs's farm. Sturgis was ten miles from the Cross Roads, and Forrest was eighteen miles away. Forrest moved very rapidly, coming, according to Gen. Chalmers, eight miles in a gallop. His wagon train was hurried south on roads east of the railroad. Notwithstanding Forrest's haste, Sturgis succeeded in getting his force south of him, and blockaded his advance at the Cross Roads. Forrest himself moved with a part of his command to the left of the Baldwyn road, and advanced, flanking the enemy's right. The Federal force was placed in the form of a fan. The movement of Forrest was very difficult, owing to thick undergrowth of black-jack which covered the surface all around the Cross Roads. But his men were dismounted, and fought as infantry. The Federal cavalry held their front until their infantry came up. Back of the Porter field the conflict was very sanguinary. At the opening of the battle Forrest ordered Gen. Buford to send a regiment (C. R. Barteau's) from Old Carrollville across the country into the rear of the enemy. This command entered the Ripley road in the rear of Sturgis, on the top of the hill west of Camp Creek, five and a half miles from the Cross Roads; and moving down the road a mile and a half, they deployed into the woods and fired on the enemy, who were beginning to fall back.

Confederate Captain James Dinkins as he appeared at age 19, while serving on the staff of Gen. James Chalmers, who commanded a division under Forrest.

In my place of concealment I heard the firing of this attack of Barteau's. About six o'clock, when this long, hot, and anxious day was drawing to a close, to my surprise shells began to fall in the woods where we were hidden. We were evidently in an unsafe place, and we retreated, going south, while the shells were flying over us. We had not gone far when I met my uncle, Joseph Agnew, who told me that our fields were filled with Yankees. The battle was evidently now raging at my father's house, and I was anxious about the dear ones at home. The enemy fought desperately, but were finally driven back. Forrest was in the front, pursuing them with vigor, and the last reports were that a desperate stand had been made at our house.

The next morning, as soon as I could see, I started to find out what had happened, and I found that the Federals had been driven away. Our once pleasant home was a wreck. Thanks to a merciful Providence, the lives of the family had been preserved, although they had been exposed to great danger. I found the females of the family all in the back piazza. They were laughing and talking, notwithstanding recent distresses. The fence around the garden and yard had been torn down. Many horses were hitched under every tree in the yard. Soldiers [Union] were stalking through the yard and house without ceremony. The public road in both directions was lined with wagons as far as could be seen. For more than half a mile, as I came home, I saw on the roadside hundreds of shoes and articles of every description, which had been thrown away by the Federals in their retreat. Several dead negroes in blue uniform were lying by the roadside not far from our dwelling. The public road was filled with soldiers passing to and fro. When I saw these things I knew that Forrest had gained a great victory, but my heart sank at the prospect of our own losses. The Yankees had taken every grain of corn and every ounce of meat, leaving us nothing to eat. The family had not eaten anything since the previous morning, and the house had been plundered. Everything was turned upside down, and much was missing. Dead and wounded men were lying in the house, upstairs and downstairs. Bullets had penetrated the walls in various places. Negroes and white men had both plundered our dwelling. Nothing could move their pity, but with vandal hands they rifled trunks and bureaus, entering every room. Destruction seemed to be their aim. They even entered the negro cabins, and robbed them of their clothing. They cut the rope, and let the bucket into the well. As they went back, panting with heat and suffering with thirst, they were glad to drink such dirty slop as they could find. [Note: all of this was illegal as it was in violation of the Geneva Conventions, as well as international law, Christian ethics, and common decency. L.S.]

The [Union] negro troops were specially insolent. As they passed down they would shake their fists at the ladies and say that they were going to show Forrest that they were his rulers. As they returned, their tune was changed. With tears in their eyes, some of them came to my mother and asked her what they must do; would Mr. Forrest kill them? On the retreat Sturgis was in the front, going at a trot.

The final stand was made at my father's house. When it began, my mother, wife, and sisters closed the window shutters, and all went into an inner room, and, lying flat on the floor, they awaited the issue of the conflict. Two Federal soldiers came into the back piazza, and surrendered to my mother just as the fight began. The yard was a battle ground. They made a breastwork of a picket fence. A Federal battery was in front of our gate. Rice's battery was just below the bend in the public road, and the fight here was nearly as stubborn as at the Cross Roads, and lasted fifty or sixty minutes. Capt. Rice told me that the artillery saved the day here. When he came up our cavalry was being repulsed. It was indeed a signal victory, for the Federal force was fully three times as great as that of Forrest. Forrest completely defeated the enemy, capturing all their artillery and their entire wagon train. To quote Sturgis's own words: "Order soon gave way to confusion, and confusion to panic." The losses incurred in such a rout were necessarily very great. According to the Official Medical History of the War, the losses on the Federal side were 617 killed and wounded, and 1,623 missing. The Confederate loss, according to the same authority, was 606 killed and wounded.

The pursuit was continued beyond Salem. On Monday, the 13th, many soldiers returned from the pursuit. Eight hundred prisoners were marched down the road that day. Some officers were among them, and they were nice-looking men. It is certain that a great many negroes were killed. They wore the badge, "Remember Fort Pillow," and it was said that they carried a black flag. This incensed the Southern soldiers [for the white and black Union troops at Fort Pillow had been abusing, robbing, and harassing the locals], and they relentlessly shot them down.[94]

Mr. Brice's house was temporarily made a hospital for wounded Confederates. Some Southern boys died there. I remember a lad who lay there dying, and whose earnest gaze and yearning for a mother's soothing presence aroused my tenderest sympathies. How gratefully did that dying boy receive the kind ministrations of Mrs. Brice, who was watching by his side! Bethany Church was occupied as a hospital, and many a Federal soldier lay wounded on benches on which worshipers had been wont to sit in days when peace reigned. A bullet [had] passed through the pulpit. The monuments and tombstones in Bethany burial ground to this day show the imprint of Minie balls. Thirty or more graves containing the bodies of brave Tennesseans and Kentuckians, who fell in battle that day, are in Bethany burial ground. The graves are unmarked, and the heroes are unknown. A man named King, of Rice's Battery, is buried a few hundred yards below my residence. The little mound which marks his grave can be seen on the roadside. King was from the vicinity of Artesia, Miss. The grave of a Tennessean, A. J. Smith, is not far away. A nice young man, who was brought wounded into my house on the day of the battle, and died there that night, was buried under a large post oak in front of my gate. His name was Rice. His friends removed his remains to the family burial ground in Lauderdale County, Tenn., in 1865.

Forrest, with his subcommanders, Buford, Lyon, Bell, Rucker, and Johnson, won laurels that day which will not soon wither. The day will not soon be forgotten by those who were present. Gen. Chalmers said it was the most brilliant victory of the war on either side. And considering the great disparity of the contending forces, the result was certainly most wonderful.[95] — REVEREND SAMUEL A. AGNEW

Miss Frances Mayes Harris, SCV Sponsor to Forrest's Cavalry Corps.

4

1901-1903

RICHARD B. ALLEY & HIS FLAG

☛ On the 7th day of December, 1864, Forrest, with his cavalry and two divisions of infantry, engaged the Federals near Murfreesboro, Tenn. The latter came out in such force and with so much pluck that the Confederate lines of infantry began to break to pieces, when Forrest rode from regiment to regiment seizing the colors from the hands of the color bearers, waving them aloft and appealing to the men to hold their ground. It is said that when Forrest found one of the color bearers running, and would not halt at his command, he shot him down; that he dismounted, took the colors

Richard B. Alley.

himself, remounted, rode again before that regiment, and waved the colors until the men rallied. To other color-bearers and officers, Forrest uttered stinging rebukes, one of which was: "Damn a man that's afraid of getting killed." He rode up to the Fifty-Fourth Virginia Regiment, and in a strong, imperious tone, at the same time reaching out his hand, said to the color bearer: "Hand me your flag." The little man, twenty years old, five feet and one or two inches high, with face as smooth as a girl's, nearly barefooted, thinly clad, and shivering with December cold, held tight to the staff of his flag, and replied: "Gen. Forrest, I can take care of my flag." The General, admiring the grit of the little fellow, said in a milder tone: "Give me your flag: I want to rally the men." The color bearer replied: "General, just show me where to plant it." The place was fixed, the flag was planted, and that portion of the line rallied and held its ground. The best troops quailed under the duties of that hour. The General then ordered the Fifty-Fourth Virginia to fall back.

Forrest never forgot the color bearer of the Fifty-Fourth. Referring to him afterwards, he called him "that little fellow that totes his own flag." Forrest never lost an opportunity to doff his hat to that flag, and the color bearer never failed to droop his colors to the General. The name of this color bearer was Richard B. Alley, of Company A. He was as proud of the flag he carried, and as jealous of its honor, as Forrest was of his commission as lieutenant general. "No man; no, not Gen. Forrest himself, shall carry my flag while I live," said Richard. Young Alley carried his colors on many bloody fields. At Missionary Ridge his regiment was thrown into great disorder. Gen. Reynolds rode up and demanded the colors, but Alley said: "No, General; just show me where to go, and I will carry the flag." Gen. Reynolds rode with him thirty or forty paces to the front, where the flag was planted, and the regiment rallied to it.

Richard B. Alley now lives at Rodgers, Montgomery County, Va., a useful man and an upright citizen, the husband of a good wife, and the father of a happy family of three sons and four daughters, every one of whom would wave the colors of their country on any field as nobly as their father did.[96] — DAVID W. BOLEN

CIRCULAR LETTER NO. 1 TO FORREST'S MEN

☛ To commanders and every soldier who, at any time, served with Forrest:

1. By invitation of the city of Memphis and the special courtesy of our General Commanding the Association of United Confederate Veterans, the reunion of Forrest's Cavalry Corps for 1901 will be held at Memphis, Tenn., on the 28th, 29th, and 30th of May.

2. In addition to the collection of historical incidents and the encouragement of good comradeship, our corps organization of Forrest veterans contemplates and purposes the erection of an equestrian statue to our great leader at the earliest date possible.

3. The circulars of the Forrest Monumental Committee of the Historical Society, and those also of the Women's Forrest Statue Association, having been extensively published, attention is called to Paragraph III, of Circular Letter No. 142, issued by Gen. George Moorman, Adjutant General of the U.C.V., of March 16.

III. Forrest's Cavalry Corps will attend the Memphis reunion in a body, and in order that due honor shall be paid to them and to the memory of their great leader, and as Memphis was his home, the General Commanding announces that Thursday, the 30th day of May, the third day of the reunion, which will be the day of the parade also, shall be designed as "Forrest Day," and on which day it is expected that the cornerstone of this great Equestrian Monument will also be laid.

George Moorman.

4. It seems to be the unanimous desire of comrades that the corner stone of the Forrest Monument at Memphis be laid as proposed in the above paragraph; therefore, all soldiers of Gen. Forrest are directed and urged to be present in parade on "Forrest Day," Thursday, May 30th—mounted, if possible.

5. Blank forms of subscription are sent out, and it is earnestly urged that all commanders distribute them to staff and line officers; also that they extend to all Forrest veterans an opportunity to contribute to the erection of an enduring monument to the memory of our renowned commander.

6. A report of all subscriptions made or obtained by those to whom subscription blanks are sent should be made to these headquarters at Murfreesboro, Tenn., not later than the 25th day of May, or at headquarters thereafter to be established at Memphis, Tenn., until May 31, so that the same may be reported to the Forrest Monumental Committee, by Col. George Dashiell, Paymaster. By order of Maj. Gen. D. C. Kelley.[97] — CHARLES W. ANDERSON, ASSISTANT ADJUTANT GENERAL

SOME MEMORIES OF MY DAYS UNDER FORREST

☛ I now look back and am amazed at the fidelity of our slaves during the trying times of those days, surrounded as they were by temptations and inducements [based on Liberal Yankee lies] to abandon us.

I told my [servant] boy Tom on several occasions that Mr. Lincoln's proclamation of January 1, 1863, pronounced him free, and at any time he was at liberty to go North, and I should put no obstacles in his way. I can never forget the expression on the face of this faithful and loved companion of my youth, as he candidly avowed his devotion to me, saying, "Why, Marse Willie, you don't suppose I'm going to leave you; didn't I promise old miss and old marster to always stay with you?" and he never did desert me through the whole war; but was always the warm-hearted, faithful creature under all circumstances. He was only a year younger than I, and we had grown up together with no distinction that his yellow skin could claim from my white; together we had been taught the prayers and catechism at my father's hearthstone, and morning and evening we daily worshiped in the family circle. If he or any other of the house servants were ill, they claimed as much care and comfort as my sisters. If I had a dollar, Tom could always claim half of it. After the war closed he and I drifted away with the great stream of struggling soldiers who were scattering here and there, seeking to earn their daily bread. Whether the honest fellow is now alive or not I do not know, but, God knows, he could always share my crust and cot.

Our removal of headquarters to Demopolis, Ala., was a matter of much congratulation, as the ease and comfort was well earned. The duties of reorganizing the department were routine, and relaxing from those previously undergone.

We had forced on us for occupancy the most palatial residence of that beautiful little town, and in the owner, Gen. Whitfield, and his charming daughter, everything that wealth and refinement could afford was extended us to add to our comfort.

In February, 1864, Gen. N. B. Forrest, commanding the cavalry of the Western Department, was busily occupied in his operations on Sherman's line of communication, stretching over an extended area from Nashville well down to Atlanta, Ga. Forrest's brilliant operations had received the well-merited promotion to the exalted rank of lieutenant general, commanding all the cavalry of the army west of the Army of Tennessee under Gen. Joseph E. Johnston.

A requisition being made by Gen. Forrest on Gen. Polk for assignment to his staff of two officers to reorganize the adjutant generals' and inspector generals' departments, Gen. Polk detailed Lieut. Sam Donelson and myself for that duty, he for the inspector generals' assistant, while I was made A. A. A. general to his chief of staff, Major J. P. Strange. I had known of Gen. Forrest in Memphis before the war, and many of his staff were my personal friends. If my previous campaigning under Stonewall Jackson's "foot cavalry" was trying, the one I was about to engage in with "Mr. Forrest's critter company" was the hardest service I had seen. What "Stonewall" was to the infantry, Forrest was his counterpart with his cavalry. Both combined the talents of great commanders, and about as different, the one from the other, as can be imagined. The one a most devout and exemplary Christian soldier; the other fearless and profane in the extreme. It has been often stated, and no doubt it is true, that the only man in the world that Gen. Bedford Forrest feared was his brother Bill; and who Bill feared, nobody ever knew, and I do not think he himself knew. Yet he was as jovial and genial a fellow as I ever cantered with. Poor fellow! we have had many a scrub quarter-mile dash together, and chaffed each other over the merits and demerits of our respective Rosinantes. After the close of the war, Bill, I hear, drifted down into Texas, where he died "with his boots on," in some shooting scrape.

Gen. Forrest moved with the celerity of a cyclone, and his blows were dealt the enemy with such sledgehammer force that the first generally so staggered him that he became "groggy," and could never recover. The same tactics were used by Stonewall Jackson.

Having reached Tupelo, Miss., and reported to Gen. Forrest, I set to work in my new duties, which gave little or no time for aught else.

A few days of "shoeing up" and provisioning, and away we clattered for West Tennessee and Kentucky. Ah! but those were glorious spring days, and we had as fine a lot of fellows under Gens. Abe Buford, William H. Jackson, and Tyree H. Bell as ever flashed a saber. Every man sat his steed as if he was part and parcel of the beast he strode, and it mattered little how mettlesome the nag, the rider was the master, and fit to fight mounted or dismounted. West Tennessee had been raided by Federal cavalry under [the notorious Yankee officers] Grierson, Hatch, and Hurst for many months, where they were always sure of finding good forage for man and beast. The latter had made himself extremely obnoxious by his indiscriminate plundering, and his command, the First Tennessee Cavalry [U.S.], had been recruited from the very worst element among what was known as "Union men," living principally amidst the mountains and valleys of East Tennessee. He had been captured in the earlier part of the war, and tried for some outlawry. Being granted his parole by Gen. Polk, at Columbus, Ky., he had deliberately violated it, and his pathway was marked by deeds of greater deviltry than ever before. It had been long the effort of our troops to capture this freebooter, but his spies and friends kept him so well advised that he always managed to elude us. He was as sly as a swamp fox. I shall refer a little later to a portion of his command that I happened to run into while traveling under a flag of truce.

Our first station appointed for a base of operations was the beautiful town of Jackson, Tenn., where Gen. Forrest was ever a welcome guest. The citizens were mostly of the refined and wealthy class, who, too old to take active service, had to remain at home, the prey of the roaming band of the enemy's cavalry and infantry, who levied heavy contributions on them for their known and avowed loyalty to the Southern cause. Our immediate headquarters were at the magnificent residence of Dr. Butler, whose hospitality was bountifully extended, aided as he was by a bevy of charming and highly cultured daughters. On the 24th of March we captured Union City, with a quantity of supplies, and what we could not utilize we destroyed.

Gen. Forrest was determined to get hold of Hurst if he could, and with that end in view instructed me to proceed to Memphis with sealed communications addressed to [Union] Gen. [Ralph P.] Buckland, commanding the Federal post there. While I was en route with my escort under flag of truce, he [Forrest] made a dash for and captured Paducah, Ky., on the 26th. This was a stunning blow to the enemy, and, becoming thoroughly alarmed, they at once commenced to provide against his crossing the river into Ohio. But Forrest had his eagle eye on the Fort Pillow garrison, and the 12th of April found him thundering at this stronghold on the Mississippi river, demanding its surrender. All day the battle raged, and being well fortified and admirably adapted by nature for defense, our cavalry, under that fiery little game cock, Gen. James R. Chalmers as advance, after stubborn resistance, drove the Federals into their last line of entrenchments. The majority of the enemy's force consisted of colored troops, and the fort was protected by a gunboat lying in the stream.

Forrest's equestrian statue, Memphis, Tenn., with some of his men. The General's son William is second from left; artillery chief John W. Morton is far right.

After carrying everything before him, Gen. Forrest made a demand on the commander of the garrison for its surrender to save further bloodshed. The demand was granted, and the white flag was raised by the Federals. Fort Pillow is well up on the bluffs, overlooking the river, the banks leading thereto being quite precipitous.

As our forces unsuspectingly entered the works, they were met by a galling fire poured into them by the fleeing Federals, who were protecting themselves in the shelter afforded by the river bank, while the gunboat opened a brisk broadside on our troops. They were maddened by such perfidy. Many of the enemy were plainly visible trying to pack their boxes of ammunition to the river bank, hoping there to continue the fight. It so exasperated our men that they drove the enemy into the river, and shot them as they tried to gain the gunboat. This is the story of the famous "Massacre of Fort Pillow," as told me by Gen. Forrest after I had rejoined him at Jackson on my return from Memphis.[98]

Journeying on my road to Memphis, bearing my flag of truce, while the above was taking place, I rode into a squadron of Federal cavalry that had been out on a foraging expedition. The men were in high spirits, for they had made a successful expedition, as the amount of various plunder packed by them testified. Wagons of feed, live cattle, poultry, and everything imaginable, useful or ornamental, or otherwise, so that they despoiled the defenseless people [of the South]. After riding rapidly through the motley crowd, I finally reached the head of the [Yankee] column, when, saluting the commanding officer, I inquired: "What command is this?" He replied, returning my salutation, "The First Tennessee Cavalry, Lieut. Col. W. J. Smith commanding." Whew! Well, this was a nest of hornets I had gotten into, sure enough. The First Tennessee Cavalry, the colonel of which was Fielding Hurst, "the outlaw," and for whose body, dead or alive, I was then bearing a demand. Fortunately my flag protected me, but if my mission had been suspected, I don't think it would. A few miles companionship was quite sufficient, and I was glad when my road separated me from these ruffians.

Time, the great assuager of grief, also heals the bitterness of battle, and is as forcibly illustrated in the case of [Union] Col. W. J. Smith, who settled in Memphis at the close of hostilities. It is great occasions of disaster that bring into play the hidden characteristics of the man.

I quote from the record of the Howard Association during the terrible yellow fever epidemic that desolated that city in the summer of 1878:

> When the Mayor of Grenada, Miss., sent an appeal to the Howards of Memphis for nurses, [Union] Gen. W. J. Smith and [Union] Col. Butler P. Anderson and other Howards found it a difficult matter to find them at once. Several hours were spent in the effort, and, finally, ten were assembled at the depot to take the special train. They were inexperienced nurses, the most of them, and without a head would have been useless. The question arose as to who should go with them. One after another had reasons for saying: "I pray thee have me excused." Gen. Smith, as the First Vice President of the Howard Association, said he would go. No one else volunteered. It was a critical moment. At the last minute Col. Anderson stepped on the train and

said: "I will go myself." After making the decision, he had only time to send a verbal message to his family. He and Gen. Smith found the city in the wildest confusion and fright. They went to work, forgetting themselves, bent only on relieving the sick and dying. They often worked from early morning until long after midnight. The Mayor fell the day after their arrival, and soon died. The six physicians of the place who remained all died. The mortality was appalling. They could not leave. The highest sense of duty and humanity impelled them to remain as they did, until one fell at his post and the other was brought away with the fever throbbing in every vein.

And incidentally here we will say, that all the terrible trials and emergencies of the yellow fever period of 1878 did not develop a nobler, braver, and more unselfish man than Gen. W. J. Smith.

Of English birth and ideas, entertaining [Liberal] political opinions at variance with those of most [Conservative] Southern people, he had been the object of dislike and coolness. But when the occasion was presented, he went to the relief of those who, in a sense, might have been considered his enemies at the risk of his life. From this circumstance we may learn a lesson of forbearance and wisdom that should never be forgotten.

Arriving at the picket post on the State line road, about three miles from the city limits, I was halted about 9 a.m., and my communication forwarded to [U.S.] post headquarters.

I was very anxious to get into the city to visit my two sisters, whom I had not seen for a year or more, they being unable to leave our home since my father's death. My request was denied [by the Yankee authorities], but my sisters were permitted to come to the picket station and meet me under escort of an officer. While grateful for this privilege I could not but complain of the rigid rule that could not permit me to visit them at our own fireside, especially as I had once a few months before been granted the permit by [Union] Gen. [Stephen A.] Hurlbut on the occasion of my father's death, but, when nearly about to gain admittance, I was suddenly and summarily ordered back. I never knew the reason of this change of heart, unless it was the grudge Hurlbut bore Forrest for his audacity in carrying his operations so far as to invade the bedchamber of that general in the Gayoso Hotel in Memphis, and capturing his uniform while Hurlbut made his escape in his night shirt, aided by the darkness and the hilarity of our troopers. [Union] Maj. Gen. Washburn was commanding the department prior to Gen. Hurlbut, and when the former heard of the latter's mishap, he gleefully railed at the War Department for relieving him from his command because he couldn't keep Forrest out of his department, and he had been succeeded by Hurlbut, who couldn't keep him out of his bedroom. He properly thought it a good joke, and so would every one else.

After waiting five or six hours in the rain for my reply, an officer finally returned from headquarters, stating that Gen. Buckland would reply by due course, after communicating with the [U.S.] War Department.

    Bidding my sisters good-by, I retraced my steps to Jackson, where I knew Forrest was waiting. I had ridden some twenty miles when I was overtaken by a cavalcade of finely mounted Federals, bearing a flag of truce. As they rode up, I was informed that they were bearing a communication to Gen. Forrest from Gen. Buckland, and the ranking officer introduced himself as [Union] Maj. Dustin, assistant adjutant general on the staff of Gen. Buckland. He proved a very companionable gentleman, and for some miles we enjoyed each other's society, chatting over our varied experience. He was, if I remember, a member of the New York Fire Department before entering the army. He knew all the young ladies in Jackson, whither we were traveling, having been stationed there quite a while during the occupancy of the country before Gen. Forrest had made it too hot to hold them, when they sought safety in Memphis.

The major had provided himself with an ambulance well filled with good cigars, champagne, and other delicacies, in anticipation of spending a day or so in Jackson, visiting and entertaining mutual friends. In fact so sure was he of being permitted to enter the town that he confided to me his plans for an evening's German at the public hall, and numerous other social events. My own experience of the refusal in not being permitted to visit my own home was too vivid, and the barb still rankled, to admit of any such courtesy being extended my adversary, and I was well convinced, in my own mind, the sole object of the flag of truce was a pretext to enable them to learn of Forrest's strength and movements. So I determined to block the little game, if possible. Within twelve or fifteen miles of Jackson, I whispered my instructions to the lieutenant of my troop to make haste slowly, and, leaving him in command, I bade adieu to the genial major, and took a short cut through Forked Deer Creek bottom, put my horse to his speed, and gained our headquarters in ample time to communicate to Gen. Forrest the news of the approaching flag, and of my ideas of its mission, as well as the anticipated pleasure of the Major in his social functions. The General immediately instructed that the cavalcade should be halted at our outposts, where, after a decorous delay, several of our staff visited the Major and enjoyed with much gusto the good things with which he had intended to regale his friends in Jackson. As anticipated, the communication he bore was of a frivolous nature, and the whole scheme was one concocted for espionage, but which failed signally.

For several weeks we rested our stock and recruited our ranks, and caused the enemy to keep themselves well within their garrison at Memphis. Orders were finally given to move south and rendezvous at Tupelo, Miss. On our arrival at Bolivar we had quite a running fight with [Union] Col. [Edward] Hatch, who undertook to intercept our line of march. It was here that the General's chief of staff, Maj. J. P. Strange, caught a ball in his arm, which, though painful, disabled him for but a short time. Brushing Hatch from our pathway as a pesky fly, we continued our journey without further trouble to Tupelo, where the whole command was soon assembled.

It was enjoyable to be able once more to sit unmolested by sight or sound of conflict, and, gathered around the great cavalry commander, join with him in a laugh at the many schemes and snares he had set to bamboozle the Federals. Forrest was very affable, and placed himself on an equal footing with each and every one of his command. Entirely free from reserve, he was as full of fun as a kitten, and as amiable likewise, always ready for a frolic or a scrub race, or poking fun at some member of his staff. One especially came in for quite a share of the General's jibes, Capt. Paul Anderson, his chief of scouts. Paul was an old Texas ranger, and affected all the vagaries of the cowboy costume, mingled with that of the Mexican greaser, as shown in the white sombrero, leather-fringed breeches, and jangling spurs. His voice had a peculiar nasal twang, and his slowness of speech caused him great difficulty in spinning his yarns.

The General had an escort of some twenty or thirty, commanded by Capt. J. C. Jackson, but their escort duty consisted in fighting, the same as the troops of the line. Forrest never ordered his men to go anywhere that he did not accompany them, generally as a leader. He enjoyed fighting more than any man I ever met in the service; he seemed to glory in it as a pastime, and frequently would, during battle, forget that as a commander he was not expected to participate personally, but, singling out some foeman worthy of his steel, go for him full tilt with drawn saber, and, swinging it in a terrific circle, cut his man down as he would a cornstalk. His eyes fairly blazed with a fiend incarnate. The contrast to Forrest in battle and in repose was the most remarkable I ever saw, and one could hardly imagine that he could possess so much docility combined with so much ferocity. Much of the latter was undoubtedly traceable to the loss in battle of a favorite brother, Brig. Gen. Jeffrey E. Forrest, who fell at Okolona, Miss., a few months before. Jeffrey, early in 1861, helped to organize a cavalry command, and soon rose to the rank of lieutenant colonel of the Sixteenth Tennessee Cavalry. Another brother, Jesse A. Forrest, who kept a livery stable in Memphis before the war, was major of the Eightieth Tennessee Cavalry, of which George G. Dibrell, as colonel, was afterwards promoted to brigadier general of cavalry.[99] Then there was Bill Forrest, a captain of cavalry, to whom reference has previously been made. Another brother, John Forrest, was a noncombatant, owing to his being a cripple and a great sufferer from rheumatism, so much so that he could with great difficulty get around unless by aid of crutch or stick. This affliction, however, did not shield him from the persecution of the enemy, who, having him a prisoner in Memphis, desired to extort information from him, and, to accomplish it, had him conveyed on one of their gunboats, and in a wooden box turned the steam on him from

Mrs. Roy W. McKinney, Chaperon for Forrest's Cavalry Corps.

the boilers of the boat in a vain endeavor to wring information from him. I saw John Forrest in the town of Grenada, Miss., a few months after the above occurrence, the particulars of which he gave me. The General had one or more half-brothers by the name of Luxton, one of whom, Mat, figured in one or two bloody feuds, the particulars of which I did not charge my memory with at the time. Gen. Forrest had only one child, William M. Forrest,[100] who was a lieutenant and aid-de-camp to his father. He partook essentially of his father's characteristics, being mild-tempered and gentle almost to effeminacy, but when aroused his temper blazed through those cold gray eyes that betokened unmistakably the danger behind them.

 The General greatly enjoyed telling the ruse he practiced on the occasion of the capture of Col. Streight, near Rome, Ga., in April, 1863.

 For daring and audacity, it is one of the most remarkable of any during the war. Streight largely outnumbered Forrest (who had only one or two parts of regiments), and was favorably posted on a commanding eminence, which would have resisted any of our assaults. A road at the base of this hill debouched from the thickly timbered country around and gave the enemy a clear and unobstructed view of our troops for fully a quarter of a mile, before again it was lost in the density of the forest. After passing this open point, the road again doubled on itself and paralleled it for fully another quarter of mile, fully hidden, however, from the Federals. By a short cut through or across this horseshoe like opening, Gen. Forrest, for an hour or more, kept his little band revolving in a circle, and Streight saw, from his perch on the hill, regiment after regiment, battery after battery, and wagon after wagon, pass before his astonished gaze.

After Forrest had thus magnified his little force into a division of solid phalanx, he halted the command, and, forming them into line of battle, preparatory to a charge, sent forward his aid-de-camp, Capt. Anderson, and demanded the unconditional surrender of Streight and his forces, stating that he had him completely surrounded, and if his demands were not complied with, he could not be responsible for the consequences. The Federal commander, satisfied in his own mind that he was outnumbered ten to one, gracefully surrendered his whole command of seventeen-hundred men without firing a gun. His subsequent mortification and rage knew no bounds when he discovered how he had been hoodwinked by the astute Forrest.

About the 1st of June we received instructions to concentrate our command at or near Florence or Tuscumbia, Ala., on the Tennessee river, which being crossed by long-established fords, we were then to push on rapidly to cut the line of communication leading from Nashville, over the Nashville and Chattanooga railroad, the only route over which Sherman could draw his supplies for the army he had at Allatoona, Ga. Could we succeed in this, his "march to the sea" would have been impossible. War is better exemplified by a game of chess than anything else. When your combination has been carefully completed, and you think you are about to make a scoop by a lucky checkmate, suddenly pops up a knight to upset all your calculations, and your well-matured schemes fall to the ground.

We left Tupelo in high spirits, glad to get back into Middle Tennessee, where most of the command were at home amidst wives and sweethearts. The rain was coming down in torrents, the streams we had to cross were running bank full, the corduroy roads in many of the bottoms had floated out, and wagons and artillery were floundering through as best they could. Poor old [Confederate Gen.] Abe Buford, commanding a brigade, was swearing his best at the muddy roads and the roaring creeks, contrasting the former, doubtless, to the macadamized and level ones of his native state, Kentucky. As I passed him I saluted him, and wished him good luck in getting his headquarters wagon out of four feet of a mud hole, which he was superintending at the time. We enjoyed a visit when Gen. Buford dropped in at our headquarters, for he was a genial, jovial companion, full of war reminiscences, and generally his chief commissary kept a supply of good Nelson County Bourbon, which he always set before us when we returned the General's visit.

Buford presented a queer appearance, either mounted or afoot. He weighed something over three hundred pounds, of powerful frame, a round, ruddy face, covered with a short, stubby, red beard, dressed in brown butternut Kentucky jeans, his pants invariably stuck in his boots, he was the most perfect picture of the Jack of Clubs, as displayed on the packs of cards made those times, before they commenced to adorn and embellish them in the present day. With all his weight he was the most graceful dancer I ever saw swing a lady on the light and fantastic. The last time I saw the General was just after the war, in Memphis, where he had brought some of his blooded stock from the blue grass region, such as Enquirer, Exchequer, Crossland, and others now forgotten.

Gen. Forrest and I greeted him at the course, after winning a fat purse, and congratulated him on his good luck. He smiled grimly and said he had been quite fortunate in his circuit, and intended getting back more of the money of which he had been robbed during the war. But the very next day a sad accident overtook him. His favorite horse, Crossland, named after a colonel of that name, who commanded one of his regiments, was entered for a four-mile heat. Crossland had won two out of five heats, and was leading the bunch on the last stretch of the winning heat, when I saw Buford throw up his hands and cry out in agony of tone: "My God! Crossland has broke his leg." Sure enough he had, and he was at once shot on the track. But the saddest ending of all was the fate of Gen. Buford himself, when, only a few years ago, his mind became unsettled, it is thought through religious mania, and it eventuated in his driving a ball through his brain. How strange sometimes do we make our exit! Here was a man who, for four years, braved battle on many a hotly contested field, and when life's closing days should have been peace, joy, and comfort, the massive brain reeled, and reason forever fled.[101] — MERCER OTEY

Lane named after Confederate Gen. Abraham Buford, Spring Hill, Tennessee. Photo by the author.

FORREST'S EQUESTRIAN MONUMENT AT MEMPHIS

☛ Few readers whose eyes fall on the attractive headlines that herald an enterprise to be set in motion, a monument to be unveiled, or a corner stone to be laid, seldom look back of the mere statement to the unswerving tirelessness of the leading mind and heart—the mainspring—that made such an event possible. Hence, upon a perusal of Gen. Gordon's circular letter, relative to the programme for Forrest Day at the Memphis Reunion, when the corner stone for the great equestrian monument will be laid, the reader does not realize that loving and loyal women have bent every energy to make this consummation an actuality.

Foremost among these faithful workers, Mrs. T. J. Latham, President of the Tennessee Division, U.D.C, has always been found. Her reelection at the State Convention on May 14 is a proof that she is a woman who is faithful in the discharge of duty. She is justly beloved by the Daughters of the Confederacy, and has the esteem and confidence of the Sons of Veterans, who are eager to lend her a helping hand. In the *Commercial Appeal* of recent date Mr. Michael Conalley heaps unstinted praise upon this rare woman, who "possesses an enthusiasm that fires all about her and melts all obstacles. She has undertaken a task which is Herculean, but she is fully competent to cope with it." The *Catholic Journal*, of Memphis, in a brilliant editorial, refers to Mrs. Latham as "one of the most learned and efficient women of Memphis, whose heart and soul are devoted to the memories of the gallant heroes who fell bravely fighting for the Southland's honor." Back of Mrs. Latham's work we must look to the brave spirit whose beauty inspired such enthusiasm, and every visitor at the Reunion will enter reverently upon the day which is to be adorned by the sacred name of "Forrest."

Phoebe F. Edmonds.

Mrs. Latham said of herself: "I am not a poetess; I am not a parliamentarian; I am not an orator; but I am strong for the Forrest monument."[102] — SUMNER ARCHIBALD CUNNINGHAM

THE CHRISTIAN FORREST

☛ Another, who is now resting in our own sacred Elmwood, a name whose echo circles the globe, Bedford Forrest, after the tempestuous storms and victories of four years' conflict, settled down a quiet and progressive citizen of Memphis. He became a meek and humble Christian, a communicant of the Court Street Cumberland Presbyterian

Church. He who commanded sits as a child at the foot of the cross, with his eagle eyes fading—fading, but fixedly upon the crown awaited him. He . . . was a citizen of Hernando for many years, with no thought of the future glory awaiting him.[103] — MRS. PHOEBE FRAZER EDMONDS

TWO OF FORREST'S SIXTY-FIVE BLACK SOLDIERS

☞ With the batteries of Capt. John W. Morton, Gen. Forrest's chief of artillery, there were two negroes, Bob Morton, a cook, and Ed Patterson, the hostler for the captain, both of whom served with the artillery throughout the war. Ed Patterson, whose fidelity and loyalty stoutly withstood the test of battle and even of capture, still survives. He is a respected householder and property owner, near Nashville, and delights to recall the time when he wore the gray in Morton's Battery. Everybody in the artillery service of Forrest knew and liked Ed. He took good care of the horses, and performed his duties with unflagging good humor.

Sumner Archibald Cunningham.

On one occasion it was feared that Ed was lost to the battery. In the terrific fight at Parker's Cross Roads, when Morton's men, behind the guns, were almost overwhelmed by superior numbers of the enemy in a sudden charge, about twenty members of the battery were run over and captured. Ed was among them. He was missed, notwithstanding the confusion of the disaster, and the temporary reverse of the almost invariably successful artillerists was regarded by them as aggravated by the loss of their diligent hostler. Capt. Morton particularly mourned his absence. One morning, a few days after the battle, he [Patterson] rode into the camp of the battery, mounted upon a superb horse, whose caparison denoted it the property of an officer of no mean rank.

"Hallo, Ed! Where did you come from?" was the artillery chief's greeting.

"I des come f'om de Yankees," responded Ed complacently, as he dismounted and stood proudly eying the steed.

"How did you get away, and where did you get that horse?"

"Wall sah, dey taken us all along. When we got out o' sight o' y'all, I notice dat dey didn't 'pear to notice me, an' when dey get to whar dey was gwine into camp, I sort o' got away. De Yankees des seed me ridin' 'roun', an' I 'spec' maybe dey thought I was waitin' on some o' de officers. I des went on th'ough de woods. I seed a heap o' dead men wid blue coats on, an' a heap of 'em what was 'live, too. D'rectly I come to a big road. I seed one o' our boys walkin' what 'ad done los' his horse. I axed him which er way Marse John [Morton] went. He knowed me, an' said 'de artillery done gone down dis road.' I kep' on, an' passed a heap o' our men walkin'. I axed 'em which er way de artillery done gone, an' de said, 'Down dis road.' I kep' on an' kep' on 'til I got here; an' dat's why I'm here, Marse John. Dey took yo' horse away f'om me, but I done got you a better one, sho. No, sah; dey didn't 'pear to notice me at all. When I was comin' on I seed some mighty nice-lookin' hosses tied in de bushes, an' ez dey wan' nobody noticin' I tuck 'n' pick me out one, an' des got on dis' 'n' and rid him to hunt y'all. I seed a blue overcoat layin' on de groun', an' I took 'n' put it on. An' it's a good one, too, Marse John."[104] — SUMNER ARCHIBALD CUNNINGHAM

FORREST & THE WESTERN ARMY

☛ The day before the battle of Trevilian's Station, on the 10th of June, 1864, Forrest, with his Western men behind him, had fought not only the greatest cavalry battle of the war, but the greatest cavalry battle of the world. Forrest and his men were the most formidable enemies with which the Federal armies contended. Gen. Sherman said of him, "Forrest is the very devil, and I think he has got some of our troops under cover"; and he declared that Forrest must be killed if it took ten thousand lives and broke the treasury, adding, "There never will be peace in Tennessee until Forrest is dead." He offered $10,000 [$300,000 in today's currency] reward for his death or capture, and a major generalship to him who would destroy this foe. But the question most serious of all to the Federal commanders was who should undertake this task. A great many Federal soldiers had gone against Forrest, only to find their plans anticipated and the objects for which they had set out defeated. At last the choice fell on Samuel D. Sturgis, [Union] brigadier general, who had achieved recent success in his battles in East Tennessee, and was regarded as a real fighter.

Three thousand four hundred cavalry, formed into two brigades, commanded by two of the best Federal officers in the West, composed the Federal advance, while 4,800 infantry, divided into three brigades, commanded by Gen. Sturgis, made up what Gen. Washburn said was a force "consisting of some of our best troops." After a march of some seventy-five miles from Memphis, on June 9, Gen. Sturgis concentrated his entire command near Brice's Crossroads, in Mississippi, with 8,100 men and twenty-two pieces of artillery. Forrest conceived the design of crushing the cavalry before the infantry, which was some eight miles away, could be brought into action. When he opened the fight he had less than 1,800 available men. At no time during the battle was Forrest able to carry into action more than 3,300 troops. With these he defeated an army composed of 3,400 cavalry and 4,800 infantry of unquestionably the best men of the West. His artillery was fourteen miles away from him when the conflict started. From ten o'clock until four, in the face of a fierce sun, these cavalrymen from Tennessee, Kentucky, Alabama, and Mississippi engaged in desperate hand-to-hand conflict with the soldiers of Indiana, Illinois, Minnesota, Iowa, and New Jersey. Sherman himself was compelled to admit that Forrest whipped Sturgis in a fair fight. He had not only whipped Sturgis, but had routed his forces; he wounded or killed or captured 2,612 men, amounting to about thirty per cent of his entire force; captured two hundred and fifty wagons and ambulances, all but four pieces of Sturgis's artillery, and made the Federal army a fleeing, panic-stricken mob. Sheridan said, "Forrest has only his cavalry. I cannot understand how he could defeat Sturgis with 8,000 men"; and yet he did. His men fought with a gallantry, a desperation, and a chivalry that may have been equaled, but never surpassed in any battle of the war. Sturgis [falsely] claimed that Forrest had fought him with fifteen or twenty thousand men, and that he had two divisions of infantry behind the cavalry, and thus had been able to accomplish his defeat and inflict such unusual humiliation.

The battle of Brice's Crossroads, thus won by Forrest, is entitled to go down through the ages as one of the most brilliant engagements ever fought. For military genius, for boldness of conception, for intrepidity of action, for reckless courage, and all that inspires men, it can have no superior while men shall live. And while the cavalry of Northern Virginia in a large part won their fame by Trevilian's Station and Hawes's Shop, two of the fiercest battles in which their cavalry participated, no man in the West envies them a single laurel, or would take from them one ray in that luminous glory which gathers round their heads; but the Western Confederate soldier holds up this conflict at Brice's Crossroads to the Army of Northern Virginia and to the world, and says: "We too bear the Confederate name, and we too have risked dangers and won triumphs that render us not unworthy an equal share in that splendid record which illumines the career of the Confederate armies."

With 1,700 of his men, Forrest whipped Grierson's 3,400 cavalry, and when reenforced by as many more, with one-half his force already worn by fierce and protracted battle, led 3,300 cavalry against 4,800 infantry, backed by the defeated Federal cavalry, and in two hours drove them in frenzied fear and confusion from the scene of conflict. The historian will search in vain amongst military archives for a parallel to such magnificent fighting and such splendid results.

The war very soon produced a new type of military procedure. The pent-up army in the field could be fed only by railway transportation. One hundred thousand men camped in any locality quickly destroyed its food supply, and army forages became as destructive as Egypt's locusts. Men and beasts alike demanded constant and enormous commissary stores, and, to secure these, the lines of communication in the rear must be kept well protected. To destroy these provision arteries became a special aim of opposing generals. The Southern forces, as they receded from the Ohio and Mississippi rivers, drew the Federals farther and farther from their base of supplies, and thus rendered a large force always necessary to defend the roads over which food and munitions were carried to the front. Stuart, Ashby, Hampton, Morgan, Forrest, and Wheeler soon taught the Union generals lessons in this great department of military science, and thousands of men were kept along the lines of transportation to guard bridges, railways, and military depots.

The Confederates gave them no rest. Operating over a wide scope of territory, they came by night and day to torment or capture these men left to defend the rear. They rode like a pestilence in the darkness, and came like the destruction at noonday. They appeared to spring up as if by magic, and to haunt the waking and sleeping dreams of their opposers.

It cannot be justly denied that the Confederate cavalry in the West not only equaled but surpassed all similar operations in the history of war. The raids into Missouri and Kentucky and through Tennessee exhibited a degree of endurance in the men, and a quality of genius in their leaders, which stamped all who engaged in them as soldiers of greatest daring, wonderful endurance, and incalculable resources. The Confederate cavalry early became masters in this new method of war, and it was months before the Federals fully comprehended the effectiveness of such work, or developed the resources and the talent which enabled them to retaliate in kind. As the man in the West, under Forrest, Morgan, and Wheeler, unfolded the enormous possibilities in this system of fighting, they became its most distinguished exponents, and made marches and fought battles, destroyed railroads, steamboats, military stores, captured garrisons, and terrorized their enemies to a degree that gave them splendid renown and world-wide fame. They quickly learned how to anticipate similar movements on the part of their enemies, and were enabled to mete out prompt and ample punishment to the Federals who undertook like enterprises.

In the East the only successful capture of those engaged in this work was that of [Union Colonel Uric] Dahlgren, who had conceived the plan of capturing, sacking, and burning Richmond. With his life he paid forfeit for failure. He himself being killed, his force, numbering less than 500 men, was scattered and a large part captured.

[Confederate] Gen. [Wade] Hampton, by his night attack, drove back Dahlgren's colleague, [Union Gen. Hugh J.] Kilpatrick, and by his gallant conduct and skillful pursuit saved Richmond from the hands of its foes. He could find his enemies only by the light of their camp fires, but in the darkness and gloom of the night, animated by a noble and unfailing courage, fearlessly he and his brave troopers rode down upon the sleeping foe, and with dashing saber and demonlike yell struck terror into the ranks, and drove them in confusion back upon their infantry support. Gen. Hampton's movements, brave in execution and brilliant in plan, won for him the gratitude of the Confederate capital, but his marches were brief and the hardships of the campaign limited to a few hours.

John H. Morgan.

[Union] Gen. Streight, with a splendidly equipped force, was sent, in April, 1863, to cut the railway communications of Gen. Bragg's army, and to destroy the arsenal at Rome, Ga. Hardly had the Federal cavalryman emerged from his supports when Gen. Forrest, prepared to destroy or capture him, was close at his heels. The moment Streight felt the first stroke of Forrest's hand, he realized that a tireless, skilled foe was on his track, and for ninety-six hours, never by day or night, was the Federal column at rest. Like some insatiate monster, Forrest followed the Federal column, and whenever and wherever found there was a vigilant and aggressive attack. In one hundred and sixty-four miles he fought eight battles by day and three by night, and in two of the latter, where artillery drawn by his men to within one hundred feet of the enemy's line, the only guide or light was the flash of rifles and the blaze of cannon.

Streight was himself a man of nerve and resource. Skillfully arranged ambuscades, fierce charges, and stubborn resistance met Forrest, and in a fair proportion of the conflicts the Federals held their own; but they greatly outnumbered the men of the gray.

The fierce onslaughts of Forrest, his impetuous attacks, his unyielding tenacity and fiery assaults, combined with his rapid movements, were enough to paralyze the stoutest heart and make the bravest soul question the outcome. Like a tireless bloodhound following his prey, this "wizard of the saddle" pursued the swift-marching Federals, and never for a single instant in those days and nights was there other thought or plan but to destroy the invaders.

Streight found friendly guides and helping hands amongst the Union men and women of Northern Alabama; but these could not hide him from the eagle eyes or the smiting arms of those following the trail, or stay the avenging hand that was uplifted in his rear.

With horses dropping dead in the roads, with men falling in the unconsciousness of sleep from their steeds, and with their guns sliding from their paralyzed grasp, Forrest still pressed the foe. One-half of his command on the third day was killed, wounded, or broken down; but still, with only five hundred soldiers, he pursued the Federal raiders, and on May 3, within twenty miles of Rome, the objective point of his expedition, Streight and his 1,500 men laid their arms and surrendered to the Confederate general, who could then, after his terrible pursuit, muster less than five hundred followers.

Every mile of the one hundred and sixty-four was covered with war's wrecks. Dead soldiers, mutilated animals, wounded men and stricken beasts, broken wagons, abandoned trains, and scattered supplies, told the story of the relentless and pitiless assault. Near the end, in forty-eight hours, four battles and ninety miles' marching and four hours' sleeping. Surely these deeds of the cavalry of the Army of Tennessee are not unworthy of Confederate valor.

No war has a more wonderful example of genius, courage, endurance than this pursuit and capture of Streight. If Forrest had done nothing else, this one exploit would have won for him enduring fame.

On the 7th of December, 1862, [Confederate] Gen. John H. Morgan was given permission to take four regiments of Kentucky cavalry and two regiments of infantry and attack Hartsville, Tenn. It was required for the infantry to march thirty-five miles through the snow and over sloppy roads, and at all times to be subjected to great cold. In seven miles of Hartsville there were encamped 6,000 Federal troops; in the town itself

2,500. It was necessary to cross the Cumberland river without a bridge, and for the cavalry in one place to swim part of the way over. The cavalry and infantry walked and rode by turns. Day and night they kept a record breaking gait. Cold nor storm had no terrors for these Kentucky Confederates. They were engaged in brilliant and hazardous work. They knew its perils, but glory and duty called, and that was enough for them. In twenty-two hours this extraordinary march was accomplished, and at break of day, on the 8th of December, the enemy's camp was assailed. An hour's fierce fighting ended the contest; 2,000 Federals surrendered to the 1,200 Confederates, and 400 of the enemy were killed and wounded. The prisoners, with a large amount of stores, were brought off safely and forced to ford the Cumberland river, and when the Confederate guns were planted on the south shore the Federal batteries were shelling them from the opposite side, supported by several thousand Federal cavalry and infantry, three times as strong as that which Morgan commanded.

Gen. Bragg, by appropriate order, complimented the command for this valiant feat, and ordered the name "Hartsville" to be inscribed on the banners of all regiments participating. Gen. Morgan won his commission as a brigadier, and also won for himself and men the credit of one of the most brilliant exploits of the war.

History is valuable only as it is true. Opinions concerning acts are not history; acts themselves alone are historic.

The true story of the conflicts of the Army of Tennessee has never been written. This occasion does not call for a discussion of the reasons producing this omission. The West does appreciate the glorious and heroic work of the Army of Northern Virginia, but it is also true that the East has not been fully informed, and therefore does not mete out justice to the Confederates who maintained the mighty struggle in the vast West. Time must rectify and adjust this condition.

Felix Kirk Zollicoffer.

As the East speaks with pride of the glory won by the Southern hosts at Gettysburg, the West answers back, "And here is Chickamauga." As the East catches the echoes of heroism that rise in such splendid notes from the hills at Antietam, the West answers back with consciousness of duty well done and points to the blood-stained field of Shiloh as its contribution to the renown of Confederate armies. As the East lifts to view the gory form of Malvern Hill, the West responds, "We have Perryville"; and when Second Manassas is named, the mention of which touches the deepest emotions of every man who wore the gray, the West answers back with the requiem of its slain and the heroism of its dead who sleep at Franklin.

When the East so justly sings the praises of Stuart and Hampton and their valiant hosts, the West says "We gave Forrest and Morgan and their knightly riders."

And from the regions beyond the "Father of Waters" comes the refrain of the fearless deeds of our brothers at Wilson's Creek, Elkhorn, Mansfield, Pleasant Hill, and Sabine Pass, and the world listens in rapturous wonder and admiration, as from all sections of our Southland comes the same story of illustrious courage and splendid patriotism and unselfish consecration to the cause of liberty. In ages to come there will be no page of human history with brighter or fairer record than was written by the people of the Confederate States in the four years of their struggle for freedom. The courage, patience, and gallantry of its men, the devotion, constancy and sublime sacrifices of its women, contributed to the world's history priceless treasure.

Bennett H. Young.

As we call from the roll of the world's record the immortal names of our martyrs—Jackson, Stuart, the Garnetts, A. P. Hill, Pegram, Ashby, and Armistead, from Virginia; Strahl, Zollicoffer, Adams, Hatton, Carter, Rains, and Smith, from Tennessee; Cleburne, from Arkansas; Walker, Cobb, Semmes, Deshler, and Doles, from Georgia; Rhodes, Garrott, Tracey, Saunders, Kelly, Gracey, from Alabama; Little, Slack, and Green, from Missouri; Bee, Dunovant, Gist, Jenkins, and Gregg, from South Carolina; Pender, Gordon, Ramseur, Branch, and Pettigrew, from North Carolina; McCullough, Randall, Scurry, Granbury, and Gregg, from Texas; Polk, Morton, Stark, and Gladden, from Louisiana; Barksdale, Benton, Griffith, and Posey, from Mississippi; McIntosh, from Florida; Winder, from Maryland; Albert Sidney Johnston, Hanson, Morgan, Helm, and Tilghman, from Kentucky—and say, "These and two hundred thousand others are our offering on the battlefield for freedom; tell us, O Time, thou keeper of all human history, tell us if in the corridors where are kept the records of ages there has been nobler sacrifice or richer offering on liberty's altar?"

Time answers back: "Amongst those who have answered the call of duty and stood for all mankind among all nations, kingdoms, and people, I find none who brought more glorious contribution to freedom, or who made greater sacrifice for truth, than these men you have named, who went down to death at their country's call, 'nor braver bled for brighter land, nor brighter land had cause so grand.'"[105] — CONFEDERATE COLONEL BENNETT H. YOUNG

A YANKEE TRIBUTE TO FORREST

☛ Dear Sir: In this [letter] please find inclosed my check on the Bank of Commerce, this city, for $250, in aid of the Forrest Monumental Association. I thank you very much for giving me an opportunity to join my old ex-Confederate friends in aid of a monument commemorative of one of the greatest soldiers of ancient or modern times. . . . Much more could be said in praise of this wonderful soldier. In war [he was] as terrible and masterful as a lion; in peace gentle, mindful, and considerate of the feelings and prerogatives of others. It was my good fortune and pleasure to have known him well from 1865 to the time of his death, October, 1877. I esteemed him as much for his worth as a citizen in peace as I feared him as a soldier in war.

As the passions and prejudices growing out of the war subside, the more will this man's military career be appreciated by his countrymen, North as well as South. Never did a general recognize the inevitable and lay down his sword with a sadder heart; and never did a fallen hero rise to the sublimity of a loyal and patriotic citizen more earnestly and honestly.

Had he been living at the outbreak of the Spanish war, he would have been among the first to have offered his services, and if need be die on the altar of his country, in defense of its institutions and its flag. When living he talked frequently with me of his desire to live long enough to see his country reunited in bonds of brotherly and soldierly love, to the end that each by the other would be forgiven (but not forgotten) for all that happened in that terrible conflict. The present historian has recorded and the future will record the fact that Gen. Forrest accomplished more with less resources at his command than any other soldier or officer on either side in our civil war.

I have long since been on record as favoring the erection of monuments all over the South in memory of her dead heroes, and I want to say of him, as I said of them, that while the monument itself can but feebly emphasize the veneration felt by the living for the dead, yet the memory of his brave deeds and wonderful achievements will be cherished in the hearts of his countrymen, and will live in other lands and speak in other tongues and to other times than ours.[106] — UNION CAPTAIN SAMUEL WESLEY FORDYCE (Ohio)

A SCHOOL TEXTBOOK SLANDERS FORREST

☛ The attention of the committee has been called to a paragraph found on pages 257 and 258 of a book known as the *Young People's Story of the Greater Republic*, by Ella Hines Stratton, where, in speaking of the capture of Fort Pillow by Gen. N. B. Forrest, a most false and misleading account is given of that battle not sustained by the facts of the occurrence, as brought out by the reports and correspondence, as shown in Vol. 32, Series 1, Part 1, of the *War of the Rebellion—Official Records of the Union and Confederate Armies*. The committee is pained at this late date to see such paragraphs breathing all the bad blood of the bitterest war of the centuries, and endeavoring to undermine the respect of American youth for their ancestry, in a book which is generally fair in other respects. Until those paragraphs are expunged by the author, your committee states that the book should not be bought or allowed in the home of any Southern family, where Southern youth can read such a misrepresentation of history.

Stephen Dill Lee reviewing a Confederate parade at Louisville, Kentucky, circa 1905.

Gen. N. B. Forrest was not only the most distinguished cavalry leader of the Confederacy, but his memory and that of his heroic followers have the respect and love of every true Southern man and woman; and no slander of that great American soldier can hold in any true American heart in our reunited country, now beloved by all of its citizens.[107] — CONFEDERATE GENERAL STEPHEN DILL LEE, CHAIRMAN OF THE HISTORY COMMITTEE

A LIFE-SIZE PORTRAIT OF FORREST

☛ An occasion of very notable interest at Nashville, Tenn., was the unveiling, with appropriate ceremonies, in the State Capitol of a life-size portrait of the famous Confederate cavalry general, Nathan Bedford Forrest, painted for the State by Mr. Hankins. Among the distinguished company present were a number of veterans who followed the thrilling fortunes of the "Wizard of the Saddle" through the war, including Capt. John W. Morton, the present Secretary of State of Tennessee, who was his chief of artillery; Maj. Charles W. Anderson of Murfreesboro, his adjutant general; and Capt. William M. Forrest, of Memphis, his son and aid-de-camp.

Capt. Morton, the chairman of the committee appointed to pass upon the skill and fidelity of the artist, after stating that the portrait was satisfactory [made a short speech].

. . . At the conclusion of Capt. Morton's remarks, Mrs. Lulu B. Epperson, the gifted and beautiful daughter of a gallant Confederate soldier, drew the cords of the Confederate flag which covered the portrait—the flag of the Thirty-Second Tennessee, stolen at Fort Donelson and secured from a pawn shop in Ohio, when the life-sized figure and martial features of the great cavalry general were revealed in vivid colors and the audience burst into enthusiastic applause.[108] — SUMNER ARCHIBALD CUNNINGHAM

PERFECT ONE-SENTENCE DESCRIPTION OF FORREST
☛ [He] swept through the ranks of the foe as a tempest through a forest of oaks, leaving wreck and ruin behind.[109] — W. L. SANFORD

RECKLESS & WICKED WORDS Of SHERMAN
☛ I see that [Union Gen. William T.] Sherman has characterized our cavalrymen and their leaders in a manner much more discreditable to himself than to them, so preposterously unjust it is. He says in his *Memoirs*:

> The young bloods of the South, sons of planters, lawyers about town, good billiard players, and sportsmen, who never did work and never will. . . . They care not a sou for niggers, land, or anything—the most dangerous set of men this war has turned loose upon the world. They have no past, present, or future. They are splendid riders, first-rate shots, and utterly reckless. These men must all be killed or employed by us before we can hope for peace. Stuart, John Morgan, Forrest, and Jackson are the types of this class. They have no property or future, and therefore cannot be influenced by anything but personal considerations.

If they were sons of planters or farmers, how is it that they had no property or hope of ever having any? If they cared "nothing for niggers, land, or anything,"[110] how was it that they could be influenced by personal considerations—bribes? Are these nothing in the ordinary sense of the term? And how could he say that such sensible, industrious, high-toned, honorable gentlemen as Stuart, Morgan, Forrest, and Jackson were types of the men he so loosely describes? He writes like a crazy man. Both Morgan and Forrest [the latter who owned numerous plantations and was worth today's equivalent of $50 million at the start of the War] were industrious business men of means; and were they alive, they would be well off and enjoying a wonderful fame and popularity, and with Stuart and Jackson they would have had a brilliant future, even had they come out of the war penniless. Insurance companies, etc., even in the North, would have given them fine salaries simply for the weight their names would carry.[111] — CONFEDERATE COLONEL JAMES W. BOWLES

FORREST'S RAID INTO MEMPHIS

☛ About 4 A.M., Sunday, August 21, 1864, Gen. Forrest, with part each of Bell's and Neely's Brigades and two pieces of artillery, moved briskly through the hazy twilight in columns of fours along the Hernando road, toward Memphis. The General, on his superb charger, soon glided toward the head of the column.

The river wharf at Memphis, Tenn., 1860s.

His command, in low, firm tones, was: "Forward, men!" Capt. William H. Forrest moved into the lead with his company, to clear the way of pickets. Our detachment was led by Col. T. H. Logwood, with orders to proceed to the Gayoso Hotel and capture [Union] Gen. [Stephen A.] Hurlbut, whose headquarters were there. Col. Jesse Forrest was directed to make for Gen. C. C. Washburn's headquarters, on Union Street, and to send one detachment to capture Gen. R. P. Buckland, and another to the Irving Block, on Second Street, to release the Confederate prisoners held there. Gen. Forrest, with Col. Bell and parts of Barteau's, Newsom's, and Russell's regiments, and Lieut. Sale, with his two pieces of artillery, were to remain in the neighborhood of the State Female College, to cover the return of the columns sent into town.

Onward sped the troopers. A shot was heard, the outmost pickets having been reached and captured. When the second reserve was reached a few more shots were heard. Faster moved the column, and the excitement was intense, but the injunction of silence had to be observed. Some delay was caused by the column proceeding due north toward the college, then countermarching to follow the Hernando road around to the left. Our detachment closely followed the lead of Capt. Forrest, and passed by a Federal battery on the left side of the road, which had been swept of its men by the onrush of Capt. Forrest. Though daylight was abroad, a thick fog enveloped our right, from which a Federal officer was heard trying to rally his scattered men, saying: "Fall in here, men! It is nothing but a band of guerrillas."

Treasured memories came to mind as we passed places familiar from my childhood: the Provine residence, McKinney's, the old bed of the Memphis and Lagrange railroad, over which only one train ever passed, but it is now the much-used Broadway; the residences of Col. R. F. Looney and Gen. Preston Smith; just opposite, at the intersection of Hernando road by Lauderdale Street, the home of my mother, three sisters, and two young brothers. There were three of us then who could not really call it our home, for we had dared to fight for that home.

I had hoped to see my home folks as we passed, and perchance breakfast with them that Sunday morning, but it was so early that there was no one astir. Sweeping past like an avalanche along Hernando Street to Beale, thence to Gayoso Street, we dismounted. Just then from a window above some Federal cried out: "Hello, boys! What luck on your raid?" We hastened to the Gayoso Hotel, where we found Capt. Forrest with some of his men on horseback in the rotunda of the hotel. As we entered I heard him call to them: "Come out of here, you forty thieves!" Some were upstairs, making so much noise battering doors with the butts of their guns that it sounded like a skirmish. A cigar case in the hotel was broken, and occasionally in passing a Confederate would grab something. I got two pipes and a few cigars. This incident, among others, is why I could not stand up at one of Sam Jones's meetings when he called on any one who did not steal anything during the war to stand up. Col. Logwood conscripted a clerk in the hotel, and commanded me to take him in charge and go with him to his room to get his pistol and such other articles as he desired to take with him. His room was upstairs, and I waited at the door. He [the clerk] seemed slow; but as he was an acquaintance of Col. Logwood, I did not unduly hurry him. Some ladies—hotel attendants, I suppose—entreated me not to take him. When he was ready we hastened downstairs. The command was mounted and in the act of leaving, I asked Col. Logwood what to do with the man, and he said: "Turn him loose and mount your horse. We are going to leave here immediately." The clerk was overjoyed. He bowed humbly, thanking the Colonel. I felt thankful also, for the task was unpleasant to me. I have forgotten his name, but should like to hear from him.

Squads of Federals began to gather and fire at us from house corners. Not finding Col. Hurlbut at the hotel, he having spent the night with Col. Eddy, our mission in that respect was a failure, and the other detachment also failed to accomplish the object of its mission.

Hurriedly we retraced our way down Beale to Hernando Street. At every cross street we were fired at by scattered bands. One or two of our horses were killed here, and one man wounded. I was told that a large, strong woman, a Mrs. Beethe, succeeded in getting the wounded man into her store, near by, and with an ax successfully kept off some negroes who were anxious to kill him. We moved out down Vance to Echols Street, thence to the Hernando road. On Echols Street Comrade Perkins was killed. As we passed him several ladies were seen going to where he lay dead with upturned face.

On passing my old home I turned to the gate, where I saw standing my mother, sisters, brothers, and one or two others, watching our column pass. Just then some Federals from Stewart Avenue fired across our yard at the passing Confederates, when mother and the others ran toward the house to get out of the way of the flying balls. I called to my youngest brother, but in the confusion he did not realize who it was.

The command moved down Lauderdale Street to Trigg, thence east to Hernando, and in passing a battery stable we had orders not to break ranks, even to get the horses. I tried in vain, however, to grab the halter of a fine claybank horse.

We soon reached the command, where Gen. Forrest was. After remaining there an hour or so skirmishing, we moved out toward Nonconnah Creek, where we halted two or three hours to communicate with Gen. Washburn in regard to exchanging and paroling prisoners and furnishing the Federal prisoners, four or five hundred, with food and clothing. Many of them were taken in their nightclothes, and our stock of provisions, as well as of clothing, was running low.

Being convinced, though without positive knowledge, that our camp that night would be near Horn Lake Depot road, I concluded to spend the night with Stephen Lester, an old friend of our family. The Lesters welcomed me heartily, and on leaving the next morning they filled my haversack.

My command did not stay where I expected, but had moved on to Hernando. After riding two or three miles, I suddenly approached a squad of bluecoats, and was too close to escape. Another trial of prison

life seemed to be my fate. I had been a prisoner at Alton, Ill., and had no desire to be one again. I soon saw a white flag, when I felt relieved. It was [Union] Col. W. P. Hepburne and Capt. H. S. Lee, with a detachment, who had gone to Hernando with clothing and provisions for the Federal prisoners. As they passed me Capt. Lee asked: "How far back to our men?" "Three or four miles," I replied. I came near telling the truth, but did not know it. The Federals had camped the night before within one mile of where I stayed. Hastening on, I reached Hernando. The first man I met in the edge of town was [Confederate] Capt. W. M. Forrest looking for stragglers, to which class I belonged.[112]
— W. B. STEWART

HOLDING A BRIDGE FOR FORREST

☛ It is not always the largest battles that are the bloodiest, as witnessed by the little fight of which I wish to write, and mention of which I have never seen.

During the latter part of 1863 there was organized in Attala, Leake, and Holmes Counties, Miss., a [Confederate] company of boys. None of us were over eighteen years of age, except our captain, John Kennedy, who was nineteen and had seen two years' service in the cavalry. I was just eighteen, and was first lieutenant. As soon as mustered in we were ordered to report to Gen. Wirt Adams at Jackson, Miss., and he assigned us to Col. Griffith's Eleventh and Seventeenth consolidated Arkansas Regiment. In a short time we were ordered to report to Gen. Forrest at Tupelo. From that time on we were in all the battles fought by that great military genius. At Harrisburg we had six killed and ten wounded out of our boy company.

But the bloody little fight of which I write was a few days after that. Our troops were on the move when Kennedy was ordered to report in person to Gen. Forrest, who ordered him to take his company and a detail of twenty-five from another company, making about seventy-five in all, and to hold a long, tall bridge that spanned a river (Big Black, I think it was), and extending some distance out in the swamp on each side. Kennedy's orders were to hold the bridge at all hazards until sundown, and under no circumstances was he to burn it. It was about 2 p.m. before the troops had all passed over, and we began to make preparation for emergencies, confident that the enemy would soon be up.

We first took up some planks about the middle of the bridge, which was about three hundred yards long; then began to fortify our position, which commanded the bridge. On our side of the river there was a rail-fence along the road, and a low, marshy swamp on the other. We had scarcely finished making breastworks out of the rails before the enemy appeared on the opposite side. Their advance guard rode out on the bridge until they reached the opening we made by removing the planks, which they had not noticed until they were right on it. We opened on them in their huddled-up position a murderous fire, which we kept up until the few that were left, and able to do so, retreated rapidly.

After the smoke cleared away we saw that the passage by the bridge was completely blocked with dead men and horses. Their reenforcements were hurried up, with three pieces of artillery. Fortunately the ground was such that their shells went over us, and our rail breastworks protected us fairly well from the rifles of their dismounted men. Up to this time we had only two killed and three or four wounded. We were congratulating ourselves on our success when some one discovered a line of Yankees advancing on the rear of our right. When first discovered they were not more than a hundred yards away, deployed as skirmishers, slowly feeling their way through the switch cane that covered the swamp. Orders were whispered down our line to hold our fire, for as yet they had not located us exactly.

A Confederate monument at Lexington, Kentucky, 1898.

When they came within fifty or sixty yards of us we opened on them. For a moment they were in confusion, but their officer soon rallied them and, ordered a charge, placing himself at their head. They made a rush, firing as they came, but when within forty steps of us they were stopped by a deep slough (of which we were not aware) filled with water.

Under our rapid fire they were compelled to fall back again, which they did in great confusion, but leaving seven of our boys dead and a number wounded.

Again we were congratulating ourselves that the bridge was safe and the fight over, when we saw the enemy coming, the same line re-formed, still farther to our right and rear, evidently with the purpose of avoiding the slough that had stopped their first attempt; but they were mistaken, for the slough, as we discovered afterwards, was an old cut-off of the river in the shape of a horseshoe, and filled with water when the river rose as it then was.

Their second charge was as dashing as their first. This time the bend in the slough brought them within thirty steps of us before they came to a halt. As they began to give away again under our fire, Capt. Kennedy ordered us to charge, which we did up to the slough from our side, and some of the boys went in up to their shoulders; but our exposure cost us dear. The enemy on the opposite side of the river, as well as those in front, were pouring their fire upon us. It was now sundown, and we prepared to withdraw according to our orders.

We found that sixteen of our little command were dead and eighteen wounded. We counted thirty-seven dead Yankees along the edges of the slough and as far in the switch cane as we could see, to say nothing of those on the bridge, which we could not see for the dead horses. We reached Gen. Forrest's headquarters about midnight. He was so well pleased with Capt. Kennedy's report that the latter ventured to ask him how he happened to select him with such a small force for such a perilous job, to which the "old man" [Forrest] replied: "Because I thought you were damned fool enough to stay there."

Our company was paroled at Crystal Springs, Miss. If Capt. Kennedy is alive, and will write me, I will return him his old army pistol, which I've kept all these years in remembrance of him.[113] — D. MILLER

5

1864-1865

CAMPAIGNING UNDER FORREST

☛ I don't claim to be an encyclopedia of the war, but of events that my regiment took part in I know something. I have been too busy hustling to make an honest living. Handicapped as I am, it has been a hard fight (I was knocked down by the concussion of a shell at Harrisburg, Miss., and rendered almost deaf) to give much thought or time to those stirring old war times. We of the Third Kentucky always gave the Fifteenth Mississippi credit for being one of the best regiments in the service. The men proved it on many a hard-fought field, but there were "others."

But don't throw mud at Kentuckians. Of the eight hundred men who participated in the Canton drill, less than one hundred ever saw their "old Kentucky homes'" again. As long as we were in Loring's Division we carried our "Canton flag," and it was in all the fights of the division.

We were mounted and joined Gen. Forrest in North Mississippi. Forrest had a very small command at that time. Nobody thought then that he had sense enough to manage a separate command. He had raised Bell's Brigade; but the men were poorly equipped, and many of them had never been in a fight. His batteries were light guns of poor quality. We captured the guns and horses that afterwards made Morton and Rice famous.

In every raid that Forrest went on in Kentucky or Middle Tennessee our old Canton flag appeared. Gen. Forrest always favored the Tennesseans; but when he wanted Bell to get down to his level best, he would say, "Watch those damn Kentuckians and stay with them." At the fight at Brice's Cross Roads, when we had our last man in the fight, and the Yanks were still rushing men that had not fired a shot, Morton was "crowding them with artillery." Gen. Buford got uneasy about our battery, and called Gen. Forrest's attention to the danger. Forrest looked around and saw our Canton flag flying close to the guns. Then turning to Gen. Buford, he said: "There are not Yankees here or to come that can capture that battery."

At Harrisburg we planted our flag on Gen. Smith's breastworks, while twenty thousand infantrymen and eighteen guns were firing on our one brigade; but it took sixty-two and a half percent of the regiment to do it. It was among the first to cross the Tennessee River in front of Hood, and from there to Nashville it was in the front all the way. On the retreat, Wilson tried, day after day, to ride over it, but never could.

Miss Kathleen Malone, Maid of Honor for Forrest's Cavalry.

We found Gen. Forrest a major general, with a small, badly equipped command. In three months we were the best-mounted and equipped cavalry in the C.S.A.; we had the finest batteries, and got all from the Yanks. In six months we made Forrest a lieutenant general, with a name that will stand as long as the American people care for heroic deeds. The few of us that got home are proud to think we did our duty always.[114] — CONFEDERATE PRIVATE HENRY EWELL HORD

FOLLOWING THE IMMORTAL FORREST

☛ I, with five other men from [James W.] Starnes's Fourth Tennessee Cavalry Regiment, was captured on the same day on the fighting line near a small village called Lawrenceville, Ga. That day's fighting may never be mentioned in history, although it was about the hardest fight I was in during the years that I followed the immortal Forrest, lasting from early in the morning till late in the afternoon, when we were offered the alternative of surrendering or being killed, and some of the boys already had more Yankee lead in their bodies than they could carry comfortably. After a short consultation, allowed us before the killing would begin, we decided, on account of the wounded, we would surrender.

One thing happened there that was not often the case after a hard fight: We were complimented by the Yankee major commanding as the best fighters he had ever met, and when I informed him that we belonged to, and were trained up in, Forrest's old brigade, he gave me his hand with the remark that no wonder Gen. Forrest accomplished everything he undertook when followed by such men.[115] — CONFEDERATE CAPTAIN J. M. KILLOUGH

NAMES OF THE MEN IN FORREST'S ESCORT
☛ The following [is a] roll of members who surrendered at Gainesville, Ala., May 5, 1865:

Staff: Majs. J. P. Strange and C. W. Anderson; Lieuts. William M. Forrest, Sam Donelson, C. S. Severson, R. M. Mason, and G. V. Rambaut; Capts. George Dashields, Charles H. Hill, and J. G. Mann; Drs. J. B. Cowan and G. W. Jones.

Officers: J. C. Jackson, captain; Nathan Boone, Math Cortner, and George L. Cowan, lieutenants; M. L. Parks, first sergeant; W. E. Sims, second sergeant; W. A. F. Rutledge, third sergeant; C. C. McLemore, fourth sergeant; W. H. Mathews, first corporal; H. J. Crenshaw, second corporal; W. T. H. Wharton, third corporal; P. C. Richardson, fourth corporal; R. C. Keeble, fifth corporal; W. F. Watson, bugler.

Privates: J. N. Anderson, A. D. Adair, H. L. W. Boone, J. H. Bivins, P. P. Bennett, J. W. Bridges, W. A. Bailey, S. E. Batts, W. F. Buchanan, J. O. Crump, W. C. Cooper, Alex Cortner, Sam Carter, Joe Cunningham, Silas J. Clark, E. C. Clark, Thomas Childs, T. G. Chairs, S. W. Carmack, D. H. Call, C. A. Crenshaw, George R. Dismukes, W. R. Dyer, H. F. Dusenberry, Phil Dodd, L. A. Dwiggins, J. G. Davidson, G. W. Davidson, F. M. Dance, T. J. Eaton, John Eaton, W. D. Elder, S. W. Edens, M. M. Emmons, M. A. L. Enochs, A. Forrest, J. D. Fletcher, George W. Foster, George W. Felps, R. E. B. Floyd, R. C. Garrett, J. S. Garrett, George C. Gillespie, G. W. Hooper, H. A. Holland, D. C. Jackson, John F. Key, A. W. Key, W. S. Livingston, H. D. Lipscomb, C. T. Latimer, E. E. Linch, Thomas C. Little, W. T. McGehee, T. N. McCord, R. F. McKnight, B. F. Martin, J. O. Martin, R. H. Maxwell, O. W. McKissick, A. McEwin, T. H. Moore, J. M. McNabb, J. W. Newsom, F. C. Nolan, J. K. P. Neece, E. P. Oakly, D. C. Padgett, B. A. Pearson, J. B. Pearson, T. R. Priest, W. R. Poplin, D. G. Roland, C. H. Ruffin, R. Felix Renfro, J. K. Reaves, John W. Snell, Joel Reese, W. L. Shofner, J. K. Stephenson, G. W. Stevenson, C. Searback, W. R. Shofner, A. M. Spencer, Noah Scales, H. C. Troxler, J. N. Taylor, W. F. Taylor, L. E. Thompson, W. A. Thompson, J. R. Troop, E. F. Tucker, A. (Sandy) White, T. H. Wood, Mark G. Watson, W. A. Woodard, J. H. Womack, J. H. Word, W. D. Ward, Flinch

Woodard, A. A. Pearson.

L. H. Pass and W. H. Moon were both in prison at the time of the surrender, and there were other members of the company who were entitled to be paroled at Gainesville, who were unavoidably absent on detached duty or were sick in hospitals.[116] — J. N. TAYLOR, SECRETARY OF FORREST'S STAFF & ESCORT

MISREPRESENTING FORREST

☛ "To git thar fustest with the mostest," Samuel Emerson's reference to a remark imputed to Gen. N. B. Forrest in an article in *Munsey's Magazine* on "Japan's Naval Heroes," goes so far beyond consistency that to cultured people it is ridiculous, but others will accept it as literal truth. A worthy criticism concludes as follows: "The sacred memory of Gen. Forrest is beloved in every home in the Southland, his military career is the pride of the nation, and foreign military authorities have been unstinted in their praise of his genius as the world's greatest cavalry leader. Mr. Emerson shows not only a surprising lack of knowledge of a historic character but also of the Southern people. 'To git thar fustest with the mostest' is certainly not a Southern idiom, neither could it be found among the extreme provincial classes. The magazine mentioned is criticised for permitting such a gross error to appear."[117] — UNKNOWN

☛ CONFEDERATE CANNON AT GAINESVILLE, ALA.

Mrs. D. H. Williams writes that the Ladies' Memorial Association of Gainesville, Ala., has succeeded in having removed to their Confederate Cemetery, after many unsuccessful attempts, an old siege gun left there by Gen. Forrest when he surrendered that place, May, 1865.

"It was quite an undertaking, as it lay near the river, partly buried in the sand, for so many years. This was the only relic of our great 'war for the Constitution' that we could boast of, and now that we have accomplished the difficult work we feel that our cemetery, where lie buried one hundred and ninety-two brave heroes, is complete with its modest shaft of white marble; and when our old soldiers have answered their last call something will remain to remind our younger generations of the brave deeds of their fathers, those who fought for what they knew was right." In regard to the old gun's having been left by Gen. Forrest, Charles Bean wrote from Brownwood, Tex.: "I was under Gen. Bedford Forrest and surrendered to [Union] Gen. [Edward R. S.] Canby at Gainesville, Ala. The old cannon was left by Gen. Forrest."[118] — SUMNER ARCHIBALD CUNNINGHAM

FORREST & THE SCIENCE OF WAR

☛ There existed once a man by the name of Hannibal; later a Corsican, Napoleon Bonaparte by name; earlier another Italian from Rome, of the genus Julius, surnamed Caesar—all of whom thought they knew something about the importance of time in military operations, something about marching infantry, so as to be "at the point of crisis with the largest numbers first"; but one Thomas Jonathan Jackson, surnamed "Stonewall," because he could, when that was the thing to do, stand still like a stone wall, might, in this game of marching, have given either of these world captains an advantage of three out of five and beaten them to the goal; and an unlettered man, guiltless of military training, untutored in the science of war, half West Tennessean and half North-Mississippian, by name Bedford Forrest, could not only have taught them how to move cavalry quicker than they knew, but could have revolutionized for them, as he did for the modern world, the art of war by changing cavalry into "mounted infantry," with all the advantage of cavalry on the march, and all the advantage of infantry in the fight.[119]
— JOHN SHARP WILLIAMS

BRICE'S CROSS ROADS FROM A PRIVATE'S VIEW

Edmund W. Rucker.

☛ Reading the various reports of this fight, one would think that Gen. Forrest had the battle of Brice's Cross Roads all planned and figured out days before it was fought, even to time and place, whereas Gens. Buford, Lyon, and Rucker had all insisted on fighting at the council held at Baldwyn only the night before the battle, and they should have some credit. Gen. Buford particularly contended we could whip the Yankee cavalry before the infantry got up. "Fight 'em, and fight damned quick," were his words. Three of Gen. Buford's staff had been members of our company, and we fellows of Company D, Third Kentucky Regiment, knew everything that was said or ordered at headquarters almost as soon as "old Abe" [Confederate Gen. Abraham Buford] himself. The facts of the case are that the Sturgis raid was a great surprise to us. Scouts had reported all quiet at Memphis. Gen. Forrest had started with Buford's Division, composed of Bell's and Lyon's Brigades and Morton's and Rice's Batteries, to Middle Tennessee, and while we were making tracks for Tennessee, overjoyed at the idea of being again among our kind-hearted Tennessee friends, and incidentally hitting Sherman in the back, Gen. Sturgis was behind us in Mississippi, burning, plundering, and laying the country in ruins. We were three days on our march before we got news of Sturgis, and had all that distance to retrace, through the worst mud I ever traveled over.

We reached Baldwyn, ten miles from Brice's Cross Roads, on the evening before the fight. There Gen. Forrest found out the enemy's cavalry were at Brice's Cross Roads and his infantry camped at Stubb's farm, nine miles farther west, in the Ripley Road. He held a council with his officers, and it was determined to try and whip the cavalry before the infantry could get up. Buford went back to bring up Bell's Brigade and place the Second Tennessee, Col. Barteau, so they would reach the flank of the enemy west of Brice's; orders were sent to Rucker and Capt. Morton to "move up," and Forrest started with Lyon's Brigade toward Brice's Cross Roads at daylight. We met the enemy a mile or so north of Brice's house, on the Baldwyn road, early in the morning. Two companies of the Twelfth Kentucky were sent forward, mounted, to feel of [that is, for] them.

They did not like the way they felt, and came back faster than they went. The Third Kentucky was then dismounted and thrown forward to take their places. The Third, Seventh, and Eighth Kentucky had served nearly three years as infantry before they were mounted, and had all an infantryman's contempt for cavalry fighting; but they changed their opinion before they had been with old Bedford long. We deployed in skirmish order on the left of the road, moved forward, and soon had our brigade in line, driving the enemy in front of us through a densely wooded country. Rucker came up and took position on our left, and was soon heavily engaged. We, having served as infantry, were agreeably surprised to see him with his dismounted cavalry keep up his side so well; and all day long, when Rucker got "busy," our boys would shout out: "O, my Rucker," "Stay with him, Rucker." Even when we had trouble of our own in front, we found time to cheer Rucker.

Johnson came up and took position on our right. We found we had a heavy force in our front armed with Spencer rifles that shot seven times to our once, for we still had our old Enfields. We never tried to keep up with the enemy in number of shots, but we had had so much practice that when we did shoot we mostly "got meat." We had no trouble driving them whenever we cared to, but Gen. Lyon cautioned us to "go slow; we don't want to crowd them too much till Bell and Morton get up."

From early in the morning till 12 o'clock Rucker and Lyon fought three times their number, and all the time their lines were close up—had to be to see anything in that dense undergrowth, and we could hear every order the Yankee officers gave. The roar of their batteries, bursting shells, falling timber, ceaseless cackle of their Spencers, and deadly work of our old Enfields will never be forgotten by any of that command. We fought back and forth over the same ground so often that it was strewn with the dead and dying, and—hot! with not a drop of water to drink.

At last we heard the welcome sound of Morton's men and saw his guns coming down the road under whip and spur, the horses reeling with exhaustion from the pace and the distance they had come over the heavy roads. Our alignment then was right across the road, and the first gun was placed in front of our company, and soon opened on the Yankees, but after a few shots Morton found a better elevation in an old field just in the rear of our line, where he could do better work, and moved over there.

We had the enemy driven back to the Brice house when Morton came up. They had drawn in their lines and planted their guns so as to rake both roads; and back of the guns they had dismounted cavalry, with such infantry as had reached them, and were trying to hold their own till more could come up. Shortly after Morton arrived Lyon got word from Gen. Forrest that Bell also had reached the field, had taken position on Rucker's left, and to move everything forward. Between us and the house was a strip of heavily timbered land, and then the lawn fence, with a gentle slope of one hundred and fifty or two hundred yards back to the house. The Yankee battery was behind the house and supported by infantry. Our skirmishers moved forward through the woods; Morton limbered up and followed down the road just behind us. We reached the fence and ceased firing, dressed up our line, and, at the word "Charge!" cleared the fence at a bound and started straight for the guns.

Adam R. Johnson, one of Forrest's most renowned scouts.

Now could be seen the effect of drill and thorough discipline on troops. Our old infantry regiment swept up toward the house, lines straight, double-quick, trailing arms. Shot and shell tore great gaps out, but they were closed so quickly one would scarcely notice it. Rucker's and Bell's men jumped the fence the same time, farther along, and started pell mell toward the house, some of the men forty yards in front of the others, and some firing as they ran. Johnson, over on our right, advanced also, but I could not see him. Pool, Rosencrantz, and two comrades were within forty yards of the battery, when all of us went down at once.

Miss Duncan, Maid of Honor for Forrest's Cavalry Corps, Birmingham Reunion.

I had pulled my cartridge box around on my hip, so that I could get at it handier. A ball struck one corner of it, spun me around and knocked me down, but I was not hurt. I jumped up and started again, but luck was against me. I had drawn a pair of pants sometime before that would come nearer fitting Gen. Buford, who weighed three hundred and twenty pounds, than me, a slender boy; and the only way I could keep them up was with my belt. The ball that struck my cartridge box jerked the belt up over the waist of the pants, and the first jump I made to go forward they dropped around my ankles like a pair of hobbles and threw me flat. I whirled over on my back and gave a vicious kick with both of my feet, and they went off my heels like a shot, striking square in the face one of our boys just rushing by with his eyes fixed on the Yankee battery. He thought it was a shell and could not understand why his head was still on. Pool was struck in the head, making a scalp wound. I left him flopping around like a chicken with his head cut off. Rosencrantz was struck in the face, the ball ranging back into his neck and killing him.

I got up to the house at last. Mrs. Brice's daughter ran out on the porch when she saw us coming, and waved her handkerchief to us.

The gunners left the guns. We stopped about ten steps in front of their supporting line, and delivered our first volley; it was a "deadener." They began to retire, firing as they went. I had fallen heir to a Spencer that morning, and had just recharged the magazine when I felt a sharp rap on my shoulder. I looked around, and was surprised to find it was a saber in the hand of Gen. Forrest, who pointed down the road toward Ripley. I looked and saw, about one hundred yards of, one [Union] gunner making desperate efforts to save his gun; all the rest had run away and left him. There were three pairs of horses hitched to the gun, and he was mounted on the lead team, lashing and spurring furiously. The wheel team did not care to hurry. I fired at the fellow's back, and he tumbled off. I looked up to see if that was what old Bedford wanted. He smiled down on me as sweetly as some young girl that had just received her first proposal.

The horses, missing the hand and voice that controlled them, took fright and bolted down the road as hard as they could go, found the bridge blocked, and, in trying to cross the creek, bogged down. I expect Capt. Morton or some of the battery fellows remember fishing it out. Morton had followed close behind our lines and taken position on the right of our regiment, commanding the road to the creek, along which any reenforcements coming to the enemy were bound to pass, the battery boys working like double-geared lightning and firing double charges. The gun would jump off the ground at every discharge, but would hardly hit the earth before they would have another charge in. They kept a constant stream of old iron going down the road after the Yankees, but they retired slowly, firing as they went.

We drove them through a strip of wood and across a bottom field on the creek, where they got some reenforcements, formed a line with their backs to the creek, and stood us off for some time—in fact, it looked as if we had got to the end of our rope, with only about a hundred yards between us, and it fairly raining bullets. From where we were we could see a long line of their infantry coming up the Ripley road as fast as they could lay foot to ground, and fresh batteries rushing across the fields beyond the creek, taking up commanding positions, while we had every man in the fight we could put in, even to some horse holders.

Morton was crowding them with his guns almost at pistol shot range, and yet they stood their ground manfully. It was all open country in front of us now, and away across to our right we could see Barteau and his gallant old Second Tennessee beginning their move on the flank and rear of the Yankees. They were deployed mounted, long distance apart, advancing toward the Ripley road, and firing as they came. We could see the smoke from their guns, but it was too far off to hear them.

The good news that Barteau was on their flank had scarcely passed down the line, when some one found Capt. Tyler with two companies of the Twelfth Kentucky over on the other flank of the enemy creating wild consternation. Barteau and Tyler could not have timed their attack better if they had practiced a week.

Just then we heard old Buford's voice. He had been with Barteau and Bell all day, and that was the first time we had heard or seen him. He was an old West Pointer, and had a voice one could hear two miles.

"Attention, battalion! Cease firing," he called out. We ceased instantly, Rucker partially, and Bell not at all. Down the line old Abe came, making the dirt fly, and reined up in front of Bell. "Damn you, cease firing," he yelled. They stopped.

"Fix bayonets" was the next order. We had bayonets when we were first mounted, but had a fool idea when we were mounted that we would do the rest of our fighting on horseback, so we very promptly lost [that is, got rid of] our bayonets. Gen. Buford knew that as well as we did, but he was talking for the benefit of the Yankees, who could hear him as plainly as we. "Forward, guide center, march."

The whole line moved forward, and as Buford said "Charge!" they rushed forward. The enemy fired until we got pretty close, then threw down their guns and surrendered, or waded [back across] the creek. We fired a volley in their backs as they came out on the opposite side. We waded the creek after them, stopping only long enough to "dress up our line." They formed another line in front of us, and we went on to that. Morton found the bridge blocked, and had to clear that off before he could get his guns across to us. With his help we soon moved that line.

Miss Marie Brevard, Assistant Adjutant Gen. Forrest's Cavalry Corps.

I don't remember just how many lines we did rush, but I remember the last ones were the [Yankee] negroes; they had sworn before they left Memphis never to take any of Forrest's men prisoners, and they kept their oath. They did not put up much of a fight—seemed more intent on getting rid of their equipments and plunder. The Yankees had made a clean sweep for five miles on each side of the road they marched over, and all the plunder except that they destroyed fell into our hands. You could pick up anything from a lady's fine silk dress to a string of live chickens. We found their wagons (two hundred and fifty parked) loaded with ten days' rations. We kept on across the fields in line of battle till dark, and then went into camp. We lost some good soldiers at Brice's Cross Roads, but as straws show which way the wind blows, so will the dead on a battlefield show where the fighting was hardest. One of our company was on the burial detail, and he told me a few days after that he found the dead thickest around the house and on the creek: that is where our old Enfields went along.[120] —
CONFEDERATE PRIVATE HENRY EWELL HORD

PURSUIT OF GEN. STURGIS

☛ Having whipped Sturgis at Brice's Cross Roads, at daylight next morning we took the road in pursuit of him. Gens. Forrest and Buford rode together at the head of Lyon's Brigade, Third Kentucky leading. I think Gen. Lyon had been detailed to take charge of the battlefield, prisoners, plunder, etc., we had captured the day before. There was one regiment, the Twelfth Kentucky, in advance of us, though not in sight. The first thing we came upon that looked like war was a large, fine ambulance full of dead Yankees, packed in so tight that they held each other up on the two long seats on each side of the ambulance. Forrest and Buford halted to have a look at them. They had evidently been abandoned by their friends probably before they were dead, as the horses were gone. It takes a good deal to move an old soldier, but every face showed sorrow for the poor fellows left there to die by their friends. Under the seats were two little closed-up closets with a small door in the end, doubtless to carry the dead.

One of our boys noticed the doors. They excited his curiosity, and he jumped off his horse and opened one. The Yankee driver had a number of live geese, which no doubt he had stolen, confined in there, and as soon as the door opened out flew an old gander with a low hiss. The fellow was stooping down peeping into the door, his face so close he could not see what it was. He got only a glimpse of something while, which he must have taken for the ghost of the dead men overhead, for it scared him pretty nigh into fits. I never heard a fellow yell so in my life. He fought and yelled, and as fast as he knocked one out of his face another would fly out. The rest of us on our horses could see what it was, of course, and the whole command joined in the laugh. After the geese had all got out and the fellow had somewhat recovered his nerve he started to mount his horse, when somebody in the ranks told him to open the other door. He glared around at his tormentors, and answered: "I'll be damn if I do." His emphatic language started everybody to laughing again, even Gen. Forrest joining in; but the "old man" was the first to think of business, for, turning to Gen. Buford, he said, "While we are laughing at that damn fool the Yankees are getting away. I'll go on; you follow as fast as your horses can stand it;" and, striking a lope, he was soon out of sight.

It was not long till we heard firing in front, and the boys commenced yelling: "Old Bedford's treed." We soon got a "hurry up" order. The command passed down the line, "Keep closed up if it kills your horses," and away we went.

When we struck the Yankees we "formed fours" and sailed in, tore their line all to pieces, and scattered them in every direction. While we were re-forming and gathering up prisoners the next regiment would take the lead and sweep down on them, and in that way we worked a sort of endless chain attack that did not allow them to halt to rest or get water. Only once, at Ripley, I think, we were dismounted and formed a regular line of battle, and there we completely routed them and captured their last gun.

Gen. Forrest had handed out some mighty nice taffy to Capt. Morton and the battery boys on the way they handled their guns [cannon] the day before, and they had left camp that morning all "puffed up" with new guns, eight horses to each gun, and the firm determination to break all records and have old Bedford pat them on the back some more. Although they killed six horses, they never were able to get near us. It was a cavalry fight all the way through, and a friendly rivalry between the different [Confederate] regiments to see which could outdo the others. I am not sure but that we counted some of our prisoners twice. Once Gen. Forrest himself took part of Rucker's and Bell's Brigade and tried to get around the Yanks, but it did not work. When he got back into the road they were on he was in our rear.

At Salem Gen. Forrest had to be taken off his horse, he was so near fainting from fatigue. Gen. Buford was not, however. Mounted on a Kentucky thoroughbred, one of his own rearing, he hung on to that flying column, and every chance he got would rush down on them. I don't think he would ever have thought of holding up as long as anybody's horse could keep up with him. Two Yankee stragglers were the cause of our finally halting. They mistook us for their troops, and rode the whole length of our command, from rear to front. We saw them, but thought they were some of our men returning from taking prisoners to the rear. It was about eleven o'clock at night, and too dark to see the color of uniforms.

Just as they were passing Gen. Buford, who was riding at the head of our column, one of them asked: "Whose command is this?" Gen. Buford answered: "My command, A. Buford." "Good Lord!" said the Yank, and we could hear the rip, rip of their spurs as they dashed down the road. "Halt!" yelled Old Abe; bang, bang, went his pistol, but they made good their escape; then he halted his command, rode back, and wanted to know where those Yanks came from. When some one told him they came down the line, he made things blue and brimstony with his profanity, and told us, among a good many other things, that we were "a lot of damn sandlappers riding along half asleep" and let the Yanks ride over us. Some one told him it was too dark to see colors. "See, hell," yelled Old Abe; "smell 'um."

We were passing through a dense forest at the time, and the General got suspicious of an ambuscade, so he ordered one of his staff, Maj. Turk, to dismount twenty-five or thirty of us and deploy as skirmishers.

Nathan Bedford Forrest.

I was one of that unlucky lot. We had not gone fifty yards before I stumbled over something and came near falling. I looked back to see what it was, and discovered that it was a Yankee sitting at the foot of a tree sound asleep. I woke him up, told him he was a prisoner, and called to the other fellows to look close, that there were Yanks about. Pretty soon all up and down the skirmish line I could hear the boys waking up sleeping Yankees. We kept on about half an hour, and had taken quite a number of prisoners, when I heard Gen. Buford call: "Turk, where are you?" "Here, General," answered Turk, who was out in the brush with us. "Call in your skirmishers, take some of them down the road, and put out a picket. We will stay right here till morning. Every damn man with me is sound asleep."

Maj. Turk had been lieutenant in my company for years, so when I heard his order, "Skirmishers, rally on the road," I skipped back to my horse, for I was pretty certain to get a job of standing picket the rest of the night if I "rallied." I jerked my saddle off "Old Pete," crumbled up some crackers for him to eat, and was asleep before one could count a dozen.

Next morning we found we were sixty-five miles from Brice's Cross Roads, without corn or rations and nothing in the country to subsist upon. So Gen. Buford started the prisoners back under guard, and disbanded the rest of our brigade to hustle for themselves to get back to Guntown as soon as they could and pick up all the Yankee stragglers they came across.

Part of Bell's Brigade followed the Yanks still farther, but I don't think they caught up with them again. I should state that nobody cared for Old Abe's cursing; his bark was ever worse than his bite. He was one of the kindest-hearted men I ever knew, except the peerless John C. Breckinridge, the best man we ever served under. Turk told me next morning that he, as well as the pickets, went to sleep on post, and slept till daylight. The fact was, we had about reached the limit of endurance for man and horse.[121] — CONFEDERATE PRIVATE HENRY EWELL HORD

FORREST & HIS TROOPS AT CHICKAMAUGA

☛ The cavalry on our right was Forrest's Corps, and I only know positively of one of its divisions, that of Brig. Gen. John Pegram. I believe that another was composed of a division under command of Brig. Gen. Frank Armstrong, and that this consisted of Armstrong's own brigade and another under Col. Dibrell.

Gen. Pegram's Division had three brigades, his own, to the command of which Gen. H. B. Davidson had been assigned; but, as he reached it only late Friday or Friday night, the latter was handicapped by his want of knowledge of the command. It had the First Georgia (instead of First Georgia Brigade), the Sixth Georgia, Twelfth and Sixteenth Tennessee Battalions, under Lieut. Col. Rucker and composing Rucker's Legion, the Sixty-Sixth North Carolina, under Col. Folk, and the Tenth Confederate, under Col. Goode. This, with Huwald's excellent battery, composed the command which, since Murfreesboro, had been operating under Gen. Pegram, and which his West Point education and life in the regular army had enabled him to bring to a high state of discipline and efficiency.

Still farther to the right was Scott's Brigade, under Col. John Scott, of the First Louisiana Cavalry. It was in action at Red House bridge during the battle, but not near enough to Gen. Pegram to be of service to him. The Third Brigade was that of Gen. George B. Hodge, of Kentucky and Virginia troops, but it was so far off that it had no part in the fighting.

Friday night Gens. Forrest and Pegram bivouacked on the field from which Gen. Bushrod Johnson had driven a Federal force. Saturday morning, at gray daylight, Gen. Pegram awoke a staff officer of his and directed him to go to the First Georgia picket and see what that firing meant. Arriving there, no difficulty was had in determining what that firing meant, as that little company was being hard pressed by what seemed quite a heavy force. Asking that a squadron be sent him, it was quickly on hand, rapidly dismounted and put in action; but as the enemy's line still lapped ours on both right and left, another message was sent, asking for the rest of that regiment. Coming up, it was either being dismounted and moved to the right of the line engaged or was being placed in position. When Gen. Pegram came up with the brigade, which, being disposed, with Huwald on the left and the Twelfth Tennessee mounted on the left of the battery, the whole line went forward at a charge, our guns at work also. The charge developed the brigade of infantry of Col. Dan McCook, and some fifteen or sixteen prisoners were taken. We saw nothing more of that brigade that day, so far as we knew.

The brigade, remounting, was moved to our left, passing an old sawmill (since understood to have been Jay's Mill), and, moving some five or six hundred yards from it, was halted, while a conference took place between Gen. Forrest, who had just ridden up, and Gen. Pegram. During this the same staff officer was called up and ordered to take ten men and reconnoiter for a half mile in our front or in an indicated direction. Taking Sergeant Goodwin, of the First Georgia, whom he had had with him in a night reconnaissance of the position charged the next day at Murfreesboro (and who it is hoped lives to read this), they rode for three quarters of a mile through an unbroken woodland thick with undergrowth.

Riding slowly and looking in every direction, nothing was heard or seen by them, save an occasional note from small birds. Everything was as still as if two great armies were not then moving up into positions for one of the greatest and most desperately fought battles of the war. Upon returning, report was made to Gen. Pegram. He and Gen. Forrest were still talking with each other when a heavy and unexpected fire was received by the First Georgia, its men being at ease and some, perhaps, dismounted by the sides of their horses. Where those Federals came from has been ever since an unsolved puzzle to that staff officer, for that firing came from precisely the direction from which he had returned not more than fifteen or twenty minutes before, and he knows that they were not where he and Goodwin had been.

Thrown into momentary confusion, that fine command was soon in position, with Gen. Forrest directing; while the rest of the brigade were rapidly dismounted and, with Huwald's guns, took position on a small rise, with the First Georgia on the right, Twelfth and Sixteenth Tennessee on the left of the First Georgia, Huwald in the center, and on the left of his guns were the Tenth Georgia, Sixth Confederate, and the Sixty-Sixth North Carolina. Seeing at once how greatly this command was outnumbered, Gen. Forrest ordered Gen. Pegram to hold that position until he could bring reenforcements. And hold it he did, with Huwald sweeping the front with canister; while the dismounted men fought like infantry, and not an inch of ground had been yielded when, after some time (who knows of time during a fight), there was the welcome sight of the head of Ector's Brigade of Infantry, closely followed by that of Wilson. There was a lull in the firing at this time, and Pegram was ordered to mount his men and have their cartridge boxes filled, as there were but few left in the boxes after that morning's work. Forming rapidly, with Dibrell's Regiment on their right, these

commands moved in, and a bloody reception it was that met them.[122] —
CONFEDERATE CAPTAIN H. B. CLAY

FORREST ENCOURAGES A YOUNG SOLDIER

☛ [Here is an interesting incident] that I heard and witnessed during the fight [Battle of Brice's Cross Roads]. The Third Kentucky . . . had been drilled and served as infantry until they were assigned to Forrest, and evidently thought they could do no good fighting on horseback. It was after Morton's Battery had joined us at Brice's Cross Roads, and we had just started the Yankees on the go, that Gen. Forrest rode up to [Private Henry E.] Hord's regiment (the Third Kentucky) and was cursing them into shape to charge on horseback in order to overtake and capture as many prisoners as possible, when Hord, mounted on a little dun-colored mustang, rode around in front of the line near Forrest. His hat was gone, and his white [blond] head glittered in the sunshine like a ball of silver; his face, as smooth as a girl's and as red as a beet, was streaked with sweat and dirt; a liberal part of his gray shirt (he had no jacket) had worked out over the waistband of his pants and fluttered over the cantle of his saddle. He looked to be about fifteen or sixteen years old, just the right age not to be afraid of anything on earth. I was sitting on my horse near Gen. Forrest when Hord and his mustang came around to the front. He was pegging away at the Yankees as fast as he could shoot, oblivious of the fact that old Bedford was near or that he had attracted his attention, until the General shouted, "Go it, little one!" and the "little one" went. I've seen him [Hord] but once in nearly forty years, but will carry in my mind as long as I live the ludicrous but game picture of the white headed, dirty-faced boy at Brice's Cross Roads.[123] —
CONFEDERATE CAPTAIN C. F. JARRETT

INVITATION TO THE FORREST MONUMENT DEDICATION

☛ The Forrest Monument Association request the honor of your presence at the unveiling and dedication of the statue and monument erected in memory of the great Southern chieftain, Lieut. Gen. Nathan Bedford Forrest, on Tuesday, the 16th of May, 1905, at Memphis, Tenn.

Committee of Invitation: H. M. Neely, Chairman; G. W. Macrae, Hunsdon Cary.

Board of Directors: Gen. S. T. Carnes, President; Gen. George W. Gordon, Vice President; James E. Beasley, Treasurer; Judge J. P. Young, Secretary; Hon. Thomas B. Turley, Capt. H. M. Neely, George W. Macrae, S. A. Pepper, I. F. Peters, J. W. Clapp, W. A. Collier, W. P. Eckles, J. M. Goodbar, Col. W. F. Taylor, Hunsdon Cary, Capt. W.

B. Mallory, Gen. A. K. Taylor.[124] — SUMNER ARCHIBALD CUNNINGHAM

REMEMBERING GEN. FORREST
☞ Of Forrest, a born soldier. Untrained in the arts of war, sleepless vigilance, tireless energy, a quick perception, and prompt execution supplied his every deficiency. Before his native genius and force of character the science of the schools and the tactics of the books dissolved like frostwork before the sun of the tropics. Concentrating every force at his command on the object to be accomplished, no obstacle could impede his march, no resistance withstand the sudden, impetuous, and deadly energy of his assault. His guiding star was success, and he gazed at it steadfastly with the eye of the eagle and fought for it with a courage no opposition could resist. Asked how he succeeded against overwhelming numbers, he explained in an epigram the whole art of war, which Jomini, of whom Forrest may have never heard, wrote volumes to teach, he tersely said: "Get there first with the most men."[125] — CONFEDERATE COLONEL ASA S. MORGAN

Asa S. Morgan.

PERSONAL EXPERIENCES AT HARRISBURG, MISS.
☞ The Harrisburg fight was the hardest our brigade was in during the war; at least we suffered more in proportion to the time engaged. [Union] Gen. A. J. Smith, commanding the Sixteenth Army Corps, infantry, cavalry, and artillery, amounting in all to near seventeen thousand men, started from Memphis to "clean up" Gen. Forrest, march through Alabama, and join Sherman in Georgia. We had only a few small cavalry brigades at that time in North Mississippi; and Gen. Buford's Division, consisting of Lyon's and Bell's brigades, was sent out toward La Grange to delay Smith's advance and enable Gens. Forrest and Stephen D. Lee to concentrate all the troops they could to repel Smith's force. We met them south of La Grange, and immediately commenced a kind of guerrilla warfare—capturing pickets, ambushing, night attacks, rushing in while they were on the march, killing the wagon guards, burning wagons, and out again before they could get a whack at us.

Constantly annoyed in this way, Smith's Corps could not march more than six or seven miles a day on his route. He had to be ready to fight at all hours, day or night. The road in his rear was strewn with dead mules, burnt wagons, and fresh-made graves. Our loss was almost nothing, except hard riding and lack of sleep, things we were accustomed to. We were confident we should soon wear him out, get his men demoralized, and make his raid end like Gen. Sturgis's; and we would have done it if Gens. Forrest and Buford could have had their way. All the way from La Grange to Harrisburg we acted as an invisible escort to Gen. Smith. He could not water his horses without taking his army to the creek with him, and he camped every night in line of battle, with heavy skirmish lines thrown around him.

Gen. Stephen Dill Lee came up from the south just before Smith reached Harrisburg; and as he commanded the department, he took charge. All the available reenforcements that could be spared from other places were utilized. Our brigade commander, Gen. Lyon, was put in charge of a lot of dismounted militia and two batteries, and Col. Ed Crossland commanded our brigade. Mabrey and McCulloch, our old friends under Gen. Rucker, and Gen. Roddy, with his division from Alabama, were all up and eager for the fight. The night Gen. Smith reached Harrisburg our brigade had been worrying him all day, and when he finally went into camp we were so close to him that we thought we were in for a night attack.

Road named after Confederate General Stephen Dill Lee, Spring Hill, Tennessee. Photo by the author.

We were marching in line of battle, with skirmishers out, when word came down the line to "halt, dismount, and lie down." I had been asleep only a few moments when I heard a voice in a stage whisper ask: "What's the matter with Company D?" I raised up and recognized Otey O'Bryan, a member of Company B, Third Kentucky. He had made a considerable reputation as a bold and reliable scout, and Gen. Forrest very often made use of him. When Otey wanted any men to go with him, he would come to Company D and ask for volunteers. Generally the boys were eager to go; but that night every one was tired and sleepy, and no one had volunteered.

As soon as I found out what was wanted, I told him I would go; then another one of the boys, Bob , also volunteered to go. "That's all I want. Leave your horses and guns with No. 4. Bring one pistol if you want to; we are going afoot." He took us to where he had two suits of clothes, one a citizen's and the other a United States uniform. I had to take the uniform, as Bob could not get it on over his gray clothes. He then told us that Gen. Forrest was anxious to find out all he could about Gen. Smith's army, as he expected to fight him early next day, and wanted us to go inside his lines and get all the information we could. He said it was not really necessary for three to go, as each man would go alone and use his own judgment as to his movements; but it was a dangerous mission, and meant death sure and swift if we were caught, so he thought it better to have three, as some of us might never get back.

We shook hands and separated, never to meet any more in this world. Bob never got back, and Otey was killed next day on the breastworks. I never heard his report or saw him any more.

Gen. Smith was on the same ground his battle line fought on next day, and we were in the field just in front of him. As soon as we separated I went to where I was certain the enemy's skirmish line would be, and managed to locate it without being heard or seen. I then crawled up close to the sentinel and waited till the relief came around. The weeds were about as high as oats. When the guard was changed, I heard the countersign given, then I slipped back and went to another sentry, was challenged, gave the countersign, "Grant," bold as brass, told the fellow I had been outside scouting for Gen. Smith, and then, just for devilment, told him the Rebs were out there in the weeds, and he had better keep his eyes "peeled."

I made my way to where I thought Gen. Smith's main line was, and by good luck struck one end of it. They had thrown up breastworks about four feet high, stacked arms, and were all sleeping soundly around the guns. I did not see any guards at all except one sentry in front of a new tent, with a light burning in it; and as that was the only tent I saw, I supposed that it was Gen. Smith's headquarters. I went from one end of the line to the other, got the exact position of each battery, the number of guns, where the negro brigade was, etc.[126]

I got out about daylight by doing some of the fastest running a boy ever did. I found that while I was gone my command had retired to the woods in front of Gen. Smith about a mile, and in plain view. I made my report to Gen. Forrest and several of his officers, who seemed to be holding a council, Gen. Buford among them. I told them that if they attacked from that side they would have to cross that old field a mile wide and take the raking fire of those batteries. As far as I could tell from their faces, they all seemed to agree with me. I heard afterwards that Gens. Forrest and Buford were very much opposed to making the attack from that side. I don't think Gen. Lee knew how strongly the enemy were posted. . . .

[Eventually] Gen. Smith concluded that he would not go to Alabama.

Memphis was a very good town, so he began the next morning to pull his freight for that place. Gens. Forrest and Buford, thinking they could turn his retreat into a route, commenced crowding him with artillery. Smith turned on them at Town Creek, and came very near capturing four of Morton's guns. Gen. Buford had only part of our brigade supporting him at the time, and Maj. Turk came flying back after us. We went forward on the run, dismounted, and wheeled into line not a moment too soon. Morton had lost all of his horses, and, like Uncle Remus's rabbit, "he just had to climb" (fight). Gen. Buford was down on the ground helping the battery boys, and yelling: "Give 'em hell boys!"

The Yanks were charging in a long line at double-quick, and were only thirty steps or so from the battery when we got into line. We fired in their faces, which stopped them, and then we charged. They did not wait for us, but skedaddled back. We chased them across an old field, and ran up on another line, which brought us to a halt. While we were fighting that line at close range Gen. Forrest got up with McCulloch's brigade, charged, and drove them back. In that fight Forrest got the worst wound he received during the war—in the foot. We came very near losing our flag there. The color bearer was killed, and Lieut. Jarrett took the colors in falling back, closely followed by the Yanks. Jarrett fell down. He knew he would not have time to get up and away, the Yanks were so close; so he gathered the flag under him and played dead. The Yanks passed over him. We immediately made a counter charge and drove them back, and were much pleased to see Jarrett jump up and wave the old flag. Our brigade had suffered so heavily that we were excused from any more fighting on the retreat. We went back, buried the dead, and took care of the wounded.

Mrs. Davis Cox, U.D.C. member and Secretary of the Woman's Forrest Monument Association.

All of our Harrisburg wounded, as well as the enemy's, had fallen in our hands. The Yanks had never given their wounded any attention, and the poor fellows suffered fearfully. Their wounds were flyblown, and many of them died under the surgeon's knife.[127] — CONFEDERATE PRIVATE HENRY EWELL HORD

MONUMENT TO GEN. N. B. FORREST

☛ In Forrest Park, Memphis, Tenn., surrounded by fifteen thousand spectators, at 2:30 p.m. on May 16, 1905, little Miss Kathleen Bradley pulled the cord that released the veil from the magnificent equestrian statue of her illustrious great-grandfather, Lieut. Gen. Nathan Bedford Forrest. There was a momentary silence as the imposing grandeur of this colossal bronze figure of the great "Wizard of the Saddle" and his steed met the gaze of the expectant crowd, then a wild cheer broke from hundreds of his old surviving followers clustered around the base and was enthusiastically taken up by the vast multitude.

The idea of erecting a monument to Gen. Forrest was first projected in 1886, but it was not until 1891 that it took definite shape and a monument association was organized for this purpose. On November 18, 1900, the design was accepted and the order was given to the sculptor, Charles H. Niehaus. The designer of the base was Mr. B. C. Alsup, and it is built of Tennessee marble. The statue, which was made in Europe, arrived in Memphis on April 16, and was placed on its base a day or two later. The height of the entire monument is twenty-two feet. The height of the bronze figure is nine feet, and it weighs ninety-five hundred pounds. The cost of the structure approximates twenty-five thousand dollars. [See the cover of this book.]

The unveiling of the monument was attended with elaborate ceremonies. In the big parade were most of the surviving staff officers of Gen. Forrest, his general officers, and many of his old veterans who rode with him from 1861 to 1865. Judge J. P. Young, who was one of Forrest's old troopers, was master of ceremonies. In opening the proceedings he said in part: "No one who did not ride with Forrest can have so keen an appreciation of the personal qualities of the man as those who were actually under his direct command, and who, from daily, hourly observation, witnessed his fertility of resource, his vehemence in battle, and his soulful tenderness toward the stricken soldier, whether friend or foe. But it was no holiday parade. It cost something to ride with Forrest. It meant days and nights of sleepless toil and motion. It meant countless miles under a burning sun in the choking dust. It meant limitless leagues across icy wastes, with a blanket of snow at night for a covering. It meant to run down and destroy miles of freighted supply trains, to burn depots of stores, to scale the parapets of redoubts, and to plunge, mounted, into the seeming vortex of hell, lighted with the fires of a myriad rifles and scores of belching guns. It meant to meet death face to face like a drillmaster, to look into his dread eyes, to toy with the horrid trappings of his trade, to scorn the deadly chill of his breath, and to turn away unscathed or sink into the oblivion of his eternal embrace."

Judge Young then introduced Rt. Rev. Thomas F. Gailor, S.T.D., Episcopal Bishop of Tennessee, who offered the invocation. Gen. S. T. Carnes, next introduced, gave an interesting history of the monument from the organization of the association, in 1887, to its final success, in 1905.

Gen. George W. Gordon delivered the dedicatory address. He reviewed the life of Gen. Forrest from infancy to his death, and spoke eloquently of his brilliant military record.

George W. Gordon.

Of the many earnest and eloquent tributes paid the great soldier, one that was most significant was that paid by [Yankee] Col. C. A. Stanton, of the 3rd Iowa Cavalry, U.S.A., from 1861-65, and who for two years was directly opposed to Gen. Forrest. He realized Forrest's methods of war at Brice's Cross Roads, Ripley, Harrisburg, Old Town Creek, Tallahatchie, and Hurricane Creek, and was with Gen. Wilson at Montevallo, Ebenezer Church, Bogler's Creek, Selma, Montgomery, Columbus, and Macon. The spectacle of an officer who had fought in the Federal army delivering an address at the unveiling of a monument to a Confederate soldier was an interesting one, and when Col. Stanton was introduced the applause was most generous. Col. Stanton said in part:

"It is an honor which I cannot fitly acknowledge to be invited to take part in the exercises of this memorable day, and I thank the committee for giving me this opportunity to pay my tribute of respect to the memory of Tennessee's great soldier. I come before you with diffidence; but, honored by your invitation and encouraged by your greeting, I shall venture to express briefly a Northern soldier's estimate of the famous Southern leader and the brave men who followed him.

"During the War between the States I served four years in the Federal army, and what I learned then prompts what I now shall say. My knowledge of Gen. Forrest's military career was acquired while serving for a part of two years with the Federal forces that were directly opposed to him and his command. Gen. Forrest possessed the characteristic traits of the successful soldier; his personal bravery was without limit; his resources seemed to be endless, and his decisions, like Napoleon's, were instantaneous; he was aggressive, masterful, resolute, and self-reliant in the most perilous emergency; he was comprehensive in his grasp of every situation, supremely confident in himself and in his men, and inspired by his presence and example his soldiers fought as desperately as did Hannibal's fierce cavalry at Canne or the trained veterans of Caesar's Tenth Legion at Pharsalia. I think the battle at Brice's Cross Roads in June 1864 was one of the best illustrations of Gen. Forrest's daring courage, his ability in a critical moment to decide swiftly, his relentless vigor of action, and his intuitive perception of the time and place to strike fierce, stunning blows which fell like thunderbolts upon his enemy and won for him in this battle an overwhelming victory over an opposing force which greatly outnumbered his command.

"Impartial history has given Gen. Forrest high rank as one of the greatest cavalry leaders of modern times. No American, North or South, now seeks to lessen the measure of his fame, and no one can speak of him without remembrance of the men who served with him and whose soldierly qualities made it possible for him to win his wonderful victories. No military leader was ever supported by more faithful, gallant, and daring subordinate officers. It has been truly said that 'the spirit of the cavalier which was found in the Southern armies was combined with the steadfastness of Cromwell's Ironsides,' and it is equally true that no soldiers ever met more promptly every demand made upon them; no soldiers ever faced the enemies' blazing guns more fearlessly or performed greater feats of valor than did the veterans of Forrest's regiments in battles which were as hard fought as Marathon or Philippi.

"The men who wore the gray from 1861 to 1865 still treasure the memories of those heroic days; but through all the years since that time they have contributed their full share to the advancement and prosperity of our common country, and to-day the nation has no truer friends than the ex-Confederate soldiers of the South.

"The war of 1861-65 was a mighty conflict which stands without a parallel in the annals of time. Shiloh, Stone's River, Franklin, Chickamauga, and Gettysburg are names made sacred by the deeds done there and by the dead who lie there side by side in common graves, where the gray cloth and the blue have faded into dust alike.

"This monument is history in bronze; it illustrates an eventful era in our national history; it commemorates Gen. Forrest's fame and it represents all the gallant soldiers of his command; it attests the splendid courage which won triumphant victories and did not fail when reverses came; it stands for heroic deeds which are now the proud heritage of all American citizens. It is eminently fitting that this figure should stand here within the borders of the Volunteer State, whose soldiers have marched and fought 'from valley's depth to mountain height and from inland rivers to the sea,' in every war in the history of our republic, with a valor which has helped to make the name and fame of the American soldier immortal."

Hon. Thomas B. Turley, in behalf of the Monument Association and of the various Chapters of the United Daughters of the Confederacy, then turned the monument over to the city of Memphis. It was accepted by Mayor [Joseph John] Williams in a few well-chosen remarks, and the ceremonies were closed with a benediction by Rev. D. C. Kelley.

The women's part in this extraordinary achievement deserves record, and one woman in particular, Mrs. T. J. Latham, will be remembered in connection with it while the present generation lives. The United Daughters of the Confederacy will not forget the chorus to her song, "The Forrest Monument," at several conventions. She is a happy combination of amiability and unceasing courage in whatever she may undertake, and, while not a student of nor a stickler for parliamentary law, as presiding officer of Chapter or State organization (she has been also of the general officers) she never neglected her theme, "The Forrest Monument."

Mrs. T. J. Latham.

Her work was not confined to the women in their meetings, but on the highways and aboard railway trains. Proud of the enterprise in hand, she would give men and women the opportunity to contribute. Even before the U.C.V.'s in convention at Memphis in 1901 she made an appeal, asking Veterans to give her what they could spare, and in this way $118 was received, mainly in small coins. A Memphis paper, after mention of this, stated: "This is but one instance of the personal endeavor Mrs. Latham put in the work. All the members of the Sarah Law Chapter feel that Mrs. Latham is deserving of 'the lion's share' of credit for the work done by that Chapter for the Forrest monument, though she herself insists that her work would have been for naught had it not been for the assistance rendered her during the five years by the members of the Sarah Law Chapter.

In its completed beauty, the work of Mr. Niehaus, the sculptor, the monument now stands on the most conspicuous knoll of Forrest Park, a notable adornment, an object of admiration to the inhabitants of the city as well as the stranger within its gates, a new feature of interest in its development and beautification, a source of unbounded pride to all Confederate Veterans, and an inspiration to valor, courage, and patriotism for future generations.[128] — SUMNER ARCHIBALD CUNNINGHAM

TRIBUTE TO FORREST & THE TENNESSEE SOLDIER

☞ Many of my closest and dearest friends and comrades were Tennesseans, and in all that heroic host which marched and bled beneath the Southern banner there were no truer and stauncher soldiers, none braver or more devoted. I was proud then and am prouder now to claim them as my comrades. The service which these men rendered and that done by those who rode with Forrest, and the conduct of those gallant soldiers of the Tennessee Confederate infantry who never in all their history turned back from a stricken field and never looked on one they did not consecrate by acts of heroic courage, all contributed to make yet more famous the name of the "Volunteer" State . . .[129] — JUDGE S. F. WILSON

FORREST'S GUNTOWN VICTORY

☞ June 15, 1864: The greatest fight of the war has just closed, a most splendid victory has been achieved, and that victory has been followed up rapidly and every advantage secured that could be gained therefrom. This battle forms one of the most remarkable cavalry engagements on record, and no one, except an eyewitness, can well conceive of the appearance of the battlefield and the line of pursuit, strewed with wagons, ammunition, arms, accouterments, harness, Yankees dead and alive, artillery, and plunder taken from these thieving marauders on their way southward.

The news of the enemy's movement from Memphis reached Gen. Forrest while on the march with Buford's Division to Middle Tennessee. A countermarch was immediately ordered, and the command reached Tupelo on the 5th instant. This trip having been made over a rough country, entirely destitute of supplies, and a rainy season of several days' duration, placed the horses in a condition that was by no means favorable for rapid marching.

On the 6th we received information that the enemy were moving on Ripley, and a scouting party of the enemy having made a reconnaissance from Ripley toward Rienzi and thence northward to Corinth, it was supposed that the intention of the enemy was to reenforce Sherman; and, preparatory to harassing his advancing columns, our forces were ordered to Baldwyn and thence to Booneville. Col. Rucker's Brigade, which was at Oxford, had been ordered to New Albany and, crossing the Tallahatchie [River], had engaged the enemy, who, however, did not pursue the advantage gained or show any disposition so to do. Reports came in from Ripley that there was no enemy in that place, and, owing to high water, the movements of the enemy were masked from the observation of our scouts. On the evening of the 9th our scouts reported them in camp, six miles from Ripley, and moving southward on the Ripley and Fulton road.

Orders were immediately issued to march southward, obtain their front, and harass them until they reached the prairie country near Okolona, when a general engagement would take place. On the morning of the 10th the column moved forward on the road via Blackland; the Kentucky Brigade, Col. H. B. Lyon, in front; Col. Rucker's Brigade, which had passed us the day before, next; and Col. Bell's Brigade of Tennesseans in the rear. Col. Johnson's Brigade of Brig. Gen. Roddy's cavalry was camped near Guntown. When within two miles of Bryce's Cross Roads, the head of the column was fired into by the advance of the enemy and skirmishing commenced. So rapid had been the enemy's march that no one supposed that he was in force, but that this was only a scouting party. Preparations were at once made to meet any emergency, and Col. Lyon threw forward his brigade into line, deployed skirmishers, and moved forward to feel the strength of the enemy. Col. Rucker was formed on his left.

The enemy was posted near Brice's Cross Roads, between our cavalry and Tupelo, and their intention was to annihilate the cavalry and thus possess themselves of the whole country. His force was near 12,000: twelve regiments of infantry, of which two were negroes, 7,000 strong, with eighteen pieces of artillery; three brigades of cavalry, 5,000 strong; and a light battery of mounted howitzers. Our available force was 3,500 effective men and eight pieces of artillery. Col. Lyon, commanding the brigade, was ordered not to bring on a general engagement, but to move forward and obtain possession of the cross roads and enable our force to get between the enemy and Tupelo. But it was soon evident that the enemy was in force. About 12 m. Gen. Buford reached the ground with our artillery and Bell's Brigade.... The enemy was now moving up its infantry, two and three regiments at a time, pressing them up at a double-quick. Bell's Brigade having been placed in position, one whole line commenced moving forward. The artillery had been placed on a very exposed point in an open field, so as to command the Ripley and Fulton roads, and fired directly toward Brice's House. This fire was very destructive upon the enemy's batteries and upon his columns as they moved up to obtain position.

The fire from our artillery prevented, as did also the nature of the country, the enemy from using his artillery to any advantage or more than a single battery at a time. Now commenced the fight in earnest. As the Yankee regiments were pressed up they were thrown forward and received the steady fire of our gallant soldiers. A steady advance was maintained along our whole line. Our artillery advanced with the line. For three hours the fight raged equal to any infantry fight on record—in fact, it was an infantry fight. Our line moved forward in splendid order, the troops, many of them, now experiencing for the first time the rough shock of a fight, cheering and sending havoc into the exhausted ranks of the enemy. It was near 5 p.m.

On the route to the scene of conflict and after the skirmishing commenced Gen. Buford ordered Col. Barteau's regiment, 2nd Tennessee, to proceed from Carrollville on the road to Ripley, about three miles, and then move over to the road the enemy was on and attack him in the rear or the flank. Col. Barteau moved as directed, got in rear of the enemy, and attacked him vigorously. The news of this attack in the rear was soon carried to the front. Col. Barteau displayed a long line of skirmishers and deceived the enemy. Whipped in front, attacked in rear, they now commenced a retreat worse than Bull Run. Our men pressed forward rapidly, and the enemy, as their remaining regiments came into action, made an effort to stand and check the ardor of our pursuit. But their troops were demoralized; a panic seized them. The threats they had made of capturing Forrest's Cavalry and turning them over to the negroes to be dealt with operated with fearful memory on their minds, and only death was presented to them if they were captured.

Miss May Belle Lyon, Sponsor for Forrest's Cavalry.

A mile from the cross roads our advancing columns commenced passing wagons deserted, caissons left behind, and everything indicating a rout. A mile farther the evidence was more conclusive, and about three miles from the cross roads the majority of their train was left, filled with rations, forage, ammunition, and many of the luxuries of earth. On we moved, the enemy occasionally stopping and returning our fire. About four miles from the cross roads, the rout being complete, our troops were halted and awaited their horses, which were being brought from the rear.

At 10 a.m., the 11th, our troops were in the saddle, and the pursuit commenced. Ten miles from the cross roads, at the crossing of the Hatchee, the remainder of their train, their artillery, ambulances, and wounded were left in great confusion. Onward we pressed them, their cavalry turning to give us a volley once in a while in order to enable their infantry to gain a little rest.

At Ripley they made a stand, which was equal to most cavalry engagements, but they were pushed back in confusion. At Ripley Gen. Forrest, with Bell's Brigade, made a detour to the left to Salem, leaving Gen. Buford to follow the pursuit direct. Gen. Forrest's intention was to reach Salem while they were passing and cut their column in two, and thus capture the main portion of their army. The pursuit not being rapid enough for Gen. Buford, and perceiving that the enemy only had a very small rear guard of cavalry, he determined to charge through this and reach their infantry. Rucker's Brigade was in immediate pursuit, and under instructions from the General he pushed forward, charged on horseback, driving the cavalry back on their infantry, and capturing several hundred. Col. Faulkner's Kentucky Regiment, Maj. Tate commanding, of the 3rd Brigade, was now ordered to the front, and made a most gallant charge, scattering their infantry in all directions. At Ripley we captured two more pieces of artillery. Gen. Buford pursued them to Davis's Mills, about five miles to Lagrange, in person. At that point he sent forward two regiments to Lagrange and returned from the pursuit. We had pursued them this day a distance of fifty-eight miles. Their infantry marched most unprecedentedly, and their officers declared they would all have surrendered but for fear of death. The whole route was strewed with arms, cartridge boxes, bayonets, sabers, their dead, and live Yankees. The truth beggars any description.

The result of this engagement was over five hundred thousand rounds of ammunition, seventeen pieces of artillery, over two hundred wagons, immense stores (quartermaster, commissary, and ordnance), several thousand stands of small arms, and twenty-five hundred prisoners.

Our loss was severe. Many a gallant officer and brave private fell a victim to the deadly bullet, and many a household will be clothed in mourning. Our entire loss was about four hundred and fifty killed and wounded. The division of Gen. Buford immortalized themselves, and

Rucker's Brigade kept even pace throughout. The brigade commanders, Col. H. B. Lyon, of Kentucky, Col. T. H. Bell, of Tennessee, and Col. Rucker, of Tennessee, fairly earned promotion on this gallant field. It is unnecessary to mention the gallantry of Gen. Forrest and his staff. He was ever in the midst of the attacking columns.

To Gen. Buford is due the greatest praise for the quickness of his perception, the rapidity with which he moved, and the masterly manner in which he handled the troops. This officer is one among the most accomplished in the service, and deserves the highest encomium for his conspicuous gallantry on this day. His staff deported themselves, one and all, in a manner that won them a high reputation.

Col. Bell lost two members of his staff, Lieut. Porter and Capt. Bell killed, and two others wounded. Col. Lyon lost one of his staff, Cadet Skinner, wounded.

Officers and men did their duty. The action of the Kentucky Brigade was noted on that day for its steadiness, and, having been in infantry, the other brigades emulated its example and vied to keep pace with it. The 8th Kentucky captured one piece of artillery at Brice's House, the color bearer standing on the piece and holding aloft his flag. This is one of the most gallant, though one of the smallest, regiments in the service. The enemy devastated the whole country through which they passed. Their movement southward and their return formed a strong contrast. The fight from ten o'clock to about 12 m. on the 10th instant was carried on by Col. Lyon's brigade, who had driven the enemy nearly a mile before the other brigades came up. The enemy's loss was about one thousand to twelve hundred killed and some five or six hundred wounded.[130] — UNKNOWN CONFEDERATE SOLDIER (IN GEN. BUFORD'S DIVISION)

EXPLOITS OF COMMODORE FORREST

☛ There was nothing too desperate or daring for the great "wizard of the saddle" to attempt if the shadow of success lay beyond it. One of the most brilliant exploits of his military career was his Johnsonville campaign, where he captured and destroyed millions of dollars' worth of Federal army supplies, including the [Union] steamer *Mazeppa* loaded with stores of all kinds, the [Union] gunboat *Undine*, and the [Union] transport *Venus*. Capt. John W. Morton, who was chief of Forrest's artillery (now Secretary of State for Tennessee), in writing of these exploits to Mr. Julien Gracey, son of Capt. Frank P. Gracey, whose conspicuous gallantry on that occasion won him distinction in Forrest's command, says:

"I was perhaps more cognizant of your gallant father's conduct on that occasion than any one present. I personally conducted the fire on the steamer *Mazeppa*, and commanded the guns in person when the *Undine* and *Venus* were captured. It was by my suggestion that your father, Capt. Gracey, was placed in command of the *Undine* after we captured her. Gen. Forrest ordered me to take command of the gunboat, with a detachment from my different batteries to man her. I protested (mildly, mind you), thanked him for the honor, told him I was not familiar with fighting artillery on water, but that Capt. Gracey, a gallant and efficient officer and familiar with managing a boat, was at Fort Heiman, and suggested that he send for him, which he did, and in less that an hour Gracey reported. The General assigned him to the command of the gunboat, and Gracey and I went aboard. We found that two of her guns had been knocked out of position by our fire. These we readjusted. Capt. Gracey reported her 'seaworthy,' and I reported to Gen. Forrest that his navy was ready to 'move on the enemy.'

Frank P. Gracey.

"With Capt. Gracey in command, Forrest as commodore, and a number of cavalry, we 'cruised' down to Fort Heiman and 'tacked back,' as Gracey said, to Paris Landing. The transport *Venus*, in command of Col. Dawson, accompanied us, and at Fort Heiman took on her 'armament,' consisting of two twenty-pound Parrott guns. My further observation of the 'maneuvering of the fleet' was interrupted here by orders from the General to move with the artillery up the river, keeping as close to the banks as possible, to render assistance in case of a 'naval engagement.' The river makes a considerable bend several miles below Johnsonville, where we could not reach it on account of the roads, made impassable for artillery by the continuous rains and the passage of the cavalry, and the half-starved condition of my artillery horses. Here the *Venus* was abandoned and recaptured, and Capt. Gracey, after fighting seven gunboats, four above and three below, was forced to abandon the boat, and he and his men swam ashore.

"It was in 'fighting his ship,' as related to me by one of his men, that Capt. Gracey performed one of the most heroic actions of the war. He was sorely pressed by gunboats, above and below, shells exploding all around him, and fast knocking the little boat to pieces. The result was inevitable. He saw that he would be compelled to abandon her. He ordered the guns to be charged and the mattresses cut open and pressed into the magazine; he then formed his men in line and ordered them to jump into the river and swim ashore. Waiting until they had reached the bank, he walked back and set fire to the mattresses; then going deliberately to the bow of the boat, where the bursting shells made the heavens lurid, and, waving defiance at the enemy, he jumped into the river and swam ashore. As he was struggling up the river bank the magazine exploded, the guns discharged, and the *Undine* went to the bottom of the Tennessee River. Thus closed 'Commodore' Forrest's brief but brilliant naval career."[131] — SUMNER ARCHIBALD CUNNINGHAM

First page of a letter from Gen. Nathan Bedford Forrest to Gen. Stephen Dill Lee, dated July 1, 1865.

Page two of the above letter in Forrest's hand.

6

1986-1989

REUNION TRIBUTE TO FORREST & HIS CAVALRY

☛ Mr. Chairman, ladies, and old comrades of Forrest Cavalry Corps—survivors of as gallant a body of horsemen as ever bestrode horse, wielded saber, or carried carbine; veterans of a cause as just and sacred as any for which warrior ever "couched lance or drew blade," a cause for which thousands of as noble and gallant souls as ever mustered beneath banners of war yielded up their precious lifeblood; small remnant of one of the grandest armies the world has ever seen, an army of only six hundred thousand souls, which, ill fed and scantily clothed, defied the combined forces of the world and for four tragic years upheld upon their bloody bayonets the forces of a storm-cradled nation: Is it not, fellow-comrades, a glorious honor to have been a member, no matter how humble the rank, of that grand aggregation of patriotic warriors, fighting for homes and firesides, a proud heritage indeed to leave to posterity? Away with the sycophantic cant that we fought for what "we thought to be right"! I for one, fellow comrades, yet hold to the opinion that we fought for what we *knew* to be right [conservatism].

Now among all the corps commands of that grand army there were none the superior and but few, if any, the equal of those who rode with our grand leader, N. B. Forrest, so aptly designated the "Wizard of the Saddle," the greatest cavalry commander doubtless the world has ever produced. History tells us that in the palmy days of ancient Rome, when she as a queen "sat upon her seven hills and from her throne of beauty ruled the world," it was the common boast of her proud citizens that to be a Roman was greater than to be a king. So with us, old comrades, in view of the glorious deeds of our corps in the time that tried men's souls, it should be our proud boast to have been even humble privates in the ranks of Forrest's command.

In view of our record of the past, fellow-comrades, it is eminently proper that we, the survivors of Forrest's command, as an organization should come together annually, as long as life shall last, to greet each other, rehearse valorous deeds done, and otherwise perpetuate the memory of those who have with the immortal Jackson gone before and "crossed over the river to rest under the shade of the trees."[132] — CONFEDERATE GENERAL HENRY A. TYLER

STRAINED RELATIONS BETWEEN FORREST & WHEELER

☛ I am very anxious to know who were the three soldiers that responded to the request of General Forrest when ordered by Gen. Joe Wheeler to take two companies of cavalry and go around the left wing of the Federal army after the capture of Snodgrass Hill. I think it was on Friday. After having gone as far as prudence would permit, General Forrest called for two or three volunteers to climb one of the taller trees to get above the undergrowth and see what the Federals were doing. I was one and would like to know of the other two.

After our report, which was, "General, they are skedaddling," he said, "Come down," and down we came. The sharpshooters were sending balls in thick order, and occasionally a piece of artillery shelled the underbrush. Forrest immediately sent a courier to Wheeler and made request for a thousand men with which to attack the enemy's flank. In my opinion that was the cause of an estrangement between Forrest and Wheeler and caused Forrest to withdraw to West Tennessee.

I have always believed that the first disagreement between Generals Forrest and Wheeler began by the latter's refusal to allow the former the thousand men and to pursue the enemy. Blue bullets came thick and fast till we got out of range of the sharpshooters.[133] — DR. F. A. MOSELEY

REUNION OF GEN. FORREST'S ESCORT & STAFF

☛ Forrest's staff and escort held their annual reunion at Fayetteville, Tenn., September 6, 1906. Doubtless no company in the Army of Tennessee was more widely and favorably known or did more perilous service than Forrest's escort. It was organized in October, 1862, ninety strong, by Capt. Montgomery Little, of Bedford County, Tenn., who was killed at Thompson Station, Tenn., in March, 1863, and who was a warm personal friend of General Forrest before the war, and had been with him after the fall of Fort Donelson. Though often depleted, this company received many recruits, so that it numbered over one hundred men at the surrender at Gainesville, Ala., May 10, 1865. About thirty are still living.

Those present at Fayetteville were Dr. J. B. Cowan, Staff Chief Surgeon; Escort T. C. Little, President; W. L. Shofner, G. W. Foster, Joel Reese, O. W. McKissick, J. H. Pearson, Geo. Davidson, G. W. Enochs, H. T. Childs, E. M. McClure, E. G. Montgomery, and Col. D. C. Kelley, who commanded Forrest's old regiment. The officers elected for next year are: O. W. McKissick, President; J. N. Taylor, Corresponding Secretary; G. L. Cowan, Recording Secretary; Tom Cheairs, Treasurer; T. C. Little, Chaplain.[134] — SUMNER ARCHIBALD CUNNINGHAM

FORREST & WILKES

☛ The first time I ever saw General Forrest was in the gray dawn of the morning of the surrender [of Fort Donelson]. He was sitting on his horse in front of the old cemetery, just above Dover, gathering his boys around him. He saw I was mounted, and called to me and asked if I did not want to go out with him. I told him I did not think I ought to leave my command, but ought to share their fate. He turned with the remark: "All right; I admire your loyalty, but damn your judgment!"

In a short while I saw him at the head of his command passing out of the fort over the Wynn's Ferry road, where but for the incompetency of our generals all the garrison could have gone. What stupid blunders were perpetrated [at the Battle of Fort Donelson] has passed into history.

Again I saw General Forrest in 1872 in the lobby of the Maxwell House [in Nashville, Tenn.]. John C. Brown was then Governor. I was his private secretary, his adjutant general, and general factotum, and he trusted me with everything I could do. John C. Burch had just been appointed Comptroller. The morning papers had announced that the place [position] had been offered to me and I had declined it. General Forrest called me and asked if it was true, and why I did it. I told him it had been offered me by Governor Brown, and I had declined because I thought it to Governor Brown's interest and the best interests of the State that Colonel Burch be appointed.

He shook his finger at me, and said: "Young man, I thought you was a damned fool at Fort Donelson, and I haven't changed my opinion. You are too particular to be a politician."[135] — JUDGE JOHN S. WILKES

SOLDERING "ON THE HORSE" WITH THE GALLANT FORREST

☛ Perhaps a few words about General Forrest's West Tennessee campaign in the winter of 1862 and the capture of [the famed Yankee atheist] Col. Robert G. Ingersoll would be of interest . . . .

The incidents attending these events occurred forty-four years ago, and are now recounted without data. I was a boy at the time, just past my fourteenth birthday, and had not then joined the army; but was on a runaway from home, with a few choice associates for that purpose, trying to get South through the Federal lines, being closely followed by my father, who, while in perfect accord with the Southern cause, objected to my entering its army on account of youth.

Thus on the 18th of December, 1862, we were caught almost in the very jaws of the two hostile forces. Having quit the main road for a few miles to avoid a collision with a Federal cavalry column moving southward, upon coming into the road again we gladly, though unexpectedly, met General Forrest's advance, composed of four companies of Russell's 4th Alabama Cavalry, commanded by Capt. Frank B. Gurley, then near Lexington, in West Tennessee, and which in a very few minutes thereafter encountered the 3rd Battalion of the 5th Ohio Cavalry, some three hundred strong, commanded by Capt. James C. Harrison, which command Captain Gurley charged and drove rearward at a furious gait until the eastern limits of Lexington were reached, making many captures. There strong epaulements had been hastily erected for the Federal artillery, with dismounted cavalry on each flank and in support.

Frank B. Gurley.

Here Captain Gurley formed for battle and paused for alignment, at which juncture General Forrest arrived with the main body of his command, and, with an eye and judgment equal to any emergency, ordered the position on the Federal left carried, which order was promptly and gallantly executed by his ever-willing and resolute Tennesseans and with their characteristic impetuosity and dash, which nothing in blue withstood that day.

I sat upon my horse and stared with boyish wonderment at what appeared an apparition, the most inspiring personage my eyes had ever beheld. It was General Forrest superbly mounted upon a spirited animal, which seemed to catch the inspiration of its master as he led his battalions by our position rightward toward the Federal left; and soon we heard heavy firing in that direction, accompanied by the Rebel yell, which transmitted the result to those sturdy soldiers where we were, and they in turn announced its significance to us. At that moment Captain Gurley ordered our line forward, which, coming within the zone of the Federal artillery fire, was quickly dismounted and advanced in splendid style.

The 7th Tennessee Federal Cavalry, commanded by [Yankee] Lieut. Col. Isaac R. Hawkins, occupied the Federal left, in what was considered a strong position; but when the Tennessee Confederates advanced toward them, their line vanished like vapor, and thus the position occupied by Colonel Ingersoll with the 11th Illinois Cavalry, dismounted, was flanked and enfiladed, and he and most of his officers and men captured, together with all his artillery, small arms, and ammunition.

The Federal artillerists, commanded by Lieut. John W. H. McGuire, stood stoutly by their guns, alternating with shrapnel and canister; but so close was Gurley's line upon them that their missiles flew harmlessly overhead, and not until close quarters were reached did Gurley's line sustain any casualties, where, after a hand-to-hand encounter and an almost superhuman defense of their guns, the Federal artillerists yielded to numerical superiority, giving up their guns, and those not killed became prisoners. Lieutenant McGuire, after being exchanged, became captain of his battery.

The artillery captured here consisted of two three-inch steel Rodman guns, belonging to Capt. Merideth H. Kidd's 14th Indiana Battery, and formed the nucleus for Morton's Battery, and used thence and effectively by General Forrest until the end in 1865.

Colonel Ingersoll was a brave and skillful officer; and had the Tennessee Federals stood well to their colors, General Forrest might have been defeated, for his armament was very ineffective, being a mixture of flintlock muskets, double-barrel shotguns, and Derringer pistols, and supplied with only a few rounds of ammunition. He was therefore in poor condition to encounter such formidable equipment as Ingersoll's men possessed.

Colonel Hawkins was in no manner responsible for the bad conduct of his regiment on this or any other occasion. He was a brave, conscientious, though indulgent officer, and no truer man to his government or to his friends ever donned the Federal uniform.

Colonel Ingersoll was captured by Capt. Frank B. Gurley, of the 4th Alabama Cavalry, who, when commanded by Captain Gurley to surrender, said rather nonchalantly: "Is this your Southern Confederacy for which I have so diligently searched?" Being assured that it was,

Colonel Ingersoll replied somewhat facetiously: "Then I am your guest until the wheels of the great Cartel are put in motion." He then added: "Here are the Illinoisans; the [Union] Tennesseans have ingloriously fled."

Never in all General Forrest's captures—and they were many—did he make such timely acquisitions in war material as here or capture a foe possessed of so much wit and humor. Already aware of the aggregated number of Federal troops stationed at different points in West Tennessee and the names of the respective commanders, and being anxious to know whose command he had just encountered, General Forrest accosted Colonel Ingersoll soon after the latter's capture with the inquiry as to whose command he belonged, and was promptly answered: "To Colonel Ingersoll's, if I was not the man myself." General Forrest knew of no such command, and, being satisfied that it was only a detachment, was extremely anxious to strike the other portion at once before its commander heard of the discomfiture of the Ingersoll detachment; so he asked Colonel Ingersoll from where he came, to which the wily Colonel replied: "From everywhere but here, and I hope to be from here just as soon as I can secure your genial approbation to that effect." General Forrest greatly enjoyed such an exhibition of humor, and thereupon released Colonel Ingersoll temporarily on his verbal parole, which the Colonel faithfully observed.

My father now put in his appearance, which had a decided tendency to calm my military aspirations, for I was relieved in short order of what soldier's regalia I had become possessed of, and, like a peacock with its tail feathers plucked, started back to my "Old Kentucky Home" somewhat crestfallen, but resolved to again give the credulous old gentleman the slip.

General Forrest had on this expedition little less than two thousand men, composed of the following Tennessee cavalry organizations: Starnes's 4th, Dibrell's 8th, Biffle's 9th, and Russell's 4th Alabama Cavalry, and two companies of Woodward's 2nd Kentucky Cavalry, with Freeman's Tennessee Battery of four guns, with which was the gallant young Lieut. John W. Morton, who became successively captain of Morton's Battery and chief of Forrest's Artillery, and participated with distinguished gallantry and admiration of management of the artillery arm of Forrest's Cavalry in all the battles and campaigns of which that command formed the whole or a part except at Paducah, Ky., where only the Hudson (Miss.) Battery, Capt. Edwin S. Walton, participated.

Some ten days later this force was augmented by the arrival of Nappier's and Cox's Tennessee Battalions of Partisan Rangers, some two hundred and fifty men each, which General Forrest consolidated, forming the 10th Tennessee Cavalry. Col. Thomas Alonzo Nappier, who a few days later fell, an immolation to the Southern cause, at Parker's Crossroads while gallantly leading his regiment to a charge in the very face of enfilading Federal fire of musketry and artillery—a gallant but unnecessary sacrifice and unauthorized by General Forrest.

It was here that an old lady who chanced to live in that vicinity lost her ash hopper, as she said, by the unmitigated carelessness of one "Mr. Forrest and his hoss critters in forming a streak of fight" in her back yard, which resulted in the utter demolition of her only ash hopper and garden fence. She never forgave the General for this carelessness.

General Forrest was absent from the army under General Bragg on this expedition less than thirty days, subsisting entirely on captures from the Federal commissariat. He had crossed the Tennessee River going and coming, which was almost bank full, without adequate means of ferriage, in midwinter and almost in the presence of a hostile Federal force numerically much his superior and without loss or hindrance. He penetrated West Tennessee, then swarming with Federals perchance twenty times his numbers, his advance going as far north as Moscow, Ky., puncturing the Federal garrison at all intermediate points, with his command continually under fire. He fought two pitched battles, in both of which he was successful, and did immense damage to General Grant's communications by rail, causing frantic consternation throughout his department and the retention of several thousand Federal soldiers in West Tennessee, who otherwise would have gone to reenforce Rosecrans, then confronting Bragg in front of Murfreesboro.

Mrs. R. E. Irwin, Matron of Honor for Forrest's Cavalry, Atlanta Reunion.

Returning, his command was almost constantly in battle formation: and frequently, when his column was in motion and his advance warmly engaged with the enemy in front, another column of the enemy approaching from a different direction was at the same time hammering vigorously at his rear, and often extrication seemed impossible. Notwithstanding these environments and that no less than a half dozen different Federal columns, each of which greatly outnumbered him, were seeking his annihilation, he recrossed the Tennessee River with more men and artillery than when he entered West Tennessee, some twenty days before, gestant with an impedimenta of some seventy-five wagons laden with valuable captures of hospital and medical supplies, nearly all of which he succeeded in carrying safely through to the Confederate army, and to the great joy of General Bragg, who in a general order complimented and characterized the expedition as the most brilliant cavalry achievement of the war, a mark of appreciation manifestly due that redoubtable cavalryman.

It was under such gallant and magnificent leadership that Forrest's Cavalry learned to soldier "On the Horse" and to write the brilliant story of his campaigns across the page of the world's history, endowing him with the title, the "Wizard of the Saddle," and as an intrepid champion.[136]
— CONFEDERATE COLONEL V. Y. COOK

FORREST'S FIRST CAVALRY FIGHT

☛ In September, 1861, David and John Prewitt and I left Perryville, Ky., after Church on Sunday night and rode to and through Bloomfield to the home of Mr. William Huston, about five miles south from Bloomfield, where we were fed and slept through the day. After supper we fell in with an old fox hunter, who was piloting Hon. R. W. Wooley, and started for Dixie. After several days and nights of hard riding and dodging the home guards, we arrived at Munfordsville, then inside Dixie's line. From there the two Prewitts and I rode over to Bowling Green, where we got transported to Memphis. There we enlisted in Capt. Dave Logan's company of Forrest's Regiment. About ten days afterwards we were ordered into Kentucky.

After a short stop at Fort Donelson, we moved on to Hopkinsville, Ky., and went into winter quarters. There we began scouting the country, and did it thoroughly from Canton, on the Cumberland, to Morganfield, back to Eddyville, on the Ohio, to Princeton, back to camp. We were not in camp many days at a time, just enough to rest the horses, when we would be off on another scout.

During Christmas week we started on a scout. The weather was very cold, with snow on ground, and often we suffered severely. One night some of us boys got in a shuck pen and buried ourselves in the shucks and passed a comfortable night. After almost two days of marching, Colonel Forrest took one half of the command and went off a side road, leaving Major Kelley to march on to Greenville with the rest. We had about three hundred men on this scout. On the second night Major Kelley went into camp about one half mile north of Greenville, where the good people sent out an invitation to supper.

They gave us a real royal feast at the courthouse. Just as we were finishing supper Colonel [James W.] Starnes rode up and reported a Yankee scouting party out. Major Kelley took us back to camp. He sent Lieutenant Cowan out with twelve men as pickets to picket the road. We went about three miles, when our road ran into another. We halted here and prepared for a fight.

It was so cold that it seemed as if we would freeze, so we went to work and tore out about a hundred panels of fence to our rear and came up with them and built a big, strong fence across our road and staked and ridered it and braced it. Then day began to break. We mounted our horses and rode back to camp about sunrise. We fed our horses and lay down by a good fire to sleep, when "Boots and Saddles" was blown. O, Lordy! No sleep all night and no breakfast. Colonel Forrest came in just as we got covered up. We got up and saddled, mounted our horses, and took up our line of march over the same road we had picketed all night before. When we came to our base of the night before, we received information that the Yankees were a mile or two ahead of us. Colonel Forrest called a halt and said: "Now, boys, keep quiet." He then ordered the trot march.

We rode probably a mile or two when a halt was called. We all tightened our saddle girths. Colonel Forrest spoke to the bugler: "Blow the charge, Isham." With that, we raised the yell and away we went. The ground had begun to thaw by this time, and we were soon covered with mud from head to foot. Our company was in the rear, and our boys began cursing the two companies ahead of us, whom we thought were riding too slow, and threatened to ride over them. Colonel Starnes was riding with us. He told Lieutenant Cowan to pass them with his men right and left, which we did, reaching the open woods where Forrest had just engaged the Yankees. We went in red-hot, and in about ten minutes we had them going. We chased them through Sacramento and about two miles beyond, when a halt was called. We killed over twenty and captured about twenty-five without the loss of a man.[137] — H. T. GRAY

FORREST WITH HOOD AFTER NASHVILLE

☛ [Shortly after December 16, 1864:] As we were moving along the pike near Columbia [Tenn.], General Hood rode up to our brigade. He seemed in nowise disconcerted by the misfortune that had befallen his army. [The Confederate Army of Tennessee had been badly beaten at Nashville just days before.] He asked my what my command was. I told him Strahl's Brigade. He then said he wished to form a reserved infantry force, and consolidated eight old brigades under Palmer, Featherston, Field, and Reynolds, with an effective total of 1,940 men, under Walthall, to report to Forrest in covering the retreat to the Tennessee River. He asked me if the brigade would volunteer for that service. I replied: "We are soldiers, General." He then said: "You will report to Colonel Field. I know no soldiers upon whom I can rely with greater confidence that the work will be done well than you Tennesseans." He then ordered those without shoes to go to the wagon train. I recall, however, that some soldiers without shoes remained with the reserve.

An incident here illustrates the freedom of speech between the men and their officers. General Hood, upon being asked when he would give the boys a furlough, said, "After we cross the Tennessee," adding: "The cards have been fairly dealt, for I cut them and dealt them myself, and the Yankees have beat us in the game." Thereupon a soldier of the 19th Tennessee said: "Yes, General, but they were badly shuffled." This, save the yells of comrades in appreciation of the comment, closed the matter, and the General rode off.

Otho French Strahl.

A snowstorm came up and it turned very cold. Here Col. C. W. Heiskell took command of the brigade. We went into bivouac on the north side of the pike. I had just lain down in the open before a good log fire at eleven o'clock when an orderly from Colonel Field summoned me to his quarters. Upon my reporting, he said: "I have two messages for you. You will take two hundred men, and at four o'clock to-morrow morning relieve the soldiers guarding the crossings of Duck River, from the old mill above to the fort below. This is under an order from General Forrest. The other is more agreeable. I wish you to share that pot of coffee with me." I did so; it was most refreshing.

I returned to bivouac, went to sleep, and about 3:30 in the morning I started with two hundred men to relieve the command guarding Duck River. It was bitterly cold. Our boys, without notice to me, but of which I had knowledge, made an agreement with the Federal soldiers not to fire without notice; so no firing took place between them that day. Some negroes belonging to the Federal command started to kill some sheep just across Duck River, and our boys fired on them, which caused a shout of "All right!" from the enemy.

We had had up to that time nothing to eat that day. A young lady whom I knew in Memphis was then living in Columbia. I wrote her a note on a small piece of paper to send me some cold victuals. In about forty minutes a servant came with a large waiter [tray] bearing us a fine dinner. I placed it on a table in the old house in which I had my quarters and called the lieutenant, sergeant, and corporal who were with me, and we enjoyed it as soldiers without rations could.

At 9 a.m. the next day my command was relieved by Maj. William E. Estes, a companion and friend of my boyhood, who came in command of two Texas regiments, and I ordered my men to report to their respective regiments. The Federals found that some of our cavalry pickets had gone into a cabin on our side some distance above the old mill, and immediately shoved a pontoon bridge across Duck River and crossed. This made Forrest furious. He at once sent J. P. Young (a boy then, but now a circuit judge at Memphis) to tell Armstrong to come to him at once with his brigade. He rode for six miles against the northwest wind; and when he reached Armstrong's quarters, he was so nearly frozen that he could not get off his horse. They carried him into the house, and he managed to say: "Boots and saddles." After thawing, he delivered the message to General Armstrong, who, with his men who were already mounted, dashed off with Young to meet Forrest. The Federal officer, with his magnificently furnished command, was endeavoring to break Forrest's rear line.

As we approached Pulaski I received an order from General Walthall near sundown to place some guards across the road where the two ridges approached each other near the town. A severe fight was going on about two miles in the rear; Armstrong was engaging them. An officer on horseback dashed up, and the guard would not let him pass, in compliance with my orders that none but wounded soldiers or men with a pass from Forrest should pass. He was neither. He asked the guard under whose command he was. He pointed him to the sergeant. He rushed up to him on his horse and said: "What are you men stopping me for? I am on Forrest's staff, and don't have to carry a pass." The sergeant was obdurate, and he referred him to me. He met with the same answer, when he said: "I will go, anyhow." I said to the sergeant: "Shoot him if he does." Thinking that the sergeant would do it, the man rode back across the pike, saying he would report him to General Forrest. It was after sunset, and soon General Forrest and his subordinate officers and staff rode up. To my surprise, he dashed up to Forrest and said to him: "That officer won't let me pass." Forrest, turning to me said, "Damn him, shoot him," and the officer rode hurriedly back to his own command.

That night we bivouacked near Pulaski. The next day, Christmas, we reached Anthony's Hill, seven miles south of Pulaski. I had dismounted and was standing near my command. The men were resting, and Forrest rode up. He was, as usual, quiet, mild, and self-possessed. He likewise dismounted. While he engaged with me in conversation a straggler rode up. He [Forrest] pointed to a sapling about one hundred and fifty yards distant and ordered him to take his position there and remain there until he came. In like manner another and another, until some thirty odd [men] were ordered to take position by the sapling. He then told me that the Yankees were coming, that he was going to tell them so, and that the man would be shot who turned his back on them, adding that he would put a line of infantry behind them to do it. In about an hour the fight, which was then imminent, came on, and the shots of the pickets along the line announced its coming. The fight took place, and the well-equipped Federal command gave way, and the reserve force captured a splendid piece of artillery and the United States flag; and as they passed through our lines with them, it caused great, good cheer.

The following story from that field is related by Hon. J. P. Young, mentioned previously, who was with Forrest:

William Hicks "Red" Jackson.

"During the battle, when General Forrest was returning from the sortie made with his infantry, and which proved so successful, he found a group of officers in the old orchard at his field headquarters. He was explaining to them with great glee the capture of two brass Napoleons by the infantry in charge. The guns had just been brought up on the hill. At this juncture his eye happened to observe a section of a battery retiring from the crest of the ridge at the infantry line. Instantly his brow became clouded, and he cried out impatiently to the officer in charge of the section: "Where are you going? Who ordered you away from there?" General [William Hicks "Red"] Jackson, who was standing by, replied: "I ordered him away, General. The guns were unsupported and liable to capture." Forrest instantly replied in great wrath as he rode toward the gun: "What did you do that for, Jackson? I put the guns out there. That's always the way. I can't do a thing but that there's forty ordering around me."

Gen. George H. Thomas, U.S.A., says in *United States Record*: "The enemy, with something of his former boldness, sallied from his breastworks and drove back Harrison's skirmishers, capturing and carrying off one gun belonging to Battery I, 4th United States Artillery, which was not recovered by us, notwithstanding the ground lost was almost immediately regained."

General Forrest, C.S.A., says in the same volume: "Seven miles from Pulaski I took position on King's [properly Anthony's] Hill, and, awaiting the advance of the enemy, repulsed him with a loss of one hundred and fifty killed and wounded, besides capturing many prisoners and one piece of artillery. The enemy made no further demonstrations during that day. I called my command at Sugar Creek, where it encamped during the night."

Members of the N. B. Forrest Camp, U.C.V. Louisville Reunion.

About eighteen miles south of Sugar Creek we formed a line of battle, and the Tennesseans, under Field, and the Arkansans and Texans, under Reynolds, were on the front line. The Federal officer was approaching with his forces. Forrest called Reynolds, Field, and the regimental officers, including Colonel Heiskell and myself, together on a little knoll in front of our line and said: "The Yankees are coming. We are going to have a fight; and when the infantry break their lines, I'll throw Ross's Cavalry on them." Field, a wiry, brave soldier, misunderstanding Forrest, with a stutter in his speech said: "We have got no such infantry, General. They will not break our lines." Forrest, laughing, said: "I don't mean when they break our lines, but when we break theirs." Fields instantly said, "That's the kind of infantry we have, General," which created a big laugh all around.

Sure enough, the enemy soon appeared; and after a short, decisive fight, we broke their line, and Ross, with his Texans, dashed after them and put them to rout. Colonel Heiskell captured a fine saddle on the field. Here occurred an amusing little incident. Just before the engagement of our command, while the fight was hot on our right and left, our boys were ordered to hold their fire until the enemy's line came above the knoll in our front. Their bugler appeared on the top of the ridge and blew his bugle for a charge. A [Confederate] soldier stationed in the line near James E. Beasley, A.A.G., asked permission of him to shoot the Yank. He was insistent on this, but he was refused the privilege. The bugler appeared the second time and repeated his effort for a charge, and each time the adjutant general was asked to let him shoot. Just at this juncture the order was given our line to advance, and quickly they went over the slight breastwork, and soon were busily engaged with advancing Federals, which ended their pursuit.

General Beauregard says of the retreat: "Untoward and calamitous as were the issues of this campaign, never in the course of this war have the best qualities of our soldiery been more conspicuously shown; never more enthusiasm evinced than when our troops once more crossed the Tennessee River; never greater fortitude and uncomplaining devotion than were displayed on the retreat from Nashville to Tupelo; never greater gallantry than that which was so general at Franklin. The heroic dead of that campaign will ever be recollected with honor by their countrymen, and the survivors have the proud consolation that no share of the disaster can be laid to them, who have so worthily served their country and have stood by their colors even to the last dark hours of the republic."

Another incident occurred just before the Sugar Creek fight. General Forrest told the infantry soldiers that when the Yanks were put to flight every infantry soldier that captured a horse might ride it; and the boys believed it, and did capture several. Mounted on their steeds, they rode toward the Tennessee River with much glee. Arriving at the river, however, they found a guard at the pontoon bridge, who accosted them with: "What command do you belong to?" Our boys, proud of their command, promptly replied: "Cheatham's Division." Then came the woeful order: "Get down off that horse," and they had to do it, as it appeared that the cavalry needed all the horses; but that fact did not keep the boys from criticising the act all the same. Thus closed the disastrous campaign in Tennessee.

The splendid assault, not surpassed during the war, upon the works at Franklin, so well prepared and so obstinately defended, showed the character of this remarkable body of men under Hood. If every soldier saw and comprehended the situation before Nashville on December 16, 1864, the army, if obedient to orders, perhaps could not have eluded the grasp of Thomas to better purpose than it did. It was in the lion's mouth. Its spirits were not broken in getting out. The covering of the retreat by Forrest was as unmistakably well done as the courage of the soldiery was determined and superb. Whenever a point of danger presented itself, there instantly appeared on the scene the ever-watchful Forrest. It was a military masterpiece.

In that trying hour a compact body obeyed his orders; his foes, fully equipped, bore the ordeal well, and staggered before the determined few who stood in their pathway. Forrest was present and directed every movement, and successfully covered the retreat. All the generals who figured in that campaign save two or three are gone. A few of that rear guard are now bringing up the rear guard and nearing the approach to another river [that is, death]. They did their duty well in that difficult period under adverse circumstances. May we not hope that they too may deserve for their fidelity to duty in the discharge of life's demands a commendation equally as grand as that with which [Union General] Thomas spoke of them when he used these remarkable words: "The rearguard, however, was undaunted and firm, and did its work bravely to the last!"[138] — CONFEDERATE COLONEL LUKE W. FINLAY

PROPOSED FORREST STATUE, ROME, GEORGIA, 1907

☛ The N. B. Forrest Chapter, U.D.C, of Rome, Ga., has in hand a movement to erect a monument there in honor of Gen. N. B. Forrest. The monument will be of granite, twenty-five feet with ten feet base; all ornamentation will be symbolic of the cavalry arm of the service. Surmounting the granite will be a figure of pure Italian marble (made in Italy) facsimile of General Forrest in his height of six feet, two inches. This small Chapter of only thirty-four members has already a neat sum in the treasury for this purpose, and expects to secure the balance needed with little trouble. Any of General Forrest's command who desire to contribute to this monument fund can send it to Miss Mattie B. Sheibley, President N. B. Forrest Chapter, Rome, Ga.[139] — SUMNER ARCHIBALD CUNNINGHAM

THE DARING OF FORREST'S MEN

☛ In the latter part of March, 1865—when the War between the States was on the verge of collapse, when General Grant had closed in on Richmond, when Sherman was burning his way through our homes, when Hood had been driven out of Tennessee, and when Gen. N. B.

Forrest, with about three thousand men, was camped at West Point, Miss.—a feat of dash and dare occurred which showed the mettle of his men.

Ben Brown, of Company L, 3rd Kentucky (now dead), and Tom J. Milner, of Company I, 12th Kentucky (now a leading physician at Greenville, Tex.), having failed to secure fresh horses at their homes in Kentucky, as ordered to do by their officers, came back into Mississippi and forced some farmers to give them some good horses for their broken-down ones. This would have been all right and no crime in Kentucky, simply a war necessity; but not so in Mississippi. Our boys needed those horses in defending Mississippi against the Federal invaders. Ben and Tom were followed, arrested, and put into the guardhouse by some of Forrest's Mississippi Cavalry and charged with stealing.

This [Confederate] prison was very close to Forrest's headquarters, was surrounded by many regiments of soldiers, companies of scouts, field artillery, etc., and was guarded by thirty soldiers, who kept about twenty prisoners in an upper room, with a stairway on the outside. Four guards stood at the foot of these steps, two at the top, and twenty-four were in reserve in the lower story, with double doors open at the stairway. Our Kentucky troops, Buford's Brigade, were camped some nine miles northeast, and pickets guarded every road.

Our prison comrades wrote to us and told us the whole story. We, through our officers, who freely sympathized with them, tried hard to get them released, but utterly failed. Ben and Tom were good, true soldiers; therefore fourteen veterans—namely, Add Brown, John Bushart, Bob Bushart, Newt Bushart, Rufus Johnson (all dead), Bill Murphy, Sam Stone, George Strather, John Smith, James H. Saunders, Don Singletary, Jap Nall, Mike Ward, W. P. Butler—hastily volunteered to go to the release of our comrades at any hazard.

After a hasty caucus, John Bushart and Don Singletary were sent to the prison to see the situation, warn our comrades of our intentions, and make every arrangement for our move that night at 11 p.m. After going into the prison and talking with Ben and Tom, comrades Bushart and Singletary took in the lay of troops, Forrest's quarters, batteries, etc., and then went back toward camp, some five miles, and met their comrades. This squad of four reached West Point in due time, and rode in between a fence and a small clump of hazel bushes within fifty yards of the prison and Forrest's headquarters. Add Brown and John Smith held all horses. John Bushart and Jap Nall took charge of a small cabin of jolly folks, who seemed to be dancing, and the rest of the men went quickly in the darkness of the night to the prison, surprising and capturing the guards on post. Each one of the rescuers was armed with two revolvers, and ready for war, if war must come. We knew our business. But little was said. It took us perhaps three minutes. The reserve guards were aroused, surprised, and confused; but they caught up their guns, and we had a hand-to-hand encounter, and barely escaped war to the finish. One shot or casualty would have meant death and destruction for many.

One of our men ordered them to be quiet and no harm would occur, and they obeyed. In the meantime James H. Saunders and Bill Murphy had secured Ben and Tom, and had warned the guards that we were taking one of their men along, and would kill him if they made an alarm; but had not taken either of their men. They were afraid to alarm until they called their roll and found no one missing. So our tactics worked to perfection. Every one was at his best and acted well his part. We escaped with our comrades, flanked all pickets, got into camp, cleaned the mud off our horses, hid our two comrades, and lay down just before a courier from Forrest's quarter dashed up and ordered roll call and absentees noted.

Capt. J. E. Morris (now Dr. Morris, of Madisonville, Tex.) was happy that all were present. But alas! Our greatest trouble was yet to come. We had committed mutiny, and the penalty was death.

The next morning Gen. B. H. Lyon had Companies L, 3rd Kentucky, and I, 12th Kentucky, arrested and put in the very prison we raided the night before; and the day following Generals Forrest, Lyon, and Jackson sat as a court of inquiry to find out the leaders or men who were guilty; but we were up to our business, and played a little tactics. We held a council and agreed that in this court we were not to know or tell anything on each other. We were to know nothing about our comrades, to forget it all, but to tell whatever we wanted to about ourselves except the truth of our trips. This worked well; we outgeneraled the generals, and all were released except Bob and John Bushart and John Beard. Yet the generals got no proof against them. A little later Captain Morris assisted in getting these released and exonerated. Ben Brown (now dead) and T. J. Milner (now a leading physician at Greenville, Tex.) were hid out near our camp and cared for.

General Forrest soon moved for a raid. We were on the scout when the war closed, and made our way home without ever being paroled.

In Memphis, Tenn., soon after the war, First Lieut. Wiley Bushart talked over the above facts with General Forrest; and when the General learned that fourteen men had done this feat and outwitted his court, he said: "Lieutenant Bushart, that was the only time I was ever outgeneraled; and if ever I go into war again, I want every one of those men as my staff officers or couriers."

In 1906 (Capt.) Dr. Morris, of Madisonville, Tex., wrote to this scribe concerning this West Point raid in part as follows: "I am free to state that you were a brave, good, gallant soldier, and a gentleman possessing the highest type of manhood. The release of Ben Brown and Tom Milner (now Dr. Milner, of Greenville, Tex.) from the West Point Prison was, in my opinion, an honorable, manly, and valorous deed. I indorsed it. I was at Meridian, Miss., when Ben Brown was recaptured and brought there and thrown in the stockade in irons. In the meantime three of the Bushart boys were sent there by General Forrest on suspicion. We succeeded in freeing Ben Brown from cuffs and turning him loose; and as there were no charges against the Bushart boys, I demanded of the provost marshal their trial or release. He turned them over to me, and we returned to camp. Not only our regimental and brigade officers commended the raid, but, you remember, General Forrest himself after the surrender complimented the boys who were engaged on their bravery. You all were exonerated. Ben and Tom had obeyed orders in obtaining fresh horses. Your chivalry should go down in history among the [most] brilliant of our victories. You fought a good fight."[140] — SUMNER ARCHIBALD CUNNINGHAM

THE FORTUNES OF A BOY UNDER FORREST

☛ The journey of Jacob with his son to Mount Moriah was not more sacrificial in aim than that of William Metcalfe, of Lincoln County [Tennessee], who in the autumn of 1862 traveled with his son, James Martin Metcalfe, to Lavergne, there to bind him upon Bedford Forrest's fiery altar of war.

Nathan Bedford Forrest.

Yet widely different was the spirit in which the victim went to be offered up for his country. To the nineteen-year-old youth, whose small stature and thin frame would have passed him for three years younger, it was a day of exultant pride. It was an hour of desire fulfilled, and more. For truly he could not have hoped to reach Lavergne as he did when Forrest's command was deployed in line of battle awaiting an immediate attack from the Yankees. Rare luck for a boy on his first day out as a soldier! Here was a fight ready to hand. At once he was enlisted and became part of the line as a driver in Freeman's Battery. This farmer boy, at ease on his horse (one of the swing team), was elated with eager courage and high resolve. He had been lifted at a bound from the commonplace into a life wherein great deeds are as natural as breathing. He was to act a man's part with men. The hour passed, however, and the enemy did not appear. Dark came, and no Yankee was in sight. For the time the chance of conflict seemed over. Yet, as nothing is certain in war, the father lay all night awake, anxious; and the seasoned cavalrymen and artillerists slept but lightly on their arms, while the inexperienced recruit, with no worse feeling than chagrin, fell into quiet slumber that lasted until morning.

At dawn his sense of disappointment had hardly come back with waking when brisk orders came hurtling along the line, and presently, amid clatter of swords, jingle of spurs, shouts of command, and the rattle of gun carriages, the whole force was in motion. Off to the southwestward on a long, forced march, they went to sweep through Columbia and beyond into the dreary stretches of the "Barrens" of Lawrence and Wayne Counties, whence they turned westward to the Tennessee River at Clifton and across it in flatboats as quickly as might be, and still on into West Tennessee, led by the "Wizard of the Saddle" so swiftly that no Union spy could locate them, no Federal force forestall them until they reached their quarry at Lexington. This was Forrest's way, and the boy liked it. War under Forrest was every whit as stirring as had been pictured in his daydreams. Nothing could be finer than the dash into Lexington, followed by the short, sharp fight and the capture of an Indiana regiment. Unfortunately, though, Hawkins's Federal regiment of [Unionized] Tennesseans made good their escape. The colonel of the captured 11th Illinois proved to be the since renowned [atheist] Robert G. Ingersoll.

"Where are you from?" Forrest demanded of him.

"From almost everywhere but here, and with your consent I will be from here before long," said Ingersoll with dry humor.

"Are these all of your men?" asked Forrest impatiently.

"Yes, all of the Illinoisans," replied Ingersoll, adding after a pause: "All the Tennesseans ran away."

If Forrest saw the joke [actually, an insult], he did not take time from his business of war to smile. His next move was to whirl his men off toward Jackson. But when the troopers, with their flying artillery, approached that place, they found it too well fortified to attack, and they turned aside to swoop down upon Trenton. They shelled the fortified depot building, stormed the intrenchments, and took the town.

In Trenton they captured large army stores of clothing, provisions, arms, etc., which Forrest ordered to be burned after allowing the men to supply themselves with such part of them as they needed. In the scramble that followed young Metcalfe seized a pair of new boots. His feeling of prowess in wresting them from the enemy was not lessened by the ill luck that one was a [size] six and the other a [size] seven.

From Trenton Forrest struck out for Union City in his hunt for weak or unguarded parties of the enemy. On his way he destroyed stockades, tore up railroads, and injured the enemy in every possible way. Yet his movements, however dashing, were not without caution. To avoid the large Federal forces that were closing in on every side of his band of raiders, he marched at night across country, through prohibitive swamps, and over almost impassable roads. At sunrise near Parker's Crossroads they again caught sight of the bluecoats, gave chase, and drove them back to the crossroads, where a stand was made and a brisk fight took place.

The Federals were losing ground. Many fell. Among them was an officer whose valise [a small traveling bag] came temptingly to the hand of young Jim Metcalfe. With the spirit of war and reprisal upon him, he was bearing it off when an older comrade rebuked him, saying: "You may be in the same fix as that dead Yankee before night. Forrest is going to get the worst licking a soldier ever got."

But for the slur on his commander the boy might have accepted the reproof. But to allow any one to predict that the invincible Forrest would be whipped? Impossible! And the boy gave the older man the lie, then joined in the gallant attack which soon brought out a white flag from the Federals. The order to "cease firing" came from the Confederate officers, and the day seemed won.

Forrest's maneuvers had thrown a body of cavalry in rear of the enemy. Others of his troops were flanking them. They could do nothing but surrender, being surrounded.

At this crisis a sudden change took place. Heavy columns of [Union] infantry, supported by cavalry, were seen coming rapidly in Forrest's rear. It was he who was hemmed in. The trapper was trapped. To cut his way out seemed hopeless, but it must be done. It was Forrest's way. Part of his forces, obeying his call to come on, pressed through a weak place in the enemy's line and out to safety. The artillery, accustomed as they were under the influence of Forrest's spirit to making a charge as though they were cavalry, dashed after him, and some got through. The cannon on which Jim Metcalfe was a driver bounded forward to follow with the rest. But the gap closed in their faces, and at close range a volley was fired into the gunners. The two drivers in front of Metcalfe were shot down. He turned to ask the man behind him what he must do at the instant that that man also went down. The riderless horses plunged madly. Turning squarely around, they tore down the blue ranks, making a running target for the Federal firing line.

At the first volley Metcalfe's horse reared. The girth broke as he came down, and the rider was thrown under the hoofs of the rear horse and trampled. One iron shoe pounded his chest and another his arm before the cannon wheels rolled over his body, crushing the breast bones and pressing out the breath. When the boy regained consciousness, a Yankee soldier was standing over him cursing him and saying: "I have a notion to stamp the life out of you." At that moment a Federal officer came forward and ordered the soldier to be off. Then, stooping tenderly to the wounded boy, he gave him a drink from his canteen, unstrapped it from his own neck, put it over the shoulder of his fallen enemy, and offered him a piece of corn bread. "No," said the boy feebly, "I'll never need anything of that sort any more." "O," said his friend of the other side, "don't give up. You are worth ten dead men yet. But you ought never to have been here at all"; and, glancing at the boy's slight form, added feelingly, "You ought to be at home with your mother." As he moved off he said: "When I get through with this thing, I'm coming back to look after you."

Miss Rose E. Dickinson, Sponsor for Forrest's Cavalry.

He was true to his word. With four others he gently placed the wounded boy on a blanket and carried him to a temporary [Yankee] hospital. There Metcalfe lay for several days on a pallet, with very little attention from any one and with full time to consider what war really is. The scenes about him were not enlivening. Surgical knives and probing instruments were at work above the table in the middle of the room. One case was that of an officer to be operated upon. The surgeon cut his belt in haste and threw it aside. The pistol it held rolled under a bureau in plain view of the disarmed, crippled Confederate boy. From his pallet he could see it where it was lying out of sight of every one else. He eyed the pistol with the determination to have it. Several days passed with this sole thought in his fevered brain.

One day he found himself the only patient in the room. Finally the attendants went out and he was alone, when an unsophisticated country boy strolled in. "Buddy," said Jim Metcalfe in the pleading tone of a very sick person, "hand me my pistol from under the bureau." And "buddy" obligingly stooped for the weapon and gave it to the wounded boy.

How he clung to his treasure! Tied in a corner of his blanket, it was kept concealed through all changes and under all difficulties until one day a girl nurse untied the blanket and found the pistol. But being a girl, a Tennessee girl [that is, sympathetic to the South], she was easily persuaded not to tell. The weapon was a safeguard to the weak, wounded boy when, as a paroled Confederate, he made his way back alone through a multitude of dangers to the farm in Lincoln County. His wounds were of such a nature as to disable him from further military service as well as to unfit him in after life for the active pursuit of business. Yet never has he regretted the sacrifice he was called on to make for his country. J. M. Metcalfe is one of the three thousand Confederate soldiers of Lincoln County to whom the monument in Fayetteville is dedicated.[141] — OCTAVIA ZOLLICOFFER BOND

A GROUP OF OFFICERS OF FORREST'S CAVALRY

☞ Maj. Charles W. Anderson is designated in the records as "Acting Assistant Adjutant and Inspector General of Staff of General Forrest," he having served in much of the latter part of the war as if the actual adjutant general to the Wizard of the Saddle.

Col. D. C. Kelley, who was nearly all of the war under General Forrest, furnishes the following:

"Writing from memory, it was about September, 1863, that General Forrest and Major Anderson met. Forrest, though writing but little himself, was very exacting as to what was written by his order. He was about to start on an expedition on one occasion, and while getting ready a few days before the meeting he had found some difficulty, in the absence of Major Strange, his adjutant general, in the procurement of a man who could write his orders in the exact form he desired. Turning to a soldier he had seen writing at another desk, he said: 'You try, will you?' When the order was written, he said: 'Well done. I need you. Will you consent to go with me?' This was Charles Anderson, of Murfreesboro, Tenn. When the writer was next in headquarters, a hundred miles or more southwest, he slept on Major Anderson's blanket and was his close friend and comrade until we separated at Gainesville, Ala., May 9, 1865.

"Forrest's surrender brought out some of Anderson's finest and wisest qualities. All was gloom, broken only by wild rumors, causing almost reckless despair. Again and again soldiers worn out with delay in camp and uncertainty were questioning superiors and threatening disbandment. Anderson stood nobly, kindly advising and with consummate skill answering every question as best he might, heart breaking, but with face and voice kindly. Two successive nights were spent in long rides with General Forrest, the first in helping the General to overcome his first thought of going to Mexico, the second in maturing his address to the troops. Since this noble address truly represents General Forrest, the great soldier, and his daily and often nightly companion, our Charlie, his adjutant and lifelong friend, it seems fitting now, since both have gone, that the address should represent both."

The extracts referred to in General Forrest's farewell address to his soldiers are as follows:

"I do not think it proper or necessary at this time to refer to the causes which have reduced us to this extremity; nor is it now a matter of material consequence as to how such results were brought about. That we are beaten is a self evident fact, and any further resistance on our part would be justly regarded as the very height of folly and rashness.

"The cause [conservatism] for which you have so long and manfully struggled, and for which you have braved dangers, endured privations and sufferings, and made so many sacrifices, is to-day hopeless. Reason dictates and humanity demands that no more blood be shed. Fully realizing and feeling that such is the case, it is your duty and mine to lay down our arms, submit to the 'powers that be,' and aid in restoring peace and establishing law and order throughout the land.

"Civil war, such as you have just passed through, naturally engenders feelings of animosity, hatred, and revenge. It is our duty to divest ourselves of all such feelings, and as far as in our power to do so to cultivate friendly feelings toward those with whom we have so long contended and heretofore so widely but honestly differed. Neighborhood feuds, personal animosities, and private differences should be blotted out; and when you return home, a manly, straightforward course of conduct will secure the respect even of your enemies. Whatever your responsibilities may be to government, to society, or to individuals, meet them like men.

"I have never on the field of battle sent you where I was unwilling to go myself; nor would I now advise you to a course which I felt myself unwilling to pursue. You have been good soldiers; you can be good citizens. Obey the laws, preserve your honor, and the government to which you have surrendered can afford to be, and will be, magnanimous."

Major Anderson was buried from his Murfreesboro home, where he had lived from childhood, known, loved, and trusted by all. It was the privilege of the writer to participate in the burial service, as he had done for six members of the old Forrest staff before.

But a few weeks later Capt. William Forrest, son of Gen. N. B. Forrest, the youngest and gentlest of the above group, we buried from the church of his mother in Memphis. He blended the cool courage and active service of his father with the modesty and gentleness of his refined and beautiful mother [Mary Ann Forrest].

The writer was associated with General Forrest from a very early period in the war, first in the Forrest Cavalry Regiment, our regimental headquarters being one. We had one table and, for a while, one tent; family prayers in the evening and grace at meals. The son was a member with his mother of the First Cumberland Presbyterian Church in Memphis. By his father's consent he became my deacon and elder, performing both functions. Later, when General Forrest was commanding a division or corps, the son was still charged with conveying orders for religious services to be held at headquarters. With the genteel and devout bearing of his mother, commingled with the activities of his father, he conveyed the orders for headquarter services or cared for the preacher's comfort, so we came to know and love each other well.

It was not until since the close of the war that I was able to decipher one problem or connect it, especially with William. General Forrest made a visit to General Polk's headquarters, about two days' ride distant, and returned with two soldier youths who possessed the highest blood of our Southland—one the son of Bishop Otey, of the Episcopal Church; the other a son of General Donelson, of Tennessee. For more than two years they had been under the care of Bishop-General Polk. Forrest never told us that it was for companions to Willie in that life, to meet the anxiety and Christian culture of the mother when her health would no longer allow her to keep near headquarters, watching over this boy. The General had for once forgotten battle and hardship that she might feel comfort in the knowledge that the companionship of the only son was with charming youths of the highest birth and truest courage. This is written that the fame of the father in battle may not obscure the higher and nobler characteristic of desire for Christian training and pure association for the son. Yet Willie was brave as pure. Many a night the writer shared his blanket.

We buried him from the old Memphis home, and were gratified to have this last Christian service to him in the Memphis church where the mother first, then Willie, and later General Forrest had held membership.

This service was conducted by Rev. D. C. Kelley, D.D., L.L.D., who was colonel of Forrest's old cavalry regiment, and who when called to Forrest's headquarters by courtesy was recognized as headquarters chaplain. Later the Confederate Veterans elected him to the rank of Lieutenant General of Forrest's Cavalry Corps.

The death of Major Anderson recalls to the [writer] . . . a visit from General Forrest to his office in Nashville a short while before his death [in October 1877]. He was on a brief visit to Nashville. His hair was white, and there was a gentleness of manner that conformed to his reformed life. His greatest manifest desire was to see Major Anderson, as if it were his last opportunity.[142] — SUMNER ARCHIBALD CUNNINGHAM

GENERALS BRAGG & FORREST

☞ My attention has just been called to a publication made in *Trotwood's Magazine* for February of the current year entitled the "Storm Center of the Rebellion" and signed "Geo. T. Moffett," in which this paragraph appears: "And what of Bragg? Had he done that for which the fearless Forrest cursed him to his face so loud and deep and branded him as a coward for not doing?"

There is no foundation for this story. General Forrest was incapable of such conduct. He had the sense and knowledge to know that it was a high military crime that would have resulted in a court-martial and in his disgrace. But without resistance to that question, I am surprised that a Southern magazine would give circulation to a slander on a patriotic soldier long since dead. A public journal or magazine is impersonal, but it is never legitimate to print words that are suspicious or actionable in a court of law.

Benjamin F. Cheatham.

If General Forrest had denounced General Bragg in the terms used by the writer, General Bragg would have resented it on the spot. He was a man with a combative nature, and was possessed of lofty personal courage. Those of us who saw him on the field of Shiloh were witnesses of a display of courage not surpassed by any soldier of any rank on any field of any war known to history. I recall the fact that the morning following that great battle I said to Gen. Frank Cheatham, himself a hero: "General Bragg is the hero of this battle." He replied without hesitation: "Yes, beyond all question."

He added: "When we were in action with him yesterday and saw him push nearer and nearer to the front, I could but think of the battle of Buena Vista [Mexican American War] and of the critical moment when General [Zachary] Taylor galloped up to his battery and said, 'Give them a little more grape, Captain Bragg,' and the Captain replied, 'I will push the guns a little nearer the enemy.'"

    General Bragg possessed the confidence of President Davis at all times. He rated him above Lee, the Johnstons, and Jackson. After the great disaster at Mission Ridge, and after Forrest's alleged denunciation, he [Davis] made him chief of staff of the army, and he was his virtual commander. When a movement was made to place General Johnston or Stonewall Jackson in command of the Army of Tennessee after the Kentucky campaign and again after the battle of Murfreesboro, the President could not be moved by army or political influence, replying to all importunities that General Bragg was the better soldier. After Missionary Ridge General Bragg was relieved at his own request, and was immediately made chief of the staff. In this service he continued until the last sad days. He took the field in command of Hoke's small division, reenforced by the still smaller division of D. H. Hill, met Cox, of Sherman's army, at Kinston, N.C., with an army corps, and gave him a a bloody repulse. Cox sustained a loss of over twelve hundred, while Bragg's loss was less than two hundred. After the repulse of Cox, Bragg reported to General Johnston, and served under him as a division commander at the Battle of Bentonville.

    It was a fine illustration of his patriotism that he could come from the command of a great army to a division without a murmur.[143] — CONFEDERATE ADJUTANT GENERAL JAMES D. PORTER

EMMA SANSOM'S VERSION OF EVENTS

☛ As we [Emma and her mother] got to the top of the hill we saw the rails were already piled on the bridge and were on fire, and the Yankees were in line on the other side guarding it. We turned back toward the house, and had gone but a few steps before we saw a Yankee coming at full speed, and behind were some more men on horses. I heard them shout: "Halt! and surrender!" The man stopped, threw up his hand, and handed over his gun. The officer to whom the soldier surrendered said: "Ladies, do not be alarmed: I am General Forrest. I and my men will protect you from harm." He inquired: "Where are the Yankees?" Mother said: "They have set the bridge on fire and are standing in line on the other side; and if you go down that hill, they will kill the last one of you."

By this time our men had come up, and some went out in the field and both sides commenced shooting. We ran to the house, and I got there ahead of all. General Forrest dashed up to the gate and said to me:

Emma Sansom.

"Can you tell me where I can get across that creek?" I told him there was an unsafe bridge about two miles farther down the stream, but that I knew of a trail about two hundred yards above the bridge on our farm where our cows used to cross in low water, and I believed he could get his men over there, and that if he would have my saddle put on a horse I would show him the way. He said: "There is no time to saddle a horse; get up here behind me." As he said this he rode close to the bank on the side of the road, and I jumped up behind him. Just as we started off mother came up out of breath and gasped: "Emma, what do you mean?" General Forrest said: "She is going to show me a ford where I can get my men over in time to catch those Yankees before they get to Rome. Don't be uneasy; I will bring her back safe."

We rode out into a field through which ran a branch or small ravine and along which there was a thick undergrowth that protected us a while from being seen by the Yankees at the bridge or on the other side of the creek. This branch emptied into the creek just above the ford. When we got close to the creek, I said: "General Forrest, I think we had better get off the horse, as we are now where we can be seen." We both got down and crept through the bushes, and when we were right at the ford I happened to be in front. I stepped quickly between me and the Yankees, saying: "I am glad to have you for a pilot, but I am not going to make breastworks of you." The cannon and the other guns were firing fast by this time, as I pointed out to him where to go into the water and out on the other bank, and then we went back toward the house. He asked me my name and asked me to give him a lock of my hair. The cannon balls were screaming over us so loud that we were told to leave and hide in some place out of danger, which we did.

Soon all the firing stopped, and I started back home. On the way I met General Forrest again, and he told me that he had written a note for me and left it on the bureau. He asked me again for a lock of my hair.[144]
— EMMA SANSOM

FORREST AS DESCRIBED BY A FELLOW REBEL GENERAL

☛ . . . Forrest had a genius for war. He was a man of great courage and had inspiration. Now here is an instance to show it. He always had about him a chosen company which was his bodyguard, and in critical moments he would charge with them to decide a case, to decide the fact; but he made a charge one time through the enemy and found himself in a position with hostile soldiers between him and his line of communications. One of his men remarked in alarm: "General, the enemy is in our rear." Said he: "Ain't we in their rayer too?" He saw the point exactly.

He was a gallant fellow. When Forrest captured Streight, his forces were inferior; but he maneuvered them in such a way as to convince Streight that he was going to overwhelm him. When Forrest got back to Huntsville, Ala., the people were so gratified that they subscribed and got him a fine horse that was presented to him by the ladies of Huntsville. That horse was brought out, flowers adorning it everywhere, richly caparisoned, and they made a speech presenting the horse to him. He replied: "I am much obliged to you for this present. I certainly appreciate it. But take them roses and flowers off of there; that is no place for them—on this horse—take them away."

Simon B. Buckner.

Looking around at the crowd and seeing a good many young men, he said: "I see in this crowd a good many young men who ought to be in the army fighting for their country. For my part, I have lost all self-respect for any young man that I see out not in the army." Everybody knew what he meant. He wasn't always accurate in his language, but they always knew what he was aiming at.[145] — CONFEDERATE GENERAL SIMON BOLIVAR BUCKNER

EXECUTIONS PREVENTED BY GENERAL FORREST

☛ Twenty [Confederate] prisoners belonging to Forrest's Cavalry incarcerated in Fort Delaware were ordered to be shot in retaliation for the shooting of some slaves and white men in 1864. Forrest sent in a flag of truce with a message that he would shoot twenty Federals for every one of his men who was executed. The execution was abandoned.[146] — "AN OLD VETERAN"

MY SERVICE UNDER GENERAL FORREST

☞ The weakness of the defense of Chattanooga made it necessary that the post should be strengthened. Governor Harris secured the services of General Forrest to lead an expedition, and a command was organized for the purpose. The design of this movement was for General Forrest to occupy and hold any available territory in Middle Tennessee, while I should enlist the needed troops and encamp near Chattanooga.

In obedience to Order Number 4 I organized all the facilities, transportation, commissary stores, arms, etc., for the campaign and moved across the mountain to meet General Forrest, who was to go in advance to Rock Martin, about six or eight miles from McMinnville. I had been delayed some hours by the breaking down of a wagon loaded with arms coming down the mountain. When I reached his camp, General Forrest was in his saddle ready to march on Murfreesboro. I expressed surprise about his contemplated movement, and stated that from the activity of the Federal forces I would be in a perilous condition, and I was fearful I would not be successful in enrolling volunteers. He thought there was no danger and said he wanted to leave with me for the time being his wagon trains and army stores. I told him that he would have to leave some force to protect them. He replied that he would leave a company.

Colonel Lawton with a Georgia regiment, under command of General Forrest at the time, was lacking in arms, and General Forrest ordered me to turn over to them about sixty muskets, which I did. When I took charge of the camp, consisting of seventy-five or eighty Confederate wagons and about ten Tennessee wagons, I found only about fifteen men instead of a company, which he said he would leave. I detained all straggling troops that came up afterwards, armed them and the teamsters, and prepared to make the best defense possible in the event of an attack.

I had the country around well scouted and captured four Federal soldiers clothed in citizens' garb. I inquired why they had put on citizens' dress. They said they had heard of a contemplated move into Middle Tennessee by the Confederates and they had been sent out as scouts to ascertain the facts, and they had put on citizens' clothes to keep from being bushwacked. I turned them over to General Forrest.

I put out notice of my presence at Rock Martin Camp as secretly as I could and that my object was to enroll Tennessee troops for State service. Quite a number came to me, and I commissioned them to raise companies, furnishing them subsistence for troops in State service. I had heard of Forrest's great victory at Murfreesboro and his capture of about eleven hundred prisoners and that he expected to return to McMinnville. I had been informed that there was a considerable force of Federal infantry and cavalry at Tullahoma and the railroad in full operation between Tullahoma and McMinnville. I saw that they might strike General Forrest in the flank, and in the disordered condition of his troops might deprive him of the fruits of his victory. I therefore ordered Captain Brewster, of the Tennessee troops, to take a squad of men the following night and destroy the railroad bridge at Manchester, and he executed the order. I was ordered by General Forrest through Colonel Wharton, of Texas, to move the train up to McMinnville, which I did, and met General Forrest in the vicinity of McMinnville with his prisoners, and they were all impounded in Judge Marchbanks's yard.

I found great confusion in General Forrest's command. Troops were scattered, and I was informed that quite a number loaded with plunder were on their way to Chattanooga. I spent the night in the room with General Forrest in company with Hon. Andrew Ewing, of Nashville. I mentioned to Forrest the capture of four prisoners in citizens' dress. I asked what I should do with them, and he replied: "Try them as spies." I said I was not willing to do that, and remarked that Colonel Ewing and I were in citizens' dress and we were not spies, and our motive was to avoid recognition by bushwhackers, and according to my theory it was the office that made the spy and not the dress. He just remarked that they were my prisoners and to do what I pleased with them. They were paroled next morning with other prisoners.

I told him, apprehending danger from the force at Tullahoma striking him in the flank about McMinnville, I had sent a squad of Tennessee troops and had the bridge destroyed the night before. He said he thought there was no danger; but I differed with him. Early the next morning I asked him about the parole of his prisoners, and he replied that he had spoken to some clerks in McMinnville to come out that morning and parole them. I remarked that I thought haste was expedient; that I had an adjutant, Col. Robert McKee, who was a fine scribe, and who, with myself, would change the caption on the muster rolls of Tennessee into parole lists. He agreed to it, and in a little while the parole lists were ready, and one was handed to each officer highest in command of the prisoners to take the names of the members of his command. In a very short time the prisoners had all signed the parole lists, and they were immediately supplied with rations and sent back.

The prisoners had not left more than an hour perhaps before Colonel Shedd, of Coffee County, rode up to General Forrest's headquarters and informed him that a large force of Federal cavalry had passed his house early in the morning on their way to McMinnville, and that a considerable force of Federal infantry was to come by railroad to unite with them at McMinnville. General Forrest's men were scattered and in confusion, and some of them loaded with captured spoils on their way to Chattanooga. General Forrest mounted his horse and dashed through his troops giving his rallying command, and soon brought order out of confusion.

He marched his command some three or four miles out and formed them into line of battle and waited the most of the day for the coming of the enemy. The Federal cavalry came up within five miles of McMinnville and waited nearly all day for the Federal infantry, but they got no farther than the demolished bridge. The wreck of the bridge probably saved the fruits of Forrest's victory. I requested General Forrest not to insert my name in connection with the wreck of the bridge in his report, as I did not wish it known that I was in that section at this juncture. I then left General Forrest and proceeded, with some disadvantages, to the enlistment of Tennessee troops.[147] — CONFEDERATE GENERAL JOHN MORGAN BRIGHT

GENERAL GRANT'S ASSESSMENT OF FORREST
☞ Grant expressed very high admiration for Gen. N. B. Forrest and spoke of him as a "natural-born soldier."[148] — CONFEDERATE GENERAL MARCUS J. WRIGHT

SKETCH OF FORREST BY HIS CHIEF OF ARTILLERY
☞ For nearly three years preceding the close of the Civil War, as a member of General Forrest's military family and an officer of his staff, I had unlimited opportunities for observing and studying him as a man and as a commander, and that too under all the varying conditions of the camp, the march, and the battlefield.

[As has been noted:] "Every structure in nature and in art necessarily rests upon a base, a foundation, and it has been said that man himself is in no wise exempt from this primal necessity; that for him, as a living temple, heredity lays a foundation, while environment becomes the dominant factor in shaping and developing the superstructure." If this be true, my association with and daily observation of the

John W. Morton.

man warrants the assertion that a massive brain, an inflexible purpose, unflinching courage, tireless energy, and a will that could brook no opposition were the bed rocks of the foundation upon which General Forrest built—truly a combination of characteristics and attributes rarely found in any one man.

Early in life General Forrest fell upon hard lines. The death of his father left him, when only sixteen years of age, the sole dependence for support and protection of a widowed mother and eight young brothers and sisters. It was then he began building on that foundation upon which all his subsequent career rested.

Deprived at this early age of every advantage of fortune, save a resolute soul and a robust constitution, he faced his duties and responsibilities with all that force of character displayed by him twenty years later as a cavalry commander. With no one to look to or lean upon, and so many dependent upon him, he was forced to think and act for himself, and thus, amid toil, privations, and hardships, he began the development of that complete self-reliance which characterized his whole military career.

As a soldier, by his intelligence, energy, and bravery, he carved his way unaided from obscurity to fame—from the ranks [private] to a Lieutenant-Generalship [one step shy of the highest rank].

General Forrest, as a commander, was, in many respects, the negative of a West Pointer. He regarded evolution, maneuvers, and exhaustive cavalry drill an unnecessary tax upon men and horses. He cared nothing for tactics further than the movement by twos or fours in column, and from column right or left into line, dismounting, charging, and fighting. As attested by his unparalleled successes, these simple movements proved sufficient.

Except for officers, as an insignia of rank, General Forrest banished the saber from his command. In the hands of troopers he regarded them as a dangling, clattering appendage—of no value as offensive weapons. He armed his men with a Sharp's rifle, or short carbine, and two navy sixes, better in every way for either attack or defense. By his captures the Federal Government supplied him with guns and artillery and more ordnance, commissary, and quartermaster's stores than he could use.

With vastly inferior numbers he met on different fields and defeated [Union] Generals Hatch, Grierson, William Sooy Smith, and Sturgis, all of whom were veteran soldiers and graduates of West Point. The two last named were specially selected by Generals Grant and Sherman, and sent out with splendidly equipped commands for no other purpose than to whip or kill that "devil Forrest." In the light of such events General

Forrest can be excused for holding in contempt the idea that only West Pointers were fitted to command, and also for saying on one occasion: "Whenever I met one of them fellers that fit by note, I generally whipped hell out of him before he got his tune pitched."

By nature General Forrest was aggressive, consequently he was always an offensive fighter. He believed the moral effect was with the attacking party, and never failed, when it was possible to do so, to take the initiative and deliver the first blow. He believed that one man advancing in attack was equal to two men standing in line of battle and awaiting attack. When charged by the enemy, no matter in what numbers, it was his invariable rule to meet a charge with a counter charge.

His restless nature would not allow him to remain in camp any longer than was necessary to rest his men and shoe his horses. Unlike some generals, who seemed content with holding their ground and keeping from being whipped, General Forrest was ever on the move, and never content unless he was whipping somebody. He cared little for army regulations or tactics; disobeyed or went outside of them whenever the good of the service or surrounding circumstances demanded it. Nor was he free from inconsistencies common to us all. While he could not tolerate insubordination in his own command, he was himself at times the most insubordinate of men. However contrary to his own judgment a movement might be, an order from his superior officer on the battlefield was always obeyed, except in matters affecting himself or his command unwisely or unjustly.

An instance of this kind I well remember. When General Hood crossed his army over the Tennessee to Florence, Ala., General Forrest was in command of all the cavalry of his army. We had our headquarters at a church a few miles out in the country. An officer came out with an order reducing the number of mules in wagons and ordering all surplus mules to be turned over to the quartermaster of transportation. General Forrest happened to be out, and the officer left after giving specific directions to have the mules sent in the next morning. It was read to the General when he came in, and he said very quietly: "None of my mules will be sent in on that order." The next evening Maj. A. L. Landis came out and asked the General if he had received the order, and wanted to know why the mules had not been sent in as ordered. If the good people accustomed to sit in the "amen corner" had dropped in just at that time, they would have concluded that the good Lord had been ousted and old Nick had taken full possession of the sanctuary. The atmosphere was blue for a while.

Stripped of General Forrest's bad words, he said to Major Landis: "Go back to your quarters and don't you come here again or send anybody here about mules. The order will not be obeyed; and, moreover, if Major Ewing bothers me any further about this matter, I'll come down to his office, tie his long legs into a double bowknot around his neck, and choke him to death with his own shins. It's a fool order anyway. General Hood had better send his inspectors to overhaul your wagons, rid them of all surplus baggage, tents, adjutant desks, and everything that can be spared. Reduce the number of his wagons instead of reducing the strength of his teams. Besides, I know what is before me; and if he knew the road from here to Pulaski, this order would be countermanded. I whipped the enemy and captured every mule wagon and ambulance in my command; have not made a requisition on the government for anything of the kind for two years, and now that they are indispensable my teams will go as they are or not at all."

Insubordination may be justified, but it cannot be defended. General Forrest's insubordination in this case was a Godsend and a saving cause to General Hood's retreating army. From Richland Creek to the Tennessee River the road was strewn with his abandoned wagons, and but for the help afforded the pontoon train by General Forrest's fine six-mule teams great delay and probable disaster to the army would have occurred before a passage of the river was effected.

American patriot Miss Decca Lamar West.

Long after the gray-haired veterans of the Confederate armies shall have passed away, and when, as far as possible, all error shall have been expunged from the pages of history, which should be illuminated by truth alone, a glorious constellation will shine undimmed in the sky of the Confederate States of America. It will be an empyrean of exalted memories in which these fixed stars, differing from one another in their own peculiar glory, will beam in their appropriate places, an enduring revelation to the world of the virtues and genius of our greatest commanders.

In the zenith of the grand constellation will be a trinity of stars. The greatest and central luminary will send forth earth-wide rays, sustained and brilliant beyond all others, but beaming everywhere with softened radiance. The other two, different of element, but alike calling forth our admiration, will shine with their own brightness and effulgence to the right and left of the noble central star; one, Sirius-like, with far-flashing radiance of a light divine, from a Christian warrior's armor; the other with a rich, dazzling splendor that seems to fling lightnings of defiance to the sun's fiercest rays from the burnished shield of a dauntless heart. These stars are Robert E. Lee, T. J. (Stonewall) Jackson, and Nathan Bedford Forrest.

The first was preeminent by reason of a superlatively noble nature and exalted purity of character, combined with world-wide fame as the commander of incomparable armies that loved him with a love as near adoration as ever blessed a mortal; the other two startled the solitudes of space and made the chasms of time to ring with the echoes of their matchlessly adroit and marvelously swift achievements. General Jackson prayed and marched, and prayed and fought. General Forrest, like a ruthless besom of destruction, charged the air with electric energy as he hurled himself upon the foe.

He was indeed the "Wizard of the Saddle," self-reliant and aggressive, with the consciousness of one who seemed to know intuitively when, where, and how to strike. Without military training he forced his way from the ranks of the company in which he enlisted to a commander's fame as complete and brilliant as ever reflected honor upon any school of arms.

We can picture him one spring morning at reveille, taking his place with comrades who barely knew his name, and four years later a lieutenant general, the resplendent and fiery star of whose glory still sheds a light that makes his deeds and his genius the theme of eager discussion in every camp and school where military science and skill enlist a thought.

He had absolutely no knowledge or experience of war gleaned from the study of what others had wrought. General Forrest grasped intuitively and instantaneously the strategic possibilities of every situation which confronted him, and with inspired native genius, and complete confidence put into practice the tactics of the most famous generals in all history. His knowledge of men was in most cases unerring; and his ability to inspire and bring out the greatest power and endurance of his men was unsurpassed even by the great Napoleon himself. His eye for position was almost infallible, and his knowledge of the effect of a given movement on the enemy was intuitive and seemed to come rather from an inner than an outer source of information. His plans of battle were not chalked out on blackboards nor drawn on charts; they were conceived on the instant and as instantaneously carried out. He struck as the lightning strikes, and his tactics were as incalculable as those of the electric fluid and as mysterious to the enemy, for his movements were so rapid and his endurance and daring so remarkable that they could not be computed by any known rules of warfare.[149] — CONFEDERATE CAPTAIN JOHN WATSON MORTON

John W. Morton.

7

1910-1913

FROM AN ADDRESS TO THE WEST POINT CLASS OF 1910

☛ . . . In our early [U.S.] history there was no regular education of officers. Washington, Jackson, Harrison, and Taylor became successful soldiers by force of their genius and only the training obtained in the school of hard and costly experience. We had trained officers when our Civil War began, and they made a wonderful fame for this institution; but the war was so stupendous that many with no previous knowledge of war were forced into leadership.

Jacob McGavock Dickinson.

Forrest, one of the greatest generals developed by our Civil War, which endured long enough to make as good soldiers as the world ever saw, had at the beginning no soldierly training and was ignorant of military history. One of his officers told me that when he first saw his artillery come into action, the guns whirled into position, unlimbered, and the caissons started to the rear, the distance fixed by the tactics, conceiving the idea that the drivers were panic-stricken and were running away with the ammunition, he drew his pistols, charged down upon the leaders, and halted them with a terrible imprecation upon their cowardice. A long-drawn-out war and splendid genius made good all such deficiencies in him and in many others who won immortal fame in that great contest.[150] — HONORABLE JACOB MCGAVOCK DICKINSON, U.S. SECRETARY OF WAR, 1910

GEN. FORREST IN THE BATTLE OF SELMA, ALA.
☛ On April 2, 1865, when [Union] General [James Harrison] Wilson was marching on Selma, Ala., with about eight or ten thousand cavalry, General Forrest opposed him and contested his way constantly; but having only about 3,500 men, he was forced to fall back and take shelter inside of the breastworks of the city, extending from the Alabama River above to the same protection below. The line was so long that General Forrest had not half enough men to hold it; so he dismounted his men on April 3 and ordered all detailed men and citizens to the breastworks, and soon the men had to stretch out eight or ten feet apart.

The enemy made charge after charge, but were again and again repulsed. Finally, however, they broke through our lines, and then came a great stampede of riderless horses running all through the city, while men were fighting all along the streets. General Forrest, brave and fearless, ran into Water Street all alone on a beautiful black horse, with about one hundred Yankee soldiers after him. He had been wounded in the left arm that morning. As he turned into Broad Street he threw the reins over the pommel of his saddle, drew his pistol, turned in his saddle, and gave them every shot he had. Then he spurred his noble horse to run for his life, the gang of howling soldiers following him; but by the swiftness of his noble steed the dashing General was safely carried through the lines.

The house of the surgeon who had charge of the hospitals of the city was on the outskirts of the city and in range of the artillery from the enemy; so the doctor's family (six in number) was compelled to vacate the house and seek safety in the wayside hospital, and there they had to remain for two weeks or more, as [Union] General [Emory] Upton took the house for his headquarters. While there his men burned everything they could find; and when they left, his men broke up every piece of furniture in the house. The Union army became a perfect mob, breaking open the saloons and stores, taking anything they wanted, and then setting the city on fire, burning the entire water front and nearly all of one side of Broad Street, including the Episcopal church. Our hospital, with the wounded from both armies, was in imminent danger; but it was saved by ordering the troops to man the fire engines with steady streams, while three blocks were on fire near the hospital.

The Union troops remained in Selma about two weeks or more, building pontoon bridges to throw across the Alabama River and also removing powder and shell from the Confederate arsenal, which was the largest in the South, and throwing them in the river. The night before they left the city they set fire to this arsenal; and but for its raining that night, the whole city possibly might have been burned up. There was explosion after explosion of shells and cartridges all through the night. The Union army had taken all the horses and mules they could find on their march to the city, and there were a number in the city also, all of which, several hundred in number, were penned in the quartermaster's yard in the heart of the city. As General Wilson was unable to carry them with him, and fearing they would fall into the hands of the farmers and Confederate soldiers, he issued an order to his quartermaster to have them all shot, which was done, and left them there for the citizens to get away the best they could. So without ox, horse, or mule to haul them away, the people got together, swung the dead animals to "carry logs," hauled them off by hand, and dumped them into the Alabama River. The Union army then crossed over the river on their pontoon bridge and pushed on to Montgomery.

This ended the invasion of Selma, Ala., by the forces commanded by General Wilson, General Upton, and others of the United States army, which [the end of the invasion, that is] will long be gratefully remembered.[151] — S. Y. BROWNE

"HERE'S YOUR MULE"
☞ After coming out of Tennessee the cavalry under General Jackson was encamped at Tupelo and Verona, while we (Harvey's Scouts) were sent out to look after some Federal troops who had come out of Memphis and were making their way down through Pontotoc County, Miss. We intercepted them some twenty miles or more from Verona, and in the encounter my horse was killed, and I was ordered to go back to our camp at Verona.

While walking on the way I met a very nice-looking mule ridden by an old family negro servant. I ordered him to dismount. He obeyed, but was scared for fear I intended to kill him. He begged most piteously for his life, and I told him it was his mule and not his life that I wanted. I gave him my name and command; also told him where he could get the mule in Verona. He hurried home with the news that one of Forrest's cavalrymen had taken his mule, and that his life was saved only by tearful pleadings.

The mule happened to be owned by an officer on Forrest's staff, who was immediately notified of his great loss, and at once the whole machinery of Forrest's Cavalry was put in motion to catch the vandal who had the audacity to steal a mule from the stalls of the great cavalry leader.

Capt. Sam Henderson, who was around Forrest's headquarters at Meridian at this time, was detailed to capture me. By a singular coincidence I was at headquarters, having a transportation pass to Corinth, Miss., approved by General Forrest, and to get a furlough, but I was not recognized as the party wanted. Going back to Tupelo on the train was Capt. Sam Henderson. That gentleman always appeared in a new officer's dress suit, with white gauntlets, and in his usual suave and at the same time highly impressive and bombastic manner he was telling all about the war and how near Henderson's Scouts came to catching Grant before he caught Vicksburg. Finally he discovered me, still unknown to him, tucked away in a corner asleep.

We reached Tupelo about 10:30 p.m., after a weary ride. As we alighted from the train he requested me to show him where Captain Harvey was camped. When we reached the tent, he doffed his hat with a grand bow, at the same time giving a sweeping salute with his highly befeathered hat, remarking: "My dear Captain Harvey, how is your most excellent health? I owe you an apology for coming so late at night, but I am up here on a most unpleasant duty; and when you hear the details you will appreciate the delicacy of my position. It seems that one of your men, Wallace Wood, has stolen a mule from Lieutenant Colonel _____, of Forrest's staff, and I volunteered to come up and see you and to save you some annoyance. So if you will have the young man arrested and keep him under guard, you will oblige your old friend."

I was standing by listening, and do not know which was the most surprised. However, Captain Harvey was equal to the occasion. He invited Captain Henderson to take a seat, and then sent for me. As we passed out of the tent Captain Harvey said to me: "What the devil does this mean? Don't you know that General Forrest has issued an order threatening most dire punishment to any soldier who 'presses' a horse or mule?" That was what we called it in those days. After I explained, Captain Harvey said to me: "Get away from here on the first train, and keep out of the way."

I have forgotten how he fixed it up with Captain Henderson; but I had many a laugh with Captain Henderson after the war about this trip and his waterhaul.

This raid of the Federals was of such importance that General Forrest with his staff came up the Memphis and Ohio Railroad and disembarked from the train at Verona and started out to meet the raiders. When I met General Forrest going out to where I came from, I reported the facts to him as to the enemy. He wanted to know where I got the mule I was riding, and I told him that I borrowed him from a farmer to ride to the railroad. My lieutenant colonel failed to recognize his favorite mule when I was on him, but afterwards recovered him at Verona. This is a true tale of my "pressing" a mule during the war.[152] — WALLACE WOOD

FORREST & SAMUAL FREEMAN

☛ . . . in regard to the killing of [Confederate] Capt. Samuel Freeman, of Freeman's Battery, Forrest's Cavalry. I was a member of that battery and in the fight that day on the Lewisburg Pike near Douglas Church, and was taken prisoner with twenty-eight others, as brave soldiers and noble men as ever lived. Lieut. Nathaniel Baxter, now Speaker of the Tennessee State Senate, was of the number. My recollection is that General Forrest was moving on Franklin that day, intending to make an attack. Our videttes on the east side of the pike were captured by the United States regulars; then they charged our battery. We were completely surprised, and they were on us before we could unlimber and load.

Mrs. C. E. Buek, Matron of Honor, Forrest's Cavalry Corps, Jacksonville, Fla., 1914.

After Captain Freeman had surrendered, a Yankee cavalryman rode up and shot him in the head while he was still on his horse, and Captain Freeman fell to the ground. I was within ten yards of him. His horse ran back toward General Dibrell's regiment, which was in our rear. General Starnes's regiment was in front of us in the line of march. The Yankees double-quicked us out of the way; they came in and threatened to shoot us if we did not keep moving. Dr. Skelton, our company physician, was wounded, as was Dick Routon also. We were guarded that night in Franklin, and taken to Nashville next day and put in the penitentiary. From there we were sent to Louisville, Ky., and thence to Baltimore, Md. Later we were sent to City Point, Va. We were among the last prisoners exchanged.

I don't know who the young man was who was crying and cursing the Yankees for the brutal murder of Captain Freeman, but my impression is that it must have been Glewes McWhirter or Tom Allen, for we three were the youngest of the company—each about seventeen.

General Forrest loved Captain Freeman devotedly, and I heard that he burst into tears when he heard of Captain Freeman's fate. Our battery always held to the name of Freeman. In the noted West Tennessee raid made by General Forrest he took our battery with him, and we were in the battle of Parker's Crossroads, where we captured a battery and a brigade of Yankees. When shot and shell were flying thick as hail, Lieutenant Baxter (we called him "Nat") walked among his men, encouraging them with his manly bearing and words of cheer. At one stage of the battle, when part of Dibrell's Regiment was supporting our battery (and braver men than Dibrell's never lived), they moved a little farther to our right. Not being aware of what the move meant, Lieutenant Baxter ran up to them and said: "Boys, for God's sake, don't leave us. We will whip them." They soon convinced him that he need have no fear of their leaving him, and then they poured the shot into the Yankees thick and fast. I think, with Judge Henderson, that a shaft of some kind should be erected on the spot where the gallant Freeman fell.[153] — O. V. ANDERSON

MORE ON FORREST & FREEMAN

☛ General Forrest and his men believed that Captain Freeman was murdered, and they ever afterwards held a grudge against the 4th Regular Cavalry [U.S.] which did this deed. Some of his troopers made a bloody reprisal near Selma in 1865.

I was under the impression that Captain Freeman was on foot when killed, and that the excuse for the shooting was that he would not [actually, being overweight, he *could* not] run faster to keep up with the mounted Federals, who were trying to get away from Starnes, who was in hot pursuit.

Dr. Skelton said Captain Freeman told the Federal who shot him that he could go no faster, and that he made no resistance and did not try to escape. As he and Captain Freeman were being hurried from the field they were ordered to "double-quick," or they would shoot them.

I have always associated Freeman with our Alabama artilleryman, the "Gallant Pelham," who was killed in the Army of Northern Virginia.[154] — DR. JOHN ALLAN WYETH

GENERAL FORREST'S RIDE INTO MEMPHIS

☛ This is a correct account of one of the most daring and brilliant exploits of the war of the States—an exploit great in conception, execution, and achievement. The writer was a member of [Confederate] Company B; Zillman Voss, Captain, 14th Tennessee Cavalry; J. J. Neely, Colonel. Our regiment was a part of the command of 1,500 men. We took two small pieces of artillery and went into the city of Memphis, where there were 10,000 or more Federal soldiers, and remained there several hours, leaving in good order with 400 or 500 prisoners (many of them in their night clothes) and about 300 fine horses.

In August, 1864, our command was in line of battle on the south side of Hurricane Creek, eight or ten miles north of Oxford, Miss., a mere skirmish line stretched out to make a show and conceal our weakness. Across the creek about three miles north the Federal army was camped, Gen. A. J. Smith in command. It was one of the best-equipped and largest forces that had been "sent out from Memphis to crush Forrest." It was 22,000 strong of infantry, artillery, and cavalry.

(Other expeditions had tried it. Gen. William Sooy Smith was the first, and on meeting General Forrest at West Point and then at Okolona his greatest effort was to see how quickly he could get back to Memphis with a whipped and demoralized army, making the trip in much less time than it took in coming out. General Sturgis came next, and met his Waterloo at Brice's Crossroads after a most desperate conflict, losing his artillery, entire wagon train of 250 wagons, with many prisoners, and with many killed and wounded. Then Gen. A. J. Smith tried it when the severe battle of Harrisburg was fought; and although it was not decisive, he had enough and retreated to Memphis. Now he was in front of us again with a force more than five times as great as ours. Part of their daily routine was to shell us every morning, but they made no attempt to cross the creek.)

General Forrest had in all 3,500 to 4,000 effective fighting men. Something had to be done, and the plan of going to Memphis was here conceived and carried out. Of course the private soldier knew nothing of the plan. The difficulties in the way were very great. Between us and Memphis there were two streams nearly bank full from recent rains. There were no bridges, and just now they could not be forded. To bridge them trees were cut down that would reach across. They were trimmed up and pulled in position and cabled fast to each bank with grapevines. One stream was much wider than the other, and here trees had to be cut on opposite banks, so that they would lap, and some light logs were found and tied under to prevent sinking. Then flooring from gin houses, two to four miles distant, was torn up and carried on horseback to the creeks, and the bridges were made, crude, rough affairs; but they answered the purpose, and we crossed over with little delay. This work was done by a special detail of 300 men. The road was very muddy in many places from continued rains, and at times ten horses had to be used for one little cannon. To go around General Smith's army without being detected was another difficulty; but nothing ever deterred General Forrest from accomplishing anything that he had made up his mind to do, and all of these obstacles were overcome.

One evening about three o'clock we had orders to prepare three days' rations and to be ready to march at eight o'clock. We were to go as light as possible, carrying nothing but what was absolutely necessary. Men with the best horses were picked. We started with 2,000 men and four pieces of artillery for Memphis (as we learned later on), sixty to sixty-five miles distant. Orders were passed down the line that no noise was to be made. It was a little cloudy, and at times quite dark. All night long we rode in a trot or gallop. The road was very rough, with ditches, stumps, and mud galore. We went into camp about daybreak in a thick woods back of a cornfield near Hernando, Miss. It had been a most strenuous ride, and it was truly a case of the survival of the fittest, as fully 500 had fallen by the wayside and two pieces of the artillery had to be abandoned. Orders were given that no fires were to be made, no lights or noise. We fed our horses from the corn field and watered them at a little branch running through the woods, where there was also good grazing; so they fared well, while we gave ourselves up to rest or gathered in little groups to surmise where we were and wonder what our destination might be.

As soon as it was dark we started again for another all night ride; but it was not so wild and rough as the night before, and the road was better. We went in a brisk trot, and when within three or four miles of Memphis the command was halted and we were informed that we were going into the city, strict orders being given that any soldier caught out of line plundering would be shot. We went in at daybreak, about 4:30, riding in a gallop through a cavalry regiment camp, then an infantry camp, then artillery, then another infantry camp, as if they were not there, shooting at every human being on foot and into their tents; some were shot in their beds. The Federals were completely surprised, panic-stricken, and dazed. They fled in all directions; their greatest terror, the "Wizard of the Saddle," was in their midst, and little resistance was made.

There were three major generals in Memphis at this time, [Union] General [Cadwallader Colden] Washburn and General Herbert being two, while I don't recall the third. General Forrest had the location of the headquarters of each, and expected to capture them. Special details went to the quarters of each, but two had stayed elsewhere that night. General Washburn was awakened just in time to run out the back way in his night clothes, and escaped to one of the forts just as the Confederates were coming in the front door. The Federals were so demoralized that their only thought was to find a place of safety, and all that could took refuge in the forts. Although we were in the city about three hours, no organized effort was made to attack or follow us when we left, though by that time they were shooting at us from all directions, but with little effect, and our loss in the whole affair was very slight. The object of the expedition was accomplished. General Smith retreated to Memphis in great haste. General Forrest was still very much alive, and he had again saved Mississippi from desolation and ruin.[155] — CHARLES G. JOY

Before he became a multimillionaire Forrest lived in this house in Hernando, Mississippi.

GENERAL FORREST'S MARRIAGE
☛ From a faded old clipping is taken the following notice of General Forrest's marriage, which took place at Hernando, Miss., on September 25, 1845: "Married.—On Thursday evening, the 25th inst., by the Rev. S. M. Cowan, Mr. N. B. Forrest to Miss Mary Ann Montgomery, all of this county.

"The above came to hand accompanied by a good, sweet morsel of cake and a bottle of the best wine. May the happy couple live long to enjoy the felicity of this world! is our sentiment, and we heartily thank them for remembering us in the midst of their hymeneal joy."

After the marriage Forrest resided in Hernando for some time.[156] — SUMNER ARCHIBALD CUNNINGHAM

HOW FORREST WON OVER STREIGHT
☛ I can see the little home now where we had the pleasure of entertaining Gen. N. B. Forrest and his staff on May 3, 1863, a day made memorable by one of the greatest Southern victories during the War of the States. We were living temporarily thirteen miles south of Rome on the old Alabama road, my husband, Judge Thomas E. Williamson, having sold his river bottom farm, Glen Willie, seven miles below Rome on the

Coosa River.

While at breakfast Sunday morning Maria, the maid, came in saying that a soldier was at the gate calling for buttermilk. He was invited in to breakfast, but declined, asking only for milk. Before he was supplied a comrade joined him, and yet another, until quite a number had collected at the front gate. Maria appeared the second time, saying: "The buttermilk is all gone." She was ordered to give the milk in the churn, which she did, and that soon disappeared. Later I went to the front door and bade the men good morning, not noticing the absence of guns nor the color of uniforms, so dust-soiled were they. One soldier looked up and said: "We had the biggest fight yesterday, and I'll tell you we gave the Yankees hell." I answered, "I wish you had given them more," not knowing that they were captured [paroled] Federals.

They then rode on toward Rome. Others were passing all morning. Upon finding that they were bluecoats, we put our valuables out of sight as well as we could. Gathering up the silver and gold, Maria and I went to the henhouse, removed an old speckled hen, and deposited our treasures underground, carefully replacing the nest and persuading the hen to resume her occupation. The soldiers quietly passed on. Horace, the groom, had brought the carriage, but we did not go to Sunday school that day.

Everyone was excited, the neighbors going from house to house. While at my sister's home near by I was called to come home and bring the keys to the sideboard, where the wines were kept. On my arrival the house was full of soldiers, both the blue and the gray. I thought the whole army was upon us and said to my guest: "O, Mr. Choat, let your prayers ascend on high!"

I was introduced to Generals Forrest and Streight, and wines were passed to the exhausted officers. [Note: Forrest did not consume alcohol.]

General Forrest was a brave and noble general. Streight's forces had been sent out for the purpose of reaching Rome, destroying railroads and bridges, liberating the Federal prisoners, and taking the commissaries, thus cutting off communication with Bragg's army and the supplies of Gen. Joseph E. Johnston. Forrest was ordered to pursue Streight and save Rome. The armies had been skirmishing four or five days.

Near Gadsden Streight and his men crossed Black Creek, burning the bridge behind them. Forrest, arriving a few hours later, found himself cut off by the high waters, and inquired of a family the best place to ford the creek. While the lady, Mrs. Sansom, was giving directions, Emma, the eighteen-year old daughter, offered to show him the "shallows," where she had driven the cows across. Taking her behind him on his horse, she piloted the way, his brave men following. She was sent back to her home in safety. Some years after Emma Sansom was granted a section of land by the State of Alabama and the Governor presented her with a medal properly engraved.

Before finding the "shallows"' Forrest shouted across the stream that he would give one thousand dollars to the man who would take the news to Rome that Streight was on the way. John H. Wisdom volunteered, saying that he would go, but did not want any reward. The citizens of Rome years after presented Mr. Wisdom with a silver service in recognition of his deed. He died four years ago at his home, Hoke's Bluff, Ala.

Forrest was known as a strategist, never endangering the lives of his men when it could be avoided. His forces had been reduced to a part of a regiment, about five hundred men, with but two field pieces; while Streight's number was nearly two thousand, as we understood.

There was a knoll around which the soldiers had to pass, and, knowing that sentinels were watching, Forrest's men were made to go round and round many times to show their "vast numbers."

While Forrest was demanding Streight's surrender, couriers were dispatched from various directions asking for General Forrest's headquarters and announcing that reenforcements were arriving. Forrest seemed not to notice their coming, directing his attention to the opposing general. Streight reluctantly surrendered, deeming it unwise to enter a battle with such odds against him. When the ruse was discovered, Streight wept with disappointment.

Their arms were stacked a half mile from our house, and the hungry men poured in. The large gate was opened in front of our house and wagons and tents were taken into the grove. Every negro on the place was put to work with pot, oven, and skillet cooking for the exhausted soldiers. I continued till midnight serving one table after another. The advance guard who had passed in the morning were turned back by a fabricated report that the cannon had been planted on the hills of Rome, and that the Confederates were ready to meet them. This story was told them by Mrs. Meyers, whose husband was a Confederate soldier and whose father, Curtis Bailey, was at her home hidden in a thicket.

Among Forrest's men were the late Col. Moses Clift and W. T. Skelton, whose families still reside in Chattanooga.

In the fall of 1863 we moved to a large plantation six miles north of Rome, taking with us more than a hundred negroes, with horses, mules, and cattle, to cultivate a very large farm. For eighteen months we were undisturbed. Many of our neighbors refugeed [that is, sent their loved ones and servants further south for added protection], but Mr. Williamson remained, quietly pursuing his agricultural interests.

Sherman's campaign began the last of November, and while stationed at Rome two Federal officers rode up to our house one day and discovered our well-stocked farm, full cribs, etc. Then the foraging began, and for six months, excepting two weeks, army wagons came every day, taking away to their camps the corn and meat, oats, fodder, potatoes, and, lastly, the green corn in the field. I stood on the porch and saw them take twenty-five horses and mules to recruit their army. There was left only a yoke of young oxen, and some wanton soldier was careful to shoot them. However, the oxen recovered, and I asked a Federal officer to give me protection for them to haul our firewood the next winter. A little slip of paper served the purpose; and although frequent attempts were made, no one molested my property, and the next spring we rode to church in an oxcart, thankful for our lives.

Mrs. Caroline E. Mitchell.

Some negroes reported that we were hiding Confederates in a cave on our place, and two [Union] officers came to investigate. Mr. Williamson went with them and showed them the empty cave. They dined with us. Before leaving, one of them remarked that they had looked for a spy, but found a gentleman.

Not only our home but the whole country was devastated. Mr. Williamson never recovered from the shock, but died six years later. Somehow I was given the strength to withstand the loss better than he, and for my children and my country I have done my best.[157] — MRS. CAROLINE E. MITCHELL

HONOR FOR THE OLD-TIME NEGRO
☛ The time is not far distant when a monument will be erected in Montgomery, Ala., or Richmond, Va., as a tribute to the memory of the old-time Southern negro. The loyal devotion of the men and women who were slaves has had no equal in all history. They took care of the women and children whose natural protectors were with Lee and Jackson, Forrest and Joe Johnston, and were faithful to the trust.

Women during the great war did not fear to ride alone through large plantations to give directions as to the crops. These women were protected and never outraged. It was the coming of the [Left-wing] carpetbagger, with his social equality teachings [liberalism and socialism], that caused many negroes to become brutes.

The old-time negro will soon be but a memory, and while a remnant survive an imposing monument should be erected as a tribute to their faithfulness. It should be a monument worth fifty thousand dollars. This money could be easily raised if the religious and secular papers in the South would take up the matter in the spirit that the cause merits.[158] —
JOHN W. PAULETT

BEING A PRIVATE UNDER FORREST

☞ There was little red tape in our command. Our officers were our friends and comrades. As officers they had our greatest respect and obedience. There never was a body of soldiers that obeyed orders and performed duties more faithfully than Forrest's command. Rarely was even a trivial order violated. Off duty we were equals [with the officers]; they were gentlemen, so were we. We had confidence in them and they in us, and this cordiality and friendship elevated and helped us, made us better soldiers and better men of officers and privates.

 . . . We did a great deal of hard riding or marching, day or night, rain or shine. Sometimes we left our camp after dark and appeared next morning miles away where least expected. Sometimes we were in the saddle continuously for weeks. We were rough and ready riders, healthy and strong, and could endure all kinds of hardships, and our horses were the same way. General Forrest was always ready for a fight, and at any odds. He fought many battles, killed, wounded, and captured thousands of men; captured thousands of guns and ammunition, many pieces of artillery, hundreds of wagons, horses, mules, ambulances, clothing, provisions; tore up railroads, burned bridges, trestles, cars, engines, and much other property.

In November, 1864, General Forrest was ordered to join General Hood on his march into Middle Tennessee and take command of all the cavalry. We crossed the Tennessee River about the middle of the month, and the second day after leaving Florence, Ala., we met the Yankee cavalry, and then it was skirmishing and fighting every day, sometimes even into the night. In the first night's fight Cannon Justice, of Hall's Company, our regiment, had an eye shot out, and several others were wounded. As the cavalry led the advance, this work fell to them, and the way was stubbornly contested. At Fouche's Springs we had quite a sharp fight. There was a heavy snow on the ground and we were on foot. Here part of a regiment of Yankee cavalry that had been cut off rode through our skirmish line at a fast run without firing a gun and joined their command in front of us. We moved on, fighting every day.

The battle of Franklin was fought on November 30 [1864]. It was one of the most desperate engagements of the war and a fatal blow to our army. The Federals were superior in numbers, behind fortifications and breastworks. The Southern troops charged across open fields in plain view of the enemy, and were mowed down like weeds. It might well have been called the field of blood. Hood's army lost in killed and wounded about 5,000 and the Federals about 2,500; and although they retreated that night, it was a dearly won victory. Many of the best and most able generals and other officers were killed or wounded. The spirit of the men was crushed.

Hood's view (looking north) of Franklin, Tenn., from the top of Winstead Hill prior to the Battle of Franklin II, November 30, 1864. Columbia Pike, then a single lane dirt road, can be seen in the center crossing from right to left into town. Had Hood listened to Forrest the entire tragedy could have been avoided.

Our army was in front of Nashville about the 2nd of December. General Forrest was sent to Murfreesboro with part of his command. Hood's army had terrible experiences. The weather was very severe, raining and snowing every day, freezing and thawing, ice, snow, and water in the trenches, without shelter, and many without overcoats or blankets and with but scant and irregular rations. The suffering was indeed great. About the middle of December commenced the great battle of Nashville; and after two days' hard fighting against a force of fresh troops well armed and well fed fully three times as great, Hood's army was completely routed. It was very cold, still raining and snowing, the roads heavy with mud, the men suffering from hunger, cold, and exhaustion. Their clothing was ragged, often exposing the flesh. They looked like an army of tramps. Many were barefooted and had cut their feet on the ice and frozen ground, leaving blood marks in the snow. Hundreds of them whose feet had become sore and inflamed were hauled in the wagons, as were also some of the sick and wounded. The retreat was covered by the cavalry, fighting day and night, often hand-to-hand conflicts, the muskets used as clubs, the six-shooter against the saber, both sides displaying the greatest bravery and fearlessness. That Hood's entire army was not captured was due to the stubborn, reckless, and desperate fighting of the cavalry. General Forrest with his command and some infantry that he had gathered up from various commands under General Walthall formed the rear guard and saved the army from destruction.

Miss Rosalie Eva Elcan, Sponsor for Second Brigade, First Division, Forrest's Cavalry.

At last the Tennessee River was reached. There was a pontoon bridge, a frail-looking affair, as if it were nothing but inch boards laid on top of the water, the current being so strong that it was in the shape of a rainbow; yet all the command passed over safely, the cavalry being the last to cross. The bridge was cut loose from the north bank, the retreat was over, our endurance nearly exhausted, and we gave a sigh of relief.

The suffering and hardships endured by the soldiers on that retreat cannot be described. It stands without a parallel in history. It was the roughest, the severest, the hardest and most desperate fighting, the saddest and most pitiable, the bloodiest and most disastrous of the war to the Southern soldiers. The Army of Northern Virginia will recall the last days before Appomattox.

The foregoing tells in a feeble way of the life of the soldiers of Forrest's Cavalry in '63, '64, and '65. The brief account of the invasion of Middle Tennessee is related to portray the part performed by that great cavalry leader and his command in that memorable campaign.[159]—
CHARLES GORE JOY

HONORING THE NEGRO SERVANTS IN FORREST'S COMMAND

☞ [In regards] to monuments to our servants in the Confederate army . . . [this] recalls a work of that grand patriot, William H. Howcott, of

New Orleans. With the hearty approval of the citizens of Canton, Miss., from which locality many of us enlisted in Harvey's Scouts, of General Forrest's army, he [Howcott], at his individual expense, bought a lot adjoining the Canton Cemetery and erected a very imposing monument to our faithful negroes. It is splendid and cost about $3,000.

[Incidentally] my "boy" [black servant] Ben was captured by the Federals, escaped, and returned to our company. Mr. Howcott belonged to it.[160] — JAMES L. GOODLOE

DESCRIPTION OF FORREST BY A CONFEDERATE NOVELIST
☛ [Forrest was] a strange figure, an uneducated countryman, with no military training or influence; a man of violence and magnanimities; a big smoky personality; here dark, here broadly, clearly lighted.[161] — MARY JOHNSTON (from the pro-South romantic fiction, *Cease Firing*, 1912)

FORREST ON THE TENNESSEE RIVER
☛ I had an uncle and cousin with Forrest when he captured three Yankee transports at Paris Landing, on the Tennessee River, two miles from where my father lived. The vessels were loaded with [Union] army supplies en route for Johnsonville. When the boats were unloaded and the General about to leave, Uncle John asked him where he must report. "Meet me at Johnsonville, which place I will capture tomorrow," answered Forrest. Uncle John, being familiar with the General, then asked him if he was not counting chickens before they hatched, to which Forrest replied: "They are nearly hatched."

General Forrest had to fire two or three shots at the boats before they would surrender, and one of the shots cut a dining table down while the occupants were eating dinner. A Captain Wolf and his wife came off the boat and went to my father's home, where they remained a week. The Captain brought from the boat a very large and handsome salt cellar which had been knocked from the table and gave it to my father. I have it now.

Before General Forrest left, an old lady who lived in the country was present and asked him for a pair of shoes for her little boy. "What number does he wear?" asked the General. "Number eleven," she replied. "Bring your little boy to me and I will fit him," said Forrest.

Forrest captured Johnsonville the next day, as foretold.[162] — C. S. WILLIAMS

FORREST'S CAVALRY
☛ After Shiloh the year 1862 was one of active, strenuous service for

Forrest's men. These troops were always in conflict with the enemy's outposts, and their scouting parties rendered invaluable service at no expense to the Confederate government. The enemy furnished horses, arms, ammunition, and subsistence to these intrepid horsemen.

About December 10, 1862, General Bragg ordered Forrest, with his brigade of two thousand men and a four-gun battery, on a raid into West Tennessee. The command crossed the Tennessee River at Clifton on December 15. It was a daring venture. Winter had set in with cold rain, snow, sleet, and exposure of every sort for these unprotected men, and the country was swarming with Federal soldiers. The first fight was at Lexington, where Forrest's men captured Bob Ingersoll, with his entire regiment, and two rifled Rodman guns, three hundred small arms, two hundred horses, some wagons, ammunition, and other army stores.

The Federal authorities were greatly disturbed at this daring foray into their very midst, and plans were laid for the capture and destruction of the raiders before they could make their way back across the Tennessee River.

At Trenton there was a sharp fight which resulted in the capture on Forrest's part of twelve hundred prisoners, together with one thousand horses and mules, thirteen wagons, and an immense amount of ammunition, food, and clothing.

The Morris Hotel, a portion of the first floor which was used as headquarters for Forrest's Cavalry Corps, U.C.V., during the Reunion in the early 1900s.

From Trenton Forrest pushed on to Union City, and there captured a small garrison and about fifteen hundred paroled prisoners, and all without the firing of a gun.

By December 25 every bridge and trestle on the Mobile and Ohio Railroad from Jackson, Tenn., to Moscow, Ky., had been destroyed. But Forrest had stirred up a hornet's nest. From every quarter he learned that the enemy was planning his destruction, and it was evidently time to get out. He began his retreat toward his own country, and at Parker's Crossroads the hardest battle of the expedition was fought. Here Forrest outgeneraled and outfought a superior force and made his escape to the river, which he recrossed in safety.

This raid of two weeks may be summed up as follows: Three battles—Lexington, Trenton, and Parker's Crossroads—and innumerable skirmishes, many bridges destroyed, twenty stockades captured and burned, twenty five hundred of the enemy killed and captured, ten pieces of artillery and fifty wagons and teams, ten thousand small arms, one million rounds of ammunition, and eighteen hundred blankets taken from the enemy, and then the Tennessee River recrossed.[163] — REVEREND J. N. HUNTER

REMEMBERING THE MIGHTY FORREST

☞ [Let us recall the] wondrous strategy by which Forrest ensnared Streight and his raiders, the capture by Wheeler of the immense wagon train loaded with supplies for the Federal army, which, after disastrous defeat at Chickamauga, was beleaguered in Chattanooga, and Morgan's raid, in which he captured nine towns in Kentucky, fourteen in Indiana, and twenty-nine in Ohio, form a galaxy of wonderful exploits unequaled on the pages of history.

The turning back of Sherman's army by Forrest's victory at Okolona was a fitting prelude to the marvelous deeds of the Confederate horsemen of the West during the campaign of 1864. Who does not remember Tishomingo Creek,

> "Where the dread 'wizard of the saddle's' name
> Struck terror deep into the foeman's soul,
> While the fierce battle cry did upward roll,
> As his gray columns with resistless might
> Swept all before them in disastrous plight
> And utter rout, when in confusion blent
> Horsemen and footmen, guns and wagons went
> In headlong haste to find a safe retreat
> From gleaming blades they dared not wait to meet,
> The while that Forrest kept his border free
> In Mississippi and in Tennessee"?

It was by his reckless but skillful aggressiveness that Forrest held his ground so successfully in North Mississippi and West Tennessee during the time when Sherman was slowly yet surely moving on in the conquest of Northwest Georgia. When A. J. Smith came against him with too strong a force, Forrest swept around him and, in a sixty four-hour ride, entered Memphis, compelling Smith to make a rapid retreat. Then, after playing havoc with Federal transportation, garrisons, and depots of Tennessee, Forrest crowned his wondrous deeds by the capture and destruction of six million dollars' worth of Federal supplies and a gunboat fleet at Johnsonville—"a feat of arms," said Sherman, "which, I must confess, excited my admiration."[164] — J. T. DERRY

FORREST, MURAT, & NEY
☞ Forrest was the greatest cavalry officer since [French military commander] Marshal [Michel] Ney, without Ney's opportunities. His impetuosity and insubordinate temper toward his less capable superior officers would class him with [French military commander Joachim] Murat rather than with Ney.[165] — Dr. B. F. Ward

FORREST AFTER THE SPRING HILL FIASCO
☞ As we started in pursuit [of the Yanks, now fleeing north toward Franklin, Tenn.,] I saw General Forrest sitting on his horse by the roadside. As I had never been close to him, I availed myself of my privilege as chaplain to march at will; so I went up to where he sat. I was in rags like the rest and never wore any mark of rank, and of course he never noticed me. He seemed to be in a rage. As I looked on his splendid physique and noticed his intense excitement, he seemed to me the most dangerous animal I ever saw. He was looking at the evidences of disorderly retreat.

Just then General Walthall, our division commander, rode up. He was a great favorite of the great cavalryman. Forrest spoke to him for a moment, then broke forth. His face was livid, his eyes blazed. His voice was choked, between a sob and a curse, and these were his exact words, for I wrote them down just as I heard them: "General, O General, if they had given me just one of your brigades, just one of 'em to fling across this road, I could ha' tuck the whole damn shebang." I beg pardon for reporting "cuss words," but these were his words as I wrote them at the time.

In my moving about I have lost the little diary in which I wrote them. But they were impressed on my memory forever. And in our retreat from Nashville I was one of that ragged, barefoot squad of 1,621 infantry commanded by Walthall and with the cavalry constituting the rear guard under General Forrest. In all those days, when we fought all day and marched all night, I kept near General Forrest, and I can never believe that he was withheld from "flinging a brigade across the road" by the irresponsible orders of a Yankee spy. That doesn't solve the mystery. I have seen the statement that General Hood did issue orders to General Cheatham to block the road. General Cheatham denied receiving them, and years afterwards the staff officer by whom the orders were sent confessed that he was so tired and worn out that he went to sleep and never delivered them. "Old Joe" [Wheeler] next to Lee, as a general would have seen to it that those orders got there and were obeyed.[166] — Confederate Chaplain Dr. James H. McNeilly

GEN. FORREST ENDANGERED BY HIS OWN MEN

☛ Shortly after General Bragg fell back from Murfreesboro to Tullahoma, following the great battle, Bill Robertson and Jack Peters, of the 6th Florida Regiment, were on picket. A prolific writer tells of an interview with the former of their memorable experience. Robertson states:

"Jack Peters and I were ordered as a single squad to keep watch on a dirt road a short distance from our main line of defense. There was a swamp about fifty yards from where we intersected the road, and I suggested to Jack that if the enemy advanced we should fire and break for that swamp. Our immediate stand was at the base of a tree where we continued a subdued conversation, straining our eyes at short intervals to catch the slightest indication from the enemy.

"Presently our attention was directed to advancing cavalry. 'There they are; get ready!' quickly exclaimed Jack. He proposed that I take the leading one on the left and he the leading one on the right, fire, and run for the swamp. I contended that we could postpone firing until we were sure they were the enemy and asked Jack not to fire. He was in no mood to wait, and called my attention to the fact that there was not a gray coat in the entire squad, and that we had strict orders to fire upon anything from that direction.

"My unwillingness to fire, however, was supported by the impression I had received from the general deportment of the men which up to this time remained unchanged. I called Jack's attention to the seemingly unconcerned manner in which they were traveling. They did not have the appearance of men who were advancing toward an enemy, but showed a lack of anxiety that one would naturally expect from an advance under such conditions. So I said to Jack, 'We'll let them pass; they are small in number, and if they don't belong with us they will soon know of their peril and we can get in our work on their retreat.'

"They passed within fifty yards of us when Jack remarked: 'You are right; they are some of our men.' He made his decision upon discovering that each of the men had a sheet of black oilcloth fastened about him to keep off the rain, hence the invisible gray. We noticed, however, that one of them had riding back of him on his horse a little Union soldier whom they had captured and made a prisoner—the only exhibition of real blue that we saw.

"We related our experience in camp that evening and were told that the curious cavalry was General Forrest and his staff, and so it was the General himself who was treating the little bluecoat to a ride on his own horse.

"General Forrest came to our camp that night, sought Jack and myself, and extended his congratulations for the discretion exercised and thanked us for thus sparing himself and staff."[167] — UNKNOWN

A COMPANY MADE FAVOR WITH FORREST

☛ In a meeting at Camp Cherokee Station, Memphis and Charleston Railroad, October 10, 1864, the following proceedings were had:

"Whereas Gen. N. P. Forrest has kindly offered to transfer this company to our native State, Georgia, if we so desire, a meeting of the committee was called this day to consider the matter. The captain appointed a committee who reported as follows, which report was unanimously adopted:

"Resolved: 1. That Major General Forrest has our unqualified regard as a gentleman, our profoundest respect as an officer, and our highest admiration as a leader. We consider him as a prime, if not the leading, spirit in the revolution, having written with his sword

> 'One of the few immortal names
> That were not born to die.'

"2. That this company was recruited exclusively from nonconscripts and exempts with the distinct understanding that it would report for duty to none other than General Forrest; that he has our lasting gratitude for the honorable position assigned us; that we would be guilty of base ingratitude were we to quit his command, even if we so desired. Believing as we do that his troop has accomplished more than a like number of any other command, fidelity to a glorious cause demands that we remain with him until our common country is free.

"3. That we love our native State with the most ardent devotion. The virgin soil of every Confederate State has drunk the blood of her gallant sons. Georgia needs no eulogium, no praise. There she is. Look at her. Judge for yourselves. The world knows her history by heart. She will not lack defenders, for the chivalric sons of all the other seceding States (many of whose homes and families are in the possession of the enemy) have stood for many long months as a wall of fire upon her borders, disputing inch by inch the invasion of a hateful and merciless foe. We deem it our duty, therefore, to strike a blow wherever we meet a common oppressor.

"4. That we cordially invite our brothers and friends at home to join us and fill our much-depleted company to its maximum."

Committee: Sergt. R. W. Everett (Chairman), Sergt. C. W. Fouche, Sergt. J. H. Fulton, Sergt. W. S. Scott, Lieut. C. W. Hooper, A. P.

Jones, T. H. Rentz, G. W. Morton, W. M. Towers, J. R. Dejournett, R. S. Gill, T. C. Lumpkin, A. R. Durron.

GENERAL FORREST'S REPLY: HEADQUARTERS FORREST'S CAVALRY, CORINTH, MISS., OCTOBER 13, 1864

Sergt. R. W. Everett, Lieut. C. W. Hooper, and others: Gentlemen, I have the honor to acknowledge the receipt of the resolutions of your company, commanded by Capt. H. A. Gartrell.

It was under the most complimentary and gratifying circumstances that the company you represent became a part of my escort. In offering you the privilege of a transfer to the Army of Tennessee I was actuated solely by a desire to gratify those who I supposed were anxious to defend their own State; but your determination to remain with me is certainly most gratifying to my feelings. For the complimentary terms in which your company has been pleased to speak of me permit me, gentlemen, through you to return my heartfelt thanks.

In the camp, on the march, in battle you have exhibited all the traits of the patriotic citizen and gallant soldier. In the hour of emergency you have obeyed my orders with promptness, devotion, and heroic gallantry. I have never been for a moment unappreciative of the steadiness, self-denial, and patriotism with which you have borne the hardships and privations peculiar to camp life. You deserve the gratitude of your country for these soldierly virtues.

Miss Elizabeth Carroll, Sponsor for Forrest's Cavalry Corps, granddaughter of Tennessee Governor William Carroll.

Let your future but emulate your past, and you will preserve the high estimation which your valor and patriotism have already won. May you live to return to the homes from which you are now exiled and to avenge the wrongs your people have suffered! That the God of battles may guard and protect you will be the constant prayer of one who feels honored in having you under his command and who would deeply deplore your loss.

Thanking you, gentlemen, for the kind terms in which you have discharged your duty, and asking you to make known my feelings to the company, I am, very truly yours, N. B. Forrest, Major General.

EXPLANATION OF THE FOREGOING UNUSUAL PROCEEDINGS

Maj. D. M. Scott, commander, received the following from an old soldier:

"Dear Major: At your request I mail you a short history of Captain Gartrell's company, which as an independent was under Gen. N. B. Forrest for nearly two years. This company was organized for service by a special order of Secretary [James A.] Seddon, [C.S.] Secretary of War, at the request of General Forrest.

"Lieutenant Hooper, of Stonewall Jackson's command, was in Rome, Ga., on May 2, 1863, on recruiting service when a message was received by General Black, who commanded the militia of that district, from General Forrest urging that General Black raise all the forces he could and intercept General Streight, who was headed for Rome. At the request of General Black, Lieutenant Hooper secured a mounted company of old men and boys, numbering less than two hundred. This company crossed the Etowah River at Rome and went to meet General Streight. When Streight's advance met this company, they fell back and reported to General Streight that considerable force was in their front. General Streight decided to surrender. This militia company at the request of Major Strange, General Forrest's adjutant general, took charge of the Yankee officers who surrendered, guarded them to Rome, and took care of them until they were paroled.

"General Forrest was pleased with the action of this militia company and asked if they would not like to join his command. With some effort eighty-six members were secured who were willing to enlist, six of which were over forty-five, eighty being only fifteen to eighteen years of age.

"Lieutenant Hooper and J. W. Stillwell went to Richmond to see the Secretary of War and received an order to enlist the company for special duty with General Forrest, securing all the equipments necessary excepting horses. Sixty horses were secured by members and their friends. Twenty-six members were without horses. Capt. Henry Gartrell, of the Rome *Courier* (newspaper), offered to furnish the twenty-six horses if made captain of the company. This Lieutenant Hooper agreed to, and the company went out of the State and joined General Forrest in Mississippi, although a law had been passed that no new companies should leave Georgia, but should report to General Johnson for duty in his department.

"On October 9 General Forrest received an order to send Gartrell's company back to Georgia; but his action was finally approved by the Secretary of War, as this company was organized by order of the

Secretary of War at the special request of General Forrest and for duty under him.

"Captain Gartrell was captured in November, 1864, and kept in prison for more than six months after the close of the war. The company, under the command of Lieutenant Hooper, was sent by General Forrest to watch the rear of the enemy from Columbia to Franklin, Tenn.; and being cut off from General Forrest's personal command, which went to Murfreesboro, Tenn., it joined Colonel Biffle's regiment, under General Chalmers, and was very active all around Nashville. The command was sent under special detail to the rear of the enemy at Nashville. The command it was with captured a Yankee corral, seized the horse troughs, used them as boats, crossed the Cumberland River, and routed a large party of the enemy, capturing quite a number, each member of the expedition bringing back a captured Yankee in his horse trough with him. (This occurred on the day General Hood's command retired from its advance position in front of Nashville.)

This company acted as special escort for Gen. Stephen D. Lee during the battle of Nashville and was highly complimented by him. It served night and day in the rear of Hood's army while on the retreat, almost without relief, until the Tennessee River was crossed, and it was among the very last to cross the Harpeth River on the retreat from Nashville. By special order from General Forrest the company rejoined his command at Corinth, Miss., on January 4, 1865, remaining constantly under his personal command until the surrender at Gainesville, Ala., May 11, 1865.[168] — UNKNOWN

FORREST & THE BATTLE OF JOHNSONVILLE

☛ The destruction of Johnsonville, with the events immediately preceding, form a chapter unique and unparalleled in the annals of war. Late in the fall of 1864 Gen. N. B. Forrest was ordered to destroy Johnsonville, which had become a great Federal depot. Supplies drawn from St. Louis, Cincinnati, and the surrounding country were brought up the river by boat and stored here, awaiting shipment by rail to Nashville and East Tennessee.

The Confederate force assembled at Jackson, and on the 20th of October, General Buford, who had moved forward to Lexington, was ordered to lead the advance by way of Huntingdon and Paris to the mouth of the Big Sandy River. By the 28th the entire force, not over twenty-four hundred available men, had reached and fortified Paris Landing, on Tennessee River, and another point five miles lower down, opposite old Fort Heiman. The positions were carefully chosen and the batteries well masked and supported with infantry.

About nine o'clock on the morning of the 29th the Federal transport *Mazeppa* passed the lower batteries and was soon driven ashore on the opposite bank, where all the [Union] officers and men, with the exception of the captain, escaped to the woods. A Confederate paddled across the river on a log, received the surrender of the gallant captain, and together they rowed back across the stream to the fort. The *Mazeppa* was soon pulled across to the western bank, where she was relieved of a rich cargo of stores and immediately burned. Meanwhile three gunboats appearing from below were repulsed.

W. A. Dawson.

Next day, after several sharp encounters with different boats, the gunboat *Undine* and the transport *Venus* were captured and found to be very little the worse for the encounter. General Forrest at once conceived the idea of placing detachments of his cavalry on board the boats and using them in the advance against Johnsonville. The captured pilots were pressed into service. Trial trips were successfully made amid a great display of enthusiasm by the troops on the shore. Upon the return two twenty-pound Parrott guns were placed upon the *Undine*. And now, manned by the cavalry since become famous as the "Horse Marine," this little Confederate flotilla began a brief but brilliant career that stands unique and unrivaled in the history of naval warfare.

On the morning of the 1st of November, 1864, the expedition was set in motion toward Johnsonville. Captain Gracey, who had fought with Forrest at Chickamauga, commanded the gunboat *Undine*, which became the commodore's flagship; but Lieut. Col. W. A. Dawson was placed in immediate command of the transport *Venus*. Chalmer's Division led the advance, and Buford moved in the rear to guard against gunboats from below. Morton's and the other batteries moved southward, along the western bank of the river, prepared to render immediate assistance to the boats.

The roads were in the very worst condition, while the rain poured steadily; but the troops, inspired with the novelty of the undertaking and the prospect of an early engagement, moved forward in good order and the best of spirits.

On the afternoon of the 2nd, with the *Venus* leading, the little flotilla ventured incautiously ahead of the land supports and were suddenly attacked by gunboats 29 and 32, led by Lieutenant Commander King, U.S.N. The *Undine* escaped down the river to Davidson's Ferry, where she came under the protection of the guns in Chalmers's Battery. The *Venus*, however, was soon badly damaged, run ashore, and captured. Colonel Dawson and all the other officers escaped to the shore. The gunboats soon retired up the river with the *Venus* in tow, loaded with the two Parrott guns, two hundred rounds of ammunition, five hundred and seventy-six boxes of hard bread, and much other valuable freight taken from the *Mazeppa*. The guns and ammunition were afterwards used against the Confederates at Johnsonville.

On the 3rd the *Undine* and the land forces proceeded cautiously up the river, but Federal gunboats closed in from above and below and drove the *Undine* ashore on the eastern bank. Captain Gracey and his men succeeded in firing the vessel and escaped to the canebrakes and there remained till nightfall, when they crossed the river on logs and rafts and rejoined their command. Thus ended the career of the only fleet ever manned by cavalrymen. By the evening of the 3rd the forces had reached a point near Reynoldsburg Island, about three miles below Johnsonville, and there encamped. Halfway between Johnsonville and Reynoldsburg, opposite the old Waverly Landing, Cypress Creek flows into the Tennessee River from the west. This creek is a very sluggish stream, surrounded by sloughs and treacherous swamps, and, as the Federals thought, rendered entirely impassable by the heavy rains.

Late in the afternoon Forrest, accompanied by his chief of artillery, Morton, started out to make a reconnaissance of Johnsonville. After a lengthy search along the banks of Cypress Creek, they found a crossing used by cattle wintering in the canebrakes. They crossed the stream and gained a view of the town from the opposite shore. The town, a mere hamlet, lay at the mouth of a creek along the side of a ridge of hills rising abruptly from the river to a height of a hundred feet. On two of the highest points of this ridge were strong redoubts protected by unusually heavy earthworks and armed with heavy ordnance, with rifle pits running down west and south. Scattered along the river bank stood the railway depot and storage warehouses, filled to the top with every conceivable kind of military stores. Along the landing lay immense piles of supplies not liable to damage by exposure. At the water's edge, interspersed with gunboats, floated a large fleet of transports and barges heaped with war merchandise.

On the western side the bank rises twenty feet above the water and drops back abruptly to a bottom, thus forming a natural earthwork, at that time heavily timbered and overgrown with cane. As soon as it was dark General Forrest moved up to this position. Thrall's Battery of twelve-pound howitzers was placed in the heavy timber some distance back from the bank. Meanwhile General Lyon, who had been an artillery officer in the regular army before the war, arrived with four hundred Kentucky troops. Under his direction the guns were pushed forward to within a few feet of the river and sunk below the surface of the ground in pits, with embrasures cut through the bank. The batteries were well supported by Buford's and Chalmers's Brigades concealed in the heavy timber. By noon next day preparations were complete.

To the hidden watchers the opposite shore presented an inspiring panorama. The Federals thought that Forrest had been turned back by the loss of his boats and was by this time far away in retreat. The day was dreary and misty; but the men had been very busy for the past few days preparing for the expected attack, and now, thinking that all danger was past, took this occasion for rest and a general holiday. The ladies came down the hill to stroll along the streets of the town. Along the path from the boats to the redoubts lounged soldiers, both white and black. At the dock lay the gunboats *Key West*, *Elphin*, and *Tawah* with steam up and ready for action, while the heavily loaded barges bustled with the activities of numerous deck hands.

Two o'clock was the hour set for the attack, and the timepieces of the officers had been set together; but the signal was not given till three. Exactly at three o'clock ten guns were fired as one. The scene on the opposite bank changed from quiet security to consternation and confusion. Two of the gunboats were completely disabled by the first round, while the third made only a feeble reply. The heavy guns in the redoubts opened and soon fired with great accuracy, but with little effect upon the sunken batteries. The crews of the boats jumped into the water and swam for the safety of the shore. Soon the vessels burst into flames that spread quickly to the barges and transports, till the river was filled with the burning craft. A stiff wind upstream held the boats against the bank and scattered the flames to the neighboring piles of stores. Kindled by red-hot balls and fanned by the high wind, the long line of storehouses burst into roaring flames. Thousands of bushels of grain, tons of hay, barrel upon barrel of spirits and oil, hundreds of thousands of pounds of meats, and numerous other stores fed the fury of the flames. The whole river front became a veritable wall of fire, and in one hour the great depot was destroyed.

The main object of the expedition accomplished, General Forrest moved his command six miles to the rear by the light of the conflagration. Rucker's Brigade and one section of the artillery were left to cover the retreat. The only loss sustained by the Confederates was one man killed by a falling limb shot from a great cypress tree. In the morning the redoubts guarded only charred hulks and blackened ruins. General Forrest returned in person to view the ruins. A detachment of [Union] infantry made a demonstration from one of the forts and was promptly fired upon and forced to retire. The artillery and troops under Colonel Rucker were now withdrawn. The Federal forces were hurriedly removed to Nashville. The ruins were looted and the destruction completed by guerrillas. An assistant inspector general of the United States army estimated the total money value of property destroyed in the Johnsonville raid, including barges and steamboats, at about two million two hundred thousand dollars [$55 million in today's currency]; but other estimates were much greater. The military and naval forces at Johnsonville on November 4 were as follows: 43rd Wisconsin Volunteers, seven hundred men; 13th Tennessee Colored Infantry, twelve hundred men; quartermaster's employees, eight hundred men; six ten-pound Parrott guns, four twelve-pound Napoleon guns, and two twenty-pound Parrott guns captured on the *Venus*; and the gunboats *Key West*, *Elphin*, and *Tawah*. General Forrest in his report says: "Having completed the work designed for the expedition, I moved my command six miles during the night by the light of the enemy's burning property. We reached Corinth on November 10, after an absence of two weeks, during which time I captured and destroyed four gunboats, fourteen transports, twenty barges, twenty-six pieces of artillery, and six million seven hundred thousand dollars' worth of property. My loss during the entire trip was two killed and nine wounded."

After the battle of Nashville the 13th Tennessee Colored Infantry [U.S.] returned to Johnsonville, where they remained till the close of the war. The depots were never rebuilt, and to-day all that remains to recall the fierce conflict waged there are the unusually well-preserved earthworks of the redoubts and the puny war toys of half a century past, lifting their charred ribs and iron-shod prows above the rippling waters of the Tennessee.[169] — E. G. COWEN

Remnants of Forrest's victory at Johnsonville: ribs of a burned Union gunboat in the Tennessee River shallows.

8

1914-1917

GENERAL FORREST AT SELMA, ALABAMA

☞ In the battle of Selma, Ala., I had my first and only view of General Forrest. He rode into the redoubt in which was stationed a company of the Queen Anne's, one of whom I was. His left arm was in a sling—a red handkerchief, as I remember now. The story about his hurt, as told them, was that on the day before, as he was scouting around unaccompanied at the bend in the road, he and a Federal cavalryman, also alone, bumped into each other. The Federal drew his saber and charged. Forrest reached for his pistol, which hung in the holster; so he had to throw up his left arm and take the saber blows on it until he loosened his revolver, when in a moment the Federal was ready for the burial squad.[170] — E. GUTHRIE

ANOTHER FORREST MYTH DEBUNKED

☞ I belonged to the 9th Tennessee Cavalry, one of the regiments that composed Forrest's famous old brigade, and [I] was with him from the time he was made a brigadier (except from Chickamauga by way of Atlanta back to Tennessee, about eight months, when our regiment was under Joe Wheeler) till we surrendered at Gainesville, Ala., on the 9th of May, 1865. I was with him in the quiet of the camp, on the march, in the excitement of battle, reported to him for special duty of different kinds, and received orders and personal instructions from him; but I never heard him use such an expression as "to get there fustest with the mostest men."

While General Forrest was a man of limited education and used some words then common in the South, but now obsolete, which would sound strange to us of this generation, yet he used good, old-fashioned Southern English, stronger and more impressive in times of excitement, I will admit, than it is necessary for a teacher of a Bible class in a Sunday school to use; but in ordinary times his voice was soft and low and as musical as a woman's, having a peculiar charm and attractiveness for those who listened to him. I hardly know whether those who use this expression as emanating from General Forrest intend by it to magnify his great natural military genius or to disparage him by making it appear that he was an ignoramus. In either case it is pure fiction, without one scintilla of fact to rest upon; for there never was a man who laid as little stress upon opposing numbers as he, and those who followed him knew that he used no such tactics even as "to get there first with the most men," as this myth first appeared.

He used no such tactics at Murfreesboro when he attacked an enemy of about equal numbers, protected by a fortified camp and in possession of the courthouse, jail, and other buildings, which were used as defenses; and after a six hours' fight he captured the Federal General Crittendon, all his men, and a battery of five guns, which, General Wolsley, the great English war lord, said, was one of the most brilliant achievements of the war.

He used no such tactics at Brentwood when, after capturing two forts and as many prisoners as he had men, Gen. Green Clay Smith came out from Franklin with a full brigade of Federals, charged, and stampeded our rear guard and retook a part of our captured wagons. He did not hesitate to take his escort and as many men as he could rally for that special occasion (no more than a thousand men in all), charge Smith, and send him back to Franklin in complete disorder.

He used no such tactics when, with only two regiments, the 9th and 4th Tennessee, he followed Gen. Abel D. Streight, with four full regiments of picked men, for one hundred and fifty miles across

The Hugh Moore House, Brentwood, Tenn., used by Forrest as a field hospital.

the State of Alabama, fighting him nearly every jump of the way and capturing him and all his men near Rome, Ga., and preventing his destruction of the arsenal at that place, which he had started to do, and for the third time receiving the thanks of the Confederate Congress for great services rendered by himself and men.

He used no such tactics when, with only four thousand men, he met William Sooey Smith at Sakatonchee Creek, near Westpoint, Miss., whom Generals Grant and Sherman had sent out from Memphis with a "carefully selected and well-equipped" army of seven thousand men and twenty pieces of artillery with the peremptory orders to destroy that "Devil Forrest," as General Sherman called him. Instead of which, after a sixty-mile running fight, Smith (in the lead) got back to Memphis with his army whipped and beaten and himself in disgrace, from which he never recovered.

He used no such tactics when, in order to retrieve the disgrace that had overtaken Smith and to palliate their own discomfiture, Generals Grant and Sherman, after weighing all their brigadiers in the balance, finally selected Samuel D. Sturgis as the man best fitted by military training to destroy Forrest; for General Sherman had wired [U.S.] Secretary Stanton that "Forrest must be destroyed if it takes the lives of ten thousand men and breaks the treasury." So they started Sturgis out from Memphis with another "carefully selected and well-equipped" army of eight thousand men and thirty pieces of artillery to find Forrest. He found him at Brice's Crossroads; but Forrest did not wait "to get there fustest with the mostest men," but pitched into him with his little band of four thousand devoted followers, defeated Sturgis in one of the most desperate conflicts and, according to our best military critics, one of the most masterly generaled battles of the war, and sent him back over a road in one day and two nights that it had taken him nine days to march in his advance and onto Memphis without wagons, with less than half the artillery with which he started, and with his men scattered and demoralized, some of them without guns or knapsacks, for they had stripped for a race, worse beaten and humiliated, if possible, than was William Sooey Smith.

General Forrest was unfortunate in not having a military education, for on this account he was prevented by our wise men at Richmond from the more early exemplification of that great military genius which he displayed in the last two years of the war and which, I believe, was a great loss to the South; yet he used good, plain, old-fashioned English, and all this rot about his using such an expression as "to get there fustest with the mostest men" is pure, unadulterated gammon. Maj. J. P. Strange and Capt. Charles W. Anderson, who were members of his staff and were his secretaries, both say, and it is a historical fact, that he dictated all his reports and addresses, and our "War Records" show that they compare favorably, both in composition and style, with those of our other great Southern generals. And although General Forrest was not an orator in the general acceptation of that term, yet it was just as natural for him to express himself well as it was for him to fight well.

I have a vivid recollection of a speech, or rather a talk, he made to us a few days before the surrender. It was just after the battle of Selma. Lee and Johnston had surrendered, and we had been told that Gen. Richard Taylor, who had command of that department and who ranked General Forrest, had agreed on terms of our surrender with [Union] General Canby at Mobile and that a detachment of Federal officers would soon be out to receive our arms and to parole us. Strange as it may seem to the present generation, the suggestion of giving up our arms and going home almost created a mutiny in our regiment. The same condition existed in the 7th Tennessee, and, as is stated in J. P. Young's history of that regiment, "it took all of General Forrest's powers of persuasion to induce them to surrender." The younger element among them particularly revolted against it. The truth is, we did not believe that General Forrest would do it, and we were led to this belief by the closing words of his address to us when we arrived on the south side of the Tennessee River on Hood's retreat. A move was started in which it was proposed to resist it and go to Texas, join Price (for we thought, perhaps, he would not surrender), and if this failed us to go to Mexico or to South America rather than to give up our arms, go home, and endure a condition that we then thought would be worse than death for us.

Miss Susie D. Yerger, Maid of Honor for Forrest's Cavalry.

I remember a fiery speech made by Lieut. "Pap" Nichols, of Company A, in which he called for volunteers to go with him to Texas, and it looked for a while as if the whole regiment would go with him. Our colonel tried to show us the futility of such a course, but we would not listen to him. General Bell, our brigadier, tried to reason with us, but we paid no attention to him. Then General Forrest came. He called us together and asked us to listen to him, and we did listen. He told us, among other things, that he had never asked us to do anything that he was not willing to do himself; that he had never asked us to charge the enemy when he was not willing to lead the charge; that we had followed him through the discomforts of a long war and through many hard-fought battles. Now he would ask us to follow his example and to surrender our arms on the terms agreed to by General Taylor, go home, and make as good citizens as we had made soldiers; and as our devotion to the cause of the South and our bravery in battle had won the respect of even our enemies, he believed all would be well with us. He had spoken only a few words when men who had never flinched in battle were crying like children, and when he finished we felt that we would still follow him.

That was the last time I ever saw him, now fifty years ago. Of the many who heard him then but few are left. Will we meet again? I believe we will; that

> "When our days on earth are ended
>   And we are done with things below,
> When our bark of life lies stranded,
>   We will meet again, I know
> For a spirit within me whispering
>   Says it must, it shall be so."[171] — J. G. WITHERSPOON

BRANCH OF DIXIE HIGHWAY NAMED AFTER FORREST

☛ The Southern Highway Commission, which met at Rome, Ga., on July 5 [1915], named that branch of the Dixie Highway extending from Birmingham, Ala., to Rome, Ga., for General Forrest, and a "Forrest Highway Association" was formed. The following letter from Mrs. Letitia Dowdell Ross, First Vice President General U.D.C., was read before the Commission and its suggestions indorsed. Others should profit by this and lose no opportunity to have our great men thus remembered:

"As a true Southerner, a devoted Daughter of the Confederacy, and as Chairman of the Committee on Memorials, Highways, Historic Places, and Events of the Alabama Division, U.D.C., I am writing to urge that when the Commission meets on July 5 in Rome, Ga., the members of that body use their utmost endeavors to have this branch of the great Dixie Highway from Rome, Ga., to Birmingham, Ala., named for the incomparable 'Wizard of the Saddle,' the famous cavalry leader, Nathan Bedford Forrest.

"'Poor is that country that boasts no heroes, but beggared is that people who, having them, forgets.' Forrest's terrific, relentless pursuit of Col. Abel Streight's daring and well-planned expedition from Gadsden, Ala., to Rome, Ga., and the capture of his large command with a force only one-third as numerous has been considered by capable military critics 'not only as one of Forrest's most brilliant achievements, and they were without number, but also one of the most remarkable performances known to warfare.'

"The story of the 'lost ford' and the important role played by Emma Sansom, Alabama's girl heroine, reads like a thrilling romance. 'Her presence of mind and coolness under circumstances which would have paralyzed the faculties of most older women enabled General Forrest to overcome a very formidable obstacle in his dangerous and daring pursuit of Colonel Streight and gained for him at least three hours' time, which was of inestimable value, since it enabled him to overtake and compel Colonel Streight to surrender almost within sight of Rome.'

"The Confederate soldier does not need highways to be named for him nor monuments to be erected to commemorate his matchless bravery and heroic sacrifice; for, sublime in his devotion to duty, despite overwhelming numbers and resources of the enemy, he has builded for himself monuments more enduring than granite, marble, or bronze; but highways should be built and named for our great heroes, monuments should commemorate their unrivaled deeds, not only as a patriotic duty, but to teach history to the living. Gen. Stephen D. Lee, in one of his last messages to the people of the South, urged them to honor the Confederate soldier 'first for the sake of the dead, but more for the sake of the living, that in this busy industrial age these great highways, these monuments to our soldiers, may stand like great interrogation marks to the soul of the beholder. We must not overtax posterity by expecting those who come after us to name our great highways and to erect memorials to the heroes whom our generation was unwilling to commemorate.'

Stephen Dill Lee.

"Daughters of the Confederacy, feel assured that the progressive and patriotic men composing the Commission have only to have this matter properly brought to their attention to insure the naming of this branch highway for General Forrest, and the Commission will no doubt deem it a rare privilege and opportunity thus to honor our peerless cavalry leader. They will thus write indelibly on the hearts and minds of the young as well as on the pages of history the wonderful war story of the man who at his country's call and under the inspiring strains of the immortal song 'Dixie' fearlessly gave battle to the vastly superior forces of the enemy and won for himself a place for all time in the hearts of his countrymen. In thus honoring Forrest, Alabama, Georgia, and the South will honor themselves."[172] — UNKNOWN

CHARACTERISTICS OF GENERAL FORREST

☛ A letter from Gen. Marcus J. Wright states: "In a conversation with [Union] Gen. W. T. Sherman in the presence of Col. Robert N. Scott, U.S.V., and several other persons, he said that he regarded General Forrest as one of the ablest cavalry commanders that had ever lived. [Confederate] Gen. Joseph E. Johnston expressed the same opinion and added that Forrest was a born military genius."

General Wolseley, commander in chief of the British army, acknowledged to be one of the greatest soldiers and finest military critics of the age, wrote:

"Forrest had no knowledge of military science nor of military history to teach him how he should act. He was entirely ignorant of what other generals in previous wars had done; but what he lacked in booklore was to a large extent compensated for by the soundness in his judgment upon all occasions, by his power of thinking and reasoning with great rapidity under fire and under all circumstances of surrounding or of great mental and bodily fatigue. Panic found no resting place in that calm brain of his, and no danger, no risk appalled that dauntless spirit. Born with true military instincts, he was nature's soldier. His force was largely composed of wild and reckless men, who looked on him as their master and their leader. He possessed that rare tact which enabled him not only to control effectively these fiery, turbulent spirits, but to attach them to him personally with 'hooks of steel.' They recognized in him not only the daring, able, and successful leader, but also the commanding officer who would not hesitate to punish with severity when he deemed punishment necessary. He never ventured to hamper their freedom of action by any barrack yard drill. They were irregular by nature, and he never attempted to rid them of that character. Accustomed, as they were, from boyhood to horses and the use of arms and brought up with all the devil-may-care notions of the frontier, they possessed as an inheritance all the best and most valuable qualities of the irregulars. There was something in the dark-gray eye of Forrest which warned his subordinates that he was not to be trifled with and would not stand any nonsense from friend or foe. His raids upon the enemy's line of communication were frequent and successful. No rivers stopped him, and a detailed account of the military stores he destroyed and the fortified posts he captured would alone fill a volume.

"One Federal general was removed from his command at Memphis for having failed to do anything against this now redoubtable commander. Shortly afterwards Forrest himself marched into Memphis and took possession of the newly appointed Federal general's uniform, which was found in his room. The disgraced general, referring to his dismissal, wittily said: 'They removed me because I could not keep Forrest out of West Tennessee, but my successor could not keep him out of his bedroom.'"

Concerning the capture of Fort Pillow, General Wolseley says:

"The signal for assault being then given, the place was quickly taken. There was a heavy loss on both sides; but, all things considered, including the intense ill feeling then existing between the men of Tennessee who fought on one side and those on the other, I do not think the fact that about one-half [of the men of] a small garrison in a place [like Fort Pillow were] . . . either killed or wounded evinced any unusual bloodthirstiness on the part of the assailants."

An officer who knew Forrest well gave the following description of the forces under his command about this time:

"Forrest's troops were then crossing the Tennessee River. There were about ten thousand mounted men, well provided with blankets and general equipment stamped 'U.S.,' showing whence he had obtained them, sixteen field pieces taken from the Northern army, each drawn by eight horses, two hundred and fifty wagons, and fifty-four horse ambulances. He had enlisted, armed, equipped, supplied with ammunition, and fed all this force without any help from his own government. For two years he had drawn absolutely nothing from the quartermaster or commissary department of the Confederate States. His was, indeed, a freebooter's force on a large scale, and his motto was borrowed from the old raiders on the frontier: 'I shall never want as long as my neighbor has.'

"His defeat of General Sturgis in June, 1864, was a most remarkable achievement, well worth the attention of military students. He pursued the enemy for nigh sixty miles, the battle and pursuit lasting thirty hours. Of this operation, General Sherman says: 'Forrest whipped Sturgis fair and square.'

"Forrest was wounded badly (could not sit his horse) and took to the field in a buggy. He struck Sherman's line of communication, tore up railroads, burned bridges, captured gunboats, burned transports and many million of dollars' worth of stores and supplies."

Sherman wrote General Grant in 1864: "That devil Forrest was down about Johnsonville, making havoc among the gunboats and transports."

Speaking of the end of the Confederacy, General Wolseley says:

"It was a gallant struggle from the first, a pitched battle, as it were, between a plucky boy and a full-fledged man. If ever England has to fight for her existence, may the same spirit pervade all here that was shown by both North and South! May we have . . . to lead our mounted troops as able a leader as General Forrest. . . . Forrest possessed all the best qualities of the Anglo-American frontiersmen. He was a man of great self-confidence, self-reliance, and reticence. Of quick resolve, prompt execution, inexhaustible resources, he had all the best instincts of the soldier, and his natural military genius was balanced by sound judgment. He knew what he wanted, and there was no uncertainty in his orders. There was never any languor in that determined heart nor weakness in that iron body. Panic and fear flew at his approach, and the sound of his cheer gave courage to the weakest heart.

"'In war,' said Napoleon, 'men are nothing; a man is everything.' And it would be difficult to find a stronger corroboration of this maxim than is to be found in the history of General Forrest's operations."

Gen. Joseph E. Johnston, one of the most celebrated of the Confederate leaders, regarded Forrest as one of the brightest soldiers our war produced. He achieved great things during the war and would, I am sure, have achieved greater if he had been trusted earlier and given the command of armies instead of the weak regiments and brigades which for so long were confided to him. . . . Forrest had fought like a knight-errant for the cause he believed to be that of justice and right. No man who drew his sword for his country in that fratricidal struggle deserved better of her; and as long as the chivalrous deeds of her sons find poets to describe them and fair women to sing them, the name of this gallant, though low-born and uneducated, general will be remembered with affection and sincere admiration. A man with such a record needs no ancestry, and his history proves that a general with such a head and such a military genius as he possessed can win battles without education.

John Allan Wyeth as a boy.

. . . He died about twelve years after the close of the war from the effects of a wound near the spine which he received in the battle of Shiloh. . . . It would be difficult in all history to find a more varied career than his. . . . A man who from the greatest poverty, without any learning, and by sheer force of character alone became the great fighting leader of fighting men; a man in whom an extraordinary military instinct and sound common sense supplied to a large extent his unfortunate want of military education. When all the disadvantages under which the South fought are considered, it is wonderful what her soldiers achieved; but soldiers who believe in themselves and have absolute faith in their leaders are very difficult to beat in war. Little by little this feeling grew in the officers under Forrest, and he knew well how to foster it among the wild and restless spirits that followed him.[173] — DR. JOHN ALLAN WYETH

A CATALOG OF CIVIL WAR "IFS"

☛ Here are some "ifs" contributed to the *Army and Navy Journal* by a Georgian. Students of the War between the States may find them interesting, and many will doubtless be able to add indefinitely to the list:

If—the United States in 1860 had had an army commensurate with her size. If—[Union General] McDowell's plans had been carried out at First Manassas. If—the Confederates had immediately followed up their success in the above battle.

If—the government hadn't taken McDowell's Corps away from [Union General] McClellan. If—[Confederate General] Jackson during the Seven Days' Battles had been the man of the Valley or Chancellorsville. If—McClellan's army hadn't been removed when he had solved the problem of the correct road to Richmond. If—the lost dispatch hadn't been found.

If—[Union General] Grant had been in command of the Union army at Antietam. If—[Union General] Hooker hadn't sent off his cavalry just previous to Chancellorsville. If—[Confederate General] Lee had turned over Jackson's command to Stuart after Jackson's death.

If—the Confederates had followed up their success on the first day's fight at Gettysburg. If—[Union General] Meade had pushed Lee directly after the Union victory. If—[Confederate General] Bragg had followed [Union General] Rosecrans into Chattanooga immediately after the Chickamauga fight. If—[Confederate General] Johnston had not been superseded by Hood. If—Hood had attacked at Spring Hill. If—[Union General] Hancock had known of the momentary panic of the Confederates at the Wilderness. If—Hancock's order to occupy Petersburg had been delivered to him.

But the greatest "if" of all to the Confederacy was: If—they had recognized the true worth of Forrest before it was too late.[174] — UNKNOWN

LAST REVIEW OF FORREST'S CAVALRY

☛ During the latter part of March, 1865, General Forrest reviewed his troops at West Point, Miss., and immediately thereafter marched out in the direction of Montevallo, Ala. It was whispered in camp that a large Federal cavalry was near there, and on the 31st of March, 1865, we could see volumes of smoke ascending from that direction; and the 3rd Kentucky Regiment was thrown out in a skirmish line, with Capt. T. C. Miller, of Murray, Ky., in command. We skirmished the woods for miles in the direction of the smoke and found that a force of Federals had burned rolling mills or foundries about five miles southwest of Montevallo.

When we came into the main road leading to Selma, a call was made for a volunteer advance guard. The writer and another Kentucky boy volunteered, and we were ordered to report to the officer about two hundred yards down the road toward Montevallo. When we reported, we found that the officer and the other boys were Alabamians. We proceeded in the direction of Montevallo, and when within less than two miles of the town we came upon the outpost picket at a two-story white house on the left of the road who came out, saying: "You have got me." To this our commander replied: "Hand up your arms." But instead of handing up his pistol he fired some four or five times into our squad of fifteen or twenty without hitting any one, then climbed over a fence, and went running toward Montevallo. After we had fired a few shots, with two other boys I climbed over the fence and caught him, then turned him over to some other soldiers who had overtaken us. Capt. T. C. Miller came up and threw us out as skirmishers again.

The Yankee skirmish line was just on the south side of Montevallo on a rise, and we were on the brow of a slope, without any protection whatever, and from two hundred and fifty to three hundred yards apart. They could shoot at us and drop back a few feet and be out of sight. This skirmishing lasted for some two or three hours. At this time Captain Miller was commanding the left wing of the skirmish line and Irve Nance,

Top: Miss Jane Meredith, Sponsor for Forrest's Cavalry; bottom left, Miss Sadie Gillespie and right, Miss Marjorie Weatherly, Maids of Honor to Miss Meredith.

of Oak Level, Ky., the right. Just as the Yankees charged us, dashing over the ridge within two hundred and fifty yards of us, Irve Nance said we would everyone be captured; and, sure enough, they did capture several of us, but didn't get either of our commanders.

As prisoners we went back to Montevallo, a distance of two or three miles, and were then taken on to Selma, with continued fighting along the way; at Ebenezer Church there was a considerable fight. This place, as I remember, was twenty-five miles from Selma. On the second evening of April the Federal cavalry captured Selma and most of Forrest's command, but he and his escort swam the Alabama River and made their escape.

After General Lee surrendered, we prisoners were taken to Montgomery, Ala., and on the 14th of April, 1865, Tom Lovelace, Tom Mathis, James Castleberry, and I were paroled and walked from Montgomery to our homes, in Western Kentucky. James Castleberry is dead; I don't know of Tom Lovelace or Tom Mathis.

While at the Birmingham [Confederate Veterans] Reunion I went out to Montevallo on Wednesday, the 17th, to see if I could locate the place of my capture, the house where we captured the outpost picket, and the place in the town where we were taken after being captured. Though fifty-one years had passed, I had no difficulty in recognizing the three spots indicated. Judge E. S. Lyman, a most excellent gentleman of Montevallo, showed me every courtesy, driving me to all these places, so interesting to one who was there at that terrible time facing a Federal cavalry of fifteen thousand men commanded by General Wilson. I know of but one other Kentuckian living at this time who was in that skirmish line, and that is Irve Nance, of Oak Level, Ky.[175] — D. B. CASTLEBERRY

I SURRENDERED WITH FORREST

☛ I learn that the Sumter Chapter will duly mark with an appropriate monument the spot in Gainesville, Ala., where General Forrest surrendered. The idea is surely very commendable, and I as a member of General Forrest's escort want to start your subscription with a $5 contribution.

I still have my parole, dated at Gainesville on May 10, 1865. General Forrest kept an escort of from one hundred to two hundred men, which he used largely to assist any weak spots in the fighting line when they were being hard pressed by superior numbers of the enemy and needed assistance quickly. I think there were just one hundred and two of us present with General Forrest on the day of the surrender [at Gainesville, Ala.], May 10, 1865. Our paroles were signed by [Union]

Maj. Gen. E. R. S. Canby and Brig. Gen. E. S. Dennis.

My memory runs back over the intervening space of fifty-two years since that date, and a somewhat dimmed mental picture of Gainesville shows it to me as a straggling village on the banks of the Tombigbee River. I remember well its hotel, because I and the other five men, or rather boys, of my mess made a bee line for the hotel, as we were in a chronic state of hunger in those days. We were a little surprised that we had to buy tickets at $10 each for dinner before entering the dining room. While this was about $5 higher than we had paid at any time before, it in no way deterred our going in.

We were on the waiting list, and as soon as seats were vacant we captured them and went through the menu, which was delivered orally from soup to pie. Having finished the meal, we were just ready to leave the table when a new waiter rushed up, grabbed the pie plates, thinking we had just come, and asked if we would have soup. We answered "Yes" and went clear through the meal again, thus filling up vacuums and unoccupied spaces in our "internal labyrinths" that had been accumulating for several days. In fact, when we left West Point, Miss., to dash across and intercept General Wilson's U.S.A. cavalry raid just above Selma, we did not expect 12,000 men, armed with seven-shooting rifles, to come against General Forrest's 3,500 men available, armed with the one-shot Sharp rifle mostly; but that is just what did occur.

Near Bulger's Creek, south of Plantersville, as near as I can remember, when that bunch of Yankees with those seven-shooting rifles hit our line, we decided to retire to more advantageous positions at Selma. I will not at this time describe the celerity of our actions or the absence of placidity that pervaded our boys in reaching the Selma lines. However, when we reached the Selma lines and the boys looked them over with critical eyes, our illustrious commander decided that he did not want to utilize the Selma lines as a cemetery for his boys.

Anyway, Gainesville, perched high upon the banks of the Tombigbee, would be a far more beautiful and picturesque place to go into camp. In fact, many of our boys did not go through Selma; they took a shortcut just above the town, where the water was fine and the swimming good. It was in that fight above Selma that Lieut. Nath Boone, of that escort, fat, fair, forty, and a fearless fighter, had a decoration just the shape of a horseshoe carved on the side of his head by the sharp saber of one of Wilson's men. I examined that old scar of Lieutenant Boone's in Lincoln County, Tenn., a few years after the war, and he said that big roan horse exercised uncommon good judgment in taking him away from such a mix-up of men where they were so uncouth as to say, "Go to the rear, damn you," when they decorated his head.

In conclusion, I wish you most eminent success in your laudable efforts to commemorate and pass on to the future generations the spot where one of the greatest cavalry generals, Nathan Bedford Forrest, surrendered his command, and he and they returned to the peaceful pursuits in this now reunited, greatest nation of earth.[176] — A. A. PEARSON

FORREST IN THE "OFFICIAL RECORDS"

☛ N. B. Forrest.—It is said by good authority that the "Wizard of the Saddle" killed more men with his own hand than any leader since Richard Coeur de Lion, and no doubt it is the truth, as in the affair at Sacramento, Ky., being engaged in a hand-to-hand conflict with four of the enemy, he killed three and made a prisoner of the fourth. He was undoubtedly a bad citizen to go up against, and this fact was thoroughly recognized by everybody concerned before the war was over.[177] — U.S. OFFICIAL RECORDS (VOL. 7)

A YEAR WITH FORREST

☛ I joined the army at Winchester, Tenn., the latter part of April, 1862. Having taken my only sister to school at that place in the autumn of 1861, after the battle of Shiloh I decided to visit her; so about the middle of April I went to Murfreesboro, where the Federal lines were established. I stopped with Prof. George W. Jarman, who the next morning took me to a lonely spot on the bank of Stone's River, where I took off my boots and small clothes and waded the stream. Replacing them on the farther shore, I waved mute thanks and farewells to my guide and friend and took my way on foot to Winchester, avoiding the turnpikes and traversing the entire distance of sixty miles by dirt roads.

I met at Winchester the cavalry battalion of Col. James W. Starnes, which had just come over from Chattanooga on a scouting expedition, and found a vacant saddle in Company F of this command. Company F had been raised in the beginning by Starnes, who commanded it until he was promoted to the office of lieutenant colonel and put in charge of the battalion, when he was succeeded in office by Captain McLemore. The men were recruited in the vicinity of Franklin, eighteen miles south of Nashville, where I was brought up, and I had been acquainted with a number of them in their homes. It was a choice body of troopers, most of them coming from families of wealth, position, and culture. It would have been difficult to have selected in either army a company possessing nobler blood and truer breeding than Company F.

Not long after my connection with it the period of one year for which the battalion originally enlisted ran out, and they enlisted again for three years, or during the war, and were then reorganized as a regiment, Starnes being chosen as full colonel. The following notice [by Wyeth] of Colonel Starnes is [worth citing]: "This man was James W. Starnes, who signally distinguished himself on that occasion and had won the lasting regard and friendship of Forrest, a friendship which endured until at Tullahoma in 1863 the leaden messenger of death brought to an untimely end a career full of the promise of great deeds in war. A new regiment was now organized, with Starnes as colonel, and took its place with Forrest as the 4th Tennessee Cavalry. It was destined to become famous and to sustain throughout the war the reputation it was soon to win west of the Tennessee, ending its career in a blaze of glory in a brilliant charge at Bentonville, N.C., in the last pitched battle of the Civil War."

James W. Starnes.

This estimate of the importance and services of the regiment is not overdrawn. The 4th Tennessee Cavalry was the finest fighting machine I ever saw on horseback.

Our armament at the outset was something pitiful to behold. Nearly the entire command were provided with muzzle-loading, double-barreled shotguns. There were scarcely thirty long-range rifles in the regiment. The shotguns were fowling pieces that had been contributed by gentlemen in the practice of hunting birds and other game. They were loaded with buckshot and at short range constituted a most effective weapon, but at a distance of two hundred yards they were worse than useless.

This weapon imposed a peculiar sort of tactics upon the Southern cavalry during the first year of the war. Fighting on foot, which subsequently became almost universal in the cavalry service, was rare at this time. It was the custom during the first year to charge up to a point within twenty yards of the enemy's line and to deliver the two loads of buckshot. Then those who were fortunate enough to own pistols went to work with these, while the others would load their pieces for two rounds more. But matters hardly ever got to that point. The enemy were generally thrown into disorder by the first two rounds of buckshot.

It was a favorite expedient to march all night and at the earliest dawn of day to line up before a camp of infantry and deliver a couple of charges of buckshot into the tents before anybody could wake up. But if the camp was large, the men on the opposite side of it would grasp their long-range guns and drive off the cavalry without much trouble. Indeed, it was a part of the game to run away when the long-range guns were brought into full operation.

The month of June, 1862, was a gloomy period, but the operations of Jackson in the Valley of Virginia and of Lee and Jackson in the Seven Days' battles around Richmond gave sensible relief. The whole State of Tennessee had previously been imperiled. It seemed difficult to prevent the capture of Chattanooga and even of Knoxville, but shortly afterwards the whole scene had changed. [Union General Edmund] Kirby Smith was preparing to invade Kentucky, and the regiment of Colonel Starnes was moved up to the vicinity of Cumberland Gap, where they scouted the adjacent country in Tennessee and Virginia. At the opportune moment, when roasting ears were in season, we entered Kentucky at Big Creek Gap and marched upon Richmond. Our regiment was placed in a brigade commanded by Colonel Scott, of Scott's Louisiana Cavalry, and took an active part in the battle of Richmond. When the defeat of the enemy's infantry appeared to be certain, we were sent to take a position on the turnpike leading from Richmond to Lexington, along which we found the enemy retreating in much confusion. They commonly surrendered without parley; but on passing through a dense cornfield just before we reached the main road we encountered a party who made resistance and shot through the neck my messmate and close friend, Private James Powell, killing him on the spot. The weather was intensely warm; but we were not allowed to cease pursuit until we had taken Lexington, Frankfort, Shelbyville, and were in the neighborhood of Louisville. The soldiers were hopeful and contented as long as they were kept engaged. But after the earliest spurt of energy General Smith seemed to require a season of rest. We did not understand all the details, but we felt that there was need of more activity. Finally it was announced that [Union] General [Don Carlos] Buell had entered Louisville without a pitched battle with [Confederate General Braxton] Bragg.

It was a special mercy for us that General Buell was not more vigorous and successful in the military art. If he had been a genuine soldier, we might have had some trouble getting out of Kentucky; but after delivering battle at Perryville we got off very light and made good our escape to Tennessee. Our brigade did not arrive in time to share in the conflict at Perryville; but we covered the retreat for a day or two, and then our regiment was ordered to report to General Forrest at Murfreesboro, the bulk of the army having traveled by way of Cumberland Gap to Knoxville, thence by rail to Chattanooga and Murfreesboro.

When we found General Forrest, he had a handful of raw troops with which he was trying to take Nashville, then held by a garrison of ten thousand [U.S.] infantry commanded by [Union] General [James Scott] Negley. I first saw him [Forrest] about the 1st of November, 1862, when I was ordered to report at headquarters for service as a guide, and I rode with him all day between the Nolensville and Granny White Pikes. It was my first experience of the grave responsibility of acting as guide for a considerable body of troops. General Negley was short of provisions and on that day had led a large force out the Franklin Pike as far as Brentwood to replenish his depleted stores. On this day I got my first conceptions of the *gaudium certaminis* [the

Miss Alleen Smith, Maid of Honor for Forrest's Cavalry.

"joy of battle"]. It was in Forrest a genuine and extraordinary passion. The whole tone and frame of the man were transformed; his appearance and even his voice were changed. It was a singular exaltation, which, however, appeared to leave him in absolute control of his faculties. He was never more sane nor more cool nor more terrible than in the moment of doubtful issue.

We camped that night at Nolensville, twelve miles away, and were in the saddle almost daily for a week entertaining the garrison at Nashville and trying to worry them into submission before relief might appear. We had lost our shotguns in Kentucky and were now armed with Enfield rifles, and henceforth fought chiefly as infantry. Forrest always liked to charge on horseback, but he had an unerring judgment in selecting the psychological moment for such an entertainment. He always sent one of his trustiest officers to assail the enemy in the rear, and at the earliest signs of disorder in their ranks he was glad to ride amongst them. He had likely never studied any maxims of war, but he seemed as if by instinct to understand the value of sending a force to the rear and adopted that method even in his initial fight at Sacramento, Ky.

In the fight at Murfreesboro, in July, 1862, he had also adopted the policy of beating the enemy in detail. He was swift in movement, fierce in assault, and persistent in pursuit. He had not obtained these secrets from Caesar's commentaries; they must have come to him by instinct. He was a born soldier, not made. If by any possibility he could have succeeded Albert Sidney Johnson at Shiloh, the war in the West might have run a different course. But the government at Richmond never took Forrest seriously until it was too late, and one of the greatest natural masters of the military art was buffeted by outrageous fortune almost to the wrecking of his career and to the entire destruction of his country's hopes. He was no bully nor barbarian, but a gentleman of such admirable presence that he would be observed [standing out from] among a thousand. But when the passion of battle was upon him, he was the most inspiring figure in the army. In religion he was deeply devoted to the Cumberland Presbyterian Church and a regular attendant, but I am not sure that he was a communicant. His veneration of his mother's religion and his wife's religion was beautiful to witness, and the Rev. Herschel S. Porter, pastor of the Cumberland Church in Memphis, was his standard of excellence in pulpit performance.

In the opening skirmish at Nashville I found Capt. Samuel L. Freeman, who had been one of my teachers at Mill Creek Academy, on my mother's farm, and later at Mount Juliet Academy, near Lebanon. Just prior to the war he had entered upon the practice of the law in Nashville. In the autumn of 1861 Freeman raised a company of artillery and on departing for the camps intrusted to me his law library, with the request that I should keep it safe till he returned to claim it. About noon the General [Forrest] rode up to Freeman's Battery, which at the moment was engaged in a lively duel with Negley's Artillery, and there I greeted my beloved master, six feet in height, a type of friendly dignity, shy, womanly modesty, reposeful courage—every inch a soldier.

In due time we were recalled from Nashville to Murfreesboro, whence we were ordered to Columbia, in Maury County, where Gen. Earl Van Dorn was placed in command of us. Toward the middle of December we set out for the Tennessee River, and, crossing it at Clifton, we commenced operations in West Tennessee with the purpose of crippling Grant, who was then pressing against Vicksburg, and also to prevent him from sending help to Rosecrans at Stone's River. We had less than two thousand troopers and Captain Freeman's battery of artillery. I was never sensible of the perils of that expedition until [later].

... We crossed about the 16th of December, and immediately all the great resources of the enemy were brought to bear to capture us. The first town we struck was Lexington, where we captured Colonel Ingersoll, of Illinois; but he had not then become famous, and we made nothing of him. We made a feint against Jackson and after driving the enemy within his intrenchments worked upon the railroads and burned many bridges to the north—south of the town. We captured Humboldt, Trenton, Union City, and other places of smaller note. But the problem of recrossing the Tennessee River was ever before us. It was patrolled by gunboats, but Forrest had sunk his two small ferryboats in a secluded spot where no gunboat could find them and had left a guard to watch them. On the 27th of December we became aware that forces were converging from every direction to assault us. There were two brigades of infantry close at hand, numbering in all about five thousand men, and the country swarmed with cavalry, but these did not count for much. The Northern generals still proceeded on the sleepy idea that it is the main function of cavalry to serve as eyes and ears for infantry. Forrest had gotten beyond that standpoint long before, and no cavalry trained upon the ancient maxims was able to stand against us.

Instead of moving immediately back to Clifton, raising the sunken ferryboats, and recrossing the Tennessee, Forrest, holding a position between these two infantry brigades, concluded to attack and capture one of them before the other could come up in his rear and take them home with him as prisoners of war. It was a daring conception, but he considered that he was equal to it, notwithstanding the fact that Gen. G. M. Dodge, with two other full brigades of infantry and some cavalry, was taking position between him and Clifton. We attacked Dunham's Brigade at Parker's Crossroads by sunrise of December 31, 1862, hoping to beat and crush it before any of Fuller's Brigade might arrive on the ground. We had done the work for Dunham by twelve o'clock, but Fuller just then closed in on our rear. In thirty minutes the surrender would have been completed, but in that nick of time Fuller charged us and compelled us to retreat without the prisoners who were rightfully our own.

By daylight next morning our advance had reached the river. The two ferryboats were raised from the bottom and brought over to the west side, and the work of recrossing was begun. It was completed without incident the following morning, and we made our most respectful salutations when the enemy arrived an hour later and began to shell the woods on our side. What Jackson accomplished in the Valley of Virginia was hardly more masterful than the skill of Forrest in extricating his small force from this most perilous situation.

Early in February, 1863, General Wheeler, who was in command of the entire cavalry service of Bragg's army, led a force to attack Fort Donelson and was defeated. The weather was intensely cold, and the enemy was admirably intrenched. Forrest formally protested, but the attack was made in spite of him. There was a bloody slaughter, in which our regiment suffered greatly, and Forrest notified Wheeler that he would be in his coffin before he should ever fight again under his command. Forrest understood better than Wheeler when to risk a desperate encounter.

Five of Gen. Forrest's most notable staff members. Left to right: David C. Kelley, William M. Forrest (son), Dr. J. B. Cowan (center), John W. Morton, Charles W. Anderson.

On March 5, 1863, we fought the battle of Thompson's Station under the command of Gen. Earl Van Dorn and captured the entire force of the enemy's infantry, a line brigade under Colonel Coburn, of Indiana; but Van Dorn permitted two regiments of cavalry and a battery of artillery to escape. Forrest got in the rear and rendered the escape of the infantry impossible. It was here that we captured Maj. W. R. Shaffer; but as he had not yet been to Cuba, we heard little of him. In one of the engagements of this day Capt. J. R. Dysart, of Company D, who was standing in a position just above me on the uneven ground, was shot through the head and fell over upon me with a severe crash. I thought for an instant that I myself had been killed.

On the 24th of March, 1863, we left Spring Hill, midway between Franklin and Columbia, and daylight next morning found us at Brentwood, midway between Franklin and Nashville, where we captured and brought away about eight hundred prisoners. This was a perilous expedition, as Nashville, the base of supplies of the Federal army, and Franklin also were held by a large force. On our retreat we had gotten across the last pike by which we could be attacked from Nashville and, considering ourselves at last somewhat secure, had halted for dinner. While we were thus engaged [Union] Gen. Green Clay Smith, who had been sent down from Franklin to pursue us, rushed upon our rear guard and occasioned some confusion. Forrest soon got a regiment in line, and just then Starnes, who was returning from a scouting expedition down the Hillsboro Pike toward Nashville, fell upon the flank of the enemy. Observing the confusion occasioned by that incident, Forrest instantly led a charge against the enemy and easily shook them off. It was the common verdict that General Smith displayed little stomach for fight. If Forrest had been in his position, he would have fought the Confederates every foot of the journey to [the] Harpeth River. That stream was in league against us, being swollen by the freshets of springtime; and if Smith had shown any vigor, he would have given us much annoyance.

On the 10th of April, under Van Dorn's command, a reconnaissance was made in force from Spring Hill against Franklin, with the hope of relieving the pressure upon Bragg at Tullahoma. By an unaccountable oversight the enemy's cavalry were permitted to assail our column on the right flank as we were marching down the turnpike toward Franklin. It was the brigade of [Union] General Stanley, which was striving to get in our rear. The first we saw of them the 4th United States Regulars were charging down the hill along the base of which were marching. They struck Freeman's Battery, and before a single piece could be brought into action, it had been captured. Many of the men escaped, but Captain Freeman was taken. We quickly rallied and recovered the guns and prisoners, but in the melee Captain Freeman was killed. The piece [gun] with which he had been slain was held so close to his face that the skin about the eyes was deeply burned with powder. Some of his fellow prisoners reported that he had offered no resistance; but our pursuit was so rapid that he could not keep up with his captors, and rather than give him up they concluded to take his life. He was the idol of the brigade, and it was hard to forgive the gentlemen of the 4th Regulars. Possibly the deed was done by no rightful authority; it may have been the conceit of some irresponsible private soldier.

The next day was Sunday, and I officiated at Freeman's funeral. General Forrest stood at the side of the grave, his tall form bent and swayed by his grief. It was a sight to remember always, the sternest soldier of the army bathed in womanly tears and trembling like an aspen with his pain. The whole army sympathized in the mighty sorrow.

On the 23rd of April, 1863, we were ordered from Columbia [Tenn.] to Courtland, Ala., and at Town Creek, not far away, we found our old adversary, [Union] Gen. G. M. Dodge, again with a large force of infantry and cavalry. Their purpose was to afford a proper send-off to the expedition of Col. A. D. Streight, who had a commission to visit Bragg's rear and do all the damage he might find possible in Georgia and elsewhere. General Dodge pressed us sorely all day of the 27th and also the 28th, but at midnight of the 28th a messenger appeared in our camp near Courtland to announce that a body of about twenty-five cavalry had passed through Mount Hope at dusk and had taken the road to Moulton. It was then "Boots and saddles!" and at 1 a.m. of the 20th, the same hour at which Streight quitted Moulton, Forrest set out to pursue him.

The troops of Colonel Streight were brave and formidable. They were select and seasoned infantry from Indiana, Ohio, and Illinois, who had been mounted on mules especially for this expedition. In action they always dismounted, just as we did, and they were practiced and patient fighters. During the forenoon of the 29th we reached Moulton and followed the enemy to Day's Gap, a distance of seventeen miles, where we found him in camp a little after midnight. It was suspected that with all his excellencies as a commander Colonel Streight was too slow of motion for the business he had in hand. He had been three and a half days on the march when we struck him and had traversed a distance of only sixty-five miles. What was the use of mounting his command if they were to be marched at the rate of infantry? If he had moved forty miles a day during these three days and kept up that pace, he could have reached Rome and Atlanta in spite of the world, the flesh, and the devil. He must have considered that he was on a May-day frolic; he seemed to be trying to coddle the negroes. After we had come up with him he moved at the rate of fifty miles a day and threw in some fighting besides.

At nine o'clock on the morning of the 30th of April Forrest prepared to engage Streight in his camp upon Sand Mountain. Our regiment, which for this expedition was commanded by Captain McLemore, was sent with Biffle's 9th Tennessee to climb the mountain by another gap and gain the enemy's rear. Forrest hoped to hold him with a portion of Roddy's Brigade until we might catch him in that trap. But the engagement at Day's Gap was too brief for our purpose. Streight evidently apprehended the nature of our game and slipped out of the trap.

When Forrest found us in the road on Sand Mountain, he sent General Roddy and his brigade back to the Tennessee River to observe the movements of General Dodge, and, with the two Tennessee regiments mentioned and his escort and a section of Ferrell's Battery, he closely followed the enemy, although our number was less than half of theirs. They had whipped Roddy in the initial encounter on the morning of the 29th and captured two of the guns of Morton, who commanded after the death of Freeman. But we forced Colonel Streight to deliver battle again about sunset, and when it was concluded the two pieces were left spiked on the field. This was the first night battle I had witnessed. The pine trees were very tall, the darkness of their shade was intense, the mountain where the enemy was posted was steep, and as we charged again and again under Forrest's own lead it was a grand spectacle. It seemed that the fires which blazed from their muskets were almost long enough to reach our faces. There was one advantage in being below them: they often fired above our heads in the darkness.

This battle closed about 9 p.m., and shortly afterwards the moon rose in great splendor. It seemed to have been sent for our special behoof. I have said there is no reason to suppose that the old man [Forrest] had read Caesar's commentaries either in English or in Latin, but he followed the tactics of Caesar as if by instinct. His military lore in this emergency was expressed in the following command: "Shoot at everything blue and keep up the scare." To execute this order he compelled us to hang upon the very heels of the enemy all the way. There was constant peril of ambuscade, but we waited for the moon to rise before pressing close upon the enemy after nightfall. By daylight we generally kept in sight and were able to see them and almost always to open the fighting when they attempted to surprise us.

About eleven o'clock they laid the first ambuscade, but Forrest contrived to discover it in advance and, instead of walking into it, caused us to dismount and get into line and crawl up close to the enemy's position. It would have made too much noise to have brought up a piece of artillery by horsepower, so soldiers were harnessed to it and dragged it to a point within two hundred yards of the enemy's line. When the proper moment arrived, he ordered the cannon to open and the cavalry likewise, so that we surprised the enemy instead of them surprising us. I walked along the [Union] line where they had been formed and found it littered from end to end with small bits of paper. It looked as if every man in their column must have employed the leisure afforded by that stop to tear up all the private letters found upon his person. It was clear that their alarm had become serious and would help us much if we could keep it up.

At two o'clock the next morning, when most of our command had fallen asleep on horseback, we were ambuscaded at the ford of a difficult mountain stream and caused some losses, especially among the animals. We in our turn were thrown into a degree of confusion here, but they were too much frightened to press their advantage. Indeed, most of those who fired upon us were drawn up on the other side of the stream. A small detachment lay in the undergrowth at the foot of a steep causeway upon which we were marching down to the river, but they ran away as soon as they had discharged their pieces. . . . this ambuscade at two o'clock on the morning of May 1 was "practically a repetition" of the one attempted at eleven o'clock. It was a more serious affair; and after crossing the river, a branch of the Black Warrior, the General permitted us to get down and sleep from 3 to 5 a.m.

Colonel Streight seemed to have no proper ideas of what a cavalry soldier can endure. Possibly his men, having been only recently promoted to saddle, were galled and wearied by the novelty of the exercise. He was taking his ease as if no enemy were near when we found him at Blountsville next morning, May 2. We immediately put his column in motion and kept it on the run to the Black Warrior, where he was compelled to fight us to obtain a crossing. Here we were allowed a rest from 6 p.m. until the moon arose about eleven, while two companies of Biffle's 9th Tennessee were detailed to hang upon the enemy's rear throughout the night.

We were summoned at the appointed moment and moved forward to find Colonel Streight next morning at Wilber's Creek, where Biffle's detail was relieved, and Forrest again took the chase in hand. About 11 a.m. of May 3 we came in sight of Black Creek Bridge and perceived that it was on fire, which indicated that the enemy were all on the other side. They marched away after a brief season, assured of a respite of half a day before we should be able to cross the creek and catch up with them again; but Miss Emma Sansom piloted the General to

Miss Charlie Scott, Sponsor for Forrest's Cavalry Corps at the Birmingham Reunion, early 1900s.

a ford, and we were soon across the deep and swollen stream.

It was about four o'clock in the afternoon when we struck Colonel Streight in Gadsden, four miles away on the banks of the Coosa River. Why should he be sauntering at Gadsden during those precious hours? It seemed as if he had made up his mind to fail. He ought not to have failed. He recruited his horses almost every mile. It was a common thing to find standing in the highways the wagons and carriages of citizens from which he had removed the horses, leaving his exhausted mules in the place of them. Our horses were falling out constantly, and we had no means whatever of renewing the supply.

At Gadsden Forrest took a picked company of about two hundred of his best mounted troopers and followed the retreating enemy, fighting him every step of the way to Turkey Town, where, after nightfall, Streight planned an ambuscade; but, as usual, Forrest saw his game and got the best of it. In the encounter that was occasioned by the Confederate flank movement the Federal Colonel Hathaway, with many others, was killed, and immediately all the hopes of Streight seemed to be crushed. When we caught up with Forrest about nine o'clock, I learned that Hartwell Hunt, one of my dearest friends, had been killed in the skirmish, and the rest of the night was filled with grief.

During the half hour he remained in Gadsden Forrest had procured a courier to go on horseback by a route on the opposite side of the Coosa River and advise the city of Rome of its peril. Col. John H. Wisdom was the man who rendered that service, but he was not a member of our command. At Turkey Town Streight also dispatched a force of two hundred picked men to go forward and capture the city, which was about sixty miles distant; but Colonel Wisdom outrode them and saved the day. The bottom was carefully removed from the bridge that led across the river, the State militia was under arms, and Rome was rescued from peril. When Streight's advance guard arrived, they were beaten off with small exertion, and the doom of his expedition was sealed.

We rested at Turkey Town until the moon had risen, receiving strict orders to be mounted and on the road at midnight. There was a disturbance when the General rode up and found us in line at the edge of the road; but our colonel settled it by claiming a difference of two minutes in watches, during which time we wheeled into column on the road and resumed the march.

Pursuing the enemy with renewed vigor, we found that he had burned the bridge by which he had only recently crossed Chattanooga River. Though the stream was swollen, we were ordered to plunge in, and we got across by swimming a few yards in the middle of it. There was a deal of trouble about the cannon, but they were finally pulled across, while the ammunition was transferred by means of canoes that the citizens provided.

Before ten o'clock in the morning we bore down upon the enemy's camp, and, finding him unprepared for battle, General Forrest sent Captain Pointer with a flag of truce to demand his surrender. Colonel Streight replied that he would be glad to meet General Forrest and discuss the question with him. When that message was delivered, Forrest remarked: "If he ever talks to me, then I've got him." The old man had large experience and skill in such emergencies, and before noon the surrender had been accomplished.

The place was crowded with undergrowth, and Streight proposed to march down the road until they should find an open field suitable for the business of laying down his arms. Forrest gave assent, and in a few minutes we were in the road, which shortly became a lane with immense fields of growing cotton on each side. That was the longest lane I ever traveled. It may have been a mile, but it seemed ten miles in length. Streight had about fourteen hundred and fifty men, and we had about four hundred and seventy-five in line. We were drawn up on both sides of them, and every man of them carried a loaded rifle and some likewise loaded pistols. If they had concluded to renew the struggle, it is difficult to understand how any of us could have escaped alive.

Forrest galloped up and down the column and busily gave orders to couriers to ride to the rear and order imaginary regiments and imaginary batteries to stop and feed their animals and men. But the regiments of Starnes and Biffle and Ferrell's Battery, which had been depicted to skeleton proportions, were the only available troops within a hundred miles.

Finally the lane came to an end, and there was a field of broom sedge on the right-hand side. Colonel Streight led the way, and his troops were shortly formed in line. Then at the word of command they dismounted, stacked arms, remounted, and rode away. There was an inexpressible sense of relief when they had parted company with their arms and ammunition; but we did not venture to suggest the fewness of our numbers until we had delivered them safely to the keeping of the guards whom the government had dispatched to Rome to receive them.

Our victory was embittered by a message that Stonewall Jackson had been wounded in a battle in Virginia, which was announced shortly after we reached Rome. I can never forget the sorrow and foreboding it produced. On the way back to Columbia, Tenn., a messenger arrived bringing tidings of the death of Gen. Earl Van Dorn, and Forrest was ordered shortly afterwards to take his place in command of the cavalry on the left wing of Bragg's army.

The retreat of Bragg from Shelbyville began late in June, 1863, and the duty of covering his rear was assigned to Wheeler and Forrest. At Tullahoma on the last day of the month the advance of Rosecrans's army began to press against our brigade, now commanded by Col. J. W, Starnes, of the 4th Tennessee Cavalry, and in the encounter this great soldier was fatally wounded by a sharpshooter. His loss was deeply deplored, and his name is revered by all who appreciate courage and capacity.

The alleged inefficiency of the general in command [Bragg] had become more glaringly apparent during the retreat from Shelbyville, and especially in the maneuvers that preceded the struggle at Chickamauga. Forrest, who enjoyed opportunities to observe every failure at close range, was fully convinced that the situation could not be improved as long as Bragg should be retained. The fighting at Chickamauga was more trying than the average. We always dismounted and acted as infantry, but here we were in the same line with our veteran Confederate infantry regiments. We held a portion of the front line all the morning of the 19th of September and found the enemy duly stubborn. . . . it was 1:30 p.m. when Cheatham's Division relieved us and pressed on toward Chattanooga. I always supposed it was 4 p.m. when Cheatham appeared. At any rate, the day was very long indeed.

When Cheatham took our place and went in, I must concede that the music became more lively than any we had made. We immediately got on our horses to take position on his flank and keep it from being turned. There was a short pause as the column was going into line, and half a dozen of us, standing with our horses' heads together, were listening to the tremendous din, when a grapeshot that had passed through almost a mile of undergrowth struck Coleman, of Company F, in the stomach. He fell from his horse and was dead in three minutes.

Severe as the battle of the 19th had been, that of the 20th was still more trying. We were in line with the troops of [Confederate] Gen. John C. Breckinridge on the right wing, and I have a distinct recollection of the appearance of that officer as he rode along just behind our column shortly after daylight. The action did not begin till 9:30 a.m., but we had been ready since 6:30. When it finally opened, we played the part of infantry again and kept up with the advance of Breckinridge, but that was not very great. We were face to face with [Union] General [George Henry] Thomas, a foeman worthy of our steel, who contested every inch of the ground. My impression is that this was the loudest noise and the longest day of my life, and the night which followed it was also memorable for its discomforts.

On Monday morning, September 21, Forrest pursued the enemy almost into Chattanooga and found him apparently engaged in evacuating the town. If General Bragg had pressed forward before noon of that day, there might have been a great victory. Forrest claimed that when he went in person to inform General Bragg of the importance of immediate action he caught him asleep, and that after he got him awake Bragg objected that his army had no supplies. When Forrest suggested that there were abundant supplies in Chattanooga, no reply was made, and he turned from the commanding general in unconcealed disgust.

Painting of Nathan Bedford Forrest, owned by his son William M. Forrest.

The friction had become so decided that it was now impossible for the two officers to cooperate harmoniously, and on the 28th of September Bragg issued an order for him [Forrest] to turn over his command to General Wheeler. He obeyed without delay. There was no sign of discontent or mutiny. No farewells were spoken to his companions in arms. He passed our camp at the head of his escort as if employed on customary occasions. We were not informed of the action that had been taken until he was on his way to West Tennessee to found his fortunes anew and rise to the dignity of lieutenant general of the Confederate States army.

So long as we followed Forrest we enjoyed the respect of the army. If we passed a regiment of infantry, they would heap the customary contempt upon us; but when it was suggested that we belonged to Forrest's people, they changed tune, and they fraternized with us as real soldiers, worthy companions in arms. They inquired about our battles and our leader and wondered at his genius and success. We were heroes even to the infantry. But when Wheeler took command of us, all of that was changed. The infantry could not be appeased, and it was vain to reply. General Wheeler was a brave and honorable man, but nobody ever accused him of genius.

Forrest was an extraordinary genius. He developed a new use for cavalry; that was his specific contribution to the art of war. But all the other maxims of the great masters came to him by nature. He was equally at home in infantry, cavalry, and artillery. By the readiness of his initiative he kept the whole campaign before his eye and could strike a blow at a distance of a hundred miles before anybody dreamed it was conceivable. He could discern the exigencies of the field of battle swiftly and surely. He had the sanest initiative I ever observed, not blind, not foolhardy; balanced, when retreat was essential he could perform it with more dispatch and repose than anybody. It was hard to find a soldier with intellect so strong and fertile and safe, whose will was so healthy and prompt and resistless, whose organization was so much of the hair-trigger variety, whose military education and military maxims were so admirable. If he could have commanded the Western Army after Shiloh—but I will not indulge vain regrets.

In a letter to the *Cincinnati Inquirer* George Alfred Townsend recites an interview he held with Lee at Appomattox C.H., in which he inquired: "General Lee, who is the greatest general now under your command?" Lee replied with grave deliberation: "A man I never saw, sir. His name is Forrest."

I am no military critic, but my affection inclines me to say that the War between the States developed three incomparable geniuses for war, all on the Southern side—Lee, Jackson, and Forrest.

When I first met General Forrest, he was already a famous man. He was in command of troops raised in Middle Tennessee, some 1,800 men, almost all of them raw recruits. Colonel Starnes's regiment, the 4th Tennessee Cavalry, had seen much service; four companies of Russell's 4th Alabama were also trained men. The others were newly enlisted—Dibrell's 8th Tennessee, Biffle's 9th Tennessee, and Freeman's Battery. These made up the famous Forrest Brigade.

General Forrest was a man of remarkable appearance, over six feet tall, somewhat muscular in build, powerful and graceful, giving an impression of solidity and completeness; while neatly dressed and groomed, he apparently took no thought of dress or accouterments and was altogether devoid of personal vanity.[178] — REVEREND W. H. WHITSITT

THE DISPUTE BETWEEN FORREST & WHEELER

☛ [Let us speak] of [Confederate General Joseph] Wheeler's attack on Dover, Fort Donelson, early in February, 1863, about twelve months after Grant had captured the position from the Confederate army defending it: "Forrest formally protested, but the attack was made in spite of him. There was a bloody slaughter, in which our regiment suffered greatly, and Forrest notified Wheeler that he would be in his coffin before he would ever fight again under his command."

I received the account of this unsoldierly outbreak of the great "Wizard of the Saddle" in person from a soldier who was an eyewitness within ten feet of the scene. That soldier was Samuel Lowery Robertson, later a distinguished pioneer of Birmingham, Ala., then a courier, eighteen years of age.

After the battle, the night dark and bitter cold, he [Robertson] received orders to find a home for headquarters in a general direction. He rode five miles in the direction indicated by his orders without sign of habitation, dense forests on each side. Presently he spied a flash of light under the door of a single room cabin some yards from the road. Riding back, he met the two generals and Wheeler's adjutant. They were guided to the cabin, and all took possession.

A rousing fire soon blazed from the wide hearth. Wheeler sat at one corner, the adjutant at the other, while Forrest stretched himself full length on his back, long wet boots on the hearth, his head propped on a reversed stick chair. Here history began.

General Wheeler dictating to the adjutant his report of the battle, General Forrest interrupted. Wheeler, in perfect composure, replied: "I shall state the event as it occurred, General; I shall give you full credit and your men."

Here Forrest sprang to his feet in the greatest fury. Mr. Robertson said his rage could not be described or imagined. Wheeler sat motionless. Forrest continued: "General Wheeler, I advised against this attack . . . and nothing you can now say or do can bring back my brave men lying dead or wounded and freezing around that fort to-night. I mean no disrespect to you. You know my feeling of personal friendship for you. You can take my sword if you demand it, but there is one thing that I want you to put in that report to General Bragg. Tell him that I will be put in my coffin before I will fight again under your command."

"I will not take your sword, General. I am responsible for the day," continued Wheeler, calm and self-possessed.

A few months later, June 27, 1863, before a half year had passed, Forrest was called to fight under Wheeler again; but he held fast to his self-imposed pledge, made in the little cabin, never [again] to fight under Wheeler.[179] — JOHN WITHERSPOON DUBOSE

FORREST'S LAST EXPLOIT

☛ No report was ever made of Forrest's last exploit. This was because there was nobody to report to. General Lee had surrendered on the very day that we made our last stand at Selma. [This is incorrect; see endnote for this entry.]

I was adjutant of the 1ˢᵗ Confederate Cavalry, belonging to General Wheeler; but on reaching West Point, Miss., after Hood had gone out of Tennessee, I was attached to the Kentucky Brigade, together with some one hundred men and officers, being what was left of my regiment. The brigade at the time had about seven hundred men left. I was made a staff officer of the brigade and was with it until all the fighting was over, on the 9ᵗʰ of April. Forrest guarded Hood's retreat out of that State and saved his army from capture. There was a trail of blood from footsore, barefooted infantry from Franklin to Bainbridge, Ga. After getting out himself, Forrest went to West Point, Miss., and was in camp there until early in April, recruiting his horses and fixing for the next important call upon him. In the meantime he had gathered up and got there under his command about all the cavalry not then with Wheeler in Georgia and Florida. It was early in April that he left West Point to meet [Union General James Harrison] Wilson, who was reported as starting on a raid through Alabama.

It is a fact not generally known that Forrest had more than twelve thousand men when he left West Point, or over three thousand more than Wilson had. It is also a fact that the Kentucky Brigade, cut down to eight hundred men and commanded by Col. Ed Crossland, was all of the force that ever marched to Montevallo and that ever saw Wilson, except Armstrong's Brigade, which saw him only at Selma. Just why this was so nobody ever knew, for it was never explained.

After it was all over I met Gen. Billy Jackson, who had forty-five hundred men, and he told me that before he reached Montevallo he was ordered by General Forrest to make a detour and march rapidly to Elyton and get behind Wilson, who was supposed to be fixing to go back. But it turned out that Wilson's "fixing" was to go the other way. Jackson said he marched one day rapidly toward Elyton, and, noting that the guns heard seemed to be getting farther south all the time, he turned back of his own accord, and all he had to do was to drive two thousand of the enemy found on the Tuscaloosa road back on Wilson.

[Confederate] General [James R.] Chalmers had fifty-five hundred men, and somehow he got lost and never got into the fight. He never made any report of his whereabouts, but it was understood by those of us in the fighting that Chalmers was off to one side trying to get to us; that Wilson was driving us so fast he could not keep up and really got behind Wilson, or still farther to one side. So, with Jackson's being behind him, here were one thousand more men than Wilson had, following along behind him or dodging to keep out of his way.

The result was that the Kentucky Brigade fought Wilson by itself all the way from Montevallo to Selma, the wonder being that a single man of the eight hundred ever got into Selma. But we did make it there with one hundred and fifty men. The others had been captured, killed, wounded, or run off the road and got lost. The only other troops of Forrest's command to get there was Armstrong's Brigade (1,500 men), which belonged to Chalmers. Why Chalmers was not there with his other four thousand was never known. With that many more good soldiers Wilson could not have taken Selma.

James R. Chalmers.

There were about one thousand militia there with us who had never been in a fight, and we fought him and held him out of the town all day, from sunrise until about sunset, when they broke through the militia and rushed in behind us. This settled it; and of our one hundred and fifty left of the brigade, only five got away. The others were captured, except Tobe Hurt, who crawled into a graveyard and hid there until Wilson went away. But the most of these escaped afterwards.

In the two or three days' fighting from Montevallo to Selma there were many thrilling and some ludicrous incidents. It was early in the afternoon when Wilson came out after us, and from the first jump he came like he was bound to have us. I am satisfied he drove us fifteen miles an hour a part of the time.

Wilson had with him Wilder's Brigade, composed of Indiana and Ohio troops. Among them was the 17th Indiana Cavalry, as gallant and brave a set of men as ever went to war. Wilson had this brigade in front all the way to Selma. It had been my fortune to be shoved up against these men all through the war with Joe Wheeler, and I knew them. It was no trouble to find out whom we were fighting, for occasionally just a few of the more eager of the leaders would run through us, and we got them.

Somehow about a hundred of Roddy's men got in with us. I think we just happened onto them there about their homes in North Alabama. It was said of them that early in the war they had misunderstood the call to "strike for your homes and firesides" and did that, keeping up a sort of guerrilla business of their own there in the mountains, moving against any marauding bands not too large that threatened their homes.

I remember that on coming out of a very hot place, after crossing the creek a few miles from Montevallo, we came up on Roddy's men formed on each side of the road. I had to ride in front of their line, very close to them, to get out, and while I was doing this they began firing, two or three of them shooting under my horse. No enemy at the time was in sight, and I told them so; but they had been ordered to fire and fall back, and their object was to do this while the chance was good to get away. That was the last I ever saw of them. But when the enemy did come, the rest of us undertook to check them ourselves and got into a hand-to-hand mix-up.

A ludicrous incident of this affair was that old man Conner, who was Dr. Lackey's orderly (Dr. Lackey had been our division surgeon with Wheeler), had gotten out just in time. He carried a case almost as big as a trunk swung on his back, which contained Lackey's surgical instruments. Before getting out and under good headway, the Yanks made several whacks at him with sabers, hitting the pill box instead of Conner. Down the woods, parallel with the road, two or three miles farther I came up on Conner, and he told me what his experience had been. The enemy, he said, had still kept in whacking distance of him. He thought several times of stopping to surrender, but he was afraid they would chop his head off before he could do that. He was afraid to look back, as he might lose some of his vantage. Finally he did look back, however, and not one of the enemy was in sight. The doctor's instruments had been bouncing from top to bottom of the big case they were in, and Connor thought it was the clanking of sabers.

Conner and I camped in a hazel thicket that night behind the enemy and within seventy-five yards of their camp fires. We could hear them talking of what they were going to do to us next day. But the next day we did something to them. At a long stretch in the road we came upon General Forrest with a masked battery looking down that stretch of road.

We had by this time gotten our forces down to about four hundred men, and General Forrest told us if we would check them there he would have Chalmers with us before they could get another start. What he really said was, "In twenty-five minutes." We had formed our four hundred in a little field, not fenced, just to the left of the battery, out of sight until the field was reached. Pretty soon that familiar yell of the 17th Indiana was heard, as they were again leading in column of fours. The battery was now unmasked and opened up on them until they were almost upon it. They were coming so fast that one of those Indiana boys ran into one of the pieces, knocking a wheel out of the gun carriage, killing his horse, and he himself was killed by one of the gunners. This injury to the gun carriage made us later lose the gun.

We did not fire until the battery had commenced plowing up the road. Then we turned loose on the poor fellows, and in less than three minutes we had killed and wounded eighty-seven men (fifty-two of them were killed), and we drove the whole force back half a mile. I don't mean that we followed them that far back, but that they went that far to make a new start. As the enemy whirled off the road into open woods from us, the ground was literally covered with dead men and horses. At intervals live men were caught under and held down by dead horses. Forrest, fighting over that battery, killed three men with his own hands. I am sure there was not a more complete surprise to the enemy during the war, and with either Billy Jackson or Chalmers with us right then we could have turned the tables on Wilson and driven him back. Anyhow, this drubbing we gave him made him more cautious, and they were several hours getting us started again from the next stand; and as it was near nightfall, they did not follow, letting us ride leisurely that night into Selma.

In this last fighting they had killed my horse. I had cause later for serious regret at this, for my other one couldn't swim—the thing most needed at Selma. I have often thought that an army of fifty thousand men just like Bedford Forrest, each as capable in execution as Forrest, could not have been whipped in battle. They could have killed men faster than they could be shoved up on them. General Forrest was a great commander, but a greater close-quarter fighter. In some of his more conspicuous victories he used but few of his men, as had to be done in this case against Wilson's raid. Wirt Adams had fifteen hundred men who ought to have been there too, and no account was ever given as to where they were.

From the orders to General Jackson, there appears no doubt that Forrest thought Wilson was going to retreat from Montevallo and had put his men where he could not get them back. The wonder is that all did not come to him on hearing the guns going south all the time. Jackson had come within a day's march of him after going one day the other way.

Of course there was a blunder somewhere in this instance, for we all know that General Forrest didn't expect to whip Wilson, with nine thousand men, with the Kentucky Brigade of eight hundred. The intention, no doubt, was to have the Kentucky Brigade harass and follow Wilson until he met Jackson and possibly Chalmers on another flank north of him. The mistake evidently was that they thought Wilson had no intention of going back.

In Selma General Forrest did just what he always did in a pinch. He was surrounded, of course, and was apparently in the enemy's grasp; but, seeing that all was lost, he took his escort of forty men and cut through their lines, thus getting away.

As it turned out, it seemed all for the best and saved an unnecessary sacrifice of probably one thousand lives, for our fight in Selma was made on the same day that Lee surrendered at Appomattox, and the war was ended.[180] — CONFEDERATE CAPTAIN J. M. BROWNE

Above, the original Forrest Equestrian Statue (also see cover), Forrest Park, Memphis, Tennessee. Unveiled in 1905, it stood for 112 years with little controversy, until one small but vociferous, aggressive, contemptuous, bigoted group found it politically expedient to have it removed in 2017; this after intentionally spreading both misinformation and disinformation about the monument then repeatedly vandalizing it. The self-righteous organization went on to subject Forrest's admirers to nonstop criticism, slander, and hate, *all based on the fake history they themselves fabricated*. Then and only then was the memorial taken down; this despite the bold facts that it took years to plan, design, and build and was the result of the combined energies and love of thousands of individuals; that it was originally enthusiastically welcomed by the city of Memphis; that its removal was carried out against the will of the vast majority of both Tennesseans and Americans; and that the act was illegal since the monument was supported, constructed, and funded by American taxpayers—both Southern citizens and Northern citizens, Confederate veterans and Union veterans. And who were the meddling do-gooders behind this unlawful, un-American act? An illiterate, uneducated, vengeful, intolerant, discredited, regressive, ignorant mob; an anti-intellectual thugocracy; one whose members proudly bear the name "Liberals." It is my prediction that in the future this particular monument will be replaced by *two* Forrest equestrian statues, and that with the passage of time, and the spread of the truth about this great American Conservative, dozens if not hundreds more Forrest statues will eventually be erected across the U.S. The author.

9

1918-1932

UNNECESSARY YANKEE TELEGRAM
☛ Union President Abraham Lincoln to Union General William S. Rosecrans: "Where is Forrest's headquarters?" Rosecrans to Lincoln: "Forrest has no permanent abiding place."[181] — U.S. OFFICIAL RECORDS (SER. 3, VOL. 2)

EXCERPT FROM A SOUTHERN GIRL'S DIARY (1860s)
☛ While walking out on the pike last evening I threw some roses to General Forrest as he drove by us, and my glove went, unintentionally on my part, with them. He laughed and stopped to ask me if I had "challenged him." "No, indeed!" I cried. "I would rather appoint so brave a man my champion." Whereupon he thanked me quite gallantly. [His son] Lieut. William [Montgomery] Forrest was with him.[182] — ELLEN VIRGINIA SAUNDERS (14 YEARS OLD)

ANOTHER EXCERPT FROM A SOUTHERN GIRL'S DIARY (1860s)
☛ Our struggle for independence is hourly becoming more bloody. The sad, sad news has reached us that General Forrest, our hero, noble Forrest, is wounded. How gladly would I substitute myself rather than the South should lose so able and chivalrous a defender! When peace comes, how happy would I feel could I exclaim, "My country, I too have helped to win for you your glorious independence"! Try to do all I can for our soldiers, but what is that compared with what they suffer? Were I a man, I could fight for the South, but I could not love her more.[183] — ELLEN VIRGINIA SAUNDERS (14 YEARS OLD)

WEST POINTERS & FORREST
☛ Of course discipline is necessary to efficiency, but a military martinet is generally a fool, and I believe the tendency of military schools is to make martinets. If there is really anything in a boy, experience in the army or in the world will cure him. Yet I saw some West Pointers whose buckram stiffness of uniform covered a stiffness of mind that could never adapt itself to conditions around it. Such men had great contempt for General Forrest and never forgave him for winning battles contrary to the tactics. Such men as Generals Lee, Johnston, and Stonewall Jackson knew the value of the military training, but they were not tied by it.[184] — CONFEDERATE REVEREND J. H. MCNEILLY

THE COMPLIMENT THAT LED TO DISASTER
☛ On August 9 General Forrest made an offer to the [Confederate] War Department which if they had accepted would in my opinion, have materially changed the entire aspects of the situation and would have made Sherman's march to the sea almost impossible. Forrest said:

"Give me the command of the forces on the Mississippi River from Cairo to Vicksburg, or, in other words, all the forces I may collect and organize between those points. I desire to take only four hundred men from my present command, selected entirely on account of their knowledge of the country in which I propose to operate. I have resided on the Mississippi River for over twenty years and know the territory perfectly and have officers on my staff who have rafted timber and know every foot of the ground from Commerce to Vicksburg. With the force proposed and the knowledge we possess I am confident that we could so harass and destroy boats on the river that only flats heavily protected by gunboats would be able to make the passage. In making this proposition I desire to state that I do so entirely for the good of the service. There are thousands of men where I propose to go that I am satisfied will join me and stay until all the country bordering on the Mississippi from Cairo down is retaken and permanently occupied by our forces."

General Bragg put the finish to it by paying Forrest the compliment of saying: "I know of no other officer to whom I would rather assign the duty proposed, than which none is more important, but it would deprive this army of one of its greatest elements of strength to remove General Forrest."[185] — JOHN C. STILES

FORREST SAVES A CONFEDERATE SOLDIER
☛ My father, F. E. P. Jennings, now deceased, and three brothers lived near Lebanon, Tenn., and were "Forrest's men." I once showed my

father a large painting, in a museum here, of Generals Lee and Grant. He looked at it earnestly and then said: "Well, son, they must have been great men, but they couldn't come up to old Bedford."

He said that one cold morning during the war when drawn up in line of battle just before a fight he climbed upon a large rock to look at the Yankees, who were shooting at Forrest's men. He felt a pull on the back of his jacket, and a voice said: "Get down from there! Don't you know the Yankees will shoot you?" He look around and promptly climbed down, and General Forrest climbed up.

I . . . am proud to be the son of a Confederate soldier.[186] — JOHN W. JENNINGS

A CONFEDERATE PRIVATE REMEMBERS GENERAL FORREST

W. A. Callaway.

☛ I do not see much from the plain privates of the War between the States, who endured most of the hardships. Most of those who are left are too old and feeble to write. It is always interesting to read incidents in the lives of our great generals, and I happen to have been a witness to a number of these in General Forrest's career and will relate two or three.

. . . After the Hood campaign to Franklin and Nashville [Winter 1864], we stopped in North Mississippi a few days for a much-needed rest. One morning a long, keen, razorback hog came trotting along the road through our camp. He must have looked like a "biting" hog, for one of my company pulled down on him with his revolver, making a very painful wound about his jaw. He wheeled around in the road several times with very loud squeals. Forrest's headquarters were several hundred yards up the road, and the hog went directly past it, squealing every hop of the way.

In a few minutes the General was seen coming in a gallop on a small, shaggy pony, with rope bridle reins and stirrup straps, about as sorry looking an outfit as one ever sees. Being a tall man, Forrest's long legs dangled nearly to the ground, as he was not using the stirrups, they being too short. It was an undignified appearance for our General, but he did not run on dignity; he was on business.

When he reached my company, he stopped, dismounted, and, going from one to another of the men, asked: "Who shot that hog?" Of course none of us knew that a hog had been shot. When he failed to locate the culprit, he said: "If I just knowed which one of you boys shot that hog, I would strap him across that log and hit him a thousand [times] across his naked back."

After delivering this warning, he remounted and galloped back.

On investigation we found that the pony belonged to an old farmer who owned the hog and happened to be at headquarters at that time.

I have often wondered how Forrest located that shot so correctly, as troops were camped thickly all along the way.

After a lapse of fifty-six years, I may not be betraying confidence to say that Jim Bird shot the hog, remarking that he would shoot any man's hog that tried to bite him. It was all a bluff on General Forrest's part. He often talked ugly to us in that way and then went off and laughed about it. The men were very fond of him and understood him.

During Hood's campaign into Tennessee, after the fall of Atlanta, when the advance-guard was nearing Franklin, we came to a blockhouse which the Yankees had built to protect the railroad. Forrest decided he would take it. To do this he called part of my battery (Young's)—he was leading the way, as usual—to within about two hundred yards. The blockhouse was built of logs, several thicknesses, and it was impossible with light artillery to do any damage unless we could put shells through the portholes, and these were only large enough for the defenders to stick their muskets through; so it would take a very fine marksman to hit the hole, especially as those Yankees were shooting while we were getting into position.

There were only about twenty of us in the party, including General Forrest, who was urging us to take good aim and "blow 'em up." After we had fired fifteen or twenty ineffectual shots, the General said: "Boys, we had better get back." That was mighty sweet music to our ears, and we got back.

Forrest was pretty good himself on a "git." He often exposed himself recklessly, and no one could prevent him. He was not afraid of anything or anybody.

Another incident I recall occurred on December 25, 1864, while we were acting as rear guard for Hood's defeated army. The Yankees were crowding us too closely, and about nine miles south of Pulaski we formed a fighting line on a commanding position, and when the Yankees came up they were doing much damage with their artillery. Forrest and staff sat on their horses viewing what was going on. The men were all tired and resting behind rail breastworks. All of a sudden Forrest gave the command, "Charge that battery, boys!" at the same time sticking spurs, and he and his staff went off at a rapid rate, leading the charge, and were fully fifty yards ahead of the troops. They brought back the battery.[187] — W. A. CALLAWAY

BRIEF BIOGRAPHY OF FORREST

☛ In 1861 Forrest had risen from the simple pioneer life of a Tennessee boy into a man of wealth, owning several plantations and enjoying an ample income, the result of indomitable energy and business sagacity. Throughout his life two women deeply influenced him. One was the mother [Mariam Beck], who gave him her own dauntless courage; the other his wife, the gentle and lovely Mary [Ann] Montgomery, who made for him a home of rare felicity. Every young girl should read the story of this mother, learn how she gave eight sons to the service of her country—the Napoleonic test of womanhood—consider that all of them served valiantly, one with immortal fame, and then ponder seriously how much of this proud record was due to the earnest, God-fearing woman whose horizon never extended far beyond her own fireside, but whose example and precept molded the lives of heroes. Just such mothers are needed to-day. For lack of them our race is losing its virility, and we are tending inevitably toward that easy descent to Avernus down which so many ancient empires have glided to oblivion.

Ida Saxton McKinley, wife of U.S. President William McKinley. Though he served in the Union army, the president publicly recognized the gallantry of the Confederate soldier.

When the war came Forrest enlisted as a private, but his ability was too widely recognized for him to remain long in a subordinate position. A large part of his command was raised by his own efficient methods of recruiting, and much of the equipment was paid for out of his own funds. Indeed, in securing and arming his men he showed much of the strategy which he afterwards displayed in his campaigns.

Military post-mortems are proverbially unprofitable, but in reviewing the life of Forrest, even superficially, it is necessary to dwell at some length upon the surrender of Fort Donelson. First, because it was a fatal mistake from which the Confederacy never rallied, and, second, because it was Forrest's first great opportunity to show his metal. The surrender was agreed upon over his protest after he had offered to cover the retirement of the Confederates, if they abandoned the fort, with his troopers. When his advice, in which General Pillow, concurred, was overruled, Forrest left the conference, declaring that he did not intend to surrender himself or his command.

Calling his men around him, he told them the situation and stated that he was going out if he died in the attempt. Before dawn his troopers followed him, and they escaped without the loss of a man. General Floyd and General Pillow also escaped, with a portion of their commands, and a number of officers and soldiers made their way south and were not pursued.

When the Confederates retired from Shiloh, it was Forrest who protected the retreat. The capture of Murfreesboro, then of Colonel Streight's entire command, and the hard fighting at Chickamauga followed in quick succession; and then, in consequence of differences between himself and the general commanding, Forrest asked to be transferred to a different field. What Forrest earnestly desired and asked was a command with *carte blanche* to patrol the Mississippi River and render it useless to the Federal army.

It was a bold conception and one which Forrest alone could have put into execution, but, unfortunately, the War Department did not see fit to make the attempt. He took with him to the field assigned him in West Tennessee only two hundred and seventy-one men. He very soon recruited a formidable force and fought with his accustomed skill and success; but assuredly not the least of the causes which contributed to the defeat of the Confederacy was the failure to utilize to the utmost the genius of this born leader.

Forrest survived the war twelve years. He . . . [supported] the Invisible Empire, otherwise known as the Ku-Klux Klan [at that time, a Conservative, pro-Constitution organization, and *not* connected to today's KKK], and by his proclamation it was [permanently] disbanded [in 1869].[188] His evidence before a Congressional committee in regard to this famous secret order was fearless and gave the committee some realization of the [Left-wing] evils which the Ku-Klux endeavored to resist.[189]

Forrest was always a man of high character and true chivalry; in his later days he became a devout Christian. His generosity to his needy comrades was boundless.

The object of this brief and imperfect sketch is to lead a younger generation to study the life of this remarkable man, of whom Lord Wolseley said: "Forrest had fought like a knight-errant for the cause he believed to be that of justice and right. No man who drew the sword for his country in that fratricidal struggle deserves better of her, and as long as the chivalrous deeds of her sons find poets to describe them and fair women to sing of them, the name of this gallant general will be remembered with affection and sincere admiration. A man with such a record needs no ancestry."[190] — MRS. A. A. CAMPBELL (HISTORIAN GENERAL, U.D.C.)

GEN. NATHAN BEDFORD FORREST DAY

☛ Through a bill introduced in the Tennessee Legislature by Hon. E. J. Travis, of Henry County, at the request of Mrs. Alexander B. White, the thirteenth day of July, the birthday of Gen. Nathan Bedford Forrest, has been made a legal holiday in the State of Tennessee. July 13, 1921, will be the one hundredth anniversary of the birth of the "Wizard of the Saddle" and will be observed by many Confederate organizations.[191] — UNKNOWN

FORREST'S RAID INTO MEMPHIS

☛ I joined the Confederate army in the latter part of 1863, becoming a member of Buchanan's Company of the 15th Tennessee Cavalry, of which [Francis M.] Stewart was colonel and [Thomas H.] Logwood the lieutenant colonel, Neely's Brigade.

At Holly Springs, Miss., in the summer of 1864, the Federals had assembled a large army, some 18,000 infantry and 7,000 cavalry, with artillery, all well-armed and well-equipped in every respect, and with several very eminent Federal generals in command, such as Smith, Mower, Washburn, and Grierson. Holly Springs being their base, this force moved south, and General Chalmers skirmished with them, thus keeping them from scattering all over the country.

General Forrest, with Bell's and Neely's Brigades and Morton's battery, met the Federals out north of Oxford with not more than 4,000 men and one battery of artillery. Hurricane Creek is a large creek some eight or ten miles from Oxford, running east and west, and the large range of hills on the north and south sides of this creek was a very favorable place for artillery play between the armies. The Confederates occupied the old cemetery on the south side of the creek, and in this position we skirmished with the enemy for several days, having a regular artillery duel on one or more occasions. Finally, the Federals, by their overwhelming numbers, turned our left flank, thereby necessitating our vacating the hills and falling back to Oxford.

On August 18, or thereabouts, Forrest selected about 2,000 of his best men, and, in person, started on this raid into Memphis with

Morton's battery, but without any wagon train and only two days' rations. We left Oxford in a drizzling rain traveling west in the direction of Panola, on the Tallahatchie River. There had been a pontoon bridge across the river at this place, but we had to abandon two pieces of artillery, as the roads were so bad. We started in the direction of Hernando, traveling day and night, building bridges at Hickala and Coldwater, both streams being very much swollen. The bridges were quickly built and delayed us but a short while, and about sundown of August 20 we were within twenty miles of Memphis, and then traveled all night.

The Federal outposts were only a short distance from their camps, and these we captured. Some one fired a gun and thus gave the alarm. The Federals ran off from a battery of six guns without even firing a shot; a portion of the troops dashed into their camps, while another part went into the city, the latter going in by way of the old Female College up to Main Street, where they divided. Some of them went to the Gayoso Hotel, where the Federal officers were located, the idea being to capture the Federal generals—Washburn, Hulburt, and Buckland—but they had been warned and escaped to the fort. However, we captured General Washburn's clothes and about six hundred prisoners.

We stayed in the city three or four hours and finally fell back to the old academy and fought the Federals for quite a while, giving time to get the prisoners away. We then crossed Nonconnah Creek, and sent a flag of truce to General Washburn, asking for food to feed the [Yankee] prisoners, as we had nothing to give them. We also returned General Washburn's clothes. Not a great while thereafter, General Washburn had Forrest's old tailor to make Forrest a nice Confederate suit.

The effect of this raid was to make General Smith fall back to Holly Springs, and Forrest and his men were permitted to return to Panola. After resting and recruiting the horses for some time, we then marched into northern Alabama.[192] — S. M. RAY

FORREST IN THE OFFICIAL RECORDS

☛ On March 31, General Sherman said: "Forrest was badly worsted at Paducah. I hope to catch and use him up. Tell General Hurlbut that he must not let him escape at this time."

On April 2: "I now have a force at Purdy and others coming from Memphis, which should render his escape difficult, if not impossible."

On the 3: "I know what force Forrest has and will attend to him in time."

On the 4: "Forrest is between the Tennessee and Mississippi. I want to keep him there a while, when I hope to give him a complete thrashing."

On the 6: "Dispositions are complete to make Forrest pay dear for his foolish dash at Paducah."

On the 19: "I have sent Sturgis down to take command of the cavalry and whip Forrest."

On the 21: "I fear we are too late, but I know there are troops enough at Memphis to whale Forrest if you can reach him."

On the 24: "Don't let Forrest insult you by passing in sight almost of your command."

But Sherman didn't do a thing he said he would, and Forrest did as he pleased.[193] — U.S. OFFICIAL RECORDS (SER. 3, VOL. 2)

WHEN FORREST CAPTURED FRANKLIN

Miss Anne H. Scales, Maid of Honor for Forrest's Cavalry Corps.

☛ General Forrest attacked the Federals at Franklin on June 4, 1863 [the Battle of Franklin I], driving them through the town and across the river, Forrest occupying the place.

The excitement and joy of the population over the retreat of the Northern troops was very great. People ran out of their houses into the yards and even upon the sidewalks to see and hear better. The Federal provost guards, patrolling the streets in the rear of the fighting line, remonstrated with them, saying: "Have you no sense at all? Don't you know that you may be killed or maimed by the fire of your friends? Get into the house, and in the cellar, if you have a cellar!"

After a while the town was in full possession of the Confederates. The siege guns of Fort Grainger boomed, and the rifle pieces of the Confederates, in position south of the town, crashed in a duel of artillery, the shells whistling over the town.

At our house some one raised the cry: "General Forrest is coming up the street!" Every one rushed to the front fence.

Sure enough, the general was near at hand at the head of a body of horsemen, consisting of staff officers, orderlies, and the escort troop, approaching at a walk from the direction of the public square. At the sight of our father, General Forrest turned his horse toward the sidewalk and was met just outside the sidewalk, where a low-spoken conversation was held.

Officers and men attending the general reined their horses to the other side of the street and took position in loose column formation, leaving the roadway clear.

At the conclusion of the conversation, and when shaking hands, I heard father say: "General, Major Johnson waits to pay his respects to you at his house across the street." The General, whose back was to the street, turned his horse, saying, "Yes, yes, certainly," and rode across the street toward Major Johnson's gate. I can recall how the old man tore the gate open and rushed bareheaded to meet General Forrest, both hands extended, the family standing at the fence gazing in awe at the great Forrest.

The approach to Franklin (heading North from Spring Hill and Thompson's Station), with Winstead Hill on the left and Breazy Hill on the right, the site of Hood's headquarters during the doomed Battle of Franklin II, November 30, 1864.

We remained at the fence looking at the general, his staff and escort, and passing soldiers in gray. Suddenly a horseman came from the direction of the river at utmost speed. The rider, an orderly, recognized General Forrest as he passed him and pulled his horse to a stop, and, wheeling, rode to the general, saluted and said: "General _____ (I did not catch the name) [offers you his] compliments. Armstrong is being driven back on the Murfreesboro road." General Forrest listened calmly with his eyes fastened on the man's face and said something in reply in a tone so low I could not hear what he said. I watched this episode with breathless interest. I was a student of the history of Napoleon and his marshals, and I knew the military etiquette, the prestige of rank and greatness, and the atmosphere that surrounds those in high position. And here I was witnessing the making of a report on the field of battle by a soldier to the victorious commander in chief. What would be General Forrest's attitude toward the orderly?

. . . Well, the general fulfilled my ideal of a truly great and dignified man. He regarded the man calmly, listening carefully to what he had to say, quietly and impersonally giving the man a return message to bear, and the orderly comported himself in a manner that won my boyish admiration. There was no trace of servility or embarrassment. With an impassive expression, he looked the great captain in the face and spoke in a clear, steady voice.

When the General concluded his return message, the orderly saluted punctiliously, wheeled his horse, and was gone the way he had come, his horse at full speed, *venire a terre* ["come to land"]. I knew that he was bound for the place somewhere between the Murfreesboro Road and the river, near Hughes's Mill, from which had been coming the roll of musketry, heavy, steady, without intermission, for more than an hour, so long that the ear was fatigued by the sound. This orderly, a private soldier, whose jacket of gray bore no stars or bars upon the collar nor braid upon the sleeves, was, as Burns would say, "a man for a' that."

It may not be amiss to relate a little incident illustrating the opinion of the prowess of Forrest as a military commander entertained by the people of Franklin and surrounding country based upon personal observation of the various campaigns conducted in that vicinity by the General during which there were engagements at Franklin and near by.

When Hood's army, defeated in the battle of Nashville, retreated through Franklin [The Battle of Franklin III], its rear was covered by the cavalry of Gen. Abram Buford, who contested the passage of the Harpeth River, on the northern outskirts of the town, by the pursuing Federals in a hot engagement, withdrawing late in the evening when the retreating infantry had gotten a sufficient distance away.

The river not being fordable on account of high water, a pontoon bridge was thrown across the stream and the Federals began the occupation of the town upon the retirement of Buford.

When the fighting began, the people had sought refuge in the cellars, as usual.

As it became dark, I, a lad of sixteen, climbed the fence between my home place and that of a neighbor, passing through the garden to his house for the purpose of ascertaining how the numerous persons I knew to be gathered in the large cellar had fared. In the cellar, lighted by a single lamp, I found the company seated with backs to the wall, and in a corner was a young woman crying hard. "What is Sally crying about?" I asked, but no one replied.

Thinking she had heard of some kinsman having fallen in the fighting, I went to the weeping woman and asked: "Sally, why are you crying?"

"O, Charley!" she replied, "the bridge has been swept away; only a thousand or so troops have crossed to this side. Forrest is coming from Murfreesboro to join Hood's army; Forrest will learn the situation here and will be sure to attack to-night. We shall have fighting in the town and have to go through those terrifying experiences again, and my nerves will not stand it! If it were anyone else but Forrest, I should not be so frightened, but that terrible man! Boo hoo!"

The gloomy expression of the faces of the assembly indicated that all concurred in poor Sally's view, and the worst was to be apprehended. As for myself, I reflected that home was the better place for me, especially as there was a deeper cellar there! All knew Forrest and Forrest's "way"!

However, owing to the distance, bad roads, wretched weather, and unbridged streams, General Forrest did not reach the route of the retreating army until many miles south of Franklin intervened.

In his memoirs, General Grant states that he thought (and it was so thought at Washington) that Hood's army would not be able, in view of the vigorous pursuit, to reach the distant Tennessee River and cross that wide stream to safety. "But," adds General Grant, "the rear guard was undaunted and firm and did its duty to the very end."

Forrest was in command of the rear guard![194] — CHARLES MARSHALL

INFLUENCE OF FORREST'S MOTHER ON HER SON

☞ We are here assembled to memorialize a life that apparently reached its end in 1867. I say "apparently," because that life still throbs in our midst, and it will continue to the end of time—refreshing, inspiring, edifying, and making stronger and more enduring the soul of Americanism [that is, conservatism, the "Southern Cause"].

Mariam Beck—a tall, beautiful young woman with a broad forehead, dark hair, and bluish gray eyes—was as a magnet among the young people of the Caney Springs neighborhood [near what is now Chapel Hill], in Middle Tennessee, about the time that State was admitted into the Union. Her personality was rare—and it would be to-day, even in the most populous community. It was a combination of perfect health, extraordinary physical strength, litheness, brain power, repose, and delicate charm. Such a personality is ever as the sun shining in all its strength, beauty, and glory upon the circles in which it moves.

It was not to be wondered at that William Forrest—the strong, handsome, high-toned young blacksmith of the settlement—sought her hand in marriage. It was in 1820 that the young couple started their home. They dwelt in a cabin, with a single room below and a half-room or loft overhead. However, it was a home—a real, heaven-kissed home—because the head of the house was a true man in every sense of the word, and especially because Mariam was the industrious, contented, cheer-dispensing, reigning queen.

Owing to its rich combination, Mrs. William Forrest's life in that humble home, natural and beautiful like the fragrant flowers of spring, was a benediction upon her day and generation.

However, July 13, 1821, Mariam Forrest's soul was thrilled, because on that day the Lord granted unto her the supreme joy of motherhood. A biographer, referring to William Forrest and the advent of childhood in his home, observes:

Final headquarters of General Forrest. It was in this house that Forrest reluctantly surrendered to Union General Edward R. S. Canby in May 1865. Forrest and his men were the last Confederate soldiers to leave the battlefield in the Western Theater.

"He was an honorable man and a law-abiding citizen. This I have from a perfectly reliable source, . . . from one who lived a near neighbor and knew him well. He must have been this and more to have won the love and devotion of Mariam Beck, the woman of extraordinary character who on this day held to a mother's breast her twin-born hostages to fortune, his son and daughter [Nathan Bedford and his twin sister Fanny]. If, as was natural on this eventful day, his heart swelled with pride of paternity and a father's love, what height of ecstasy might not this humble workman have reached could he have seen through the curtain of the future and read the horoscope of that first-born boy of his, who was destined to write his name on one of the loftiest tablets of the immortals in the temple of fame!"

William Forrest's home was blessed with eleven children. Six years after his decease, his widow was married to Joseph Luxton, and to this union three sons and a daughter were born.

Books on how to rear children are plentiful nowadays; but the old-time mother about whose grave we are now gathered had only one book to guide her in the rearing of fifteen children—the Bible. In its light she struggled against the adverse conditions of that pioneer day and ever pointed out the path of rectitude to her sons and daughters. My investigations reveal that she was strict, even stern, in her rulings, yet reasonable. She did not spare the rod when she considered it necessary; but the rod was not her scepter—she counseled and prayed with her children. She taught them by precept and example. In other words, she preached to them and lived her preaching in their presence.

Not a member of this large family departed from the higher walks of life. This, were there no printed data to guide us, would lead to the conclusion that the mother influence was wise and Heaven directed.

This great woman gave eight sons to the service of her beloved South, all of whom won distinction as soldiers. The name of one of her sons is now a household word, not only in the Southland, but in the North and wherever military tactics are studied and valued. She was his mentor throughout life, and her instructions, early given, lingered in his heart and shaped his destiny. A biographical statement reads: "His love for his mother amounted to adoration, and was one of the noblest features of this great man's character."

Nathan Bedford Forrest was a lad of sixteen when his father died, and upon his young shoulders fell the burden of managing the farm and supporting the large family. This he did with astonishing sagacity. Within three years after his father's death, the family enjoyed prosperity that elicited the wonder of neighbors—and probably the envy of a few. At the age of twenty-one, he entered upon a business career which changed in aspect, but continued to expand until the breaking out of the War between the States, when he was regarded as one of the rich men of the South.

With General Forrest's war record all are familiar. No career in either the Southern or Northern army shines brighter in history than does his. He was conscientious, determined, and perseverant. Defeat was something he never contemplated—the word was not in his vocabulary. The stand he took in the Fort Donelson conference illustrates his rock-ribbed courage. When Generals Floyd and Buckner argued that the situation of the Confederates was hopeless, Forrest coolly announced that the Confederate army was there to fight—not to surrender. He served with increasing distinction throughout the four black, awful years, then gracefully and philosophically accepted the inevitable—as did all the great Southerners. It may be added that as a military strategist, General Forrest has never been excelled, not even in the World War [I]—and it is doubtful if he has yet been equaled.

During the early reconstruction years, when certain sections of the South were cursed with conditions that were intolerable and the gentry had to organize and act for the protection of home and government and self-respect, General Forrest again accepted a leadership which unbiased history now exonerates and which all history will ultimately exalt. Though weary of hardship, the bugle of duty called, and he responded.

The latter years of this great man's life were spent rehabilitating his fortune, ministering unto the necessities of crippled comrades, and the widows and orphans of those who had fallen under his flag, and helping push along the work of his local Church.

Oliver Wendell Holmes said: "Apology is only egotism wrong side out." I cannot agree with this. It is human to err. The wisest make mistakes. And that man is great who, when he realizes that he has made a mistake, is ready to acknowledge it. General Forrest was such a one. He and Colonel Shepherd quarreled. Duelling was then in vogue. The matter was to have been settled at sunrise. At daybreak, General Forrest called on Colonel Shepherd, extending his hand, and said: "Colonel, I am in the wrong in this affair, and I have come to say so." It would be idle to think of Forrest as a coward. His entire life reveals indomitable courage, and, besides, in those days it required more courage to apologize than to fight a duel. I think you will agree with me when I say that when General Forrest, guided by his conscience, sought Colonel Shepherd at break o' day, he displayed [a] courage with which that of battle field cannot be compared. He, then and there, took [a] firm stand against a custom that was wrong; he dashed ahead in the fight for right, and, in another role, became a leader in the army of reform.

In dwelling at length upon the spectacular career of General Forrest, I have not departed from a discussion of which we have assembled to honor. An analysis of his life will reveal his mother in all his great acts from his boyhood to the hour of his departure. In his thrift during his early manhood and after the unfortunate national conflict, we see his mother's economy, industry, and enterprise; in his war activities and his wise, courageous leadership during the original reconstruction period, her inborn patriotism shines; in the piety and philanthropy of his later years, her Christianity and tenderness of heart are displayed; and in his apology to Colonel Shepherd, her strict insistence upon the leadings of conscience looms large. Moreover, in everything the General undertook can be seen the indefatigable will he inherited from his mother concerning whom a line in history reads: "Having undertaken any enterprise, she persisted in it until it was accomplished."

When they laid away the mortal remains of this great American woman, they said she was dead and bade her farewell. Nevertheless, she continued to live—in her posterity, and especially in the impress of her illustrious son, and in movements and things too numerous to estimate. And now after a lapse of fifty-eight years, her magnetism draws to this beautiful, sacred spot an assembly of admiring people who represent hosts not present in body but in spirit.

When, presently, we turn away from this silent little city shall we also say to her: "Farewell?" Why, love forbids the thought. Moreover, her monument in thousands of human hearts stands like Gibraltar—and it will ever enlarge.

The influence of General Forrest's mother upon the world, like that of all good mothers, and all good people, will remain while time lasts, and it will ever expand with the opportunities afforded by the passing centuries. Instead of "Farewell" we say to her: "Mother in America's Israel, we thank God that you sojourned on earth, and that you still live in our hearts and lives. You are among our great leaders, and we cheerfully follow in duty's path."[195] — DR. D. H. EVANS (FROM AN ADDRESS GIVEN AT THE DEDICATION OF THE MEMORIAL TO GENERAL FORREST'S MOTHER NEAR NAVASOTA, TEXAS, MAY 23, 1925)

FORREST AT BRICE'S CROSSROADS

☛ . . . The battle of Brice's Crossroads was the most brilliant achievement at arms in the annals of war. While the results were not so valuable as those of King's Mountain, October 8, 1780, which was the turning point of the Revolutionary War, the victory of Brice's Crossroads will forever stand as the most wonderful of all time. General Forrest, with less than four thousand men, almost totally destroyed an army of fifteen thousand. He captured, killed, and wounded nine thousand men, captured three hundred wagons, thirty-six cannon, thirty ambulances, and a large supply of flour, bacon, coffee, and other articles, and several hundred horses.

In this battle the genuine military capacity of General Forrest seems to have been demonstrated. It has been thought by many that his success was due to uncommon good luck, but it must be apparent that this brilliant victory was won by his prompt comprehension of the situation and his recognition of the possibility of taking his adversary at the disadvantage of being attacked while his column was extended. Seeing his advantage, he planned and executed with celerity. He illustrated in this affair the efficiency of employment of his whole force when the battle moment came. He launched every man and every gun and employed them as swiftly as

James Dinkins at the time he entered Confederate service in 1861.

possible. It is not amiss to say that, closely examined, Forrest's operations will be found based on the soundest principles of the art of war. His tactics, intuitively and without knowledge of what other men had done before him, were those of great masters of that art—that is, to rush down swiftly, thunderously, upon his enemy with his whole collective strength. He had the happy gift of knowing how to inspire the courage of his men, how to excite their confidence and enthusiasm, how to bend the most reckless to his iron will. He was not only very popular with his men, but he had the mysterious power of personality that made men face any danger under his direction.

In his composition there was as much sagacity as audacity. At critical instants, he was ever quick to see, swift to decide, and swift to strike. His combats appear to have been delivered, or accepted, at the right juncture. It may be justly said that no other soldier of either side during the war (Stonewall Jackson excepted) carried the genuine distinctive traits of the American character into their operation as did Forrest. Always taking the shortest line toward his object, he knew how to grasp opportunities, and was never at a loss for resources in the most sudden emergencies. Endowed by nature with as stormful, fiery a soul as ever blazed to heat and flame in any soldier, yet surely he accomplished as much by address as by swift, hard-smiting blows. Essentially as daring a cavalry leader as ever gained distinction, it may be said of him, as Napoleon said, that "his daring was not a wild cast of the net for fortune"; for it was always supported by a penetration and activity that suffered no opportunity to escape.

Forrest was a magnetic man, standing stalwart and erect, six feet one inch tall, broad shoulders, long arms, high forehead, dark gray eyes, a prominent nose, emphatic jaw, compressed lips—a face that said to all the world: "Out of my way; I'm coming." His step was firm, action impulsive, and, taken all in all, there was not a soldier of the Confederacy that acted with more celerity or effective force from the 14th of June, 1861, when he became a private at Memphis, to the 10th of May, 1865, at Gainesville, Ala., when he surrendered as lieutenant general to the United States authorities. To determine with Forrest was to act, and the flash of his saber at the head of his columns, charging the cavalry or infantry of the enemy, inspired his troops with the sunlight of victory, and they dashed into battle like the audacious warriors of Napoleon on the field of Austerlitz.

The Confederate loss at Brice's Crossroads was heavy. Some of the best officers and men of that matchless band were killed and many wounded. Looking back on the scene, I drop a tear to their memory.

Numbers of them were my friends, as well as my comrades, and I wonder who will be responsible for their loss to the South. Of the large number that never came back, may I mention one, Lieut. William S. Pope, Adjutant of the 7th Tennessee Cavalry, who was among the killed. He was the highest ideal of a Southern boy—as modest as Ruth, as brave as Forrest, as handsome as Apollo. There were others whose names and fame as soldiers deserve perpetual memory. The writer followed General Forrest in all his daring and desperate enterprises the last two years of the war, first as aide-de-camp to General Chalmers, subsequently as captain of the Escort Company of the First Division, and was the youngest captain of cavalry in the Confederate army.[196] — CONFEDERATE CAPTAIN JAMES DINKINS

THE TRUTH ABOUT FORREST & FORT PILLOW

☛ I was in twenty-nine engagements during the War between the States, but all of them could not be classified as battles. Some were little more than skirmishes. The most of them are now being correctly written in our histories, yet one seems to be still greatly misunderstood by many of our Northern friends. I refer to the Fort Pillow fight. . . . I will not attempt to reiterate the details of the fight, I only want to deny that it was a massacre.

On the morning that General Forrest left Tibbee Station, Miss., it was not his purpose to attack Fort Pillow. He made a forced march from Tibbee to Paducah, Ky., taking Union City, Tenn., on the way. At Paducah he intended only to destroy government supplies en route for [Union] General Thomas's Army of the Tennessee. After Forrest captured Union City and destroyed the supplies at Paducah, he returned to Eaton, Tenn., on his way back to Mississippi. At Eaton he was met by many of the citizens of West Tennessee, principally ladies, who besought him not to fail to take Fort Pillow before he left the State. The troops at Fort Pillow were principally negroes who formerly belonged to people that lived in West Tennessee. They had terrorized their old masters's families until they did not know what to expect next. The Rev. G. W. D. Harris, D.D., was held as a prisoner in the fort, and suffered many indignities at the hands of the negroes, and was released only a few days before Forrest's arrival. Dr. Harris was one of the most distinguished ministers in the Southern Methodist Church.

General Forrest was a man of great sympathy, and when he heard the pathetic stories told by the ladies, he changed his plans and decided to capture Fort Pillow.

In the fort, commanded by [Union] Major Bradford, whose home was in Dyersburg, Tenn., there were two hundred white and four hundred negro soldiers. Early in the afternoon of the day the ladies visited him, General Forrest sent a detail of soldiers on to capture the pickets at the fort. At 7 p.m. he mounted his command and started to the fort, getting there at 5 a.m. The advance guard had captured the pickets without the firing of a gun. After stationing his troops at strategic points, Captain Morton's battery opened fire on the fort, and this was responded to by the cannon in the fort. Then our sharpshooters began to "pick off" the gunners, and a general engagement followed. Early in the afternoon, General Forrest, under a flag of truce, ordered an unconditional surrender of the fort. Major Bradford refused, and General Forrest proceeded to take the fort. The negroes were drunk, and, when Forrest's men got into the fort, the negroes continued to fight until they were overpowered. This is why so many of them were killed. Major Bradford and many of the white troops retreated to the river, seeking protection under their gunboats. But Captain Morton soon turned the guns in the fort on the gunboats, and they sought shelter around the bend of the river. After the surrender, Major Bradford was taken from the river where, up to his chin in water, he had tried to board one of the gunboats.

Confederate President Jefferson Davis. Tragically for the South, the Union military became aware of Forrest's genius long before the authorities at Richmond. It was not until after the war that Davis, for example, came to realize that Forrest should have been given much larger command over much larger territory.

I never saw a man killed or a gun fired after the drunken negroes surrendered. The killed on the Union side was necessarily great, but it could not be helped. This fight was in no sense a massacre.[197] — THEO F. BREWER

FORREST: HISTORY'S MOST GIFTED MILITARY STRATEGIST

☞ The writer knew General Forrest as well as a boy could know a great man. I served the last two years of the war with him, and accompanied him in most of his desperate and daring enterprises. I thought of him then as the most wonderful man I had ever known. My admiration for him has grown daily during the sixty-three years since I first met him. I am familiar with the achievements of many of the great commanders of the past, but I firmly believe that Gen. Nathan Bedford Forrest was the most gifted military strategist that ever lived.

General Lee was the most perfect man for several hundred years before him. He possessed qualities that make a man great. As citizen, soldier, gentleman he never had a superior, and I doubt that he ever had an equal. The presence of General Lee and General Forrest gave to men that tingle in the blood that comes only upon momentous occasions. They could make heroes out of common mortals.[198] — CONFEDERATE CAPTAIN JAMES DINKINS

MEMORIAL TO GENERAL FORREST
☛ Nathan Bedford Forrest has been characterized—

By Robert E. Lee as "the most remarkable genius produced in the Confederate army, and a man that I never saw."

By Theodore Roosevelt as "the most remarkable man produced in either the Union or Confederate armies."

By George Creel as "the Gray Ghost of the South, whose terrible harassing embarrassed the Union forces beyond their expectations."

By one of Europe's greatest military strategists as "the greatest cavalry leader of all times."

These characterizations of Nathan Bedford Forrest could be multiplied without limit.

A memorial befitting this great leader of the Southern cause is planned to be placed where, by every show of reason, it should be, at his birthplace, Chapel Hill, Tenn.

The Daughters of the Confederacy at Chapel Hill have been appointed to raise sufficient funds to supplement a like fund appropriated by an act of the legislature of the State of Tennessee for the purchase of the house site of the birthplace of General Forrest and here erect a fitting memorial to this matchless leader.[199] — UNKNOWN

AT THE BIRTHPLACE OF GENERAL FORREST
☛ The name and fame of Nathan Bedford Forrest have been further recorded for future generations by the erection of a monument at his birthplace, the little community of Chapel Hill, in Marshall County, Tenn. In a humble home there the great Wizard of the Saddle was born one hundred and seven years ago, and on July 13, 1928, his natal day was commemorated by the dedication of this monument which perpetuates the fame of a great soldier. [Note: the original home no longer exists.]

Fitting exercises attended the dedication, beginning in the morning of the 13th and concluding in the afternoon, when the monument was unveiled in the presence of many hundreds of spectators, some of them special guests of the occasion, all of whom were welcomed to the community by Mayor W. T. Hurt, and on behalf of the county by J. N. McCord, of Lewisburg. Addresses were made by Hon. Ewin L. Davis, representative in Congress from this district, who was followed by Mrs. J. A. Hargrove, of Chapel Hill, on behalf of the U.D.C., in accepting the monument. Some of the other speakers were Gen. T. C. Little, for the Confederate Veterans; Col. Joel B. Fort, of Nashville, Scott Davis, a veteran of Forrest's Cavalry, and Charles Moss, of Lewisburg.

Cut and pasted photo of Forrest's staff members. Standing left to right: Capt. John G. Mann; Dr. J. B. Cowan; Capt. George Dashiell; Lieut. S. Donelson. Sitting: Capt. John W. Morton; Major C. W. Anderson; Capt. William M. Forrest (the General's son).

Special credit for the erection of this monument goes to Mrs. J. A. Hargrove, President of the U.D.C. Chapter at Chapel Hill, who started the movement some three years ago and had worked untiringly to its completion, ably assisted by other Daughters of the Confederacy there and friends. By their efforts the site was secured and an appropriation made by the State of Tennessee to thus honor a son who had honored his native State by his great services in time of war and in the days of peace. A splendid tribute was paid to Forrest in the address by Judge Davis, not only as a soldier, but as "a man of unimpeachable integrity, high moral courage, and constructive citizenship."

Music and readings appropriate to the occasion made the exercises complete, and the day was one of the most interesting that the old community of Chapel Hill has ever known. The tall granite shaft will ever cast its shadow over the place which once enshrined a little babe destined to immortality.[200] — E. D. POPE

FORREST: THERE CAN BE ONLY ONE!

☞ It would be idle to say that any man was the equal of Nathan Bedford Forrest. He had no counterpart in the past, and there will be no one in the future years. He will forever stand as the genius of war. There was but one Shakespeare, and there can never be but one Forrest. It has been said that the century plant blooms but once in a hundred years, and so it is with the crucibles of mankind; only once in a century does there come forth a man like Forrest—no, not in a thousand years![201] — CONFEDERATE CAPTAIN JAMES DINKINS

FORREST: AMONG THE THREE GREATEST OF THE WAR
☛ That General Forrest stands forth as the greatest military strategist is evidenced by the success he always achieved, and also by the judgment of men everywhere. I have a letter from Rev. Giles B. Cooke, of Virginia, the only survivor of Gen. R. E. Lee's staff, who states that on one occasion, while General Lee was president of Washington College, an English officer, visiting Lexington, asked the General who was the greatest military genius on both sides of the war between the States, General Lee said, "Gen. N. B. Forrest, who, with the least means, accomplished more than any other general." He then asked whom he thought was the greatest Federal general. "George B. McClellan," General Lee said.

The writer was a member of a committee sent from Mississippi in September, 1888, to Beauvoir, to persuade Mr. [Jefferson] Davis to attend the State Fair. During the visit, I asked Mr. Davis whom he regarded as his ablest general. He answered promptly, "N. B. Forrest." I then asked him how he selected Raphael Semmes to command the *Alabama*? "Because," he said, "he was the greatest naval officer and the greatest admiralty lawyer in the country." So that we can feel a pride in the comradeship of the three greatest men of the war: Gen. Robert E. Lee, Nathan Bedford Forrest, and Admiral Raphael Semmes.[202] — CONFEDERATE CAPTAIN JAMES DINKINS

FORREST & HIS WARHORSE KING PHILIP
☛ The third of that trio of famous Confederate war horses [which include first General Lee's Traveller and second General Jackson's Little Sorrel] was King Philip, the mount of Gen. Nathan Bedford Forrest, the great cavalry leader of the Confederacy, whose strategy has become immortal.

King Philip was a gift to General Forrest. The last week of May, 1863, the Federals sent an expedition of 2,200 picked men and a battery of rifled artillery commanded by Colonel Streight, distinguished Union officer, into Georgia, with orders to destroy Gen. Braxton Bragg's line of supplies and communications, and destroy, too, every source of that country's sustenance.

General Forrest, with 1,000 cavalry and one battery, went in pursuit. He killed or captured the entire command of Federals in a terrific action a short distance from Rome, Ga.

The ladies of Columbus, Ga., to express their thanks to the Confederate commander who had saved their home from pillage, bought and gave him the finest horse they could find in Georgia. Like Lee's  Traveller, King Philip was Confederate gray, with black mane and tail. He was sixteen hands high, and weighed 1,200 pounds. His name at first was simply "Philip," but presently Forrest's men christened him "King Philip." He was as unmoved amid exploding shells as Traveller, and, at close range, he was as ferocious a fighter as his master; and Forrest could fight hand-to-hand with pistol and sabre as ferociously as the strongest man under his command. Biting, kicking, and plunging, with Forrest in the saddle slashing and shooting, those two were the ideal leaders of a cavalry charge.

On the retreat of Hood's army from Nashville, in December, 1864, Forrest was in the saddle almost continuously on King Philip, five days and nights.

"I doubt if there was a horse in either army that could have endured what King Philip endured then."

In 1865, General Wilson, of the Federal army, was at Jasper, Ala., with 15,000 cavalry, 2,000 infantry and five batteries of artillery, to make a diversion to help the operations against Mobile. He had a pontoon train of fifty wagons. Forrest with 3,000 men confronted him. And Forrest, riding with his staff and escort, some seventy-five men, came in sight of a big body of Wilson's Federal cavalry moving southward. Instantly, General Forrest formed his seventy-five men in a column of fours, and at their head charged straight into the enemy. King Philip, with his mighty strength, knocked down half a dozen Federal horses and riders as the charge drove home, a stampede followed, and Forrest and his seventy-five men held the field.

As the enemy approached Selma, Ala., Forrest and his staff were engaged in a hand-to-hand combat with a party of Federal cavalrymen. Forrest himself, on King Philip, was attacked by four troopers. He shot one as they came on. The remaining three, sabres drawn, dashed upon him, with three other Federal cavalrymen galloping up to join them. Six against one, and Forrest's staff and escort were too far away to reach him in time. On either hand the roadway was hedged by a dense thicket. To the rear it was choked by a covered army wagon, which had turned over. The melee which had preceded this sudden flurry had given King Philip a pistol ball in the hip, and General Forrest's right arm was weakened from terrific sabre play in which he had killed three of the enemy. Escape looked impossible. But Forrest wheeled King Philip, drove him at the wagon, gave him the spur, and the gallant animal rose to leap clear over the wagon as a jumper would clear a barred gate.

After the war, General Forrest returned to his plantation in Coahoma County, Miss. There King Philip grazed, in peace at last. He had one final battle. A troop of Federal cavalry rode into the field where King Philip was grazing. He leaped at them like a tiger, kicking, biting, and drove them out.

Then General Forrest consented to have King Philip shown at a benefit in Memphis for sick and wounded Confederate soldiers. Jerry, the general's negro body-servant, and Pat, his Irish orderly, began grooming King Philip and feeding him quantities of green corn. Naturally, the horse died of colic, enormously swollen. Crouching beside the body, as General Forrest looked on, weeping with grief, Pat nevertheless managed to gulp out to the general: "Sir, I want you to look at the fat I put on King Philip before he died!"

A grave was dug on the Forrest plantation, and General Forrest wrapped his own old army blanket about King Philip before he was laid at rest.[203] — CONFEDERATE CAPTAIN JAMES DINKINS

General Forrest as he appeared at age 54 in 1875, two years before his death in 1877.

10

POEMS ABOUT FORREST

A CAMP SONG TO GENERAL FORREST
(Air: "Columbia, the Gem of the Ocean")

The day of our destiny was darkened,
    The heart of the nation stood still.
When Forts Henry and Donelson surrendered,
    And Johnston fell back to Nashville.
But the clouds, which then thickened around us,
    Served only the plainer to show
The form of that hero arising
    To deliver us all from the foe.

CHORUS
Here's to Forrest from the brave Tennessee,
Here's to Forrest from the brave Tennessee;
In our hearts he will triumph forever.
Here's to Forrest from the brave Tennessee.

At Shiloh he charged a division
    And covered our army's retreat;
At Murfreesboro won his promotion
    When Crittenden acknowledged defeat.
Next Streight went careering before him,

  Expecting our rear to assail.
But Forrest, with his fair maiden pilot,
  Soon landed the robber in jail.

Chickamauga, Chattanooga, Okolona,
  Memphis, and Tishomingo Creek,
Union City, Fort Pillow, and Paducah—
  All the deeds of our hero bespeak.
Now Athens, Sulphur Springs, and Pulaski
  Have aroused old Sherman from his lair,
For the boldest of Yankee commanders
  Will tremble with Forrest in his rear.

Next Johnsonville attracted his attention
  Where Sherman had collected his stores,
And the gunboats, once terrible to mention,
  Floated grandly and proudly at its doors.
But Forrest's artillery battalion,
  Morton, Rice, Ed Walton, and Thrall,
Soon set fire to his gunboats and transports.
  Nor ceased till they had burned all.[204]
CONFEDERATE GENERAL JAMES R. CHALMERS (LYRICS)

ONLY ONE OF FORREST'S MEN

Near the foot of Lookout Mountain
 Stood a farmhouse years ago,
Where the sunbeams kissed the ripples
 In the Tennessee below;
There the mocking bird in springtime,
 In its joyous, merry trill,
Answered to the distant calling
 Of the lonely whip-poor-will;

When the June leaves waved a welcome
 To the mountain laurel bloom,
And the honeysuckle scented
 The morning air with sweet perfume;

When the humming birds went flitting
   'Mong the daisies growing there,
Through the tangled wild rose bramble
   And the waving maidenhair.

In the doorway stood a woman.
   Nature seemed to pause and sigh
For the little ones about her
   And the tears that filled her eye;
For the kind and loving husband,
   Riding down the mountain's glen.
"Papa's gone," her pale lips quivered—
   "Gone to war with Forrest's men."

In the days that followed after,
   Through the years of gloom and strife,
Though his heart was on the mountain
   With his children, home, and wife,
Yet the hand that held the rammer
   Never flinched or faltered when,
Facing death, he spiked a cannon
   Bearing down on Forrest's men.

"Who was he?" the Colonel shouted,
   Glancing down the throbbing lines,
As the balls and shells reechoed
   Through the oaks and forest pines.
"Home, Sweet Home," the band was playing,
   Touching hearts of foe and friend.
Through the din a cry went ringing:
   "Only one of Forrest's men."

Shrieking balls and crash of sabers
   Spreading death on every side,
Blue and gray together falling
   In the flowing crimson tide.
Through the blazing storm of battle,
   In the lurid, fiery den
There our Lookout Mountain soldier
   Won the day with Forrest's men.

Then again at Chickamauga
  We remember still with pride,
How he with the tattered regiment
  From the morn till evening tide;
Charged the flaming iron breastworks
  Through the storm of fire, and then,
Would have faced ten thousand muskets,
  He was one of Forrest's men.

Still around old Lookout Mountain
  Birds are singing as of yore,
Flowers blooming on the hillside,
  Strangers in the farmhouse door.
Time has worn the simple headstone,
  Crumbling on the mountain glen;
There old Lookout's shadow sentinels
  Only one of Forrest's men.[205]
MRS. FRANK THOMPSON

THE WIZARD OF THE SADDLE

It was out of the South that the lion heart came,
From the ranks of the Gray like the flashing of flame,
A juggler with fortune, a master with fame—
  The rugged heart born to command.

And he rode by the star of an unconquered will,
And he struck with the might of an undaunted skill;
Unschooled, but as firm as the granite-flanked hill—
  As true and as tried as steel.

Though the Gray were outnumbered, he counted no odd,
But fought like a demon and struck like a god.
Disclaiming defeat on the blood-curdled sod,
  As he pledged to the South that he loved.

'T was saddle and spur, or on foot in the field,
Unguided by tactics that knew how to yield;

Stripped of all, save his honor, but rich in that shield,
Full armored by nature's own hand

As the rush of the storm he swept on the foe;
It was "Come!" to his legion—he never said "Go!"
With sinews unbending, how could the world know
That he rallied a starving host?

For the wondering ranks of the foe were like clay
To these men of flint in the molten day;
And the hell-hounds of war howled afar for their prey,
When the arm of a Forrest led.

Was he devil or angel? Life stirred when he spoke,
And the current of courage, if slumbering, woke
At the yell of the leader, for never was broke
The record men wondering read.

With a hundred he charged like a thousand men,
And the hoofbeats of one seemed the tattoo of ten.
What bar were burned bridges or flooded fords when
The wizard of battles was there?

But his pity could bend to a fallen foe,
The mailed hand soothe a brother's woe;
He had time to be human, for tears to flow
For the heart of the man to thrill.

Then "On!" as though never a halt befell,
With a swinging blade and the rebel yell.
Through the song of the bullets and the plowshares of hell—
The hero, half iron, half soul!

Swing rustless blade in the strong left hand—
Ride, soul of god, through the dauntless band—
Through the low, green mounds of the breadth of the land—
Wherever your legions dwell!

Swing, rebel blade, through the halls of fame,
Where courage and justice have left your name;

By the torches of glory your deeds shall flame
With the reckoning of Time!²⁰⁶
MRS. VIRGINIA FRAZER BOYLE

FORREST & LEE

If we search the wide world o'er,
Through countries bathed with patriots' gore,
   And far and near through foreign lands
   For bravest chiefs of bravest bands—
Our hearts are here, and still will be,
Back in the Southland with Forrest and Lee.

If old Scotland stand with sword in sheath,
Telling with pride of Douglas and Keith;
   If England yield her richest brood,
   From Saxon worth and Norman blood—
Our hearts are here, and still will be,
Back in the Southland with Forrest and Lee.

If we climb the grape-crowned slopes of sunny France afar,
With Napoleon she adores and the white-plumed Navarre;
   If we see Portugal's men in brave battle array
   Ne'er faltering in duty nor fleeing the fray—
Our hearts are here, and still will be,
Back in the Southland with Forrest and Lee.

If through the streets of once imperial Rome we tread,
Where Nero boasted, where Caesar bled,
   Where Horatius from the bridge with nerve in every fiber,
   Swam the swollen waters of the tawny Tiber—
Our hearts are here, and still will be,
Back in the Southland with Forrest and Lee.

If we visit the Orient, where roses in myriads swarm
About a marble Taj Mahal mid India's breezes warm;
   If where an Egyptian princess her very heart's blood shed
   For a haughty warrior lover, who life and love had fled—

Our hearts are here, and still will be,
Back in the Southland with Forrest and Lee.

And, methinks, when at last we journey to the land of endless sun
And read the long, long list of hard-fought battles won
   By honored patriots and heroes from every land and clime.
   Whom homeland's thrall and duty's call had stirred the soul sublime,
High on the honor roll of heaven, surely, yes, we'll surely see
Enscrolled in gold Nathan B. Forrest and Robert E. Lee.[207]
MRS. W. B. ROMINE

FORREST, MURAT OF THE SOUTH

Straight through the iron hail,
Smiting, as wheat by flail,
  Man, horse, munition;
Bold, grim of brow and mien.
Rode he whose glory's sheen
  Gilds war's fruition!

Who else might wield that blade,
True as Toledo made,
  Forged in war's labor,
Pond'rous as Richard's mace,
Deft, with some nameless grace,
  A Soldan's saber?

Great brained and iron-thewed,
Quick, blunt, a trifle rude,
  When his hand held it,
Havock's red lightning played
From hilt through lambent blade,
  Flawless to weld it!

On through the surge of war,
Duty his guiding star,
  Weak woman aiding,
Forrest rode down to Fame,

Carved on her scroll his name,
   Dazzling, unfading.

Racing with Death to sup,
Girt on his saddle crup,
   Shell nor steel fearing;
Careless of risk and fate,
Fierce, yet with naught of hate,
   Hurled he unerring.

Great soul and brain that gave
Lightnings that lit the glaive,
   Lending the temper,
Dentless and keen of stroke,
Shearing as axe the oak,
   Valor sic semper!

What tongue may such deeds tell
That down the ages swell,
   Grandly sonorous?
Anthem true knights shall sing
All through Time's aisles to ring
   Kings in the chorus![208]
T. C. DeLeon

THE SONG OF FORREST'S MEN

Hurrah for the carbines! and ho for the Colt!
   We have thrown all our sabers away!
And we rush to the fight with hearts that are light,
   For old Forrest leads us to-day.

And he rides to the front on his good bay mare
   (I pity the man that would lag);
Now she is down, but he is up with a frown—
   A shout on his lips for our flag!

Hurrah for the saddle! and ho for the Colt!

Here is to our sweethearts at home!
We are off on a raid, but are never afraid,
  In whatever land we may roam.

Hurrah for the bugle! and ho for the Colt!
  We are off to-day through the rain;
We are after old Streight, and we must not wait,
  Though the parting is full of pain;

For old Forrest, sitting on his good black horse,
  Is waving his saber on high;
And let the sunbeams flash or the thunder crash,
  We will follow it or we'll die![209]
CONFEDERATE CAPTAIN JAMES M. MCCANN

FORREST'S CHIEF OF ARTILLERY

Ringed with flame and sore beset
Where gunboat and rifle fire met,
Where cannon blazed from water and land
Upon the Donelson Southern band.
A gallant lad of nineteen years,
A stranger to tremor and to fears,
Stood by a battery piece and shot
The first shell in that crater hot.

His captain, Porter, smitten down
Where all the volleyed thunders frown,
Shouted when borne in pain away:
"John, don't give up that gun, I say!"
"No! not while a man is left," replied
The lad in the flush of martial pride;
And he kept his word to the utter end,
While a man could live in that river bend.

"No prison for me," grim Forrest said,
And thousands followed where he led.
But other thousands remained because

They bowed to Buckner's word and laws.
Whelmed by the girdling Northern men,
They marched to the captive's dismal den,
And the lad who fired the first gun passed
Into that solitude sad and vast.

A few months more, and the daring boy
Breathed the air that the free enjoy;
A few months more, and he gayly went
Where dauntless Forrest pitched his tent.
Saluting the hero, he quickly gave
To the South's own "bravest of the brave"
A paper that said he was to be
The Wizard's chief of artillery.

A derisive smile swept over the face
Of the stern commander in his place.
"What!" he growled, "are you to wield
Command of my guns in war's fierce field?
Nonsense, boy; go grow a beard."
And this was what the stripling heard.
But presently the Wizard's brow
Grew calm. "I'll try you, anyhow,"
He said; and from that setting sun
Morton and Forrest were as one.

Nigh four tremendous, bloody years,
Full of combat, smiles, and tears,
O'er miles of land in battles grand,
Forrest and Morton went hand in hand.
With sword and pistol the Wizard slew,
While Morton's guns mowed men in blue.
If mortal man could ever have freed
The South from the foeman's grasp and greed,
That man was Forrest; but we see
It was not destined so to be.

Long years have gone, the grass is spread
Above the bivouacs of the dead.
The mighty Wizard's wand is still,

Like his heart; but from every Southern hill
And mount and stream and vale bedight,
With sun and moon and star alight,
He lives in glorious deeds alway,
Buffing the onset of decay.

The lad who made the cannon roar
Survives on Life's tumultuous shore.
His locks are silvered, but his brain
Burns with heroic throbs amain.
Gentle and kind, but valiant yet,
Forgiving, he cannot forget
The cause he fought for with his mate,
Immortal, whatsoe'er its fate.
While from his great dark eyes there gleams
The orient of remembered dreams.

And now the old bard's final rhyme
Invokes a blessing of Easter time
Upon his people and home and race,
Like manna dew of heavenly grace.
With higher aims in war's surcease
Be thou allied with the Prince of Peace,
And never henceforth forget to be
"Soldier of Him who died for thee."[210]
CONFEDERATE COLONEL JAMES R. RANDALL

FORREST OF TENNESSEE

O sing me a song of the Southland—
   The Southland that used to be,
Of the deeds of our hallowed Grey heroes,
   So sacred to you and to me.
O Southrons, ye proud, patriotic;
   O soldiers of Jackson and Lee!
Another is sung in our South-lore—
   Famed Forrest of Tennessee.

Our leaders were daring and dauntless,
   As ever led battle array;
Each heart bore the stamp of the hero
   That rode in the ranks of the Grey;
Yet never more far-eyed or fearless,
   And never a bolder could be,
None ever more tried or triumphant
   Than Forrest of Tennessee.

Aye, matchless this victor in valor—
   A hundred hard battles and more
Saw him at the head of the horsemen,
   The brunt of the danger bore;
At Donelson he our one hero,
   Wrought wonders at Chickamauga,
And dashed lion-like down at Shiloh:
   Dread Forrest of Tennessee.

The marvel of mourned Murfreesboro
   The terror of Tishomingo,
Where with only a wearied-out handful
   Far scattered the fear-stricken foe.
And, there on the fierce field of Franklin,
   'Mong the flower of our chivalry,
'Mid the groans and the gore and the carnage,
   Charged Forrest of Tennessee.

'T was a raid thro' beloved Alabama
   Marched to our stores Gen. Streight;
All behind him was direst destruction,
   Before, the same fearful fate.
But a message went thro' to the "wizard,"
   When soon, and all suddenly—
"He is coming," rang out the glad tidings,
   "Old Forrest" of Tennessee.

On, on, the swift "knight of the saddle"
   Rushed for the foe in his lair;
But burned was the bridge, wild the waters
   And Forrest, for once in despair.

When out of a cot of the mountains
    Came a slight maid—said she:
"The way to the ford I will show you.
    Brave Forrest of Tennessee."

On, on, sped the man and the maiden,
    O'er rocks and mad-rushing stream.
And fast the few grey-coated followed
    Till full in the bayonet's gleam—
A ruse, and a shout from the Southrons,
    And the girl waved her bonnet in glee
As the federals thrice cheered Emma Sansom
    With Forrest of Tennessee.

Aye, many his perilous exploit,
    And many the death-knell his deed—
Where sword, shot and shell fell the fastest,
    There Forrest was in the lead;
Yet noble, and kind, and tender—
    As always the brave—was he,
And firm was his faith in the future—
    True Forrest of Tennessee.

O Southrons, with laurels come crown him,
    Protector, Defender of homes;
Let your praises reach up to the star-realm,
    Where the grand soul of Forrest now roams.
For all that remains of our hero
    Lies silent as silent can be.
But liveth forever in South-lore,
    Loved Forrest of Tennessee.[211]
JOSIE FRAZEE-CAPPLEMAN

THE LAST ROLL CALL

Blood red the camp fires shine to-night,
    Sleep, soldier boys in gray;
Silent the picket line, hid in the night,

Taps sobbed of comrades lost, slain in the fight;
   Sleep, soldier boys in gray.

At roll call, one his name we breathed,
His bright sword, red with blood, we sheathed;
Blood red the camp fires gleam to-night—
A star for each comrade who fell in the fight.

Far hid the distant golden shore,
   Sleep, soldier boys in gray;
Nor weep, for he, our captain bold,
Sleeps now 'neath Forrest's banner gold.
   Dreaming of thee, boys in gray.

To-morrow one shall breathe thy name,
"Come, comrade, share my deathless fame!"
And you and I shall find that land
Where Forrest waits with all his band![212]
MILLARD CROWDUS

FORREST BEFORE MURFREESBORO

So shall they tell the story in the years that are to be,
   When the crystal pen of history is dipped in living flame;
So shall the Southern mother teach the children at her knee,
   And in her song of heroes she shall sing of Forrest's fame.

Do you mind, you men who met him, when war loosed the crimson
   tide—
   Was it stratagem or science? Sound the record if you can!
Do you mind, you men who faced him when war's hell-hounds opened
   wide
   The pulses of the patriot and the passions of the man?

"Close upon his heels, harass him, keep him out of Tennessee"—
   So the Northern generals ordered their subordinates. And then,
"Destroy the Rebel Forrest—a promotion waits from me
   When I know that you have killed him," said Sherman to his men.

And the shrewd spy brought his message, and the scout his story told;
  The soldier dreamed promotion, with the star of valor nigh;
The surly blue guerrilla dreamed of capture and of gold;
  But before a Yankee bullet Forrest was not born to die!

Aye! they hounded and harassed him, but he rode through Tennessee;
  And the Federals lost their patience—some their epaulets—that day
When the ranting Rebel Forrest clanked his spurs that all might see
  Through a Union general's chamber, while they sought him miles away!

"Go, take the wizard Rebel! Kill him; let this be your care!
  The rest are mine!" said Sherman. But where was Forrest then?
Twisting cables out of grapevine, building bridges out of air.
  "We must get there first, my comrades!" said Forrest to his men.

Do you mind, you men of Forrest, you cavaliers in gray,
  That early morning sally on the thirteenth of July?
You pledged to him a victory to crown his natal day,
  While he pledged to save the Rebels who at sunrise were to die.

He had listened to the story as the anxious women thronged
  And pressed him and beset him with their sad tears rolling down;
For they begged the lives of sweethearts and of husbands, foully wronged,
  Imprisoned by the Union troops in Murfreesboro town.

O'er the distant tents of Federals swept a Forrest's eagle eye,
  Where they lay like combing billows. To the women turned he then:
"Dry your tears, you wives and sweethearts, for your loved ones shall not die!
  We will send them back by sunset," said Forrest to his men.

And how he kept that promise let the page of history tell.
  For he battered in the burning jail and set the Southrons free;
How his Texans and his Georgians blent with one wild Rebel yell
  To blazon high the glory of his rugged Tennessee!

As the blue line gave before you like the falling, wind-swept grain,
  On you charged, you men of battle, through the dawning dim and

gray;
For he rested not victorious, with a victory yet to gain,
   And the ranting Rebel Forrest won a general's spurs that day.

Do you mind, you men who followed with the zeal of youthful fire,
   Who had tried him and had proved him when his sword and cloak were new?
Do you mind, you men who loved him, when the star of his desire
   Went down with sullen glory in the overwhelming blue?

Earth shall yield to men her heroes, while the cause of nations stands;
   The breath of God shall kindle that which Earth and Nature give;
And in that blessed Valhalla, where Fame greets the warrior bands
   High upon its gleaming casements, shall the name of Forrest live![213]
MRS. VIRGINIA FRAZER BOYLE

Mrs. Virginia Frazer Boyle.

GEN. N. B. FORREST

"Those hoof beats die not upon fame's crimson sod,
But will ring through her song and her story;
He fought like a Titan, he struck like a god.
And his dust is our ashes of glory."

Virginia Frazer Boyle

APPENDICES

*Interesting and Pertinent Material
Related to Nathan Bedford Forrest
& the Confederate States of America*

Why the South fought . . .

APPENDIX A

FORREST'S LETTER TO DR. JOHN W. MORTON SR., FATHER OF HIS CHIEF OF ARTILLARY

1865

Dear Sir: It affords me pleasure to report the following to you of the conduct of your son, John W. Morton, Jr. He was ordered to report to me for duty by Gen. Bragg to take charge of my horse artillery in November, 1862.

His appearance was so youthful and form so frail, and wishing stout, active men for my service, I at first hesitated to receive him, but coming so well recommended by Col. Hallonquist, Gen. Bragg's chief of artillery, Maj. Graves, Gen. Breckinridge's chief of artillery, and others, I concluded to try him, having learned that he was first lieutenant of Porter's famous Tennessee Battery, which surrendered at Fort Donelson February 16, 1862. He was highly complimented by Gen. Buckner in his official report, and received from Gen. Buckner the high appellation of "Gallant Lieut. Morton, the beardless boy."

I gave him command of a section of artillery, and moved with my first raid into West Tennessee in December, 1862, and soon captured other guns, and placed him in command of the battery, and during this expedition the gallant and efficient manner in which he handled his guns won my confidence and esteem. He has constantly been with me since in all my engagements, never absent from his post of duty, apparently happiest when in the thickest of the fight. He has held with great credit for twelve months past the position of chief of artillery of my corps. By his soldierly bearing, generous disposition, affable manners, strict attention to duty and the welfare of his men, uniform and true gallantry on so many fields, he has made many friends, and you may feel justly proud of such a son. He was with the troops of this department, and surrendered his old battery, one of the best-equipped and finest in the service.[214] — GEN. NATHAN BEDFORD FORREST

APPENDIX B

ANNOUNCEMENT OF THE DEATH OF GENERAL N. B. FORREST'S WIFE

1893

Death of Gen. Forrest's Wife.—The lovely wife of Gen. N. Bedford Forrest died January 22nd in Memphis, where she had resided many years. She was Miss Mary Ann Montgomery [born October 24, 1826], and was married September 25, 1855. After the General's death she devoted herself to the rearing of three grandchildren, Mary [Elvira Forrest], [Nathan] Bedford [Forrest II], and William [Montgomery Forrest II], children of her only son [C.S. Captain William Montgomery "Willie" Forrest], whose mother [Jane Taylor Cook] died when they were quite small. Mrs. Forrest was a cultured Christian lady, and was devoted to the cause in which her husband was not only a hero, but a wonderful man. He was as a whirlwind in combatting the foe.[215] — SUMNER ARCHIBALD CUNNINGHAM

APPENDIX C

CHATTANOOGA NEGROES COMPLIMENT THE CONFEDERATE COMMANDER OF THE U.C.V. N. B. FORREST CAMP, CHATTANOOGA, TENN.

1895

W. P. McClatchy, Commander N. B. Forrest Camp, Chattanooga, Tenn., has been honored by the negro men of that city. They presented him with a gold-headed cane. Addresses were made by J. W. White and J. G. Burge, negro lawyers there. Comrade McClatchy held the office of City Recorder (Judge of the City Court) last year, and at the expiration of his term he was greatly surprised when these men presented it as a token of their friendship and esteem, and for the just and impartial manner in which he had dealt with their race. He asked them why they had "U.C.V., 1861-65," engraved on it, and they replied that they wished to emphasize that while he was a Southern man, and a Confederate soldier, he had administered the law justly and impartially. The N. B. Forrest Camp hearing of this compliment to its commander, by a rising vote thanked the donors for their expression of confidence in and esteem for a Confederate soldier, and a Southern Democrat [then a Conservative] who had "administered the law, in wisdom, justice and moderation."

The inscription reads: "U.C.V., 1861-1865, J. W. and J. G. to W. P. McClatchy, 1895." Which stands for United Confederate Veteran 1861 to 1865, J. B. White and J. G. Burge to W. P. McClatchy, 1895.

In a note the comrade says: "I never had a present in my life that I appreciated any more than this. *Every true Southerner understands and appreciates a good negro, while the negro understands that the Southern man is the best friend he has. But for the meddling of people [Liberals] who really care nothing for the negro, but who are prejudiced against the South, there would be no friction between the races.*"[216] — SUMNER ARCHIBALD CUNNINGHAM

APPENDIX D

U.S. PRESIDENT THEODORE ROOSEVELT EULOGIZES THE SOUTH

1910

Theodore Roosevelt was invited to address the Southern Commercial Congress which meets in Atlanta in the spring of 1911. In his reply he says that his proposed trip to California in March will, he thinks, carry him through the South, and he hopes to accept the invitation. He gives unstinted praise to the fine work being done by the Congress, and says he is in cordial sympathy with their efforts at development, and adds that what the South needs is people, but people of "the best quality." He believes that in the future the South will share growth with the West, and that on the completion of the Panama Canal she will stand at the distributing point of the oceans of the world.

Southern city street scene.

Colonel Roosevelt says he believes that more and more the "misunderstanding" between the North and South is disappearing, and that such bodies as this Commercial Congress will materially aid in its complete disappearance; that in working for a stronger South the movement must, to be effective, mean a stronger national cohesion, as the prosperity of a part must of necessity add to the prosperity of the whole.

Colonel Roosevelt says: "I earnestly hope that the young men of the South will never forget the past glories of the South, and that the young men all over America to-day will keep ever in mind those glorious memories of every section of our common country, and that the men of the North and of the West will remember the South's past with the same pride the South itself does, for the undying glory, won by the men who so valiantly and with such sincerity fought for their convictions, whether they wore the blue or the gray, is now a common heritage of all of us, wherever we dwell.

Southern farming life.

"... The statue of General Lee in Confederate uniform stands in the halls of Congress to-day,[217] and his memory is honored no more by the South than it is by the North; and in the North as in the South I think we are now learning to apply absolutely in good faith the great words of Grant: 'Let us have peace.'

"The part played by the South in the constructive statesmanship of our nation during all our earlier years was of incalculable weight and value. I firmly believe that the time has now come when the South's influence again will be felt not only in constructive statesmanship, but in the enormous field of constructive business endeavor. No part of our country has seen such progress as the South has made in the last twenty years along material lines, and I believe the next twenty years will see a greater progress."[218] — SUMNER ARCHIBALD CUNNINGHAM

President Theodore Roosevelt.

APPENDIX E

SECRETARY OF WAR DICKINSON & PRESIDENT GRANT'S SON AT A NEGRO FAIR IN NASHVILLE

1909

The occasion was but three months ago [around December 1909]. Gen. Fred [Frederick Dent] Grant [son of U.S. General and President Ulysses S. Grant], a major general of the United States army, and eminently sustaining the honors won by his father, was in Nashville and visited the Hermitage [Andrew Jackson's home]. Don't let it get out that he actually visited the Confederate Soldiers' Home of Tennessee and talked to the old men after shaking hands with them and saying kind words in a brief speech.

On the way back to Nashville he met the Secretary of War, J. [Jacob] M. [McGavock] Dickinson, at a negro fair. The two distinguished men were shown the exhibits and were invited to the auditorium, where they addressed the negroes. Judge Dickinson spoke to them as a Southerner and a Confederate, giving them practical advice, telling them that if they wanted to succeed in life they must be industrious and diligently  economical in saving their earnings. He referred to their freedom and how it came about, declaring that the war was not waged for their freedom, but that it was simply an incident of the war. He told them that the one time General Lee left the army during the war was to go to his home and formally give freedom to his slaves.

General [Fred] Grant in his address spoke kindly to them and of his pleasure in seeing their prosperity. He had known their race all of his life. His family owned slaves until they were freed by Lincoln's proclamation [actually, the Thirteenth Amendment ended slavery, not Lincoln],[219] and he said that after the war their old servants maintained an interest in the family, and in all the intervening years they had not failed to make known their needs, which had been heeded.

It was a remarkable record that in the latter years of the war Lee fought on with no interest in slavery, while Grant held his until freed by the "exigencies of war."[220] — SUMNER ARCHIBALD CUNNINGHAM

APPENDIX F
GENERAL FORREST'S GRANDSON, NATHAN BEDFORD FORREST II
1910

Nathan Bedford Forrest [II], Adjutant General and Chief of Staff of the Sons of Confederate Veterans, served on the staff of Gen. John B. Gordon from 1892 to 1897 and as aid-de-camp. He is a charter member of N. B. Forrest Camp, No. 215, U.S.C.V., Memphis, Tenn., organized in 1900; also served as Adjutant and as First Lieutenant Commander of that Camp, as Commander of the Army of Tennessee Department, and has served as Adjutant General and Chief of Staff since 1907.

Nathan B. Forrest [II] was born at Oxford, Miss., in 1872, and is a son of Capt. William Forrest [born 1846], the only son of Gen. Nathan Bedford Forrest [born 1821]. After finishing school he was connected with his father in the railroad and levee contracting business for a number of years. In the spring of 1897 he went to the Klondyke, where he remained, mining and prospecting, until December, 1900. He returned to

Nathan Bedford Forrest II.

Memphis and was in the life insurance business there until 1910. Since then he has been devoting his entire time to the work of the Sons of Confederate Veterans, and he is now at Jacksonville, Fla., in the interest of the organization in that State. [Married to Mattie Patton, with whom he had several children, he passed away in White Springs, Fla., March 13, 1931.][221] — UNKNOWN

NOTES

1. Seabrook, ARB, p. 313.
2. Woods, p. 47.
3. On Lincoln's socialistic, Marxist, and communist thoughts, ideas, and tendencies, see my books: *Lincoln's War: The Real Cause, The Real Winner, the Real Loser*; *Abraham Lincoln Was a Liberal, Jefferson Davis Was a Conservative: The Missing Key to Understanding the American Civil War*; *Abraham Lincoln: The Southern View*. Also see McCarty, passim; Browder, passim; Benson and Kennedy, passim.
4. See J. W. Jones, TDMV, pp. 144, 200-201, 273.
5. See Seabrook, TAHSR, passim. See also, Pollard, LC, p. 178; J. H. Franklin, pp. 101, 111, 130, 149; Nicolay and Hay, ALCW, Vol. 1, p. 627.
6. BISG (the "Book Industry Study Group"), for example—a Left-wing organization which describes itself as "the leading book trade association for standardized best practices, research and information, and events"—gives its BISAC ("Book Industry Standards and Communications") listing for works on the War for Southern Independence under the heading "Civil War Period, 1850-1877." Nearly all books published in the U.S.A. today are under the categorizational control of this progressive group located in New York City.
7. See e.g., Seabrook, TQJD, pp. 30, 38, 76.
8. See e.g., J. Davis, RFCG, Vol. 1, pp. 55, 422; Vol. 2, pp. 4, 161, 454, 610. Besides using the term "Civil War" himself, President Davis cites numerous other individuals who use it as well.
9. See e.g., *Confederate Veteran*, March 1912, Vol. 20, No. 3, p. 122.
10. Minutes of the Eighth Annual Meeting, July 1898, p. 87.
11. For more on the nihilistic, atheistic, anti-life, anti-tradition, anti-American, anti-Constitution, anti-capitalism, anti-South agenda of the Victorian Republican Party (then the Liberal Party) and the modern Democrat Party (now the Liberal Party), otherwise known as "The Communist/Socialist Rules for Revolution," see Hasselberg, pp. 2350-2351; Lenin, passim; Marx and Engels, passim.
12. *Confederate Veteran*, July 1901, Vol. 9, No. 7, p. 318.
13. *Confederate Veteran*, June 1896, Vol. 4, No. 6, p. 191.
14. Forrest was not nicknamed the "old Tycoon" for nothing.
15. For more on this topic, see my book: *Confederacy 101*.
16. *Vide infra*, p. 251.
17. For more on this topic, see my book: *Nathan Bedford Forrest and the Ku Klux Klan: Yankee Myth, Confederate Fact*.
18. *Confederate Veteran*, January 1898, Vol. 6, No. 1, p. 29.
19. *Vide infra*, p. 314.
20. For a detailed and historically accurate biography of Forrest, see my award-winning book: *A Rebel Born: A Defense of Nathan Bedford Forrest*.
21. *Confederate Veteran*, April 1894, Vol. 2, No. 4, p. 111.
22. *Confederate Veteran*, February 1894, Vol. 2, No. 2, p. 57.
23. *Confederate Veteran*, February 1896, Vol. 4, No. 2, p. 41.
24. *Confederate Veteran*, January 1893, Vol. 1, No. 1, p. 204. This statement is excerpted from an address Col. Lee gave at the dedication of the Confederate monument at Old Chapel, Clarke County, Virginia, probably in or around 1892.
25. *Confederate Veteran*, January 1893, Vol. 1, No. 1, p. 267. Note: I added the words "under Forrest" to the original title.
26. Blind Tom was a popular black entertainer at the time.
27. See Appendix B.
28. *Confederate Veteran*, January 1894, Vol. 2, No. 1, cover page. Note: The title of this sketch is my own.
29. *Confederate Veteran*, February 1894, Vol. 2, No. 2, p. 40. Note: The title of this entry is my own.
30. In some sources his surname is spelled Wolford.
31. *Confederate Veteran*, April 1894, Vol. 2, No. 4, p. 117.
32. *Confederate Veteran*, October 1894, Vol. 2, No. 10, p. 308.
33. This quote is attributed to Stonewall Jackson as he lay on his deathbed.
34. *Confederate Veteran*, February 1895, Vol. 3, No. 2, pp. 41-42; *Confederate Veteran*, March 1895, Vol. 3, No. 3, pp. 77-78.

35. *Confederate Veteran*, April 1895, Vol. 3, No. 4, pp. 106-107.
36. *Confederate Veteran*, May 1895, Vol. 3, No. 5, p. 133.
37. *Confederate Veteran*, July 1895, Vol. 3, No. 7, p. 212.
38. For a complete discussion on the true cause of the conflict, see my book *Lincoln's War*.
39. *Confederate Veteran*, August 1895, Vol. 3, No. 8, p. 226. Note: Wyeth never served directly under Gen. Forrest. However, he was a private in a regiment of Alabama cavalry which had once served under his son William Forrest.
40. *Confederate Veteran*, August 1895, Vol. 3, No. 8, pp. 251-252.
41. *Confederate Veteran*, September 1895, Vol. 3, No. 9, p. 279.
42. *Confederate Veteran*, October 1895, Vol. 3, No. 10, pp. 293-294.
43. *Confederate Veteran*, November 1895, Vol. 3, No. 11, pp. 322-326. For a detailed discussion of this topic, see my book: *Nathan Bedford Forrest and the Battle of Fort Pillow: Yankee Myth, Confederate Fact*.
44. *Confederate Veteran*, January 1896, Vol. 4, No. 1, p. 14.
45. *Confederate Veteran*, February 1896, Vol. 4, No. 2, pp. 41-43.
46. *Confederate Veteran*, April 1896, Vol. 4, No. 4, p. 106.
47. *Confederate Veteran*, May 1896, Vol. 4, No. 5, pp. 146-147.
48. *Confederate Veteran*, May 1896, Vol. 4, No. 5, pp. 151-152. Note: The title of this entry is my own. For a detailed discussion of this topic, see my book: *Nathan Bedford Forrest and the Battle of Fort Pillow: Yankee Myth, Confederate Fact*.
49. *Confederate Veteran*, September 1896, Vol. 4, No. 9, p. 286.
50. *Confederate Veteran*, September 1896, Vol. 4, No. 9, p. 288.
51. *Confederate Veteran*, October 1896, Vol. 4, No. 10, pp. 358-359. Note: The title of this entry is my own.
52. *Confederate Veteran*, November 1896, Vol. 4, No. 11, p. 362. Note: The title of this entry is my own.
53. *Confederate Veteran*, November 1896, Vol. 4, No. 11, p. 387.
54. *Confederate Veteran*, February 1897, Vol. 5, No. 2, p. 83.
55. *Confederate Veteran*, May 1897, Vol. 5, No. 5, pp. 212-213.
56. *Confederate Veteran*, May 1897, Vol. 5, No. 5, pp. 216-217. Note: The title of this entry is my own.
57. *Confederate Veteran*, June 1897, Vol. 5, No. 6, p. 262. Note: The title of this entry is my own.
58. *Confederate Veteran*, June 1897, Vol. 5, No. 6, pp. 265-266. Note: The title of this entry is my own.
59. *Confederate Veteran*, June 1897, Vol. 5, No. 6, pp. 277-281.
60. *Confederate Veteran*, July 1897, Vol. 5, No. 7, p. 341.
61. *Confederate Veteran*, September 1897, Vol. 5, No. 9, pp. 478-480.
62. *Confederate Veteran*, November 1897, Vol. 5, No. 11, pp. 574-575.
63. *Confederate Veteran*, December 1897, Vol. 5, No. 12, p. 623. Note: The title of this entry is my own.
64. *Confederate Veteran*, January 1898, Vol. 6, No. 1, pp. 24-25. Note: The title of this entry is my own.
65. *Confederate Veteran*, January 1898, Vol. 6, No. 1, p. 33.
66. *Confederate Veteran*, January 1898, Vol. 6, No. 1, p. 37. Note: The title of this entry is my own.
67. *Confederate Veteran*, April 1898, Vol. 6, No. 4, p. 157.
68. *Confederate Veteran*, June 1898, Vol. 6, No. 6, p. 275. Note: The title of this entry is my own.
69. *Confederate Veteran*, October 1898, Vol. 6, No. 10, p. 459. Note: The title of this entry is my own.
70. *Confederate Veteran*, October 1898, Vol. 6, No. 10, p. 487.
71. *Confederate Veteran*, October 1898, Vol. 6, No. 10, pp. 487-488. Note: The title of this entry is my own.
72. *Confederate Veteran*, January 1899, Vol. 7, No. 1, p. 30. Note: The title of this entry is my own.
73. *Confederate Veteran*, February 1899, Vol. 7, No. 2, p. 70.
74. *Confederate Veteran*, April 1899, Vol. 7, No. 4, pp. 164-165. Note: The title of this entry is my own.
75. *Confederate Veteran*, April 1899, Vol. 7, No. 4, p. 165.
76. *Confederate Veteran*, August 1899, Vol. 7, No. 8, p. 358. Note: The title of this entry is my own.
77. *Confederate Veteran*, September 1899, Vol. 7, No. 9, p. 387.
78. *Confederate Veteran*, October 1899, Vol. 7, No. 10, p. 437. Note: The title of this entry is my own.
79. *Confederate Veteran*, October 1899, Vol. 7, No. 10, p. 441. Note: The title of this entry is my own.
80. *Confederate Veteran*, October 1899, Vol. 7, No. 10, p. 446.
81. *Confederate Veteran*, November 1899, Vol. 7, No. 11, p. 499. Note: The title of this entry is my own.
82. For more on this remarkable episode, see Seabrook, ARB, pp. 307-308.
83. *Confederate Veteran*, January 1900, Vol. 8, No. 1, pp. 14-15.
84. *Confederate Veteran*, January 1900, Vol. 8, No. 1, p. 48. Note: The title of this entry is my own.

85. *Confederate Veteran*, March 1900, Vol. 8, No. 3, p. 116.
86. *Confederate Veteran*, April 1900, Vol. 8, No. 4, p. 149. Note: The title of this entry is my own.
87. *Confederate Veteran*, April 1900, Vol. 8, No. 4, p. 171.
88. *Confederate Veteran*, April 1900, Vol. 8, No. 4, p. 173.
89. *Confederate Veteran*, May 1900, Vol. 8, No. 5, p. 238.
90. *Confederate Veteran*, June 1900, Vol. 8, No. 6, pp. 262-263. Note: The title of this entry is my own.
91. *Confederate Veteran*, July 1900, Vol. 8, No. 7, pp. 301-302.
92. *Confederate Veteran*, July 1900, Vol. 8, No. 7, p. 302.
93. *Confederate Veteran*, September 1900, Vol. 8, No. 9, p. 391.
94. For more on the topic of Fort Pillow, see Seabrook, NBFATBOFP, passim.
95. Seabrook, RUACTB, pp. 524-531.
96. *Confederate Veteran*, February 1901, Vol. 9, No. 2, p. 53.
97. *Confederate Veteran*, March 1901, Vol. 9, No. 3, p. 100.
98. For a detailed discussion of this topic, see my book: *Nathan Bedford Forrest and the Battle of Fort Pillow: Yankee Myth, Confederate Fact*.
99. Some of this specific genealogical data may be inaccurate. For more on General Forrest's family history, see my book: *A Rebel Born: A Defense of Nathan Bedford Forrest*.
100. Forrest actually had two children: William, and also a daughter, Frances Ann (born 1848), the latter who died young.
101. *Confederate Veteran*, March 1901, Vol. 9, No. 3, pp. 107-110. Note: The title of this entry is my own.
102. *Confederate Veteran*, May 1901, Vol. 9, No. 5, pp. 195-196. Note: The title of this entry is my own.
103. *Confederate Veteran*, May 1901, Vol. 9, No. 5, p. 207. Note: The title of this entry is my own.
104. *Confederate Veteran*, May 1901, Vol. 9, No. 5, pp. 218-219. Note: The title of this entry is my own.
105. *Confederate Veteran*, July 1901, Vol. 9, No. 7, pp. 316-318. Note: The title of this entry is my own.
106. *Confederate Veteran*, November 1901, Vol. 9, No. 11, p. 514.
107. *Confederate Veteran*, June 1903, Vol. 11, No. 6, p. 251. Note: The title of is entry is my own.
108. *Confederate Veteran*, September 1903, Vol. 11, No. 9, pp. 398-399.
109. *Confederate Veteran*, September 1903, Vol. 11, No. 9, p. 402. Note: The title of this entry is my own.
110. For a factual and in-depth discussion on Forrest and his relationship to blacks, see my book: *Nathan Bedford Forrest and African-Americans: Yankee Myth, Confederate Fact*.
111. *Confederate Veteran*, June 1903, Vol. 11, No. 6, p. 251.
112. *Confederate Veteran*, November 1903, Vol. 11, No. 11, pp. 503-504.
113. *Confederate Veteran*, November 1903, Vol. 11, No. 11, p. 513.
114. *Confederate Veteran*, January 1904, Vol. 12, No. 1, pp. 6-7.
115. *Confederate Veteran*, March 1904, Vol. 12, No. 3, p. 121. Note: The title of this entry is my own.
116. *Confederate Veteran*, September 1904, Vol. 12, No. 9, p. 426.
117. *Confederate Veteran*, September 1904, Vol. 12, No. 9, p. 455. Note: The title of this entry is my own.
118. *Confederate Veteran*, September 1904, Vol. 12, No. 9, p. 472.
119. *Confederate Veteran*, November 1904, Vol. 12, No. 11, p. 519.
120. *Confederate Veteran*, November 1904, Vol. 12, No. 11, pp. 529-530.
121. *Confederate Veteran*, January 1905, Vol. 13, No. 1, pp. 17-18.
122. *Confederate Veteran*, February 1905, Vol. 13, No. 2, p. 72. Note: The title of this entry is my own.
123. *Confederate Veteran*, March 1905, Vol. 13, No. 3, p. 126. Note: The title of this entry is my own.
124. *Confederate Veteran*, April 1905, Vol. 13, No. 4, p. 206. Note: The title of this entry is my own.
125. *Confederate Veteran*, August 1905, Vol. 13, No. 8, p. 356.
126. In vengeance a number of black Yankee soldiers had sworn to kill Forrest and his men in cold blood for the "Fort Pillow massacre," which necessitated keeping an eye on their whereabouts from battle to battle. The so-called "massacre," however, never occurred. It was nothing more than a fabrication whipped up by South-haters, Liberals, and scallywags to divide the races, foment trouble, slander the Confederate soldier, shame Dixie, and weaken the fortitude of the Southern people. This exact ploy continues to be used by these same types of unscrupulous and intolerant bigots today. For more on this topic, see my book: *Nathan Bedford Forrest and the Battle of Fort Pillow: Yankee Myth, Confederate Fact*.
127. *Confederate Veteran*, August 1905, Vol. 13, No. 8, pp. 361, 363.
128. *Confederate Veteran*, September 1905, Vol. 13, No. 9, pp. 389-391.
129. *Confederate Veteran*, October 1905, Vol. 13, No. 10, p. 441.
130. *Confederate Veteran*, October 1905, Vol. 13, No. 10, pp. 463-465.

131. *Confederate Veteran*, December 1905, Vol. 13, No. 12, p. 566. Note: The title of this entry is my own.
132. *Confederate Veteran*, June 1906, Vol. 14, No. 6, p. 252. Note: The title of this entry is my own.
133. *Confederate Veteran*, August 1906, Vol. 14, No. 8, p. 360.
134. *Confederate Veteran*, October 1906, Vol. 14, No. 10, p. 441. Note: The title of this entry is my own.
135. *Confederate Veteran*, November 1906, Vol. 14, No. 11, p. 501. Note: The title of this entry is my own.
136. *Confederate Veteran*, January 1907, Vol.15, No. 1, pp. 54-55.
137. *Confederate Veteran*, March 1907, Vol.15, No. 3, p. 139.
138. *Confederate Veteran*, September 1907, Vol.15, No. 9, pp. 405-407. Note: The title of this entry is my own.
139. *Confederate Veteran*, October 1907, Vol.15, No. 10, p. 454. Note: The title of this entry is my own.
140. *Confederate Veteran*, November 1907, Vol.15, No. 12, p. 501. Note: The title of this entry is my own.
141. *Confederate Veteran*, March 1908, Vol. 16, No. 3, pp. 108-109.
142. *Confederate Veteran*, April 1908, Vol. 16, No. 4, pp. xxvi-xxvii.
143. *Confederate Veteran*, April 1908, Vol. 16, No. 4, p. xxvi.
144. *Confederate Veteran*, July 1908, Vol. 16, No. 7, p. 353. Note: The title of this entry is my own.
145. *Confederate Veteran*, February 1909, Vol. 17, No. 2, pp. 83-84.
146. *Confederate Veteran*, April 1909, Vol. 17, No. 4, p. 168.
147. *Confederate Veteran*, August 1909, Vol. 17, No. 8, pp. 393-394. Note: The title of this entry is my own.
148. *Confederate Veteran*, August 1909, Vol. 17, No. 8, p. 401.
149. Morton, pp. 11-17.
150. *Confederate Veteran*, August 1910, Vol. 18, No. 8, p. 374.
151. *Confederate Veteran*, February 1911, Vol. 19, No. 2, p. 67.
152. *Confederate Veteran*, May 1911, Vol. 19, No. 5, p. 223.
153. *Confederate Veteran*, September 1911, Vol. 19, No. 9, p. 435. Note: The title of this entry is my own.
154. *Confederate Veteran*, October 1911, Vol. 19, No. 10, p. 500. Note: The title of this entry is my own.
155. *Confederate Veteran*, December 1911, Vol. 19, No. 12, pp. 584-585.
156. *Confederate Veteran*, May 1912, Vol. 20, No. 5, p. 210.
157. *Confederate Veteran*, August 1912, Vol. 20, No. 8, pp. 380-381.
158. *Confederate Veteran*, September 1912, Vol. 20, No. 9, p. 410.
159. *Confederate Veteran*, October 1912, Vol. 20, No. 10, pp. 475, 476-477. Note: The title of this entry is my own.
160. *Confederate Veteran*, November 1912, Vol. 20, No. 11, p. 515. Note: The title of this entry is my own.
161. *Confederate Veteran*, January 1913, Vol. 21, No. 1, p. 40. Note: The title of this entry is my own.
162. *Confederate Veteran*, January 1913, Vol. 21, No. 1, p. 57. Note: The title of this entry is my own.
163. *Confederate Veteran*, June 1913, Vol. 21, No. 6, p. 314.
164. *Confederate Veteran*, September 1913, Vol. 21, No. 9, p. 483. Note: The title of this entry is my own.
165. *Confederate Veteran*, September 1913, Vol. 21, No. 9, p. 537. Note: The title of this entry is my own.
166. *Confederate Veteran*, February 1914, Vol. 22, No. 2, p. 60.
167. *Confederate Veteran*, February 1914, Vol. 22, No. 2, p. 69. A correction was later made to this entry by Judge W. M. Ives: "The 6th Florida was nowhere near Murfreesboro, Tenn., at the time of the battle. The 1st, 3rd, and 4th Florida were in Preston's Brigade, Breckinridge's Division, and fought gallantly December 31, 1862, and January 2, 1863. Wheeler's Cavalry acted as eyes and ears for us, and his battle at La Vergne proved it. Forrest was not there." *Confederate Veteran*, March 1914, Vol. 22, No. 3, p. 131.
168. *Confederate Veteran*, March 1914, Vol. 22, No. 3, pp. 130-131.
169. *Confederate Veteran*, April 1914, Vol. 22, No. 4, pp. 174-175.
170. *Confederate Veteran*, April 1915, Vol. 23, No. 4, p. 176.
171. *Confederate Veteran*, July 1915, Vol. 23, No. 7, pp. 317-318. Note: The title of this entry is my own.
172. *Confederate Veteran*, July 1915, Vol. 23, No. 7, p. 347. Note: The title of this entry is my own.
173. *Confederate Veteran*, October 1915, Vol. 23, No. 10, pp. 451-452.
174. *Confederate Veteran*, November 1915, Vol. 23, No. 11, p. 572.
175. *Confederate Veteran*, July 1915, Vol. 23, No. 7, pp. 307-308.
176. *Confederate Veteran*, January 1917, Vol. 25, No. 1, pp. 5-6. Note: The title of this entry is my own.
177. *Confederate Veteran*, April 1917, Vol. 25, No. 4, p. 163. Note: The title of this entry is my own.
178. *Confederate Veteran*, August 1917, Vol. 25, No. 8, pp. 357-362.

179. *Confederate Veteran*, October 1917, Vol. 25, No. 10, pp. 462-463; *Confederate Veteran*, November 1919, Vol. 27, No. 11, p. 415. Notes: I have made a few minor edits to this entry for the sake of clarity. The title is my own.
180. *Confederate Veteran*, November 1917, Vol. 25, No. 11, pp. 491-492, 526. Note: Browne has his dates off. The Battle of Selma was fought on April 2, 1865. Lee surrendered on April 9, 1865.
181. *Confederate Veteran*, September 1918, Vol. 26, No. 9, p. 403.
182. *Confederate Veteran*, December 1919, Vol. 27, No. 12, p. 452. Notes: This incident occurred at Rocky Hill, Alabama, in 1863. The title of this entry is my own.
183. *Confederate Veteran*, January 1920, Vol. 28, No. 1, p. 11. Note: From Rocky Hill, Alabama, 1863. The title of this entry is my own.
184. *Confederate Veteran*, March 1920, Vol. 28, No. 3, p. 99. Note: The title of this entry is my own.
185. *Confederate Veteran*, July 1920, Vol. 28, No. 7, p. 265. Note: The title of this entry is my own.
186. *Confederate Veteran*, July 1920, Vol. 28, No. 7, p. 278. Note: The title of this entry is my own.
187. *Confederate Veteran*, October 1920, Vol. 28, No. 10, p. 372. Note: The title of this entry is my own.
188. The modern *permanent* KKK of the 21st Century—founded in 1915—has no connection to the original post-Civil War group, which I call the Reconstruction KKK, and which, purposefully founded as a *temporary* organization, lasted only three years (late 1865 to early 1869).
189. For a detailed discussion of Forrest and the KKK, see my book: *Nathan Bedford Forrest and the Ku Klux Klan: Yankee Myth, Confederate Fact*.
190. *Confederate Veteran*, October 1920, Vol. 28, No. 10, pp. 378-379. Note: The title of this entry is my own.
191. *Confederate Veteran*, May 1921, Vol. 29, No. 5, p. 193. Note: The title of this entry is my own.
192. *Confederate Veteran*, October 1922, Vol. 30, No. 10, p. 398.
193. *Confederate Veteran*, August 1923, Vol. 31, No. 8, p. 309.
194. *Confederate Veteran*, September 1924, Vol. 32, No. 9, p. 342.
195. *Confederate Veteran*, October 1925, Vol. 33, No. 10, pp. 369-370.
196. *Confederate Veteran*, October 1925, Vol. 33, No. 10, pp. 381-382.
197. *Confederate Veteran*, December 1925, Vol. 33, No. 12, pp. 459, 478. For a detailed discussion of this topic, see my book: *Nathan Bedford Forrest and the Battle of Fort Pillow: Yankee Myth, Confederate Fact*.
198. *Confederate Veteran*, April 1926, Vol. 34, No. 4, p. 138. Note: The title of this entry is my own.
199. *Confederate Veteran*, February 1927, Vol. 35, No. 2, p. 76.
200. *Confederate Veteran*, August 1928, Vol. 36, No. 8, p. 284.
201. *Confederate Veteran*, June 1930, Vol. 38, No. 6, p. 221. Note: The title of this entry is my own.
202. *Confederate Veteran*, September 1930, Vol. 38, No. 9, p. 344. Note: The title of this entry is my own.
203. *Confederate Veteran*, December 1932, Vol. 40, No. 12, p. 425. Note: The title of this entry is my own.
204. *Confederate Veteran*, July 1906, Vol. 14, No. 7, p. 299.
205. *Confederate Veteran*, June 1905, Vol. 13, No. 6, p. 285.
206. *Confederate Veteran*, June 1901, Vol. 9, No. 6, p. 251.
207. *Confederate Veteran*, February 1907, Vol. 15, No. 2, p. 63.
208. *Confederate Veteran*, June 1911, Vol. 19, No. 6, p. 311.
209. *Confederate Veteran*, January 1908, Vol. 16, No. 1, p. 73.
210. *Confederate Veteran*, May 1908, Vol. 16, No. 5, p. 232.
211. *Confederate Veteran*, January 1917, Vol. 25, No. 1, p. 47.
212. *Confederate Veteran*, July 1925, Vol. 33, No. 7, p. 264.
213. *Confederate Veteran*, December 1906, Vol. 14, No. 12, pp. 549-550.
214. Morton, pp. 322-323. Note: The title of this letter is my own.
215. *Confederate Veteran*, January 1893, Vol. 1, No. 1, p. 63.
216. *Confederate Veteran*, June 1896, Vol. 4, No. 6, p. 178. My emphasis.
217. Cunningham is referring to National Statuary Hall, located in the U.S. Capitol Building at Washington, D.C.
218. *Confederate Veteran*, September 1910, Vol. 18, No. 9, p. 405.
219. For more on this topic, see my book: *Everything You Were Taught About American Slavery Is Wrong, Ask a Southerner!*
220. *Confederate Veteran*, February 1910, Vol. 18, No. 2, p. 56. Note: The title of this entry is my own.
221. *Confederate Veteran*, March 1914, Vol. 22, No. 3, p. 139. Note: The title of this entry is my own.

BIBLIOGRAPHY

Note: My pro-South readers are to be advised that the majority of the books listed here are anti-South in nature (some extremely so), and were written primarily by Liberal elitist, socialist, communist, and Marxist authors who loathe the South, and typically the United States and the U.S. Constitution as well. Despite this, as a scholar I find these titles indispensable, for *an honest evaluation of Lincoln's War is not possible without studying both the Southern and the Northern versions*—an attitude, unfortunately, completely lacking among pro-North historians (who read and study only their own ahistorical version). Still, it must be said that the material contained in these often mean-spirited works is largely the result of a century and a half of Yankee myth, falsehoods, cherry-picking, slander, redaction, sophistry, editorializing, anti-South propaganda, outright lies, and junk research, as modern pro-North writers merely copy one another's errors without ever looking at the original 19th-Century sources. This type of literature, filled as it is with both misinformation and disinformation, is called "scholarly" and "objective" by pro-North advocates. In the process, the mistakes and lies in these fact-free, fault-ridden, South-shaming, historically inaccurate works have been magnified over the years, and the North's version of the "Civil War" has come to be accepted as the only legitimate one. Indeed, it is now the only one known by most people. That over 95 percent of the titles in most of my bibliographies fall into the anti-South category is simply a reflection of the enormous power and influence that the pro-North movement—our nation's cultural ruling class—has long held over America's education system, libraries, publishing houses, and media (paper and electronic). My books serve as a small rampart against the overwhelming tide of anti-South Fascists, Liberals, cultural Marxists, and political elites, all who are working hard to obliterate Southern culture and guarantee that you will never learn the Truth about Lincoln and his War on the Constitution and the American people.

Ashe, Captain Samuel A'Court. *A Southern View of the Invasion of the Southern States and War of 1861-1865*. 1935. Crawfordville, GA: Ruffin Flag Company, 1938 ed.

Benson, Al, Jr., and Walter Donald Kennedy. *Lincoln's Marxists*. Gretna, LA: Pelican, 2011.

Boyd, James P. *Parties, Problems, and Leaders of 1896: An Impartial Presentation of Living National Questions*. Chicago, IL: Publishers' Union, 1896.

Brock, Robert Alonzo (ed.). *Southern Historical Society Papers*. 52 vols. Richmond, VA: Southern Historical Society, 1876-1943.

Browder, Earl. *Lincoln and the Communists*. New York, NY: Workers Library Publishers, Inc., 1936.

Bryan, William Jennings. *The First Battle: A Story of the Campaign of 1896*. Chicago, IL: W. B. Conkey Co., 1896.

Burns, James MacGregor. *The Vineyard of Liberty*. New York, NY: Alfred A. Knopf, 1982.

Christian, George Llewellyn. *Abraham Lincoln: An Address Delivered Before R. E. Lee Camp, No. 1 Confederate Veterans at Richmond, VA, October 29, 1909*. Richmond, VA: L. H. Jenkins, 1909.

———. *A Capitol Disaster: A Chapter of Reconstruction in Virginia*. Richmond, VA: self-published, 1915.

———. *Confederate Memories and Experiences*. Richmond, VA: self-published, 1915.

Confederate Veteran (Sumner A. Cunningham, ed.). 40 vols. Nashville, TN: Confederate Veteran, 1893-1932.

Davis, Jefferson. *The Rise and Fall of the Confederate Government*. 2 vols. New York, NY: D. Appleton and Co., 1881.

Evans, Clement Anselm (ed.). *Confederate Military History*. 12 vols. Atlanta, GA: Confederate Publishing Co., 1899.

Franklin, John Hope. *Reconstruction After the Civil War*. Chicago, IL: University of Chicago Press, 1961.

Hale, Will Thomas, and Dixon Lanier Merritt. *A History of Tennessee and Tennesseans: The Leaders and Representative Men in Commerce, Industry and Modern Activities*. 8 vols. Chicago, IL: The Lewis Publishing Co., 1913.

Hancock, Richard R. *Hancock's Diary: Or, A History of the Second Tennessee Cavalry, With Sketches of First and Seventh Battalions*. 2 vols. in one. Nashville, TN: self-published, 1887.

Hasselberg, P. D. (ed.). *Parliamentary Debates: First Session, Fortieth Parliament, 1982, House of Representatives* (Vol. 445). Wellington, New Zealand: Government Printer, 1982.

Johnson, Robert Underwood, and Clarence Clough Buel (eds.). *Battles and Leaders of the Civil War*. 4 vols. New York, NY: The Century Co., 1884-1888.

Johnstone, Huger William. *Truth of War Conspiracy, 1861*. Idylwild, GA: H. W. Johnstone, 1921.

Jones, John William. *The Davis Memorial Volume; Or Our Dead President, Jefferson Davis and the World's Tribute to His Memory*. Richmond, VA: B. F. Johnson, 1889.

Jordan, Thomas, and John P. Pryor. *The Campaigns of General Nathan Bedford Forrest and of Forrest's Cavalry*. New Orleans, LA: Blelock and Co., 1868.

La Bree, Benjamin. *The Confederate Soldier in the Civil War, 1861-1865*. Louisville, KY: The Prentice Press, 1897.

Lenin, Vladimir. *"Left Wing" Communism: An Infantile Disorder*. Detroit, MI: The Marxian Educational Society, 1921.

Livermore, Thomas L. *Numbers and Losses in the Civil War in America, 1861-65*. 1900. Carlisle, PA: John Kallmann, 1996 ed.

Lytle, Andrew Nelson. *Bedford Forrest and His Critter Company*. New York, NY: G. P. Putnam's Sons, 1931.

Magliocca, Gerard N. *The Tragedy of William Jennings Bryan: Constitutional Law and the Politics of Backlash*. New Haven, CT: Yale University Press, 2011.

Marx, Karl, and Frederick Engels. *Manifesto of the Communist Party*. Chicago, IL: Charles H. Kerr and Co., 1906.

Mathes, Capt. J. Harvey. *General Forrest*. New York, NY: D. Appleton and Co., 1902.

McCarty, Burke (ed.). *Little Sermons in Socialism by Abraham Lincoln*. Chicago, IL: The Chicago Daily Socialist, 1910.

McMurray, William Josiah. *History of the Twentieth Tennessee Regiment Volunteer Infantry, C.S.A*. Nashville, TN: The Publication Committee, 1904.

McPherson, James M. *Abraham Lincoln and the Second American Revolution*. New York, NY: Oxford University Press, 1991.

Meriwether, Elizabeth Avery (pseudonym, "George Edmonds"). *Facts and Falsehoods Concerning the War on the South, 1861-1865*. Memphis, TN: A. R. Taylor and Co., 1904.

Miller, Francis Trevelyan, and Robert S. Lanier (eds.). *The Photographic History of the Civil War*. 10 vols. New York, NY: The Review of Reviews Co., 1911.

Minutes of the Eighth Annual Meeting and Reunion of the United Confederate Veterans, Atlanta, GA, July 20-23, 1898. New Orleans, LA: United Confederate Veterans, 1907.

Minutes of the Ninth Annual Meeting and Reunion of the United Confederate Veterans, Charleston, SC, May 10-13, 1899. New Orleans, LA: United Confederate Veterans, 1907.

Minutes of the Twelfth Annual Meeting and Reunion of the United Confederate Veterans, Dallas, TX, April 22-25, 1902. New Orleans, LA: United Confederate Veterans, 1907.

Morton, John Watson. *The Artillery of Nathan Bedford Forrest's Cavalry*. Nashville, TN: M. E. Church, South, 1909.

Muzzey, David Saville. *The United States of America: Vol. 1, To the Civil War.* Boston, MA: Ginn and Co., 1922.

——. *The American Adventure: Vol. 2, From the Civil War.* 1924. New York, NY: Harper and Brothers, 1927 ed.

Nicolay, John G., and John Hay (eds.). *Abraham Lincoln: A History.* 10 vols. New York, NY: The Century Co., 1890.

——. *Complete Works of Abraham Lincoln.* 12 vols. 1894. New York, NY: Francis D. Tandy Co., 1905 ed.

——. *Abraham Lincoln: Complete Works.* 12 vols. 1894. New York, NY: The Century Co., 1907 ed.

ORA (full title: *The War of the Rebellion: A Compilation of the Official Records of the Union and Confederate Armies*). 70 vols. Washington, DC: Government Printing Office, 1880.

ORN (full title: *Official Records of the Union and Confederate Navies in the War of the Rebellion*). 30 vols. Washington, DC: Government Printing Office, 1894.

Pollard, Edward Alfred. *The Lost Cause.* New York, NY: E. B. Treat and Co., 1867.

Richardson, John Anderson. *Richardson's Defense of the South.* Atlanta, GA: A. B. Caldwell, 1914.

Ridley, Bromfield Lewis. *Battles and Sketches of the Army of Tennessee.* Mexico, MO: Missouri Printing and Publishing Co., 1906.

Rogers, William P. *The Three Secession Movements in the United States: Samuel J. Tilden, the Democratic Candidate for Presidency; the Advisor, Aider and Abettor of the Great Secession Movement of 1860; and One of the Authors of the Infamous Resolution of 1864; His Claims as a Statesman and Reformer Considered.* Boston, MA: John Wilson and Son, 1876.

Rove, Karl. *The Triumph of William McKinley: Why the Election of 1896 Still Matters.* New York, NY: Simon and Schuster, 2015.

Rutherford, Mildred Lewis. *Truths of History: A Fair, Unbiased, Impartial, Unprejudiced and Conscientious Study of History.* Athens, GA: n.p., 1920.

Seabrook, Lochlainn. *Carnton Plantation Ghost Stories: True Tales of the Unexplained from Tennessee's Most Haunted Civil War House!* 2005. Franklin, TN, 2016 ed.

——. *Nathan Bedford Forrest: Southern Hero, American Patriot.* 2007. Franklin, TN, 2010 ed.

——. *Abraham Lincoln: The Southern View.* 2007. Franklin, TN: Sea Raven Press, 2013 ed.

——. *The McGavocks of Carnton Plantation: A Southern History - Celebrating One of Dixie's Most Noble Confederate Families and Their Tennessee Home.* 2008. Franklin, TN, 2011ed.

——. *A Rebel Born: A Defense of Nathan Bedford Forrest.* 2010. Franklin, TN: Sea Raven Press, 2011 ed.

——. *A Rebel Born: The Screenplay* (for the film). 2011. Franklin, TN: Sea Raven Press.

——. *Everything You Were Taught About the Civil War is Wrong, Ask a Southerner!* 2010. Franklin, TN: Sea Raven Press, revised 2014 ed.

——. *The Quotable Jefferson Davis: Selections From the Writings and Speeches of the Confederacy's First President.* Franklin, TN: Sea Raven Press, 2011.

——. *The Quotable Robert E. Lee: Selections From the Writings and Speeches of the South's Most Beloved Civil War General.* Franklin, TN: Sea Raven Press, 2011 Sesquicentennial Civil War Edition.

——. *Lincolnology: The Real Abraham Lincoln Revealed In His Own Words.* Franklin, TN: Sea Raven Press, 2011.

——. *The Unquotable Abraham Lincoln: The President's Quotes They Don't Want You To Know!* Franklin, TN: Sea Raven Press, 2011.

———. *Honest Jeff and Dishonest Abe: A Southern Children's Guide to the Civil War*. Franklin, TN: Sea Raven Press, 2012.

———. *Encyclopedia of the Battle of Franklin - A Comprehensive Guide to the Conflict that Changed the Civil War*. Franklin, TN: Sea Raven Press, 2012.

———. *The Quotable Nathan Bedford Forrest: Selections From the Writings and Speeches of the Confederacy's Most Brilliant Cavalryman*. Spring Hill, TN: Sea Raven Press, 2012.

———. *Forrest! 99 Reasons to Love Nathan Bedford Forrest*. Spring Hill, TN: Sea Raven Press, 2012.

———. *Give 'Em Hell Boys! The Complete Military Correspondence of Nathan Bedford Forrest*. Spring Hill, TN: Sea Raven Press, 2012.

———. *The Constitution of the Confederate States of America Explained: A Clause-by-Clause Study of the South's Magna Carta*. Spring Hill, TN: Sea Raven Press, 2012 Sesquicentennial Civil War Edition.

———. *The Great Impersonator: 99 Reasons to Dislike Abraham Lincoln*. Spring Hill, TN: Sea Raven Press, 2012.

———. *The Old Rebel: Robert E. Lee As He Was Seen By His Contemporaries*. Spring Hill, TN: Sea Raven Press, 2012 Sesquicentennial Civil War Edition.

———. *The Quotable Stonewall Jackson: Selections From the Writings and Speeches of the South's Most Famous General*. Spring Hill, TN: Sea Raven Press, 2012 Sesquicentennial Civil War Edition.

———. *Saddle, Sword, and Gun: A Biography of Nathan Bedford Forrest for Teens*. Spring Hill, TN: Sea Raven Press, 2013.

———. *The Alexander H. Stephens Reader: Excerpts From the Works of a Confederate Founding Father*. Spring Hill, TN: Sea Raven Press, 2013.

———. *The Quotable Alexander H. Stephens: Selections From the Writings and Speeches of the Confederacy's First Vice President*. Spring Hill, TN: Sea Raven Press, 2013 Sesquicentennial Civil War Edition.

———. *Give This Book to a Yankee! A Southern Guide to the Civil War for Northerners*. Spring Hill, TN: Sea Raven Press, 2014.

———. *The Articles of Confederation Explained: A Clause-by-Clause Study of America's First Constitution*. Spring Hill, TN: Sea Raven Press, 2014.

———. *Confederate Blood and Treasure: An Interview With Lochlainn Seabrook*. Spring Hill, TN: Sea Raven Press, 2015.

———. *Nathan Bedford Forrest and the Battle of Fort Pillow: Yankee Myth, Confederate Fact*. Spring Hill, TN: Sea Raven Press, 2015.

———. *Everything You Were Taught About American Slavery War is Wrong, Ask a Southerner!* Spring Hill, TN: Sea Raven Press, 2015.

———. *Confederacy 101: Amazing Facts You Never Knew About America's Oldest Political Tradition*. Spring Hill, TN: Sea Raven Press, 2015.

———. *The Great Yankee Coverup: What the North Doesn't Want You to Know About Lincoln's War!* Spring Hill, TN: Sea Raven Press, 2015.

———. *Slavery 101: Amazing Facts You Never Knew About America's "Peculiar Institution."* Spring Hill, TN: Sea Raven Press, 2015.

———. *Confederate Flag Facts: What Every American Should Know About Dixie's Southern Cross*. Spring Hill, TN: Sea Raven Press, 2016.

———. *Nathan Bedford Forrest and the Ku Klux Klan: Yankee Myth, Confederate Fact*. Spring Hill, TN: Sea Raven Press, 2016.

———. *Seabrook's Bible Dictionary of Traditional and Mystical Christian Doctrines*. Spring Hill, TN: Sea Raven Press, 2016.

———. *Everything You Were Taught About African-Americans and the Civil War is Wrong, Ask a

Southerner! Spring Hill, TN: Sea Raven Press, 2016.
———. *Nathan Bedford Forrest and African-Americans: Yankee Myth, Confederate Fact.* Spring Hill, TN: Sea Raven Press, 2016.
———. *Women in Gray: A Tribute to the Ladies Who Supported the Southern Confederacy.* Spring Hill, TN: Sea Raven Press, 2016.
———. *Lincoln's War: The Real Cause, the Real Winner, the Real Loser.* Spring Hill, TN: Sea Raven Press, 2016.
———. *The Unholy Crusade: Lincoln's Legacy of Destruction in the American South.* Spring Hill, TN: Sea Raven Press, 2017.
———. *Abraham Lincoln Was a Liberal, Jefferson Davis Was a Conservative: The Missing Key to Understanding the American Civil War.* Spring Hill, TN: Sea Raven Press, 2017.
———. *All We Ask is to be Let Alone: The Southern Secession Fact Book.* Spring Hill, TN: Sea Raven Press, 2017.
———. *The Ultimate Civil War Quiz Book: How Much Do You Really Know About America's Most Misunderstood Conflict?* Spring Hill, TN: Sea Raven Press, 2017.
———. *Rise Up and Call Them Blessed: Victorian Tributes to the Confederate Soldier, 1861-1901.* Spring Hill, TN: Sea Raven Press, 2017.
———. *Victorian Confederate Poetry: The Southern Cause in Verse, 1861-1901.* Spring Hill, TN: Sea Raven Press, 2018.
———. *Confederate Monuments: Why Every American Should Honor Confederate Soldiers and Their Memorials.* Spring Hill, TN: Sea Raven Press, 2018.
Steel, Samuel Augustus. *The South Was Right.* Columbia, SC: R. L. Bryan Co., 1914.
Stephens, Alexander Hamilton. *Speech of Mr. Stephens, of Georgia, on the War and Taxation.* Washington, D.C.: J & G. Gideon, 1848.
———. *A Constitutional View of the Late War Between the States; Its Causes, Character, Conduct and Results.* 2 vols. Philadelphia, PA: National Publishing, Co., 1870.
———. *Recollections of Alexander H. Stephens: His Diary Kept When a Prisoner at Fort Warren, Boston Harbour, 1865.* New York, NY: Doubleday, Page, and Co., 1910.
Thompson, Holland. *The New South: A Chronicle of Social and Industrial Evolution.* New Haven, CT: Yale University Press, 1920.
Warner, Ezra J. *Generals in Gray: Lives of the Confederate Commanders.* 1959. Baton Rouge, LA: Louisiana State University Press, 1989 ed.
———. *Generals in Blue: Lives of the Union Commanders.* 1964. Baton Rouge, LA: Louisiana State University Press, 2006 ed.
Woods, Thomas E., Jr. *The Politically Incorrect Guide to American History.* Washington, D.C.: Regnery, 2004.
Wyeth, John Allan. *Life of General Nathan Bedford Forrest.* New York, NY: Harper and Brothers, 1899.
Young, Bennett Henderson. *Confederate Wizards of the Saddle: Being Reminiscences and Observations of One Who Rode With Morgan.* Boston, MA: Chapple Publishing Co., 1914.
Young, John Preston. *The Seventh Tennessee Cavalry (Confederate): A History.* Nashville, TN: M. E. Church, South, 1890.

MEET THE AUTHOR

"DEMANDING THAT THE PATRIOTIC SOUTH STOP HONORING HER CONFEDERATE ANCESTORS IS LIKE DEMANDING THE SUN NOT TO SHINE." — COLONEL LOCHLAINN SEABROOK

LOCHLAINN SEABROOK, a neo-Victorian and world acclaimed man of letters, is a Kentucky Colonel and the winner of the prestigious Jefferson Davis Historical Gold Medal for his "masterpiece," *A Rebel Born: A Defense of Nathan Bedford Forrest*. A classic littérateur and an unreconstructed Southern historian, he is an award-winning author, "Civil War" scholar, Confederate culture expert, Bible authority, the leading popularizer of American Civil War history, and a traditional Southern Agrarian of Scottish, English, Irish, Dutch, Welsh, German, and Italian extraction.

A child prodigy, Seabrook is today a true Renaissance Man whose occupational titles also include encyclopedist, lexicographer, musician, artist, graphic designer, genealogist, photographer, and award-winning poet. Also a songwriter and a screenwriter, he has a 40 year background in historical nonfiction writing and is a member of the Sons of Confederate Veterans, the Civil War Trust, and the National Grange.

Above, Colonel Lochlainn Seabrook, "the voice of the traditional South," award-winning Civil War scholar and unreconstructed Southern historian. America's most popular and prolific pro-South author, his many books have introduced hundreds of thousands to the truth about the War for Southern Independence. He coined the phrase "South-shaming" and holds the world record for writing the most books on Nathan Bedford Forrest.

Known to his many fans as the "voice of the traditional South," due to similarities in their writing styles, ideas, and literary works, Seabrook is also often referred to as the "new Shelby Foote," the "Southern Joseph Campbell," and the "American Robert Graves" (his English cousin). Seabrook coined the terms "South-shaming" and "Lincolnian liberalism," and holds the world's record for writing the most books on Nathan Bedford Forrest. In addition, Seabrook is the first Civil War scholar to connect the early American nickname for the U.S., "The Confederate States of America," with the Southern Confederacy that arose eight decades later, and the first to note that in 1860 the party platforms of the two major political parties were the opposite of what they are today (Victorian Democrats were Conservatives, Victorian Republicans were Liberals).

The son of a Kentucky trainman and the grandson of Appalachian coal-mining and farming families, Seabrook is a seventh-generation Kentuckian whose European ancestors came from Virginia, North Carolina, and Tennessee, settling in the Bluegrass State in the early 1700s, thereafter spreading into West Virginia, the Midwest, and finally the West.

Seabrook is co-chair of the Jent/Gent Family Committee (Kentucky), founder and director of the Blakeney Family Tree Project, and a board member of the Friends of Colonel Benjamin E. Caudill. His literary works have been endorsed by leading authorities, museum curators, award-winning historians, bestselling authors, celebrities, filmmakers, noted scientists, well regarded educators, TV show hosts and producers, renowned military artists, esteemed Southern organizations, and distinguished academicians from around the world.

Seabrook has authored over 50 popular adult books on the American Civil War, American and international slavery, the U.S. Confederacy (1781), the Southern Confederacy (1861), religion, theology, thealogy, Jesus, the Bible, the Apocrypha, the Law of Attraction, alternative health, spirituality, ghost stories, the paranormal, ufology, social issues, and cross-cultural studies of the family and marriage. His Confederate biographies, pro-South studies, Victorian Southern literature titles, genealogical monographs, family histories, military encyclopedias, self-help guides, and etymological dictionaries have received wide acclaim.

Seabrook's eight children's books include a Southern guide to the "Civil War," a biography of Nathan Bedford Forrest, a dictionary of religion and myth, a rewriting of the King Arthur legend (which reinstates the original pre-Christian motifs), two bedtime stories for preschoolers, a naturalist's guidebook to owls, a worldwide look at the family, and an examination of the Near-Death Experience.

Of blue-blooded Southern stock through his Kentucky, Tennessee, Virginia, North Carolina and West Virginia ancestors, he is a direct descendant of European royalty via his 6th great-grandfather, the Earl of Oxford, after which London's famous Harley Street is named. Among his celebrated male Celtic ancestors is Robert the Bruce, King of Scotland, Seabrook's 22nd great-grandfather. The 21st great-grandson of Edward I "Longshanks" Plantagenet), King of England, Seabrook is a 17th-generation Southerner through his descent from the colonists of Jamestown, Virginia (1607).

The 2nd, 3rd, and 4th great-grandson of dozens of Confederate soldiers, one of his closest connections to Lincoln's War is through his 3rd great-grandfather, Elias Jent Sr., who fought for the Confederacy

(Photo © Lochlainn Seabrook)

in the Thirteenth Cavalry Kentucky under Seabrook's 2nd cousin, Colonel Benjamin E. Caudill. The Thirteenth, also known as "Caudill's Army," fought in numerous conflicts, including the Battles of Saltville, Gladsville, Mill Cliff, Poor Fork, Whitesburg, and Leatherwood.

Seabrook is a direct descendant of the families of Alexander H. Stephens, John Singleton Mosby, William Giles Harding, and Edmund Winchester Rucker, and is related to the following Confederates and other 18th- and 19th-Century luminaries: Robert E. Lee, Stephen Dill Lee, Stonewall Jackson, Nathan Bedford Forrest, James Longstreet, John Hunt Morgan, Jeb Stuart, Pierre G. T. Beauregard (approved the Confederate Battle Flag design), George W. Gordon, John Bell Hood, Alexander Peter Stewart, Arthur M. Manigault, Joseph Manigault, Charles Scott Venable, Thornton A. Washington, John A. Washington, Abraham Buford, Edmund W. Pettus, Theodrick "Tod" Carter, John B. Womack, John H. Winder, Gideon J. Pillow, States Rights Gist, Henry R. Jackson, John Lawton Seabrook, John C. Breckinridge, Leonidas Polk, Zachary Taylor, Sarah Knox Taylor (first wife of Jefferson Davis), Richard Taylor, Davy Crockett, Daniel Boone, Meriwether Lewis (of the Lewis and Clark Expedition) Andrew Jackson, James K. Polk, Abram Poindexter Maury (founder of Franklin, TN), Zebulon Baird Vance, Thomas Jefferson, Edmund Jennings Randolph, George Wythe Randolph (grandson of Jefferson), Felix K. Zollicoffer, Fitzhugh Lee, Nathaniel F. Cheairs, Jesse James, Frank James, Robert Brank Vance, Charles Sidney Winder, John W. McGavock, Caroline E. (Winder) McGavock, David Harding McGavock, Lysander McGavock, James Randal McGavock, Randal William McGavock, Francis McGavock, Emily McGavock, William Henry F. Lee, Lucius E. Polk, Minor Meriwether (husband of noted pro-South author Elizabeth Avery Meriwether), Ellen Bourne Tynes (wife of Forrest's chief of artillery, Captain John W. Morton), South Carolina Senators Preston Smith Brooks and Andrew Pickens Butler, and famed South Carolina diarist Mary Chesnut.

Seabrook's modern day cousins include: Patrick J. Buchanan (conservative author), Cindy Crawford (model), Shelby Lee Adams (Letcher Co., Kentucky, photographer), Bertram Thomas Combs (Kentucky's 50th governor), Edith Bolling (second wife of President Woodrow Wilson), and actors Andy Griffith, Riley Keough, George C. Scott, Robert Duvall, Reese Witherspoon, Lee Marvin, Rebecca Gayheart, and Tom Cruise.

Seabrook's screenplay, *A Rebel Born*, based on his book of the same name, has been signed with acclaimed filmmaker Christopher Forbes (of Forbes Film). Set for release as a full-length feature film, it is in pre-production, awaiting the necessary funding. This will be the first movie ever made of Nathan Bedford Forrest's life story, and as a historically accurate project written from the Southern perspective, is destined to be one of the most talked about Civil War films of all time.

Born with music in his blood, Seabrook is an award-winning, multi-genre, BMI-Nashville songwriter and lyricist who has composed some 3,000 songs (250 albums) and whose original music has been heard in film (*A Rebel Born, Cowgirls 'n Angels, Confederate Cavalry, Billy the Kid: Showdown in Lincoln County, Vengeance Without Mercy, Last Step, County Line, The Mark*) and on TV and radio worldwide. A musician, producer, multi-instrumentalist, and renown performer—whose keyboard work has been variously compared to pianists from Hargus Robbins and Vince Guaraldi to Elton John and Leonard Bernstein—Seabrook has opened for groups such as the Earl Scruggs Review, Ted Nugent, and Bob Seger, and has performed privately for such public figures as President Ronald Reagan, Burt Reynolds, Loni Anderson, and Senator Edward W. Brooke. Seabrook's cousins in the music business include: Johnny Cash, Elvis Presley, Lisa Marie Presley, Billy Ray and Miley Cyrus, Patty Loveless, Tim McGraw, Lee Ann Womack, Dolly Parton, Pat Boone, Naomi, Wynonna, and Ashley Judd, Ricky Skaggs, the Sunshine Sisters, Martha Carson, and Chet Atkins.

Seabrook lives with his wife and family in historic Middle Tennessee, the heart of Forrest country and the Confederacy, where his conservative Southern ancestors fought valiantly against Liberal Lincoln and the progressive North in defense of Jeffersonianism, constitutional government, and personal liberty.

LochlainnSeabrook.com

If you enjoyed this book you will be interested in Colonel Seabrook's other popular related titles:

- ABRAHAM LINCOLN WAS A LIBERAL, JEFFERSON DAVIS WAS A CONSERVATIVE
- EVERYTHING YOU WERE TAUGHT ABOUT THE CIVIL WAR IS WRONG, ASK A SOUTHERNER!
- ALL WE ASK IS TO BE LET ALONE: THE SOUTHERN SECESSION FACT BOOK
- EVERYTHING YOU WERE TAUGHT ABOUT AMERICAN SLAVERY IS WRONG, ASK A SOUTHERNER!
- CONFEDERATE FLAG FACTS: WHAT EVERY AMERICAN SHOULD KNOW ABOUT DIXIE'S SOUTHERN CROSS
- LINCOLN'S WAR: THE REAL CAUSE, THE REAL WINNER, THE REAL LOSER

Available from Sea Raven Press and wherever fine books are sold

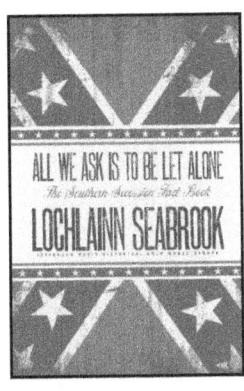

ALL OF OUR BOOK COVERS ARE AVAILABLE AS 11" X 17" POSTERS, SUITABLE FOR FRAMING

SeaRavenPress.com • NathanBedfordForrestBooks.com

www.ingramcontent.com/pod-product-compliance
Lightning Source LLC
Chambersburg PA
CBHW021141160426
43194CB00007B/651